P9-DWZ-457

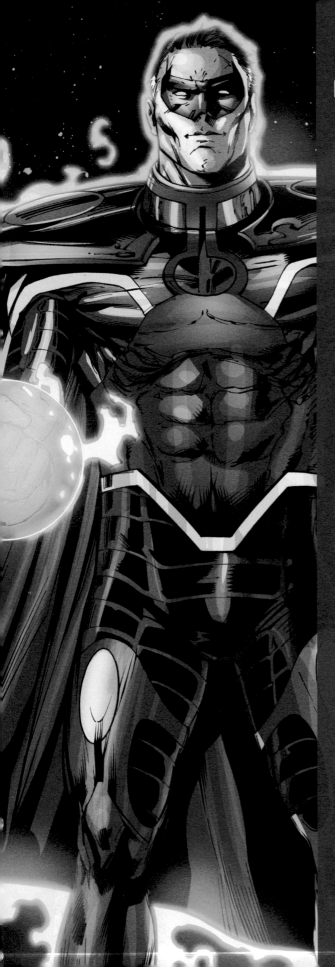

VOLUME 8
REFLECTIONS

GREEN LANTERN

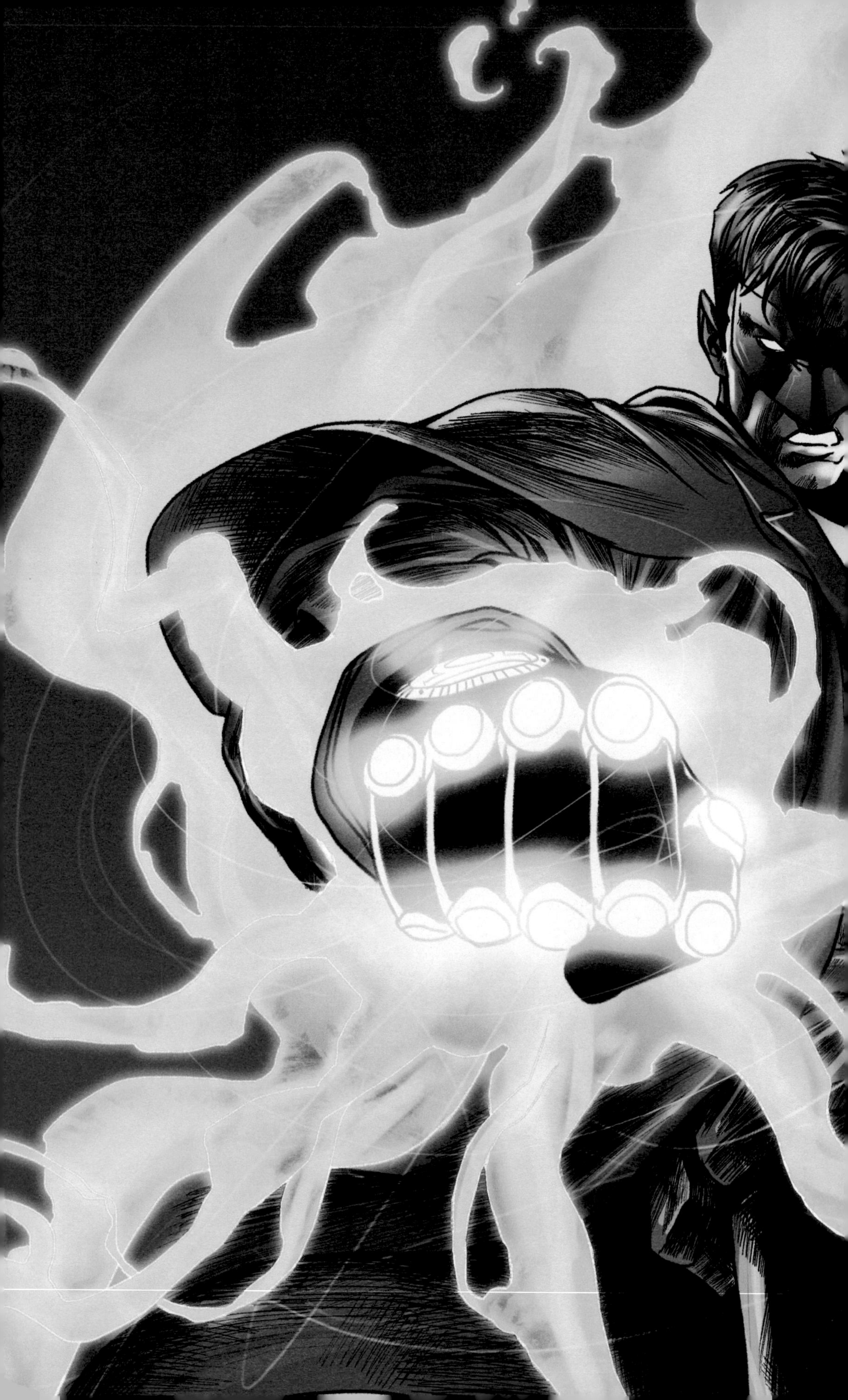

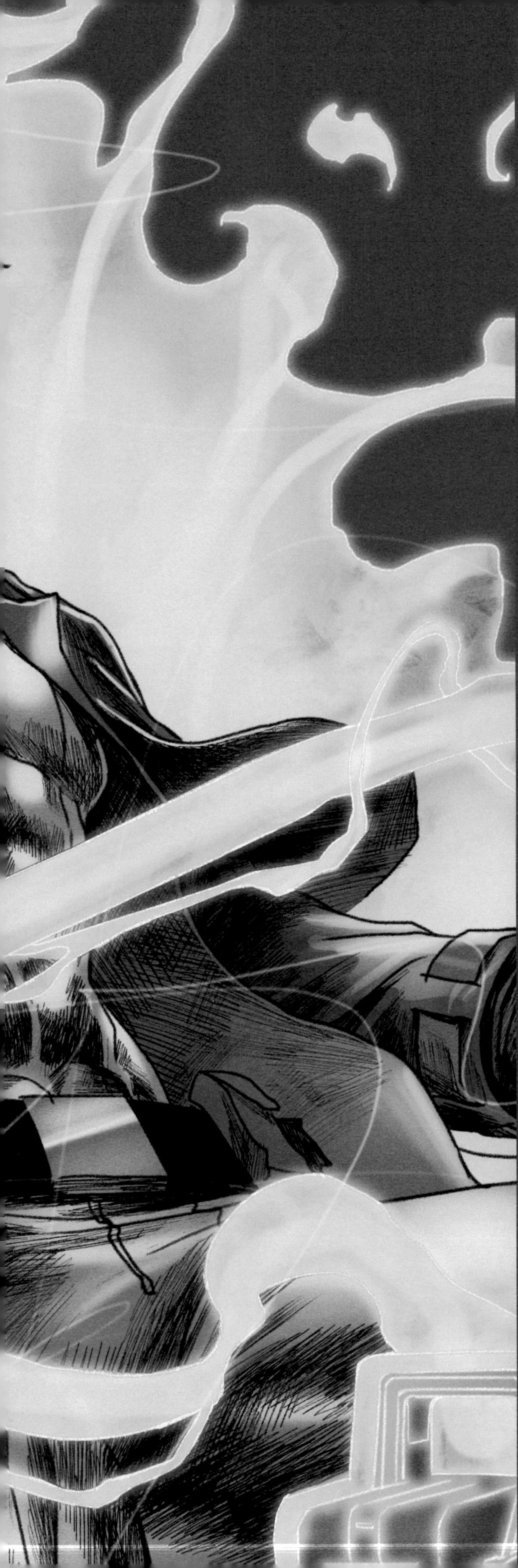

GREEN LANTERN

VOLUME 8
REFLECTIONS

WRITTEN BY
ROBERT VENDITTI

PENCILS BY
MARTIN COCCOLO
BILLY TAN
VICENTE CIFUENTES
RAFA SANDOVAL

INKS BY
MARK IRWIN
JOHN LIVESAY
VICENTE CIFUENTES
JORDI TARRAGONA

COLOR BY
TONY AVIÑA
ALEX SINCLAIR

LETTERS BY
DAVE SHARPE

COLLECTION COVER ART BY
BILLY TAN,
MARK IRWIN
& ALEX SINCLAIR

EDDIE BERGANZA MIKE COTTON Editors – Original Series
ANDREW MARINO Assistant Editor – Original Series
JEB WOODARD Group Editor – Collected Editions
STEVE COOK Design Director – Books
DAMIAN RYLAND Publication Design

BOB HARRAS Senior VP – Editor-in-Chief, DC Comics

DIANE NELSON President
DAN DIDIO and JIM LEE Co-Publishers
GEOFF JOHNS Chief Creative Officer
AMIT DESAI Senior VP – Marketing & Global Franchise Management
NAIRI GARDINER Senior VP – Finance
SAM ADES VP – Digital Marketing
BOBBIE CHASE VP – Talent Development
MARK CHIARELLO Senior VP – Art, Design & Collected Editions
JOHN CUNNINGHAM VP – Content Strategy
ANNE DEPIES VP – Strategy Planning & Reporting
DON FALLETTI VP – Manufacturing Operations
LAWRENCE GANEM VP – Editorial Administration & Talent Relations
ALISON GILL Senior VP – Manufacturing & Operations
HANK KANALZ Senior VP – Editorial Strategy & Administration
JAY KOGAN VP – Legal Affairs
DEREK MADDALENA Senior VP – Sales & Business Development
JACK MAHAN VP – Business Affairs
DAN MIRON VP – Sales Planning & Trade Development
NICK NAPOLITANO VP – Manufacturing Administration
CAROL ROEDER VP – Marketing
EDDIE SCANNELL VP – Mass Account & Digital Sales
COURTNEY SIMMONS Senior VP – Publicity & Communications
JIM (SKI) SOKOLOWSKI VP – Comic Book Specialty & Newsstand Sales
SANDY YI Senior VP – Global Franchise Management

GREEN LANTERN VOLUME 8: REFLECTIONS

Published by DC Comics. Compilation and all new material Copyright © 2016 DC Comics. All Rights Reserved. Originally
published in single magazine form in GREEN LANTERN 47-52, HAL JORDAN & THE GREEN LANTERN CORPS: REBIRTH #1.
Copyright © 2016 DC Comics. All Rights Reserved. All characters, their distinctive likenesses and related elements featured
in this publication are trademarks of DC Comics. The stories, characters and incidents featured in this publication are entirely
fictional. DC Comics does not read or accept unsolicited submissions of ideas, stories or artwork.
DC Comics, 2900 West Alameda Ave., Burbank, CA 91505
Printed by RR Donnelley, Salem, VA, USA. 8/26/16. First Printing.
ISBN: 978-1-4012-6523-6

Library of Congress Cataloging-in-Publication Data is available.

PEFC Certified

Printed on paper from
sustainably managed
forests and controlled
sources

PEFC/29-31-75   www.pefc.org

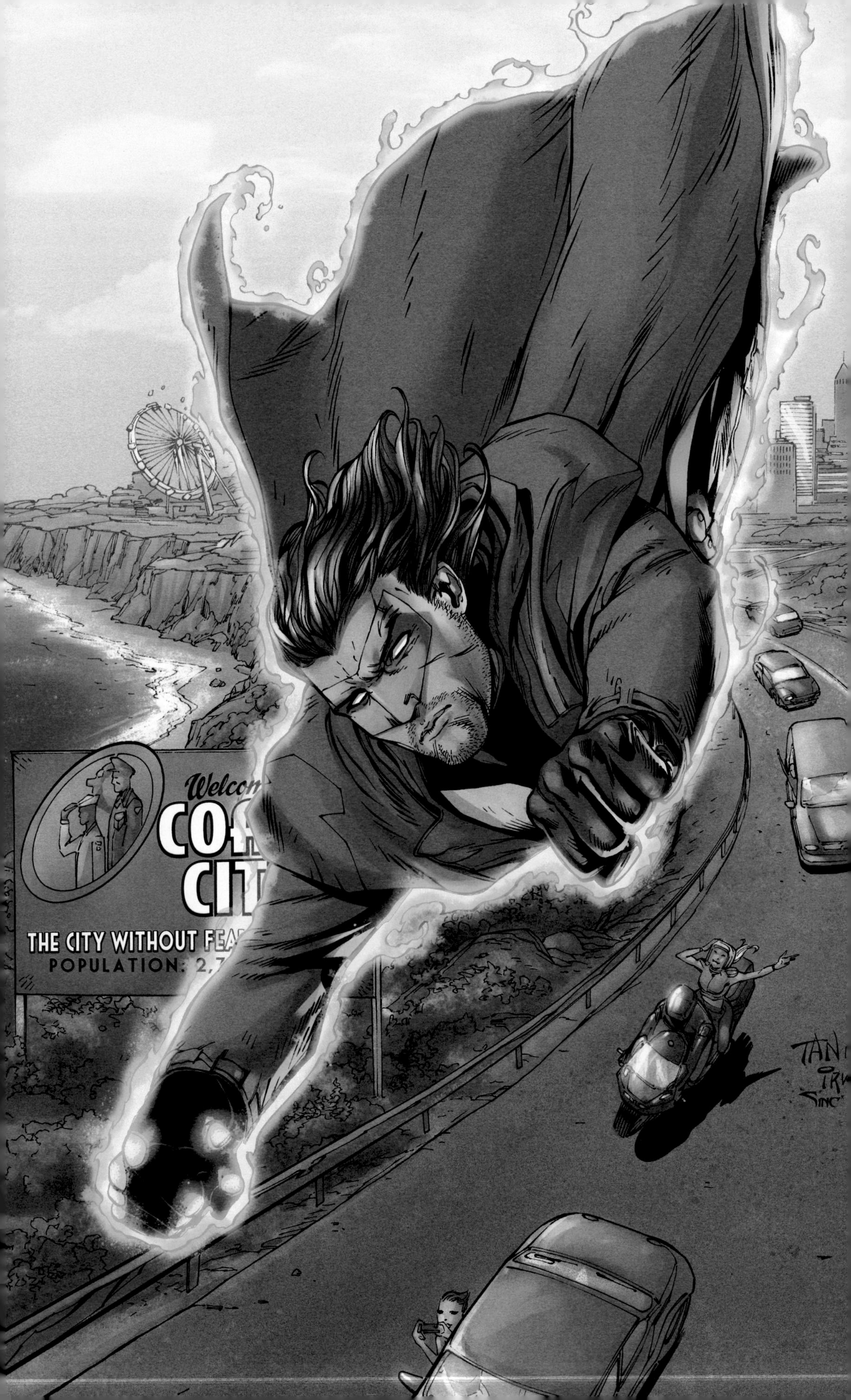
Welcom
CO
CIT
THE CITY WITHOUT FEA
POPULATION: 2,7

THE COMFORTS OF HOME

ROBERT VENDITTI writer **MARTIN COCCOLO BILLY TAN** pencillers **MARK IRWIN** inker **TONY AVIÑA** colorist **DAVE SHARPE** letterer
BILLY TAN, MARK IRWIN & ALEX SINCLAIR cover

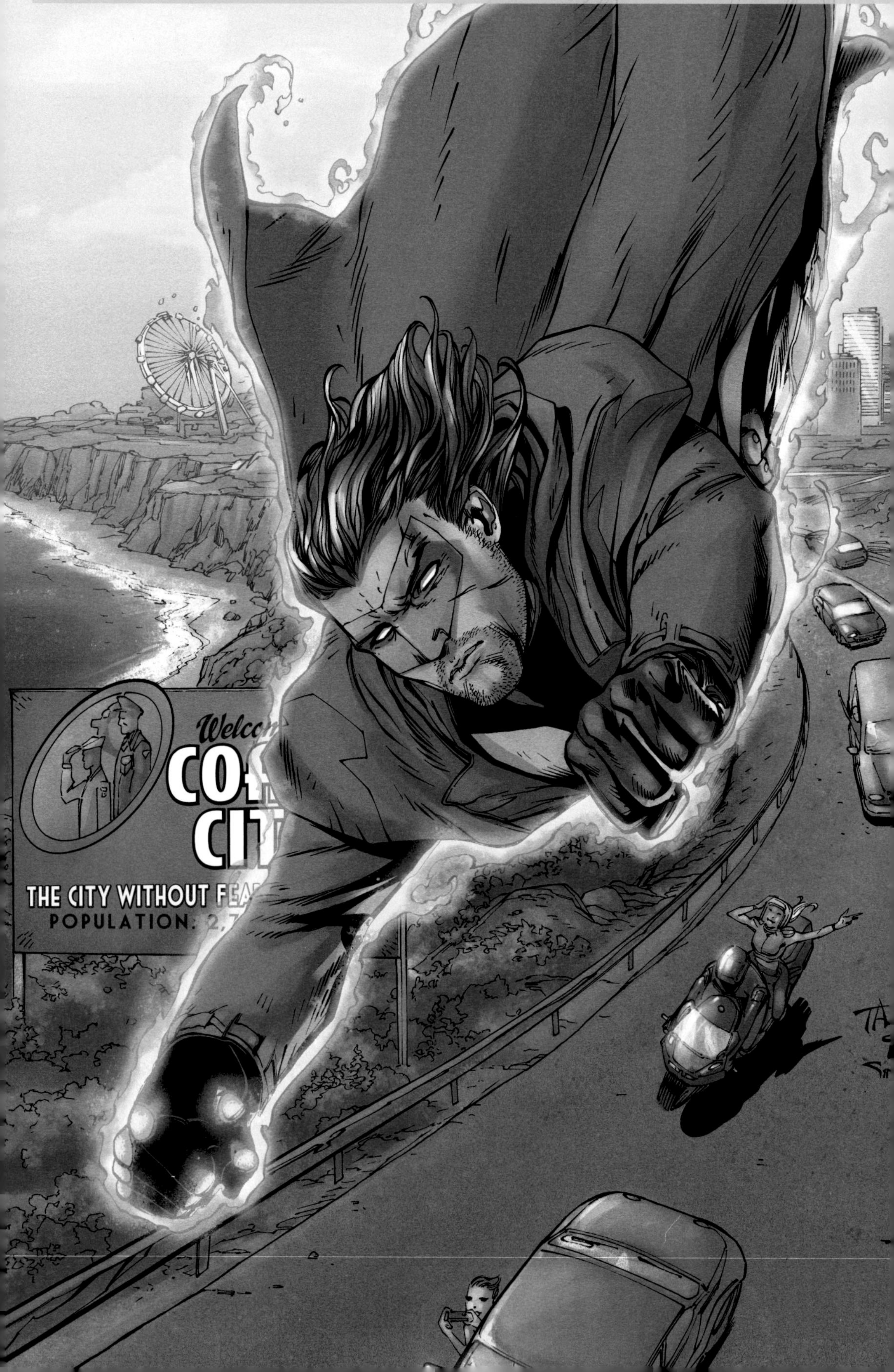
THE CITY WITHOUT FE
POPULATION:

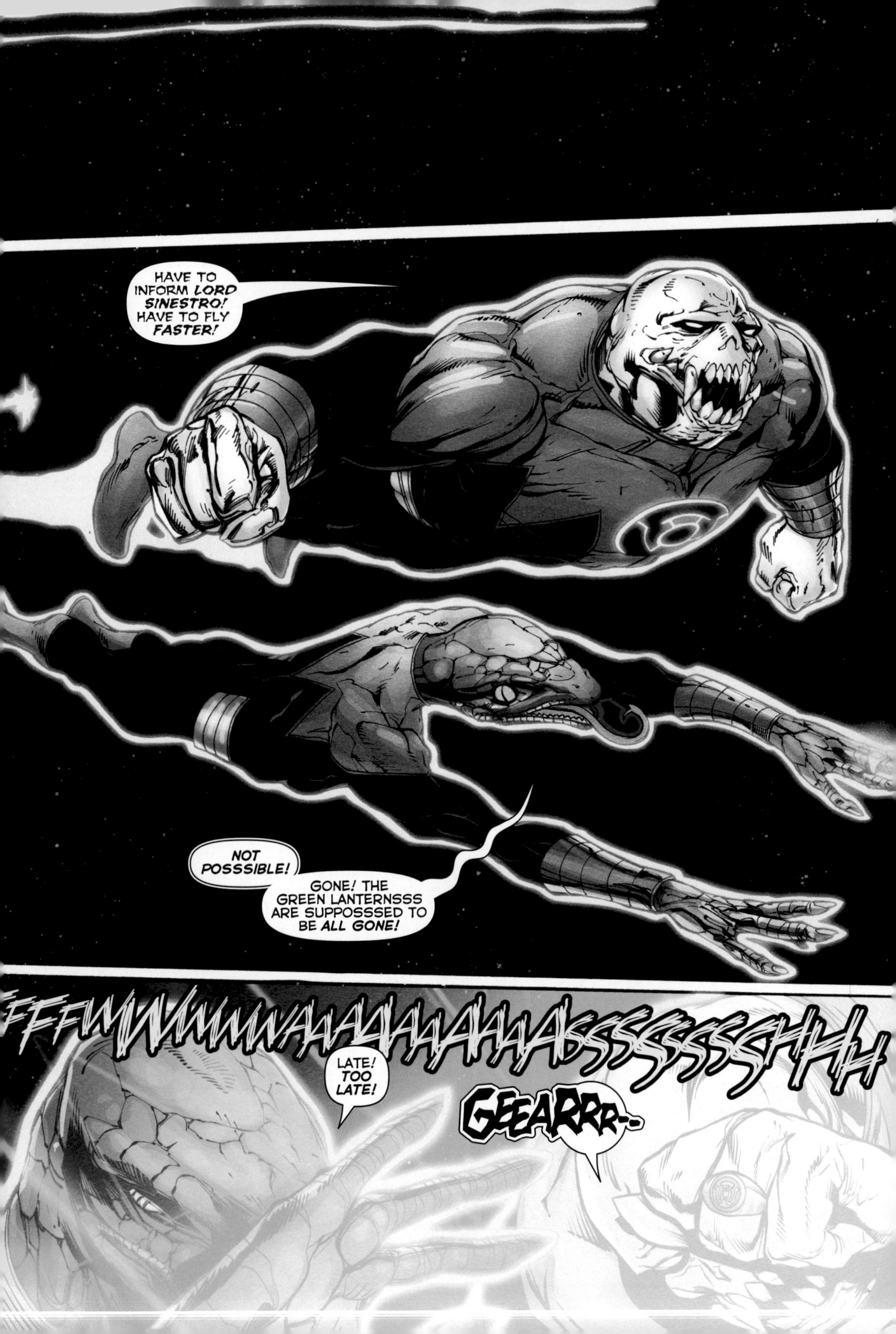
HAVE TO INFORM LORD SINESTRO! HAVE TO FLY FASTER!
NOT POSSSIBLE!
GONE! THE GREEN LANTERNSSS ARE SUPPOSSSED TO BE ALL GONE!
FFFWWWWWWAAAAAAAAASSSSSSSSSHHH
LATE! TOO LATE!
GEEARRR--

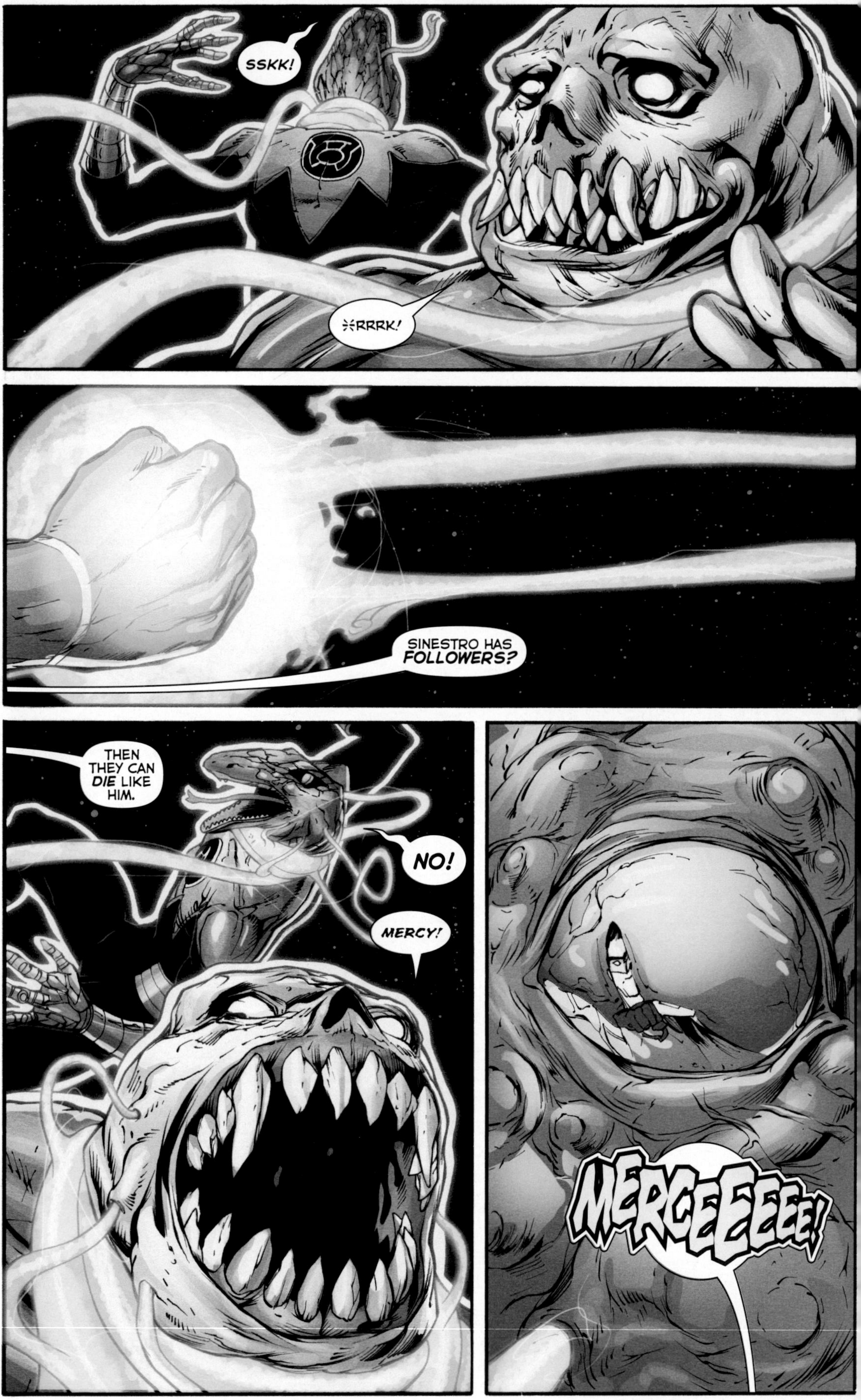
SSKK!
RRRK!
SINESTRO HAS FOLLOWERS?
THEN THEY CAN DIE LIKE HIM.
NO!
MERCY!
MERCEEEEE!

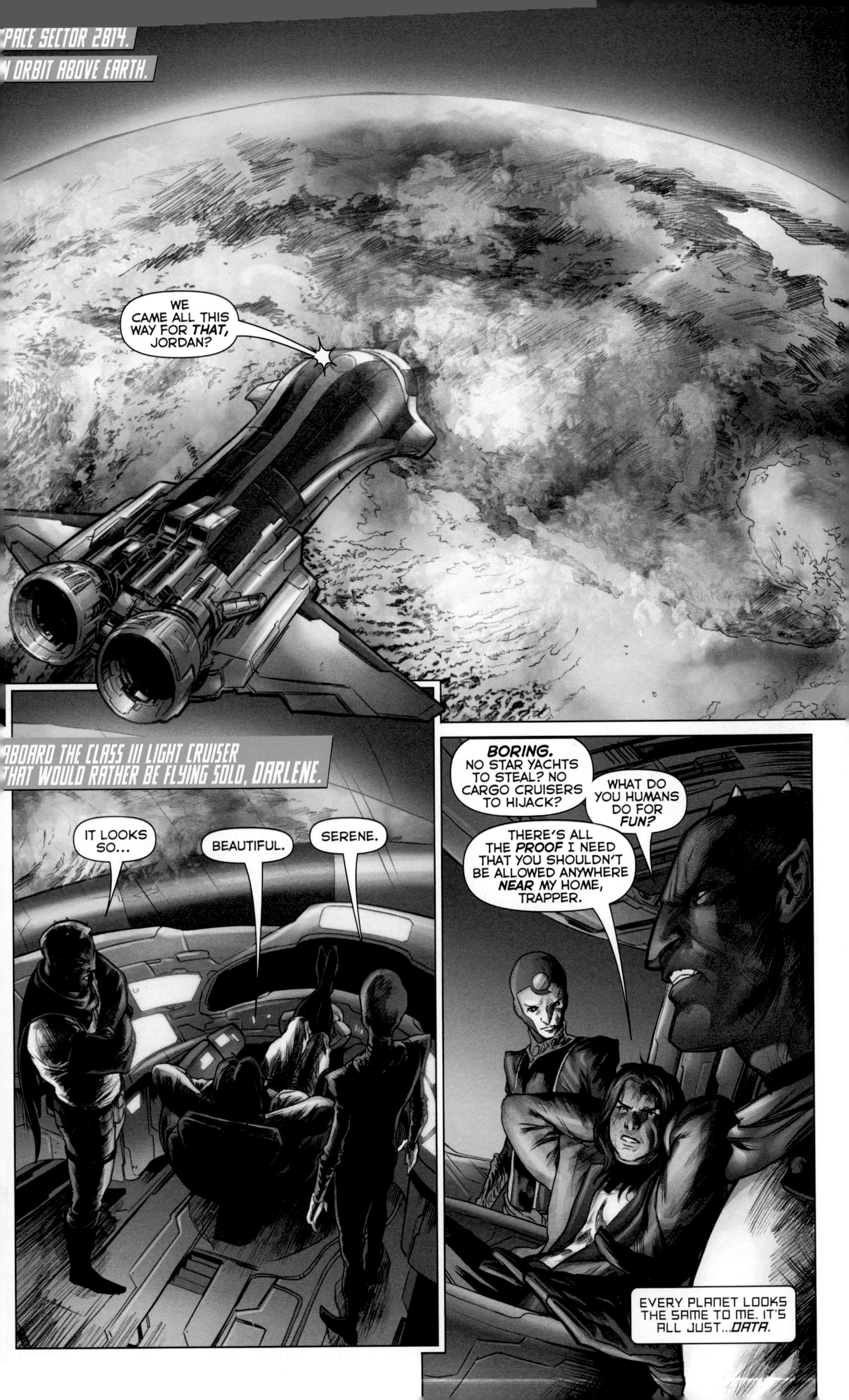
PACE SECTOR 2814.
N ORBIT ABOVE EARTH.
WE CAME ALL THIS WAY FOR THAT, JORDAN?
ABOARD THE CLASS III LIGHT CRUISER THAT WOULD RATHER BE FLYING SOLO, DARLENE.
IT LOOKS SO...
BEAUTIFUL.
SERENE.
BORING. NO STAR YACHTS TO STEAL? NO CARGO CRUISERS TO HIJACK?
WHAT DO YOU HUMANS DO FOR FUN?
THERE'S ALL THE PROOF I NEED THAT YOU SHOULDN'T BE ALLOWED ANYWHERE NEAR MY HOME, TRAPPER.
EVERY PLANET LOOKS THE SAME TO ME. IT'S ALL JUST...DATA.

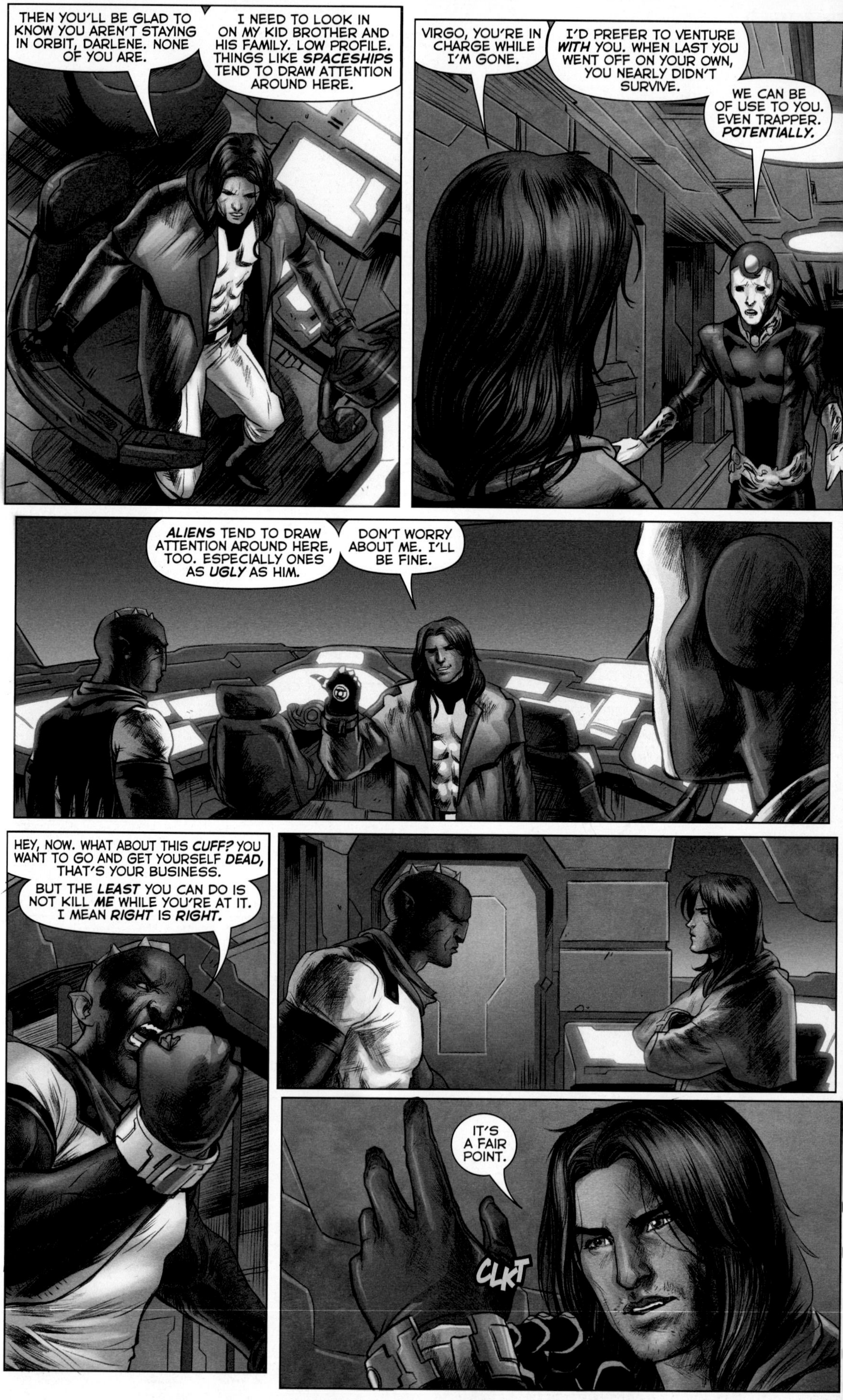

THEN YOU'LL BE GLAD TO KNOW YOU AREN'T STAYING IN ORBIT, DARLENE. NONE OF YOU ARE.
I NEED TO LOOK IN ON MY KID BROTHER AND HIS FAMILY. LOW PROFILE. THINGS LIKE SPACESHIPS TEND TO DRAW ATTENTION AROUND HERE.
VIRGO, YOU'RE IN CHARGE WHILE I'M GONE.
I'D PREFER TO VENTURE WITH YOU. WHEN LAST YOU WENT OFF ON YOUR OWN, YOU NEARLY DIDN'T SURVIVE.
WE CAN BE OF USE TO YOU. EVEN TRAPPER. POTENTIALLY.
ALIENS TEND TO DRAW ATTENTION AROUND HERE, TOO. ESPECIALLY ONES AS UGLY AS HIM.
DON'T WORRY ABOUT ME. I'LL BE FINE.
HEY, NOW. WHAT ABOUT THIS CUFF? YOU WANT TO GO AND GET YOURSELF DEAD, THAT'S YOUR BUSINESS.
BUT THE LEAST YOU CAN DO IS NOT KILL ME WHILE YOU'RE AT IT. I MEAN RIGHT IS RIGHT.
IT'S A FAIR POINT.
CLKT

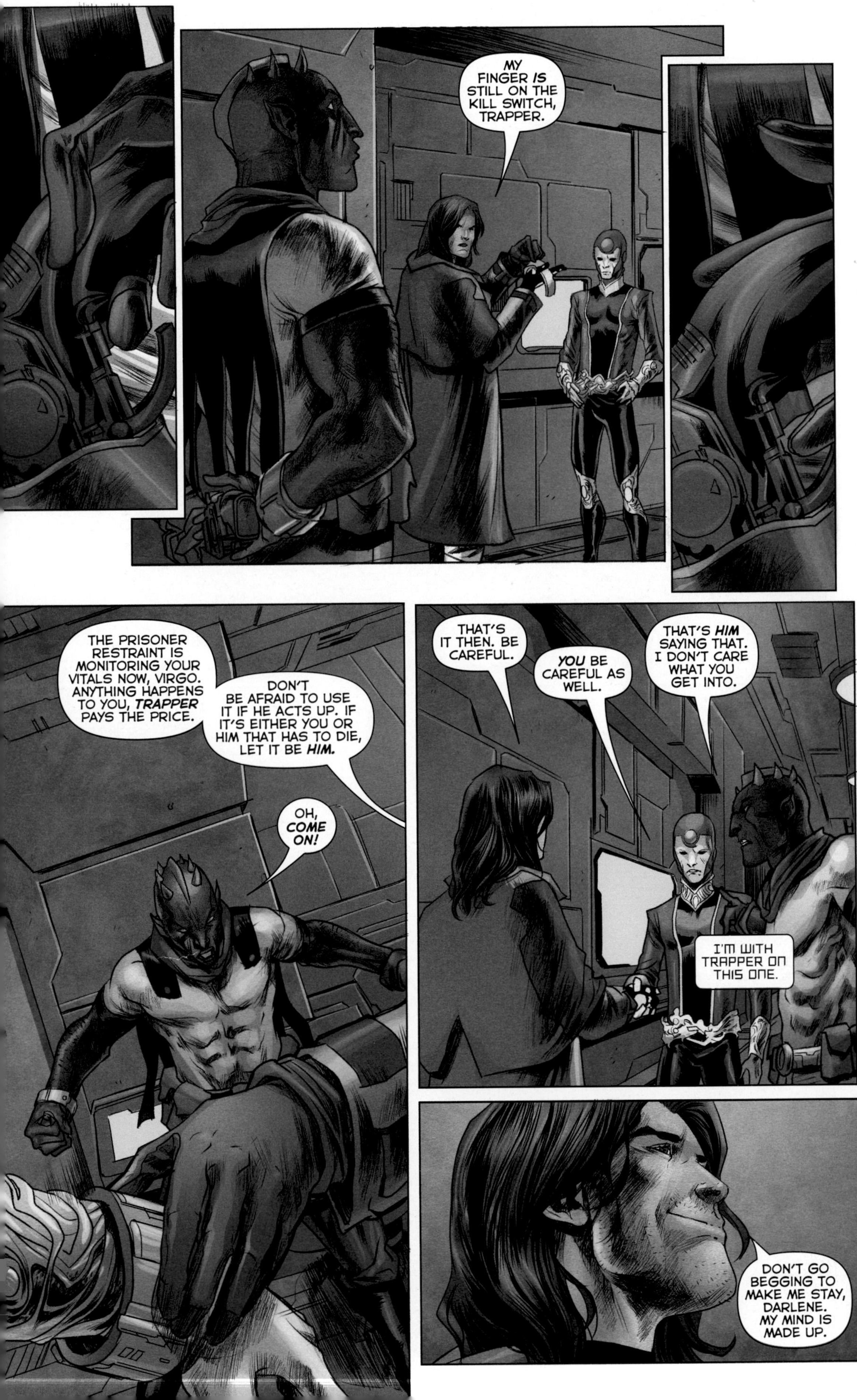
MY FINGER IS STILL ON THE KILL SWITCH, TRAPPER.
THE PRISONER RESTRAINT IS MONITORING YOUR VITALS NOW, VIRGO. ANYTHING HAPPENS TO YOU, TRAPPER PAYS THE PRICE.
DON'T BE AFRAID TO USE IT IF HE ACTS UP. IF IT'S EITHER YOU OR HIM THAT HAS TO DIE, LET IT BE HIM.
OH, COME ON!
THAT'S IT THEN. BE CAREFUL.
YOU BE CAREFUL AS WELL.
THAT'S HIM SAYING THAT. I DON'T CARE WHAT YOU GET INTO.
I'M WITH TRAPPER ON THIS ONE.
DON'T GO BEGGING TO MAKE ME STAY, DARLENE. MY MIND IS MADE UP.

"I'M GOING HOME."

COAST CITY.

JIM? SUE?

ANYBODY HOME?

NICKNAME: "THE CITY WITHOUT FEAR."

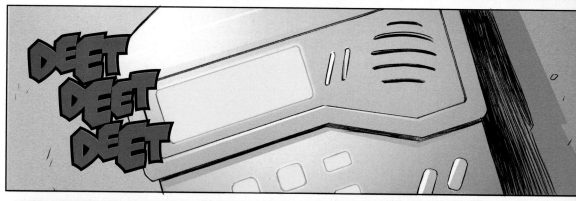

DEET DEET DEET

DEET DEET DEET

AW, HELL...

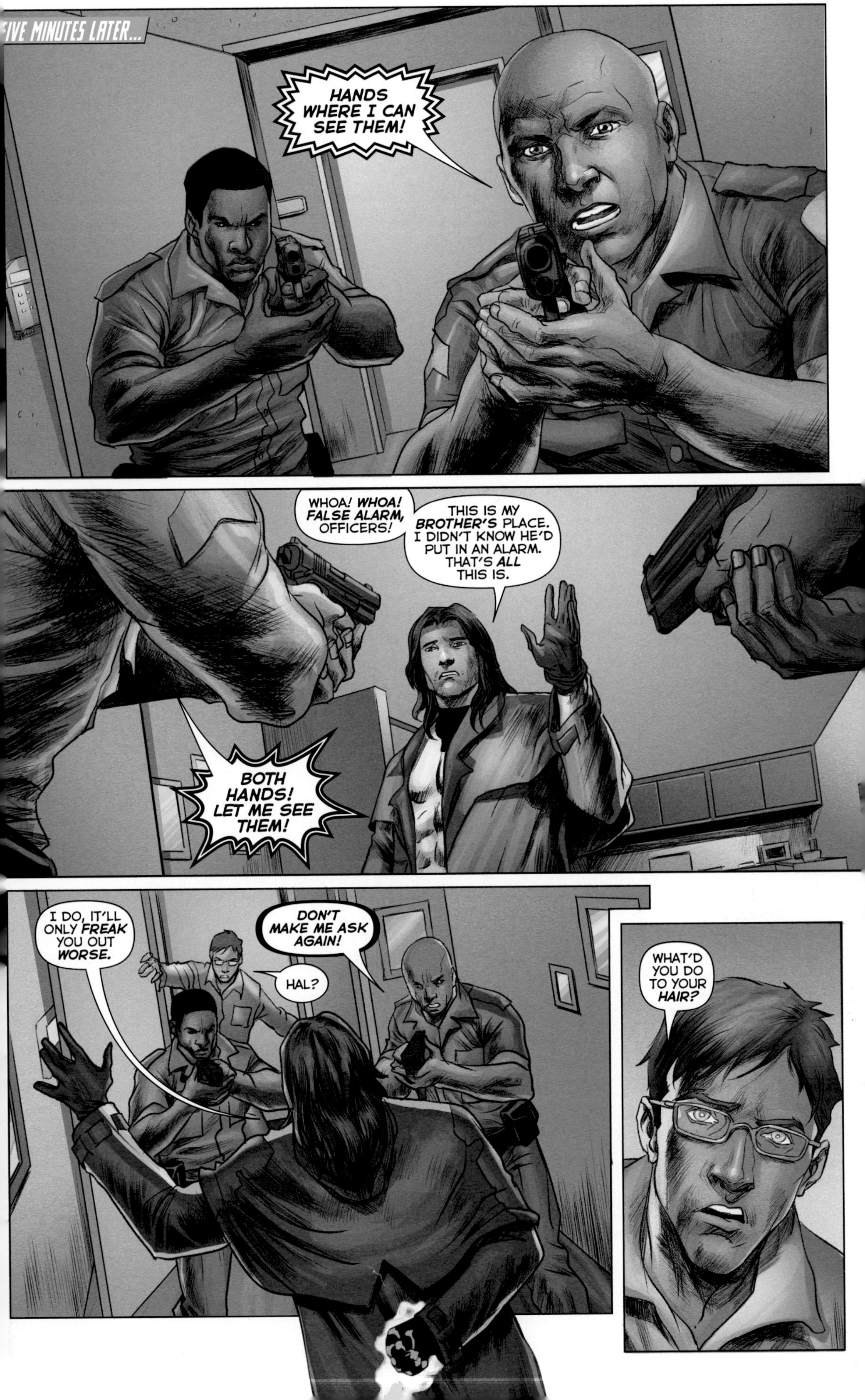
IVE MINUTES LATER...
HANDS WHERE I CAN SEE THEM!
WHOA! WHOA! FALSE ALARM, OFFICERS!
THIS IS MY BROTHER'S PLACE. I DIDN'T KNOW HE'D PUT IN AN ALARM. THAT'S ALL THIS IS.
BOTH HANDS! LET ME SEE THEM!
I DO, IT'LL ONLY FREAK YOU OUT WORSE.
DON'T MAKE ME ASK AGAIN!
HAL?
WHAT'D YOU DO TO YOUR HAIR?

THERE'LL BE A *FINE* FOR THE FALSE ALARM, MR. JORDAN.

I UNDERSTAND, OFFICER. I APOLOGIZE.

FAMILY. YOU KNOW HOW IT IS.

NEVER FAIL TO MAKE AN *ENTRANCE*, DO YOU?

SORRY, JIM. I WANTED TO SURPRISE YOU.

MISSION ACCOMPLISHED.

HOW YOU DOING? YOU LOOK... DIFFERENT.

A *LOT* OF THINGS ARE DIFFERENT. THAT'S WHY I'M HERE. I NEED TO MAKE SURE YOU'RE OKAY.

IS *SIMON BAZ* STILL COMING AROUND?

SIMON? HE WAS CHECKING IN ON US REGULARLY LIKE YOU ASKED HIM TO. BUT ALL OF A SUDDEN, HE STOPPED. I HAVEN'T SEEN HIM IN MONTHS.

THAT'S WHY I HAD THE ALARM INSTALLED. THE CODE IS YOUR *BIRTHDAY*, BY THE WAY.

YOUR PERSONAL *GREEN LANTERN BODYGUARD* QUITS SHOWING UP--

--AND YOU FIGURE THE NEXT BEST THING TO PROTECT YOU FROM MY *INTER-GALACTIC* ENEMIES IS A *HUNDRED-DOLLAR* ALARM SYSTEM?

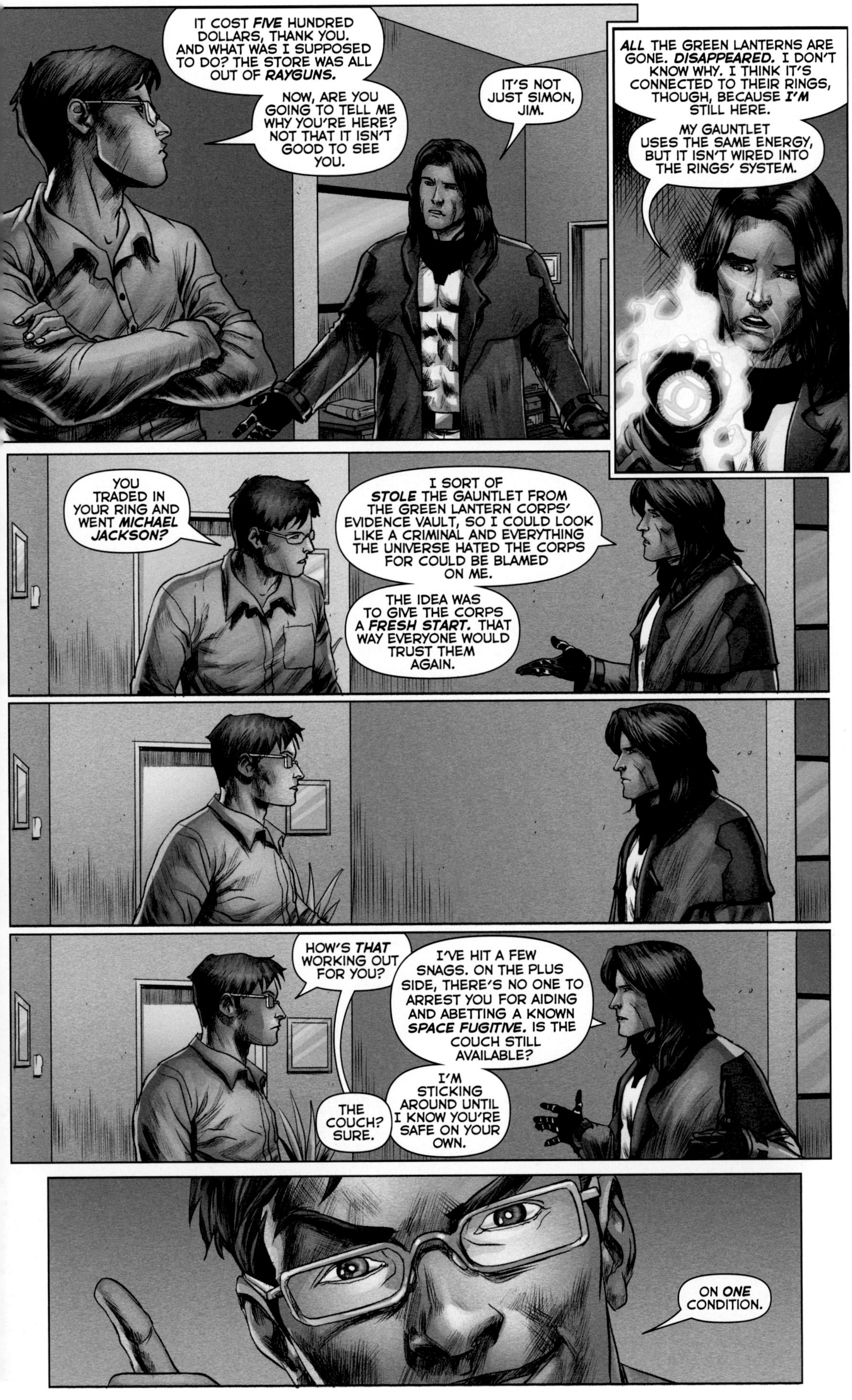
IT COST FIVE HUNDRED DOLLARS, THANK YOU. AND WHAT WAS I SUPPOSED TO DO? THE STORE WAS ALL OUT OF RAYGUNS.
NOW, ARE YOU GOING TO TELL ME WHY YOU'RE HERE? NOT THAT IT ISN'T GOOD TO SEE YOU.
IT'S NOT JUST SIMON, JIM.
ALL THE GREEN LANTERNS ARE GONE. DISAPPEARED. I DON'T KNOW WHY. I THINK IT'S CONNECTED TO THEIR RINGS, THOUGH, BECAUSE I'M STILL HERE.
MY GAUNTLET USES THE SAME ENERGY, BUT IT ISN'T WIRED INTO THE RINGS' SYSTEM.
YOU TRADED IN YOUR RING AND WENT MICHAEL JACKSON?
I SORT OF STOLE THE GAUNTLET FROM THE GREEN LANTERN CORPS' EVIDENCE VAULT, SO I COULD LOOK LIKE A CRIMINAL AND EVERYTHING THE UNIVERSE HATED THE CORPS FOR COULD BE BLAMED ON ME.
THE IDEA WAS TO GIVE THE CORPS A FRESH START. THAT WAY EVERYONE WOULD TRUST THEM AGAIN.
HOW'S THAT WORKING OUT FOR YOU?
I'VE HIT A FEW SNAGS. ON THE PLUS SIDE, THERE'S NO ONE TO ARREST YOU FOR AIDING AND ABETTING A KNOWN SPACE FUGITIVE. IS THE COUCH STILL AVAILABLE?
THE COUCH? SURE.
I'M STICKING AROUND UNTIL I KNOW YOU'RE SAFE ON YOUR OWN.
ON ONE CONDITION.

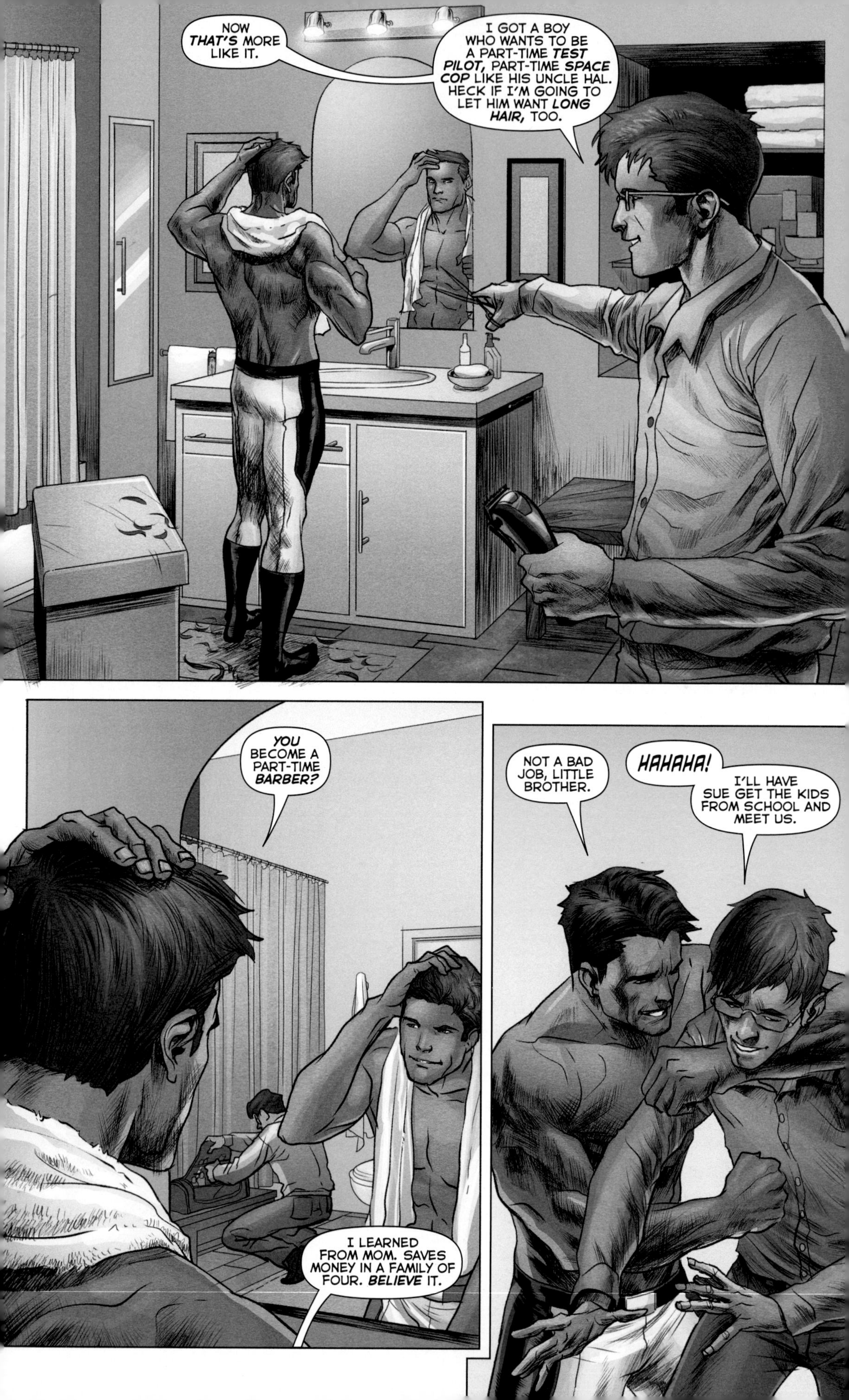
NOW THAT'S MORE LIKE IT.
I GOT A BOY WHO WANTS TO BE A PART-TIME TEST PILOT, PART-TIME SPACE COP LIKE HIS UNCLE HAL. HECK IF I'M GOING TO LET HIM WANT LONG HAIR, TOO.
YOU BECOME A PART-TIME BARBER?
I LEARNED FROM MOM. SAVES MONEY IN A FAMILY OF FOUR. BELIEVE IT.
NOT A BAD JOB, LITTLE BROTHER.
HAHAHA!
I'LL HAVE SUE GET THE KIDS FROM SCHOOL AND MEET US.

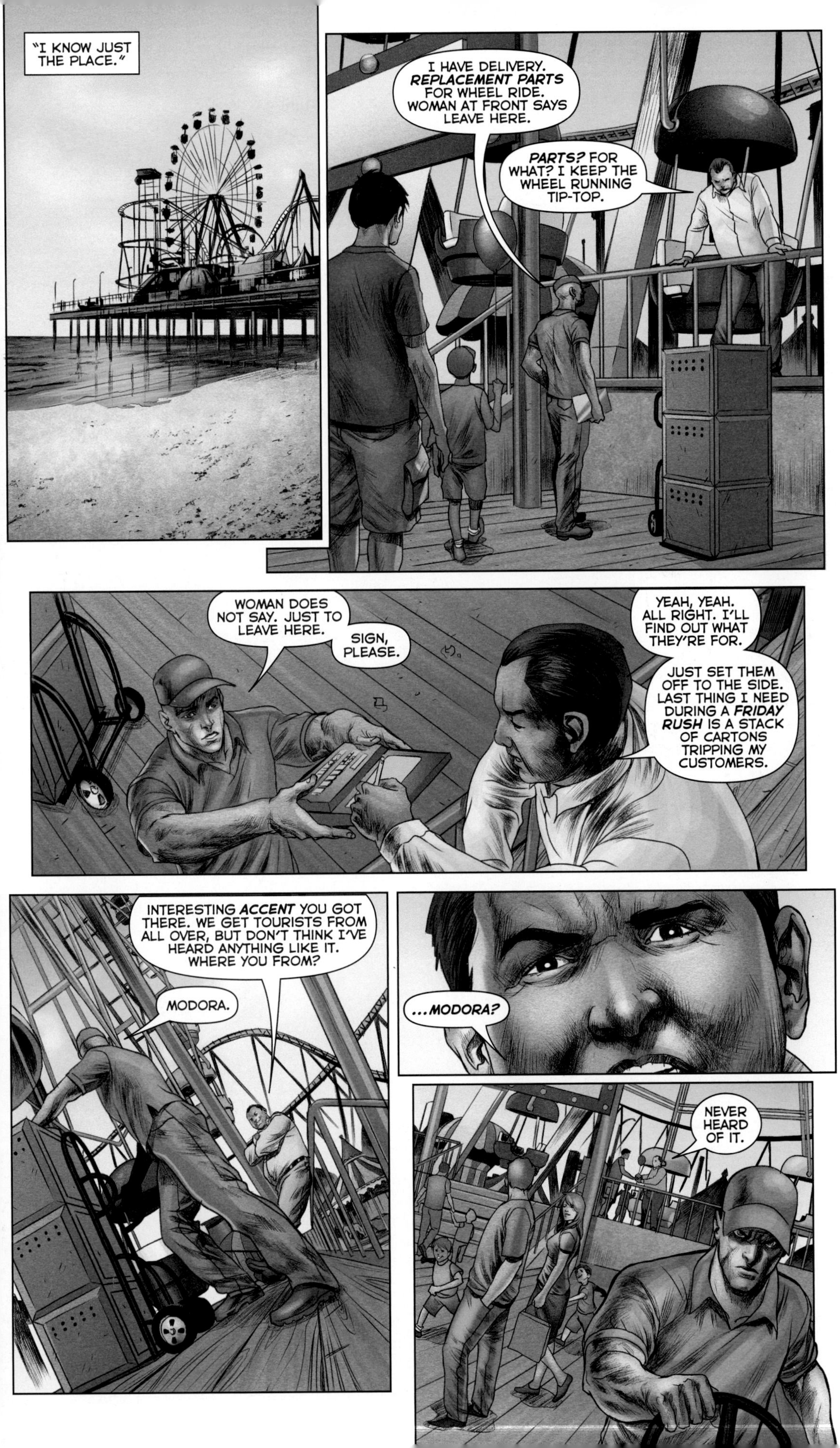
"I KNOW JUST THE PLACE."
I HAVE DELIVERY. REPLACEMENT PARTS FOR WHEEL RIDE. WOMAN AT FRONT SAYS LEAVE HERE.
PARTS? FOR WHAT? I KEEP THE WHEEL RUNNING TIP-TOP.
WOMAN DOES NOT SAY. JUST TO LEAVE HERE.
SIGN, PLEASE.
YEAH, YEAH. ALL RIGHT. I'LL FIND OUT WHAT THEY'RE FOR.
JUST SET THEM OFF TO THE SIDE. LAST THING I NEED DURING A FRIDAY RUSH IS A STACK OF CARTONS TRIPPING MY CUSTOMERS.
INTERESTING ACCENT YOU GOT THERE. WE GET TOURISTS FROM ALL OVER, BUT DON'T THINK I'VE HEARD ANYTHING LIKE IT. WHERE YOU FROM?
MODORA.
...MODORA?
NEVER HEARD OF IT.

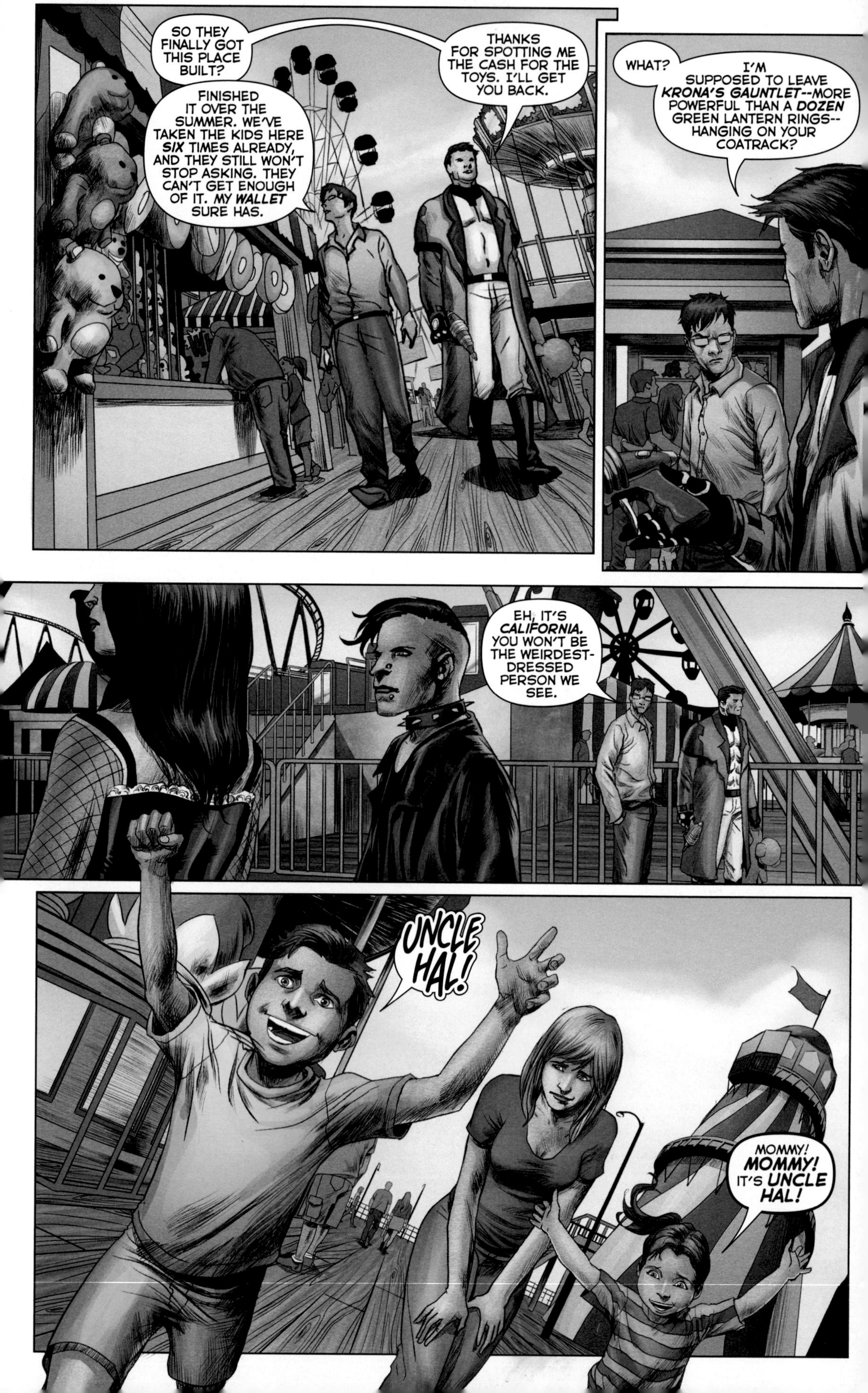
SO THEY FINALLY GOT THIS PLACE BUILT?
FINISHED IT OVER THE SUMMER. WE'VE TAKEN THE KIDS HERE SIX TIMES ALREADY, AND THEY STILL WON'T STOP ASKING. THEY CAN'T GET ENOUGH OF IT. MY WALLET SURE HAS.
THANKS FOR SPOTTING ME THE CASH FOR THE TOYS. I'LL GET YOU BACK.
WHAT?
I'M SUPPOSED TO LEAVE KRONA'S GAUNTLET--MORE POWERFUL THAN A DOZEN GREEN LANTERN RINGS--HANGING ON YOUR COATRACK?
EH, IT'S CALIFORNIA. YOU WON'T BE THE WEIRDEST-DRESSED PERSON WE SEE.
UNCLE HAL!
MOMMY! MOMMY! IT'S UNCLE HAL!

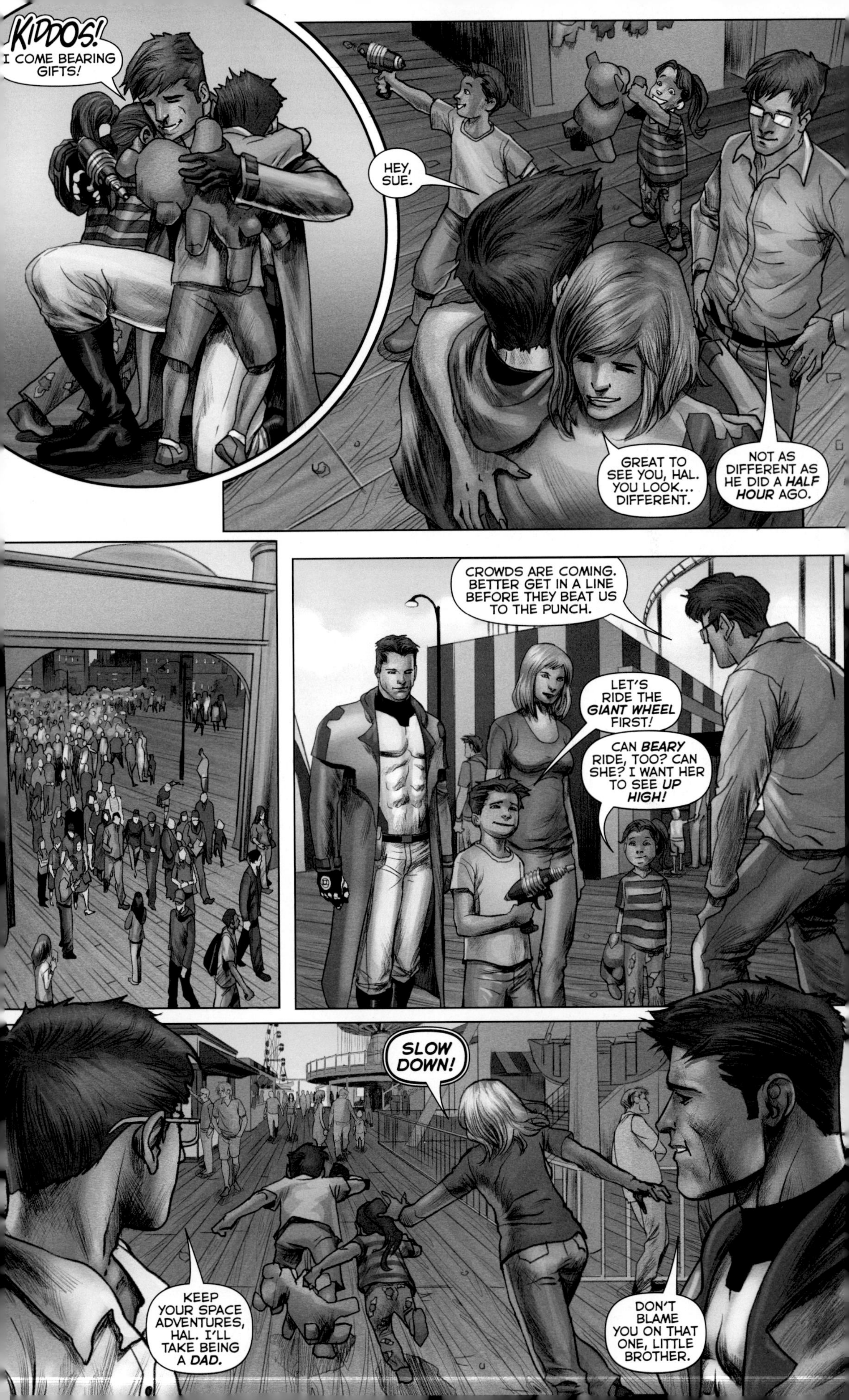
KIDDOS! I COME BEARING GIFTS!
HEY, SUE.
GREAT TO SEE YOU, HAL. YOU LOOK... DIFFERENT.
NOT AS DIFFERENT AS HE DID A HALF HOUR AGO.
CROWDS ARE COMING. BETTER GET IN A LINE BEFORE THEY BEAT US TO THE PUNCH.
LET'S RIDE THE GIANT WHEEL FIRST!
CAN BEARY RIDE, TOO? CAN SHE? I WANT HER TO SEE UP HIGH!
SLOW DOWN!
KEEP YOUR SPACE ADVENTURES, HAL. I'LL TAKE BEING A DAD.
DON'T BLAME YOU ON THAT ONE, LITTLE BROTHER.

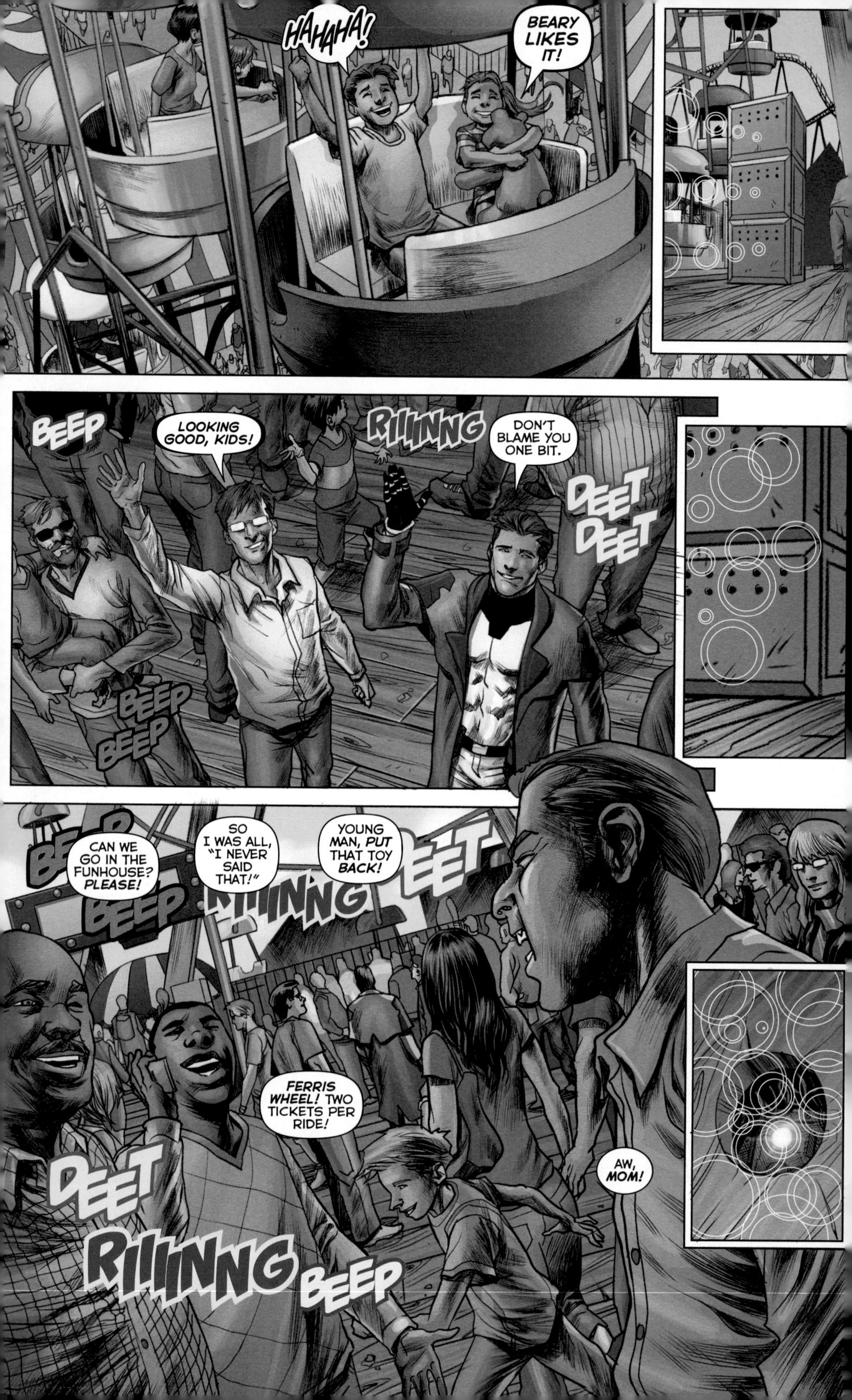
HAHAHA!
BEARY LIKES IT!
BEEP
LOOKING GOOD, KIDS!
RIIIINNG
DON'T BLAME YOU ONE BIT.
DEET DEET
BEEP BEEP
CAN WE GO IN THE FUNHOUSE? PLEASE!
SO I WAS ALL, "I NEVER SAID THAT!"
YOUNG MAN, PUT THAT TOY BACK!
BEEP
RIIIINNG
DEET
FERRIS WHEEL! TWO TICKETS PER RIDE!
AW, MOM!
DEET
RIIIINNG BEEP

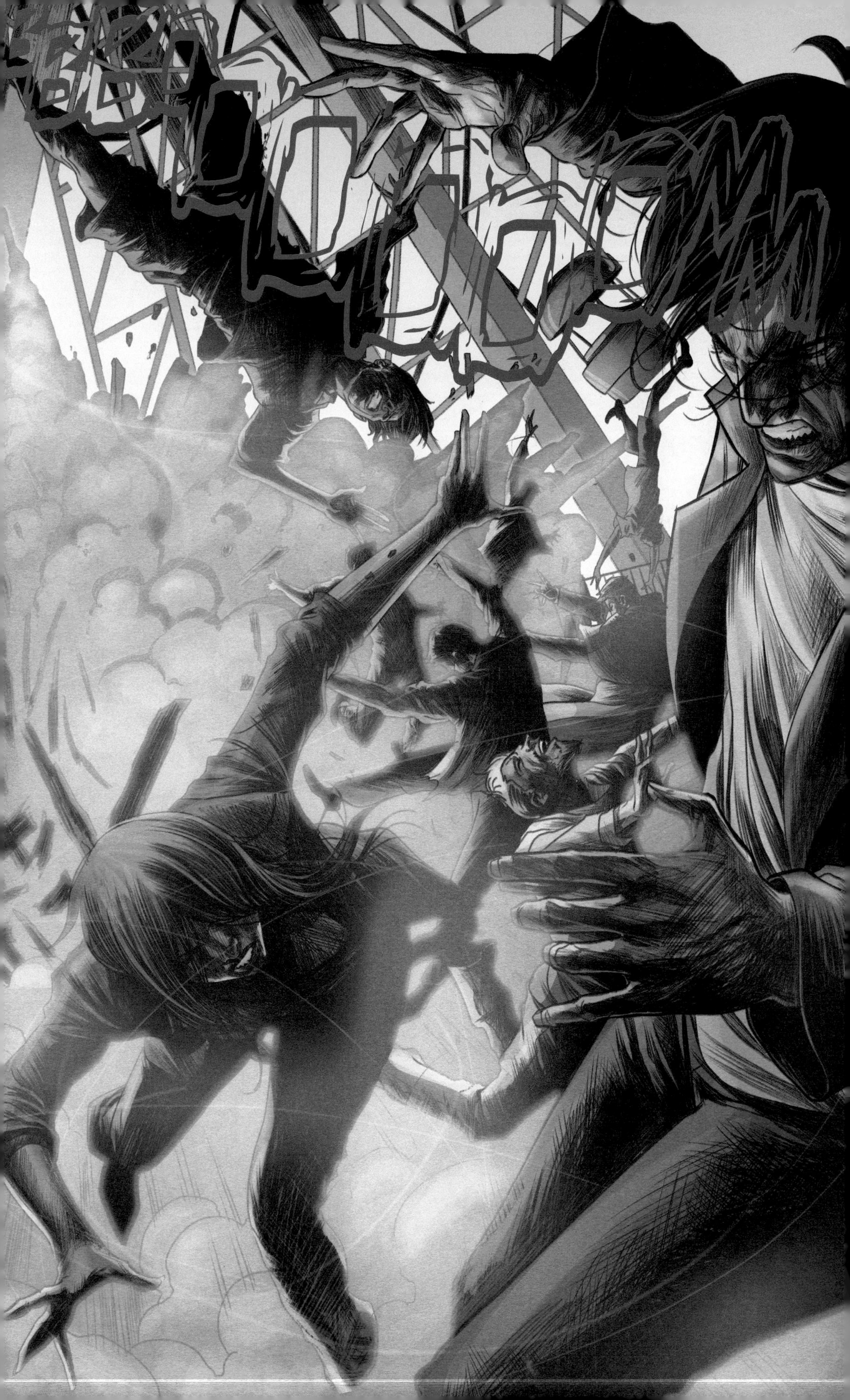

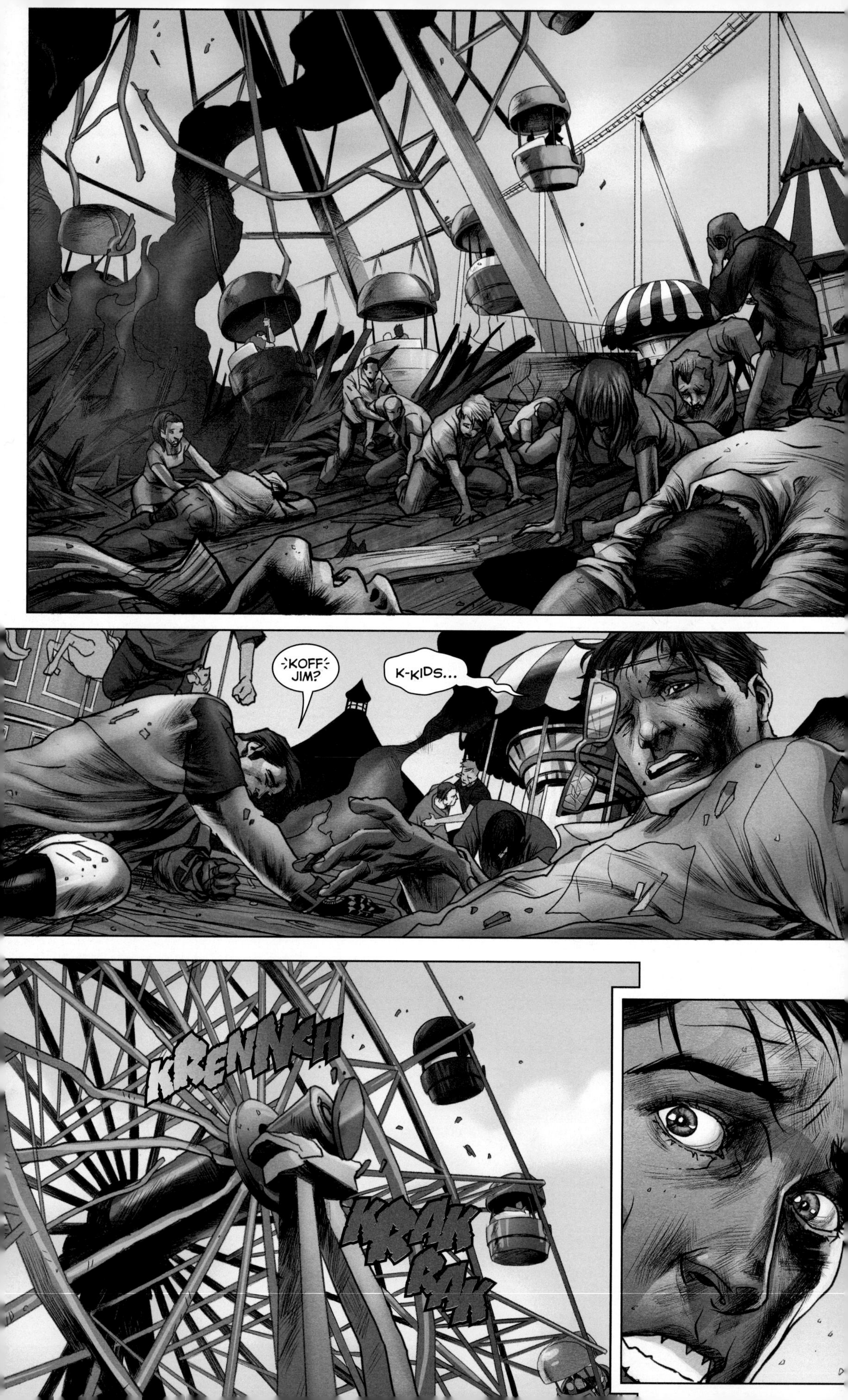

-KOFF- JIM?
K-KIDS...
KRENNCH
KRAK RAK

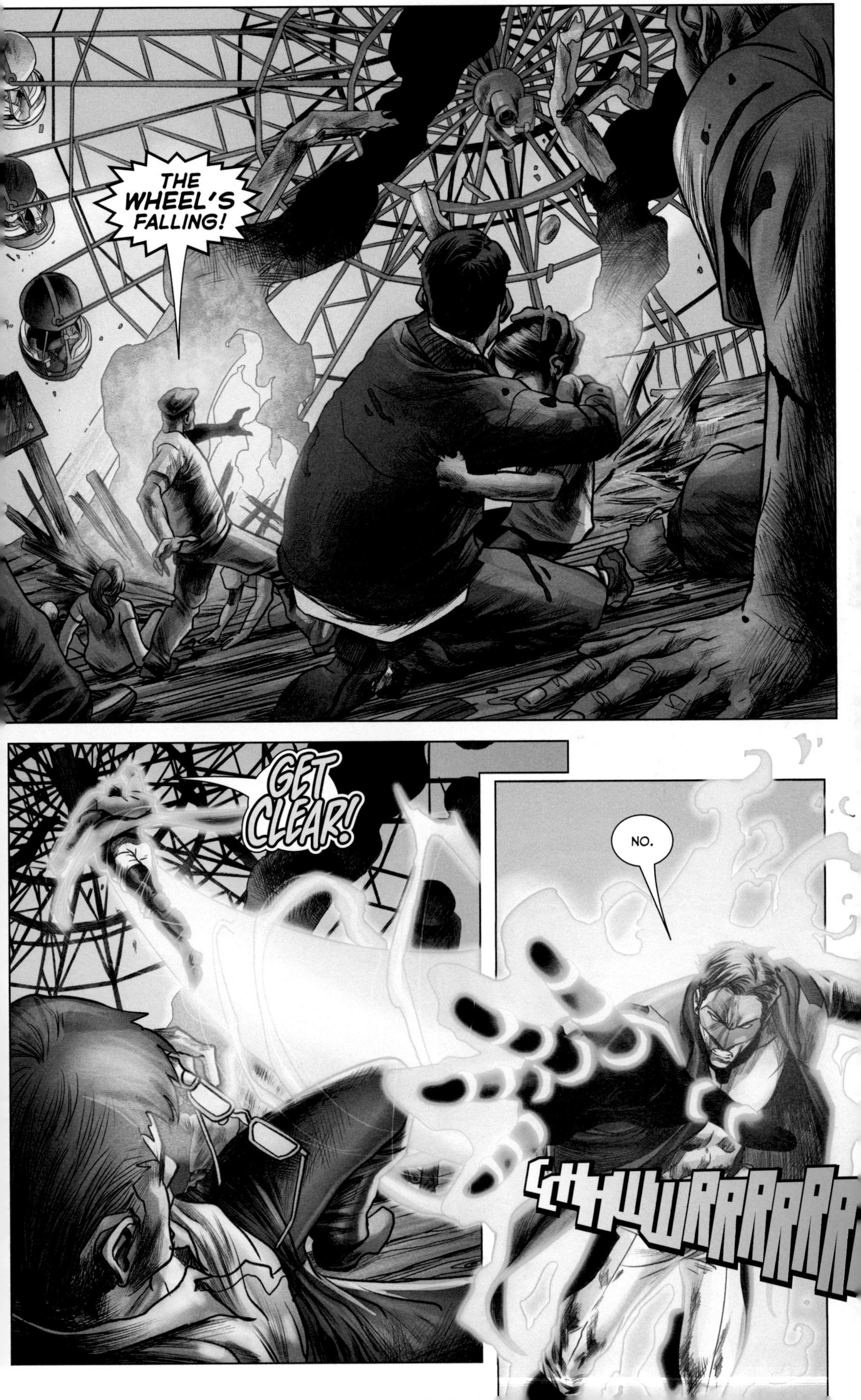
THE WHEEL'S FALLING!
GET CLEAR!
NO.
CCHHWURRRRRRR

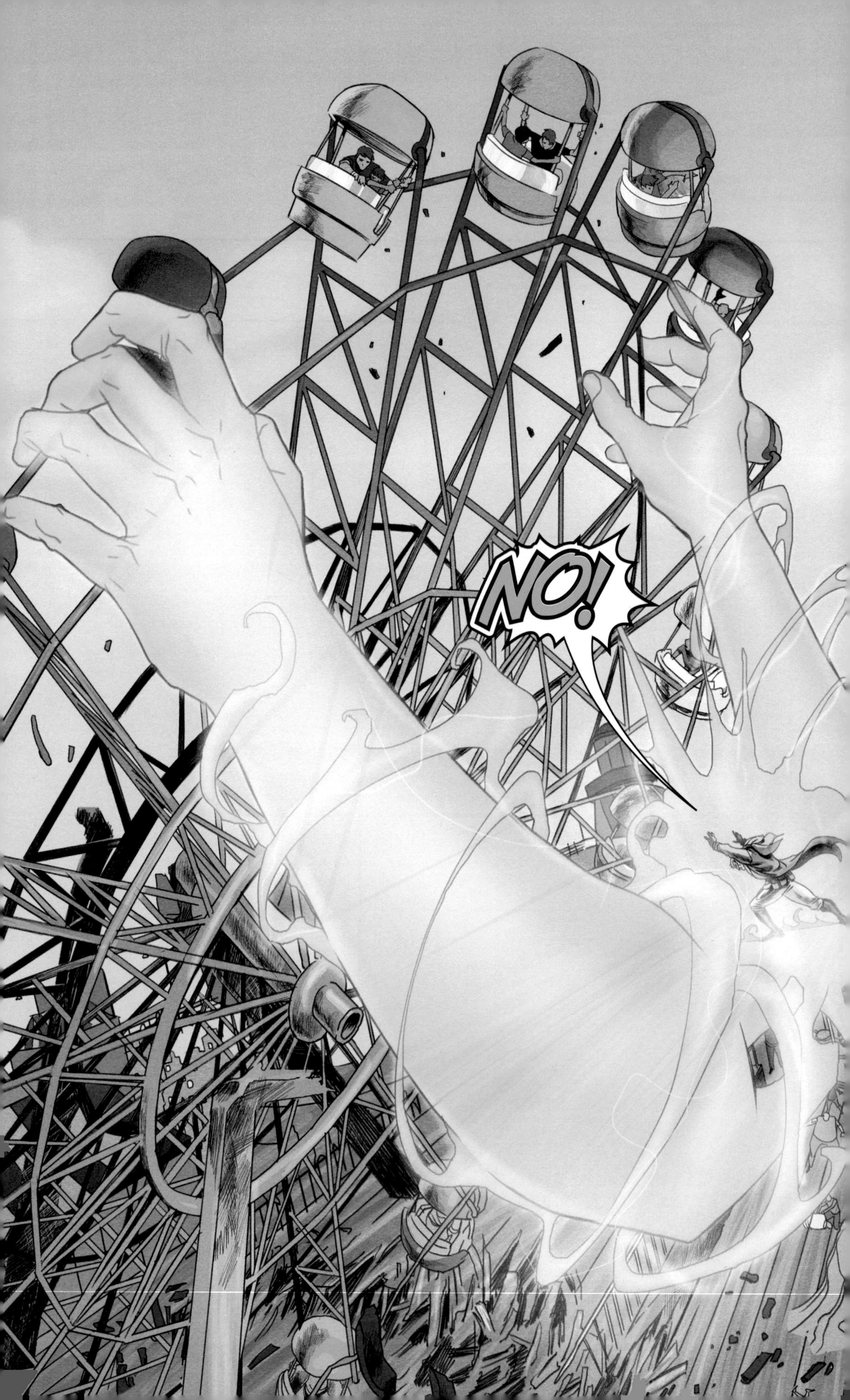
NO!

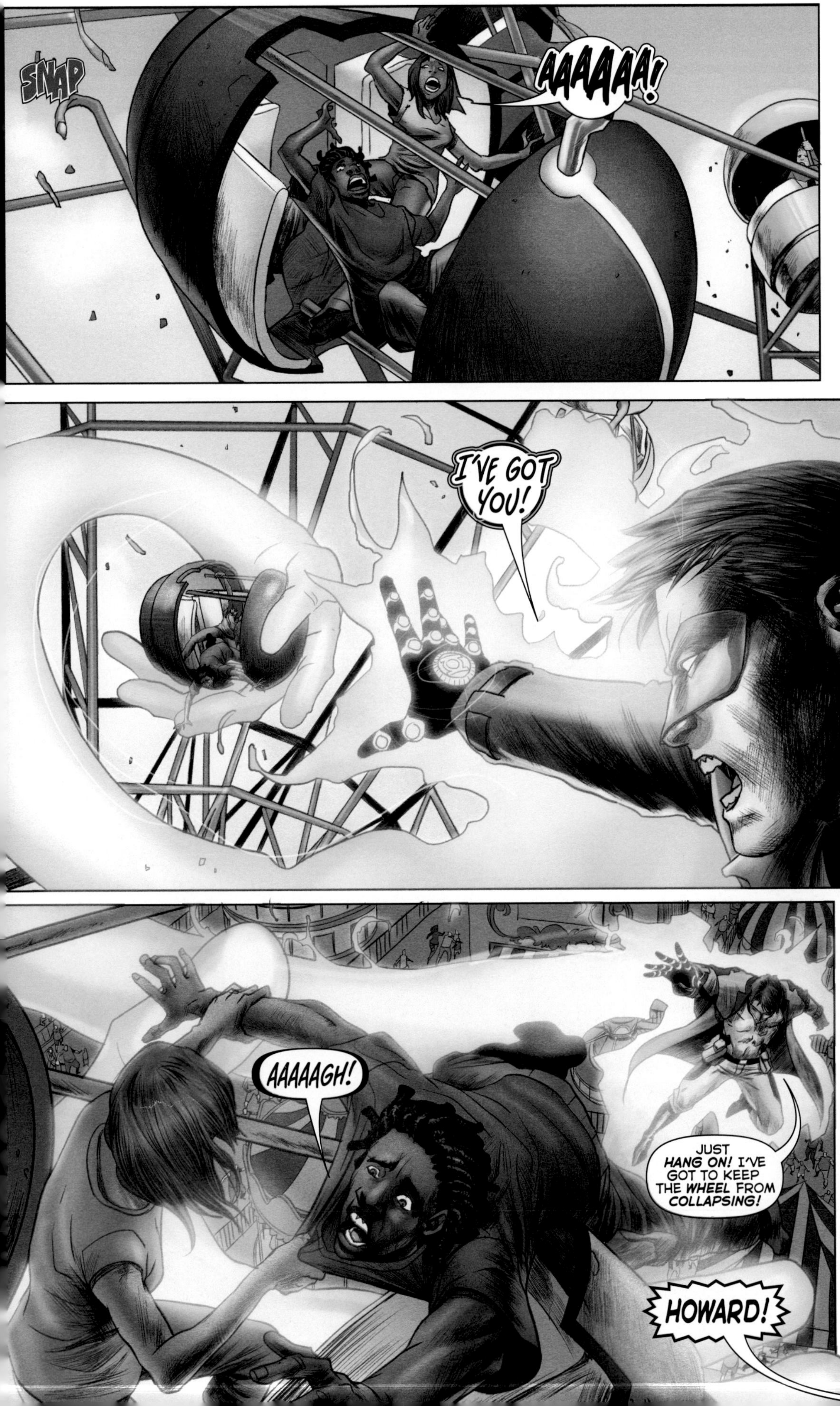
SNAP
AAAAAA!
I'VE GOT YOU!
AAAAAGH!
JUST HANG ON! I'VE GOT TO KEEP THE WHEEL FROM COLLAPSING!
HOWARD!

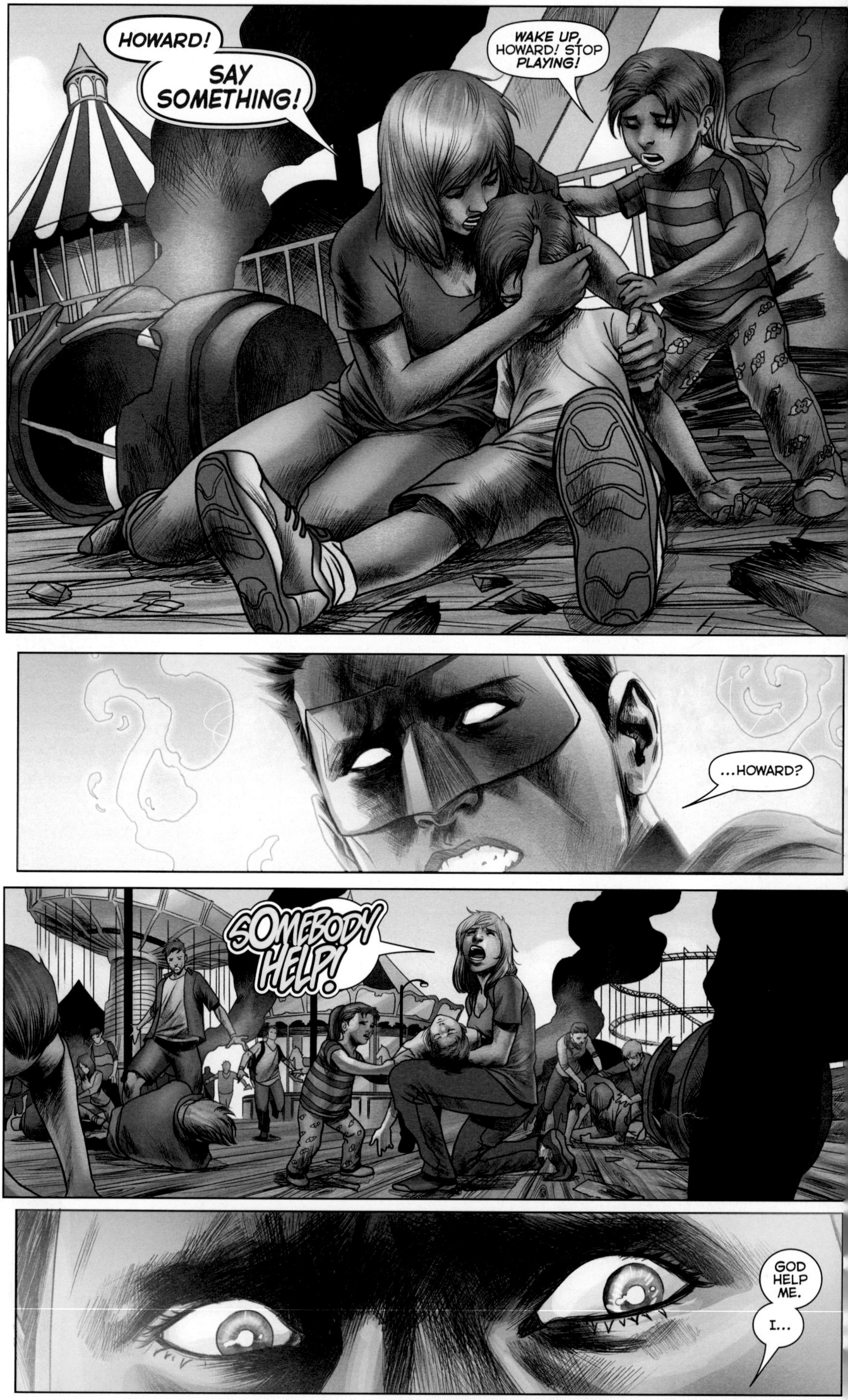
HOWARD!
SAY SOMETHING!
WAKE UP, HOWARD! STOP PLAYING!
...HOWARD?
SOMEBODY HELP!
GOD HELP ME.
I...

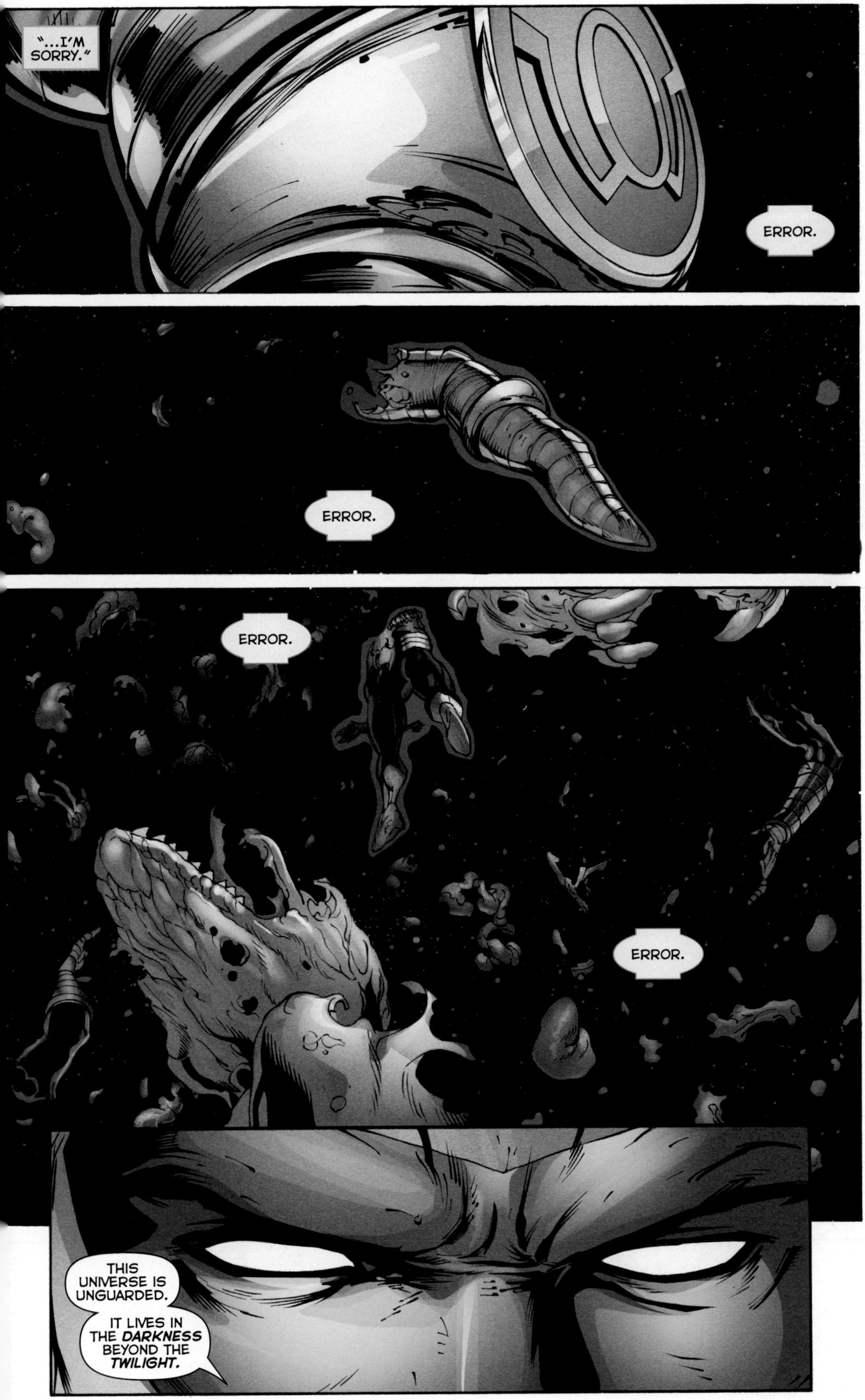
"...I'M SORRY."
ERROR.
ERROR.
ERROR.
ERROR.
THIS UNIVERSE IS UNGUARDED.
IT LIVES IN THE *DARKNESS* BEYOND THE *TWILIGHT*.

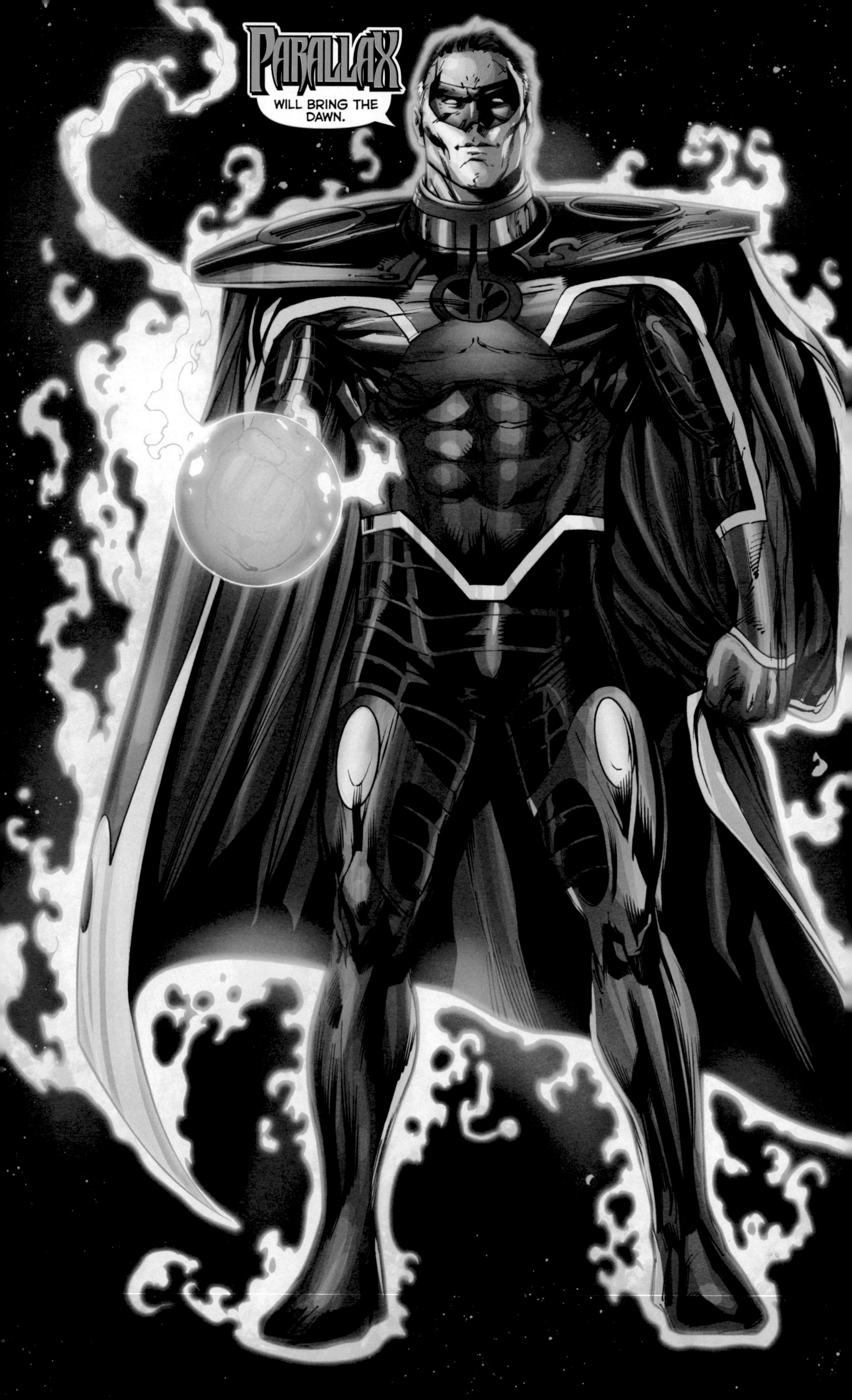
PARALLAX
WILL BRING THE DAWN.

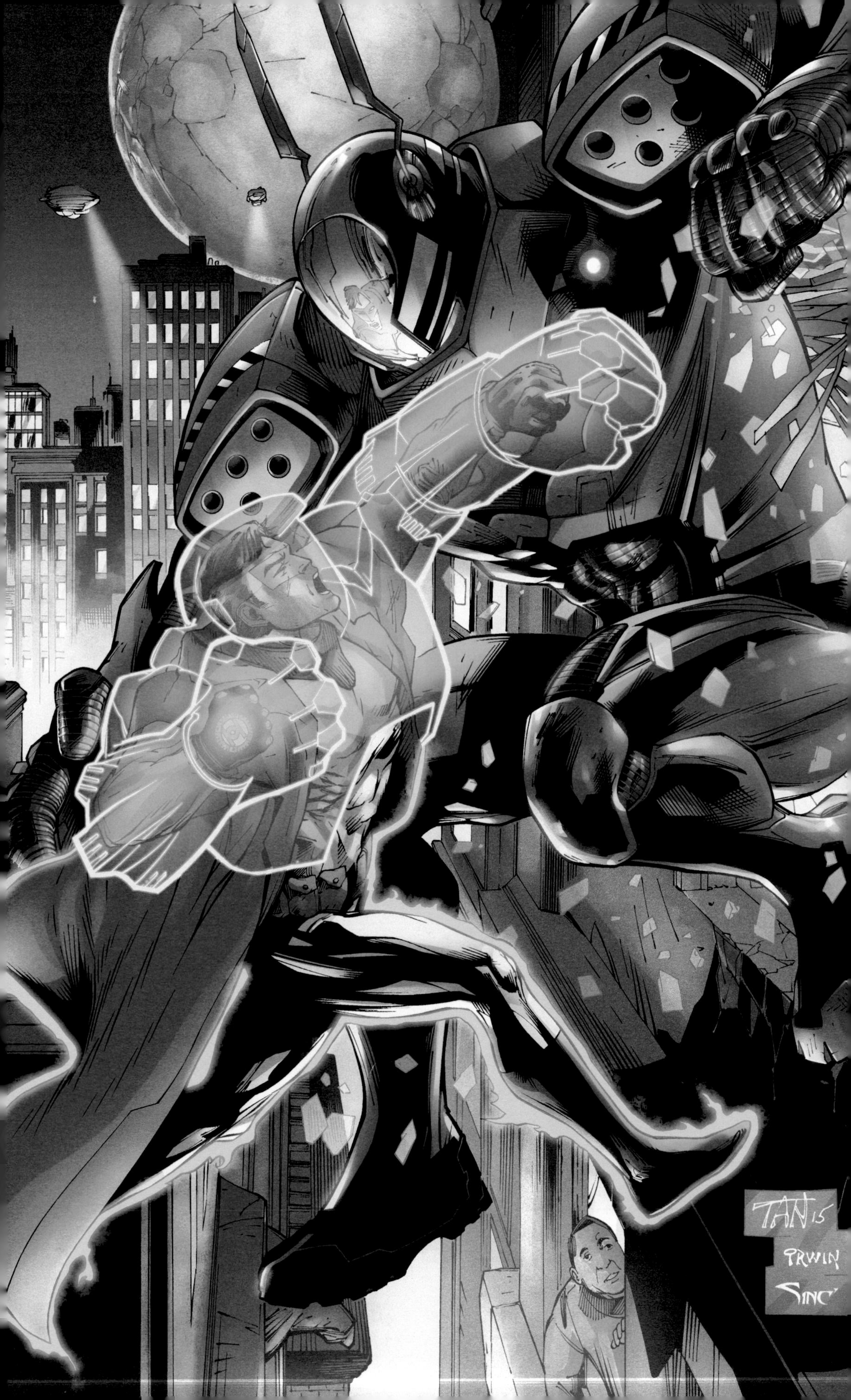
TAN 15
IRWIN
SINC'

CLOSE TO HOME

ROBERT VENDITTI writer **MARTIN COCCOLO BILLY TAN** pencillers **MARK IRWIN** inker **TONY AVIÑA** colorist **DAVE SHARPE** letterer **BILLY TAN & ALEX SINCLAIR** cover

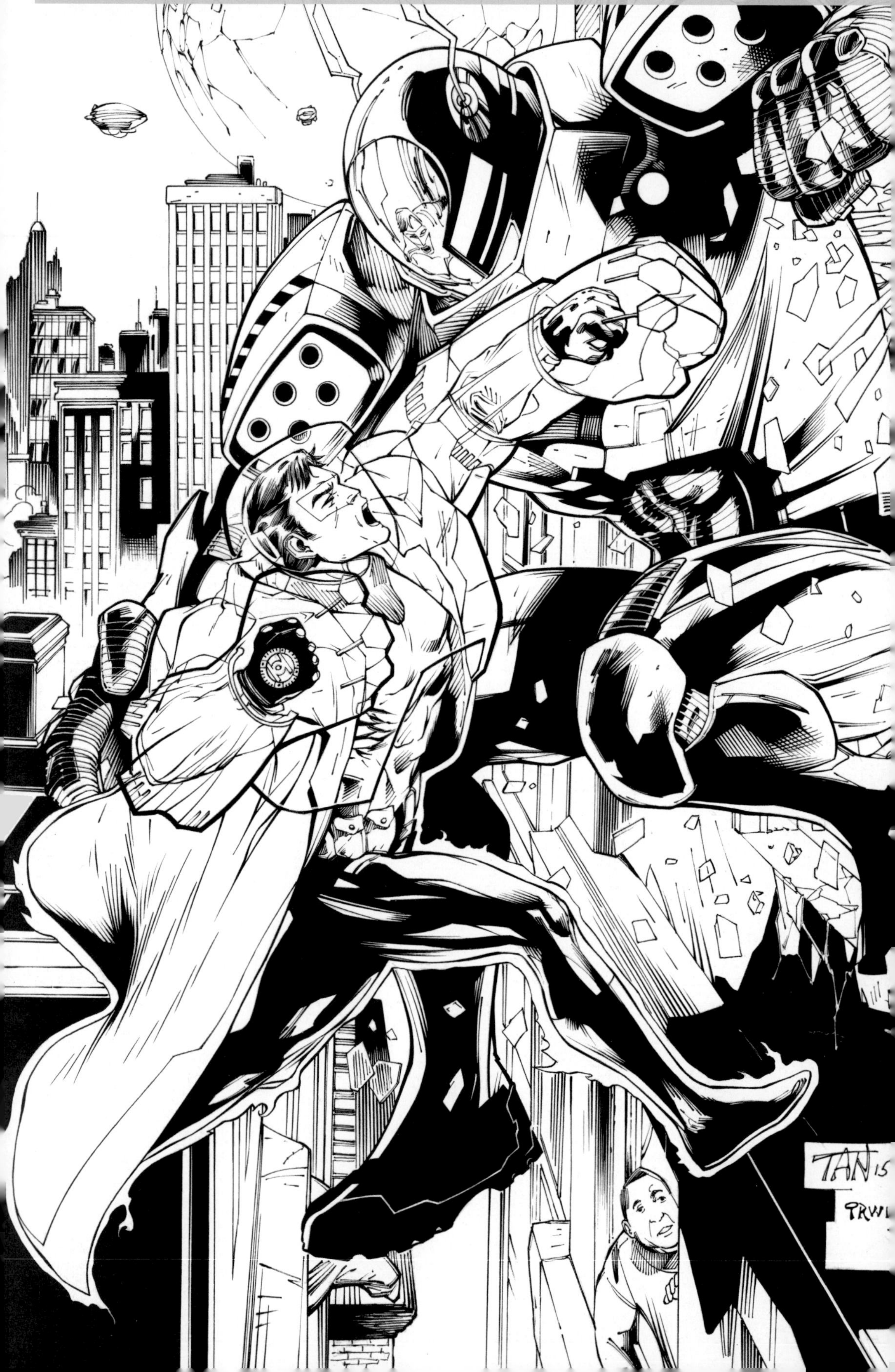

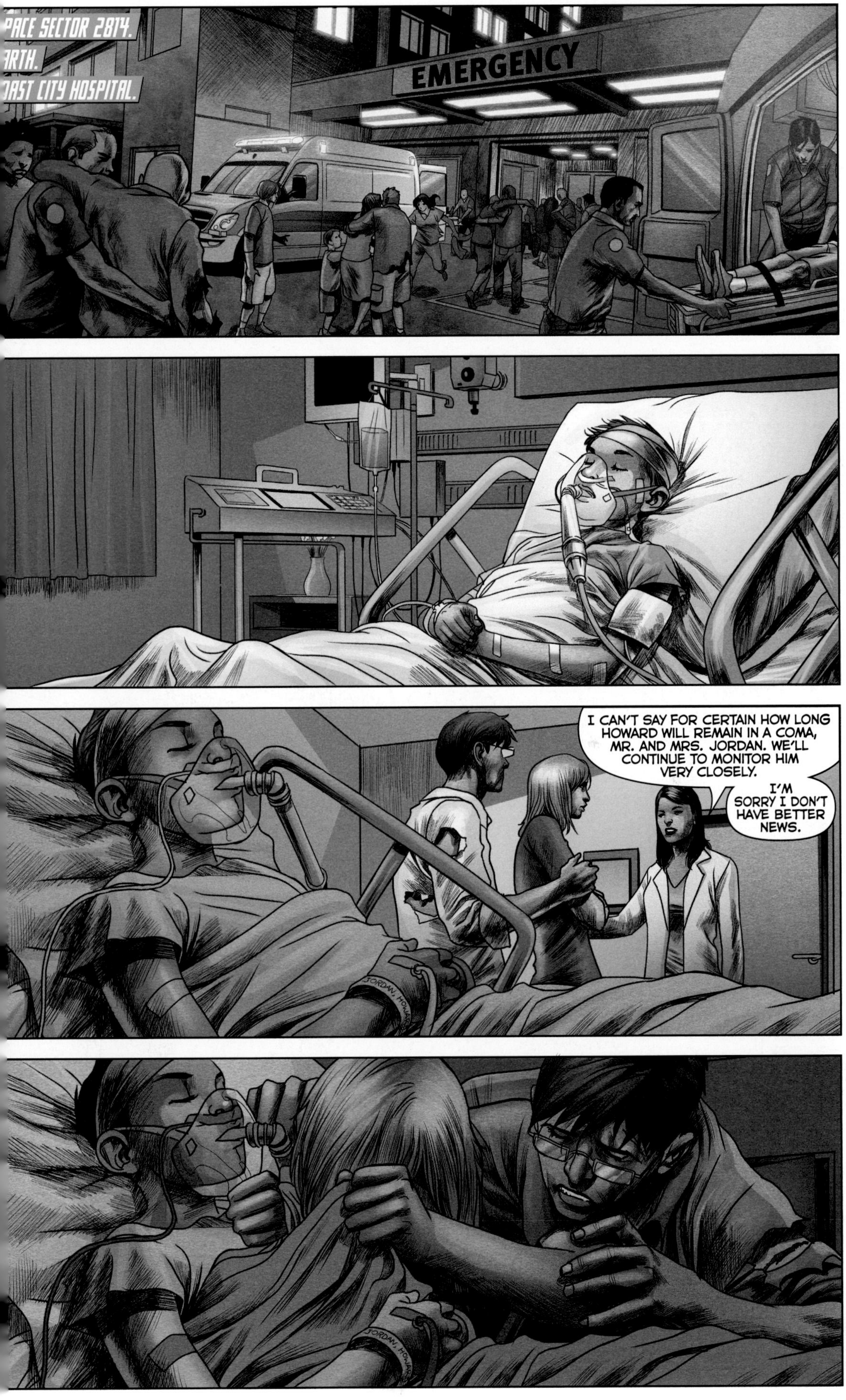
PACE SECTOR 2814.
ARTH.
OAST CITY HOSPITAL.
EMERGENCY
I CAN'T SAY FOR CERTAIN HOW LONG HOWARD WILL REMAIN IN A COMA, MR. AND MRS. JORDAN. WE'LL CONTINUE TO MONITOR HIM VERY CLOSELY.
I'M SORRY I DON'T HAVE BETTER NEWS.

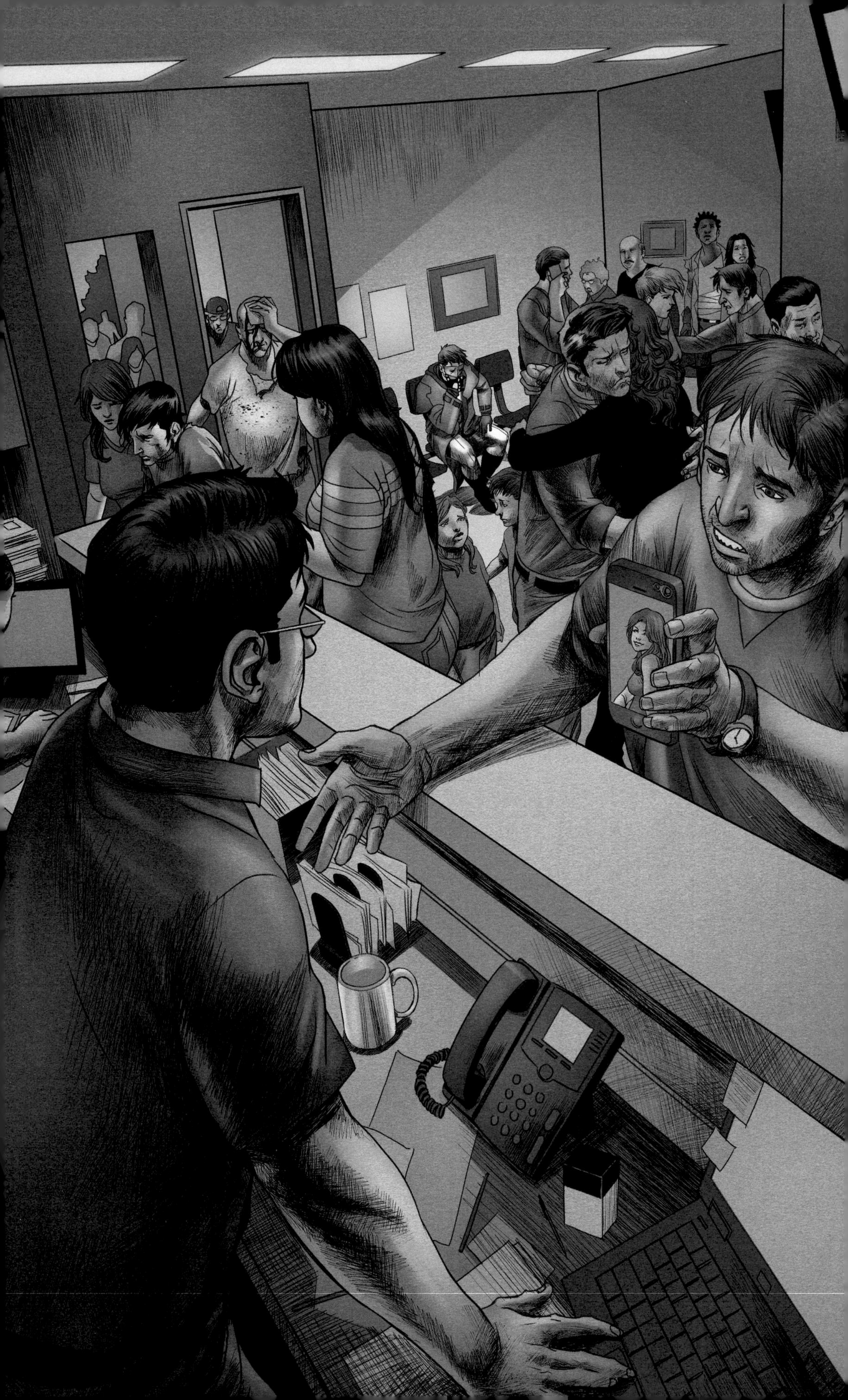

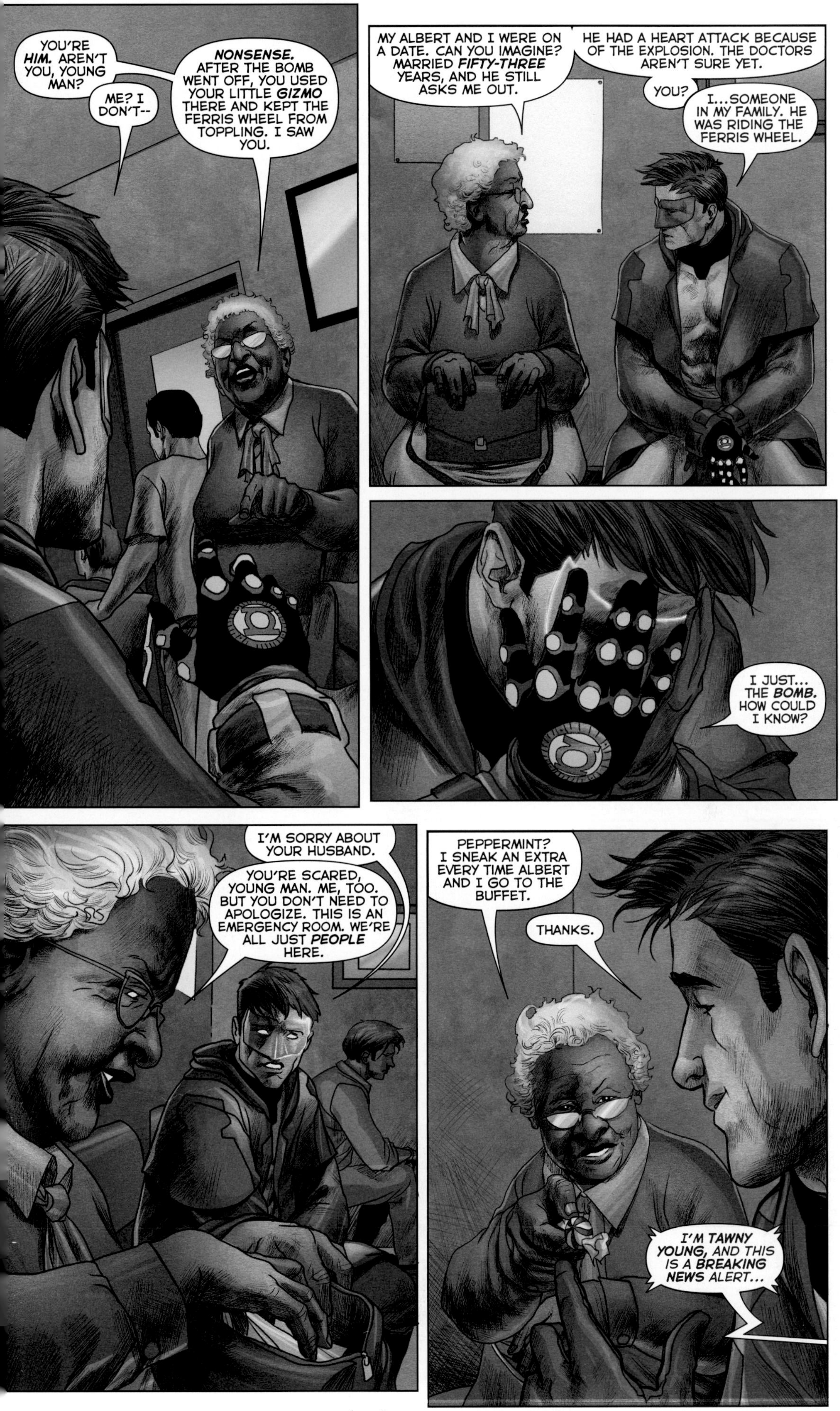
YOU'RE HIM. AREN'T YOU, YOUNG MAN?
ME? I DON'T--
NONSENSE. AFTER THE BOMB WENT OFF, YOU USED YOUR LITTLE GIZMO THERE AND KEPT THE FERRIS WHEEL FROM TOPPLING. I SAW YOU.
MY ALBERT AND I WERE ON A DATE. CAN YOU IMAGINE? MARRIED FIFTY-THREE YEARS, AND HE STILL ASKS ME OUT.
HE HAD A HEART ATTACK BECAUSE OF THE EXPLOSION. THE DOCTORS AREN'T SURE YET.
YOU?
I...SOMEONE IN MY FAMILY. HE WAS RIDING THE FERRIS WHEEL.
I JUST... THE BOMB. HOW COULD I KNOW?
I'M SORRY ABOUT YOUR HUSBAND.
YOU'RE SCARED, YOUNG MAN. ME, TOO. BUT YOU DON'T NEED TO APOLOGIZE. THIS IS AN EMERGENCY ROOM. WE'RE ALL JUST PEOPLE HERE.
PEPPERMINT? I SNEAK AN EXTRA EVERY TIME ALBERT AND I GO TO THE BUFFET.
THANKS.
I'M TAWNY YOUNG, AND THIS IS A BREAKING NEWS ALERT...

A VIDEO HAS BEEN SENT TO **WGBS NEWS** AND OTHER OUTLETS AROUND THE WORLD, IN WHICH A MAN SAYS HE AND HIS ORGANIZATION ARE RESPONSIBLE FOR THIS EVENING'S **BOMBING** IN COAST CITY.

WE ASK ALL VIEWERS TO PAY **CAREFUL ATTENTION** TO WHAT FOLLOWS.

BREAKING: COAST CITY BOMBING

MY NAME IS BITO WLADON, BUT YOU MAY CALL ME "SONAR." I TELL YOU MY NAME BECAUSE I HAVE NOTHING TO FEAR. YOU WILL **NOT** FIND ME.

TOO LONG, THE WORLD HAS **IGNORED** THE PLIGHT OF MY FELLOW MODORANS. BUT I AND MY **MODORAN SEPARATIST ARMY** HAVE YOUR ATTENTION NOW.

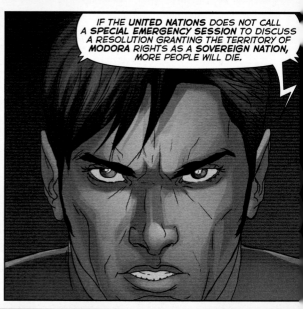

IF THE **UNITED NATIONS** DOES NOT CALL A **SPECIAL EMERGENCY SESSION** TO DISCUSS A RESOLUTION GRANTING THE TERRITORY OF **MODORA** RIGHTS AS A **SOVEREIGN NATION**, MORE PEOPLE WILL DIE.

YOU HAVE SEEN WHAT MY **BOMBS** CAN DO. EVEN IN THE HEART OF AMERICA'S SO-CALLED "CITY WITHOUT FEAR."

THE WORLD HAS **TWO DAYS.**

MODORA? WHERE THE HELL IS **MODORA?**

THAT IS THE END OF THE VIDEO. THE POLICE AND F.B.I. ASK ANYONE WITH INFORMATION ABOUT BITO WLADON TO CONTACT THEM IMMEDIATELTY.

BREAKING: COAST CITY BOMBING

YOU GO GET HIM, YOUNG MAN.

YOU TELL HIM MY **ALBERT** SENT YOU.

I'LL FIND HIM.

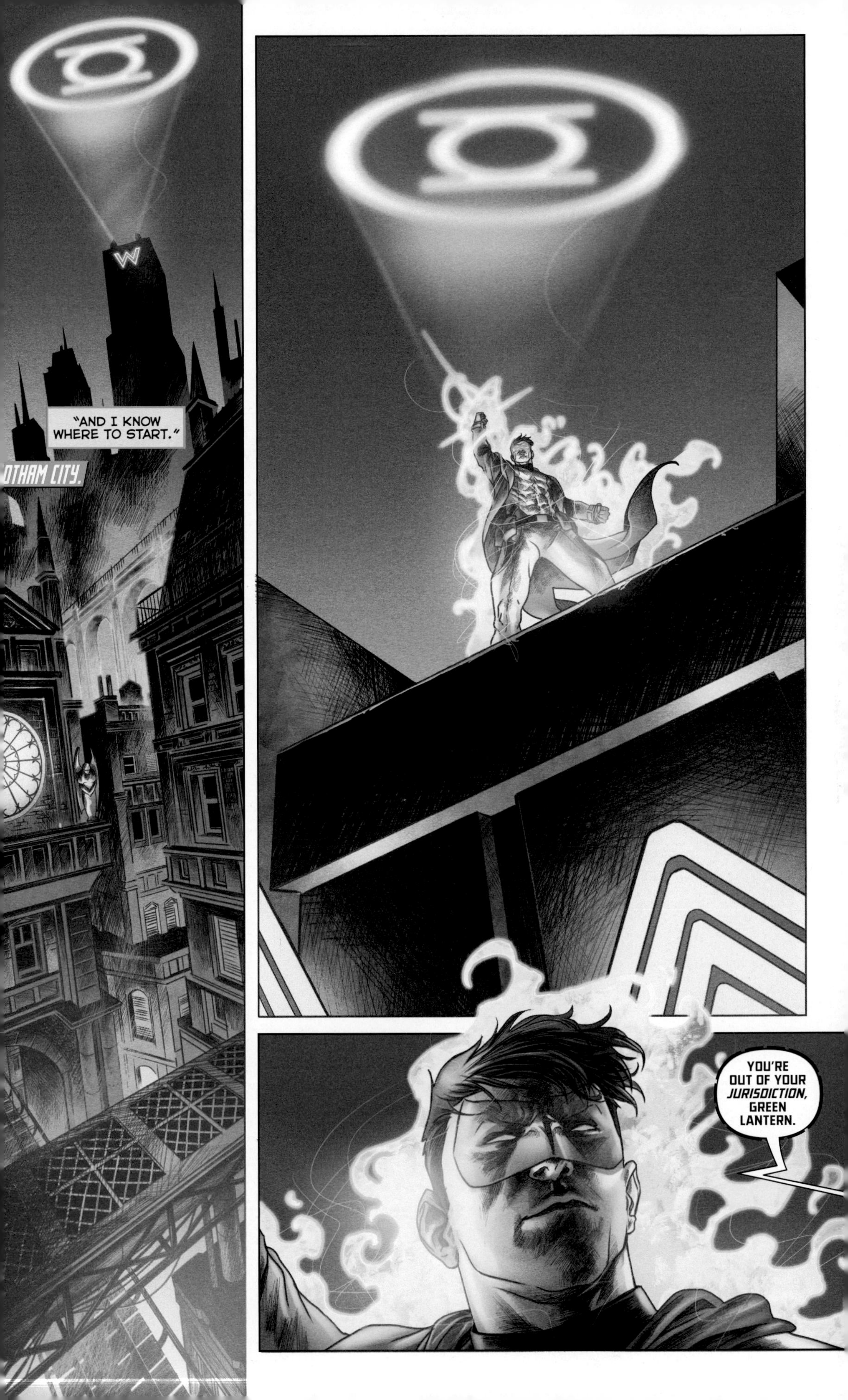
"AND I KNOW WHERE TO START."
OTHAM CITY.
YOU'RE OUT OF YOUR *JURISDICTION,* GREEN LANTERN.

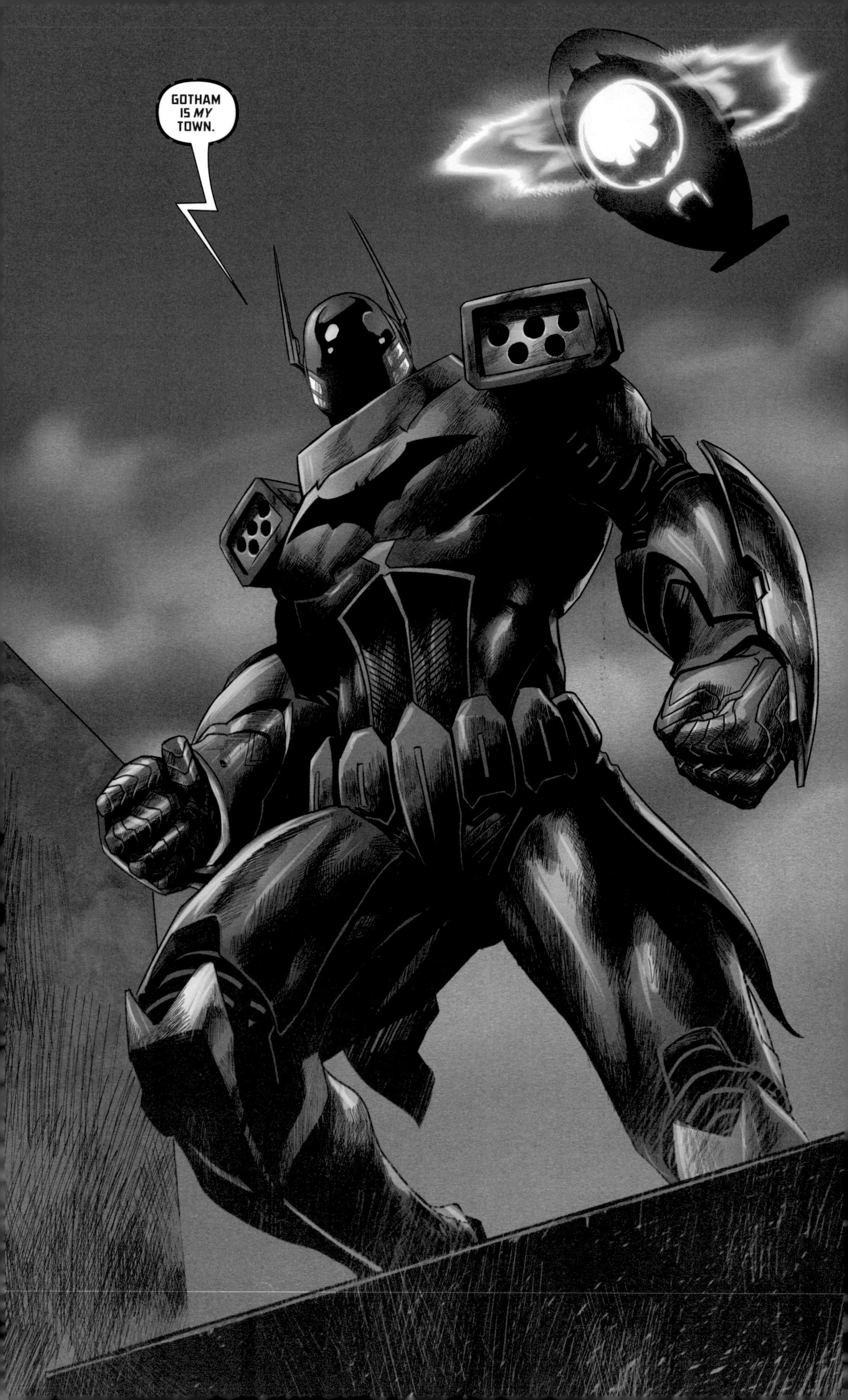
GOTHAM IS *MY* TOWN.

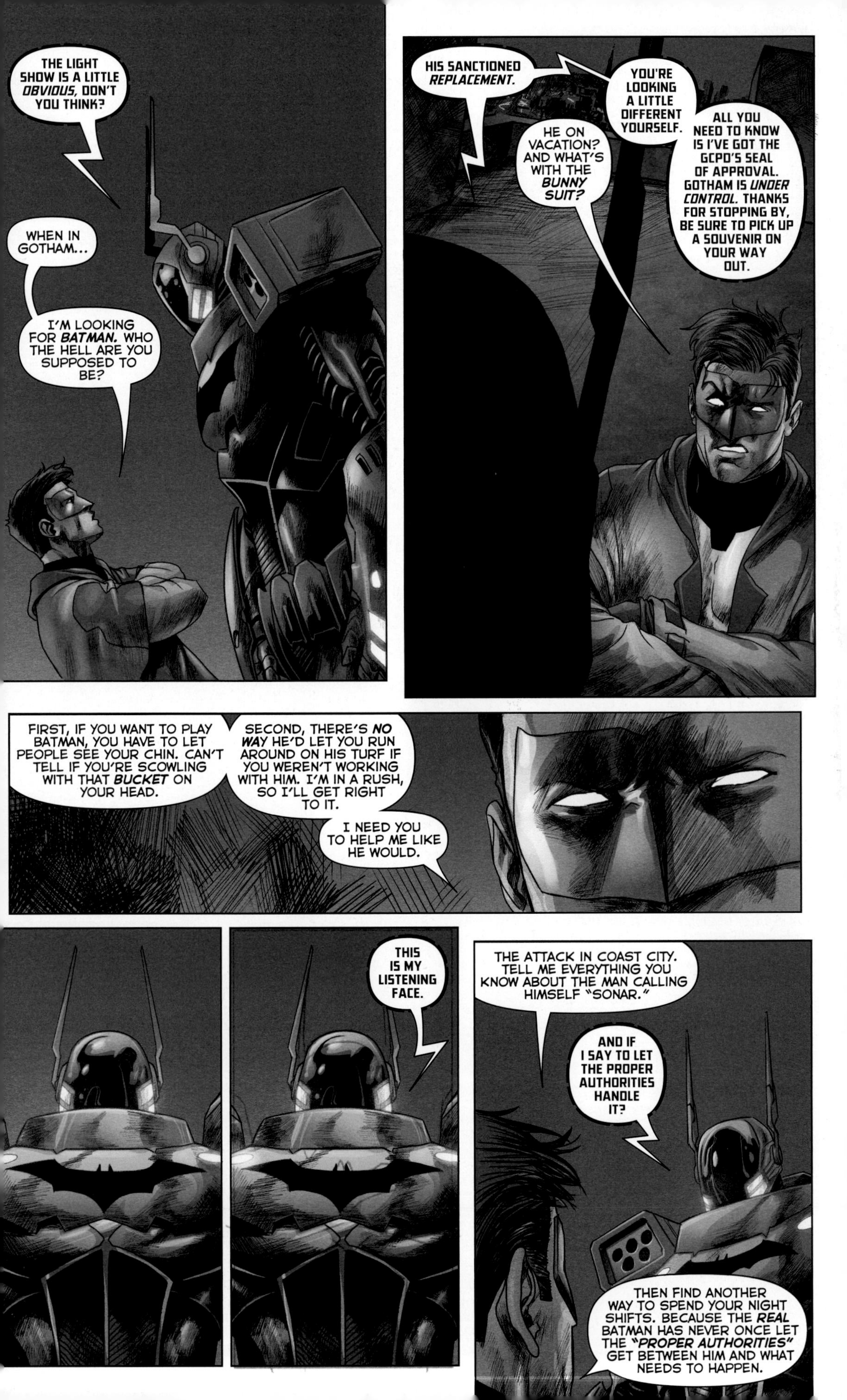
THE LIGHT SHOW IS A LITTLE *OBVIOUS*, DON'T YOU THINK?
WHEN IN GOTHAM...
I'M LOOKING FOR ***BATMAN.*** WHO THE HELL ARE YOU SUPPOSED TO BE?
HIS SANCTIONED ***REPLACEMENT.***
HE ON VACATION? AND WHAT'S WITH THE ***BUNNY SUIT?***
YOU'RE LOOKING A LITTLE DIFFERENT YOURSELF.
ALL YOU NEED TO KNOW IS I'VE GOT THE GCPD'S SEAL OF APPROVAL. GOTHAM IS *UNDER CONTROL.* THANKS FOR STOPPING BY, BE SURE TO PICK UP A SOUVENIR ON YOUR WAY OUT.
FIRST, IF YOU WANT TO PLAY BATMAN, YOU HAVE TO LET PEOPLE SEE YOUR CHIN. CAN'T TELL IF YOU'RE SCOWLING WITH THAT ***BUCKET*** ON YOUR HEAD.
SECOND, THERE'S ***NO WAY*** HE'D LET YOU RUN AROUND ON HIS TURF IF YOU WEREN'T WORKING WITH HIM. I'M IN A RUSH, SO I'LL GET RIGHT TO IT.
I NEED YOU TO HELP ME LIKE HE WOULD.
THIS IS MY LISTENING FACE.
THE ATTACK IN COAST CITY. TELL ME EVERYTHING YOU KNOW ABOUT THE MAN CALLING HIMSELF "SONAR."
AND IF I SAY TO LET THE PROPER AUTHORITIES HANDLE IT?
THEN FIND ANOTHER WAY TO SPEND YOUR NIGHT SHIFTS. BECAUSE THE ***REAL*** BATMAN HAS NEVER ONCE LET THE ***"PROPER AUTHORITIES"*** GET BETWEEN HIM AND WHAT NEEDS TO HAPPEN.

FAIR ENOUGH.

BITO WLADON. LEADER OF THE MODORAN SEPARATIST ARMY.

LAW ENFORCEMENT IN EVERY MAJOR METRO AREA IS ON *HIGHEST ALERT* BECAUSE OF HIM. THAT THING IN OAKLAND? THAT WAS THEM.

I'VE BEEN *AWAY* FOR A WHILE. NOT REALLY UP ON CURRENT EVENTS.

MODORA IS A *POSTAGE STAMP* OF A REGION IN THE EASTERN BLOC. WHEN THE BERLIN WALL CAME DOWN, THEY GOT LUMPED INSIDE SOMEONE ELSE'S BORDERS. BEEN MAD ABOUT IT EVER SINCE.

CASE IN POINT: AN M.S.A. CELL ATTACKED THE DINNER CROWD AT A RESTAURANT IN OAKLAND. OR AT LEAST TRIED TO. IT WAS SLOPPY. THE ONLY CASUALTIES WERE THEIR OWN.

THAT OP WAS RUN BY THE *OLD* LEADERSHIP. INTELLIGENCE SOURCES SAY WLADON TOOK CONTROL SOON AFTER. NOT WITHOUT BLOODSHED.

"STORY GOES, THE M.S.A.'S PREVIOUS BOSSES MET AT A SAFE HOUSE TO DISCUSS THE GROUP'S FUTURE.

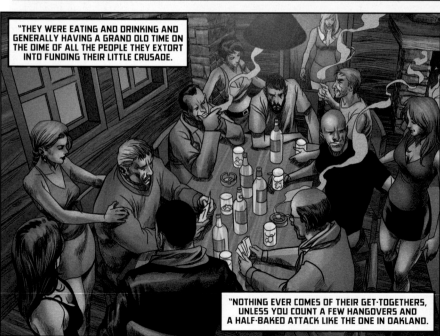

"THEY WERE EATING AND DRINKING AND GENERALLY HAVING A GRAND OLD TIME ON THE DIME OF ALL THE PEOPLE THEY EXTORT INTO FUNDING THEIR LITTLE CRUSADE.

"NOTHING EVER COMES OF THEIR GET-TOGETHERS, UNLESS YOU COUNT A FEW HANGOVERS AND A HALF-BAKED ATTACK LIKE THE ONE IN OAKLAND.

"EXCEPT THIS TIME, THE MEETING HAD RESULTS.

"WLADON WAS TIPPED OFF TO THE LOCATION. HE BUILT AN EXPLOSIVE DEVICE AND HID IT UNDER THE TABLE."

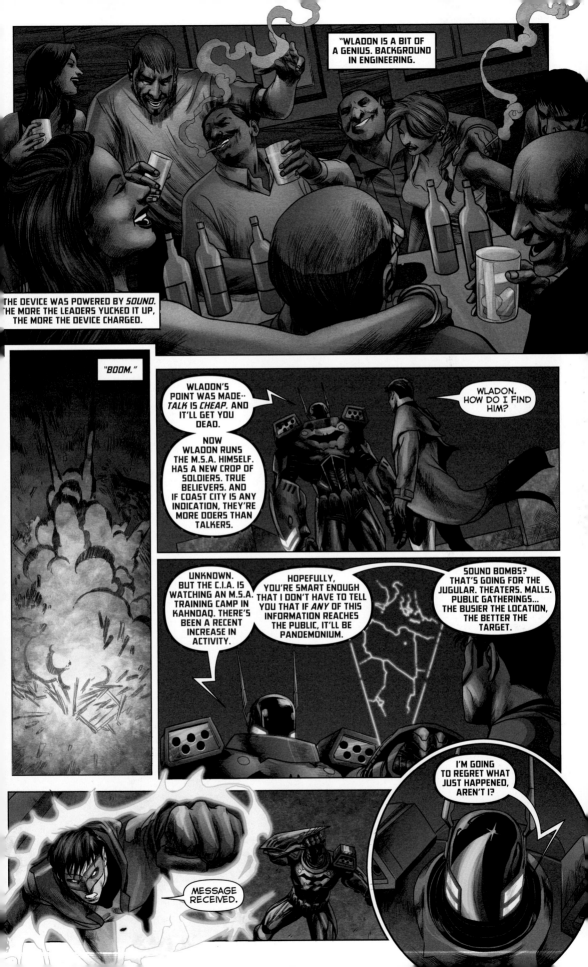

"WLADON IS A BIT OF A GENIUS. BACKGROUND IN ENGINEERING.

THE DEVICE WAS POWERED BY *SOUND*. THE MORE THE LEADERS YUCKED IT UP, THE MORE THE DEVICE CHARGED.

"BOOM."

WLADON'S POINT WAS MADE-- *TALK* IS *CHEAP*. AND IT'LL GET YOU DEAD.

NOW WLADON RUNS THE M.S.A. HIMSELF. HAS A NEW CROP OF SOLDIERS. TRUE BELIEVERS. AND IF COAST CITY IS ANY INDICATION, THEY'RE MORE DOERS THAN TALKERS.

WLADON. HOW DO I FIND HIM?

UNKNOWN. BUT THE C.I.A. IS WATCHING AN M.S.A. TRAINING CAMP IN KAHNDAQ. THERE'S BEEN A RECENT INCREASE IN ACTIVITY.

HOPEFULLY, YOU'RE SMART ENOUGH THAT I DON'T HAVE TO TELL YOU THAT IF *ANY* OF THIS INFORMATION REACHES THE PUBLIC, IT'LL BE PANDEMONIUM.

SOUND BOMBS? THAT'S GOING FOR THE JUGULAR. THEATERS. MALLS. PUBLIC GATHERINGS... THE BUSIER THE LOCATION, THE BETTER THE TARGET.

I'M GOING TO REGRET WHAT JUST HAPPENED, AREN'T I?

MESSAGE RECEIVED.

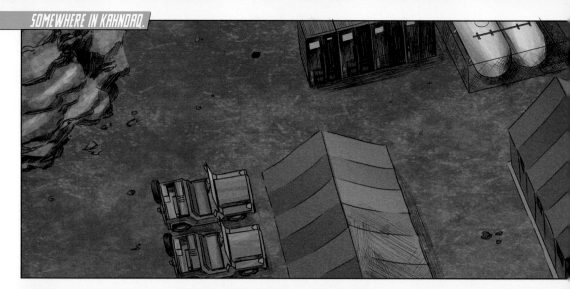

THIP THIP~

<SONAR BUILT YOUR RIFLES. AIM THEM TRUE. *SILENT* AND *LETHAL.*>

<DEATH TO *ALL* WHO DO NOT RECOGNIZE *MODORA.*>*

*TRANSLATED FROM MODORAN.

HM?

<NO ONE GAVE THE COMMAND TO CEASE-->

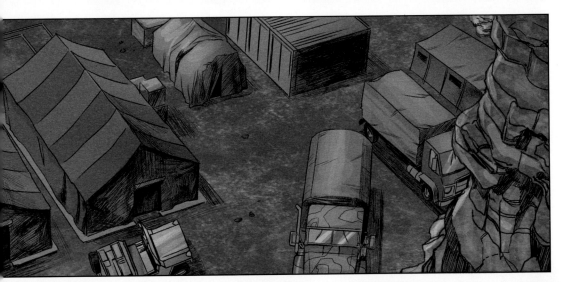

THIP THIP THIP THIP THIP THIP THIP

<...FIRE?>

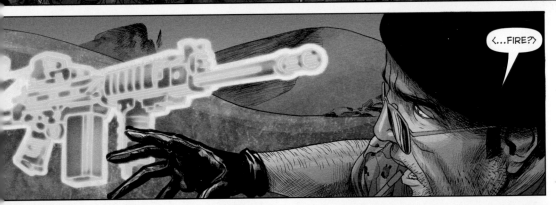

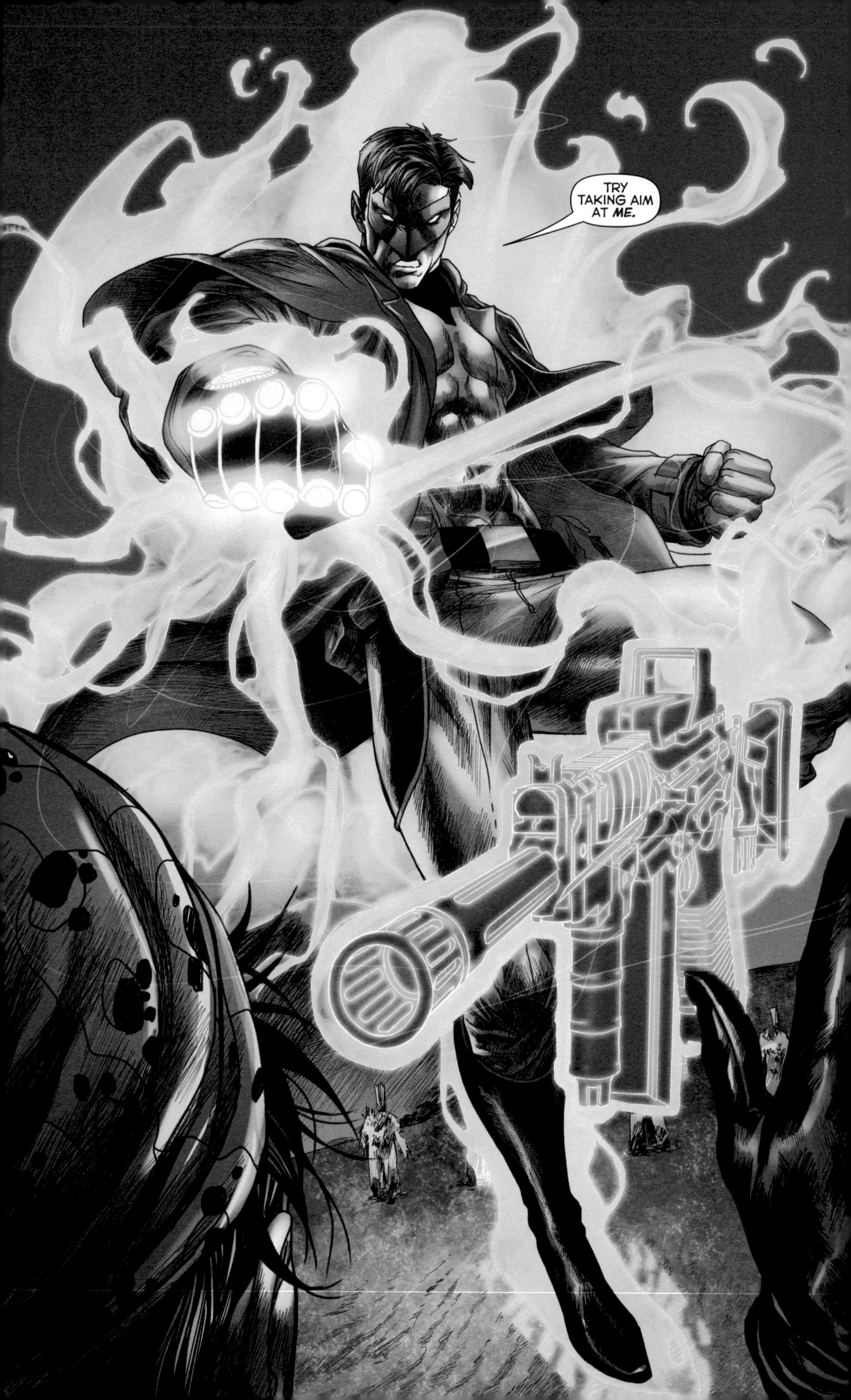
TRY TAKING AIM AT *ME.*

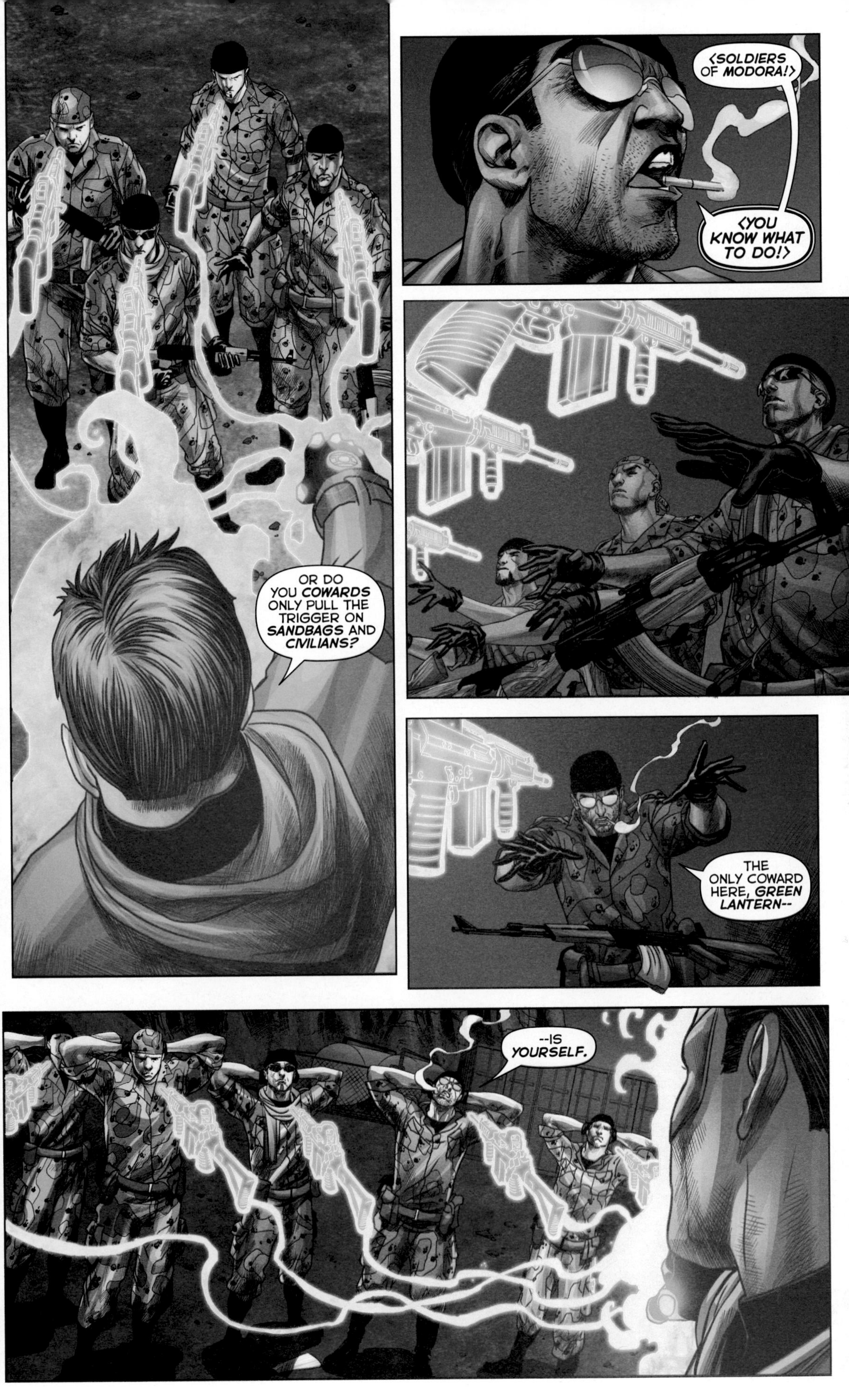
OR DO YOU COWARDS ONLY PULL THE TRIGGER ON SANDBAGS AND CIVILIANS?
<SOLDIERS OF MODORA!>
<YOU KNOW WHAT TO DO!>
THE ONLY COWARD HERE, GREEN LANTERN--
--IS YOURSELF.

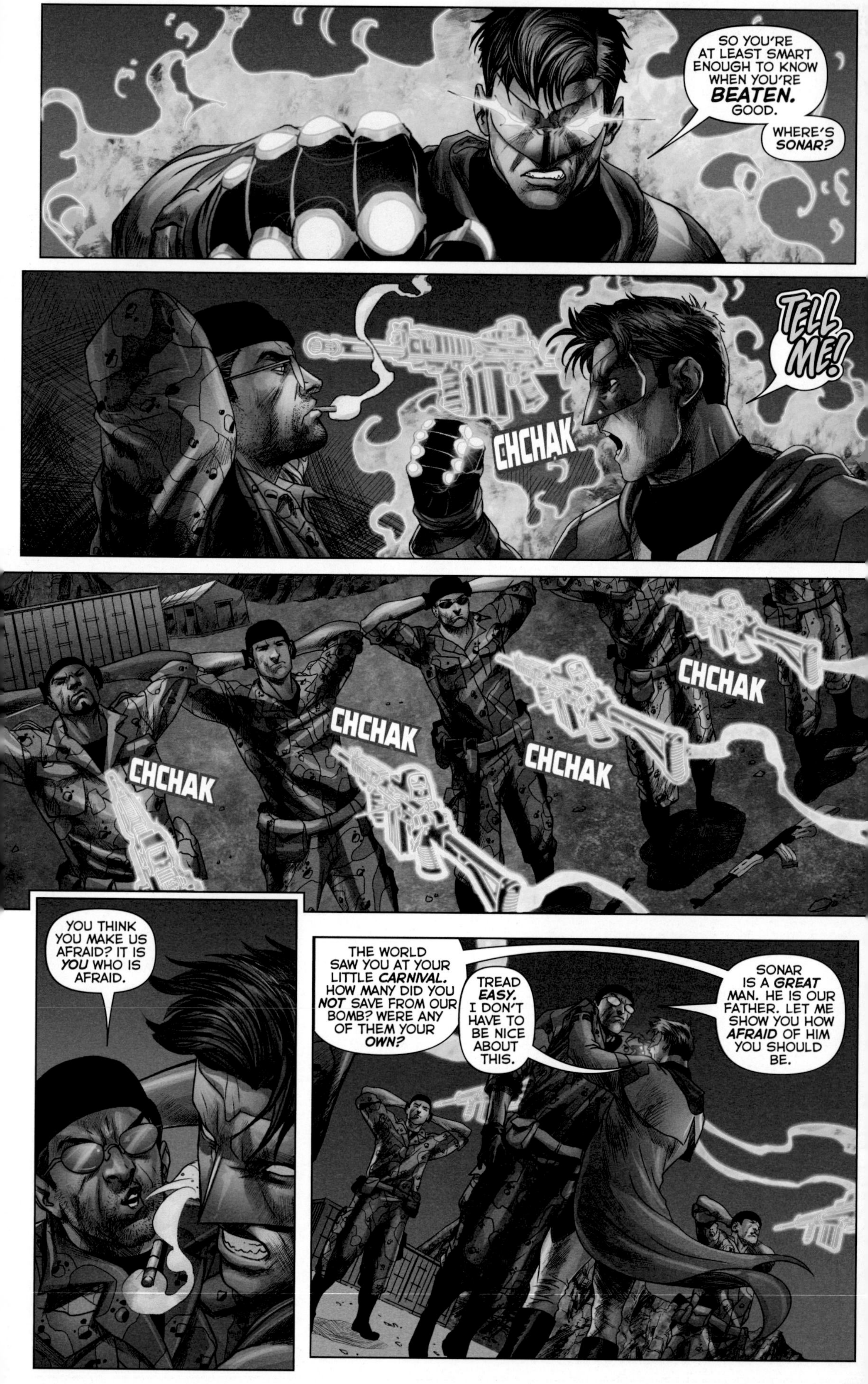

SO YOU'RE AT LEAST SMART ENOUGH TO KNOW WHEN YOU'RE BEATEN. GOOD.
WHERE'S SONAR?
TELL ME!
CHCHAK
CHCHAK
CHCHAK
CHCHAK
CHCHAK
YOU THINK YOU MAKE US AFRAID? IT IS YOU WHO IS AFRAID.
THE WORLD SAW YOU AT YOUR LITTLE CARNIVAL. HOW MANY DID YOU NOT SAVE FROM OUR BOMB? WERE ANY OF THEM YOUR OWN?
TREAD EASY. I DON'T HAVE TO BE NICE ABOUT THIS.
SONAR IS A GREAT MAN. HE IS OUR FATHER. LET ME SHOW YOU HOW AFRAID OF HIM YOU SHOULD BE.

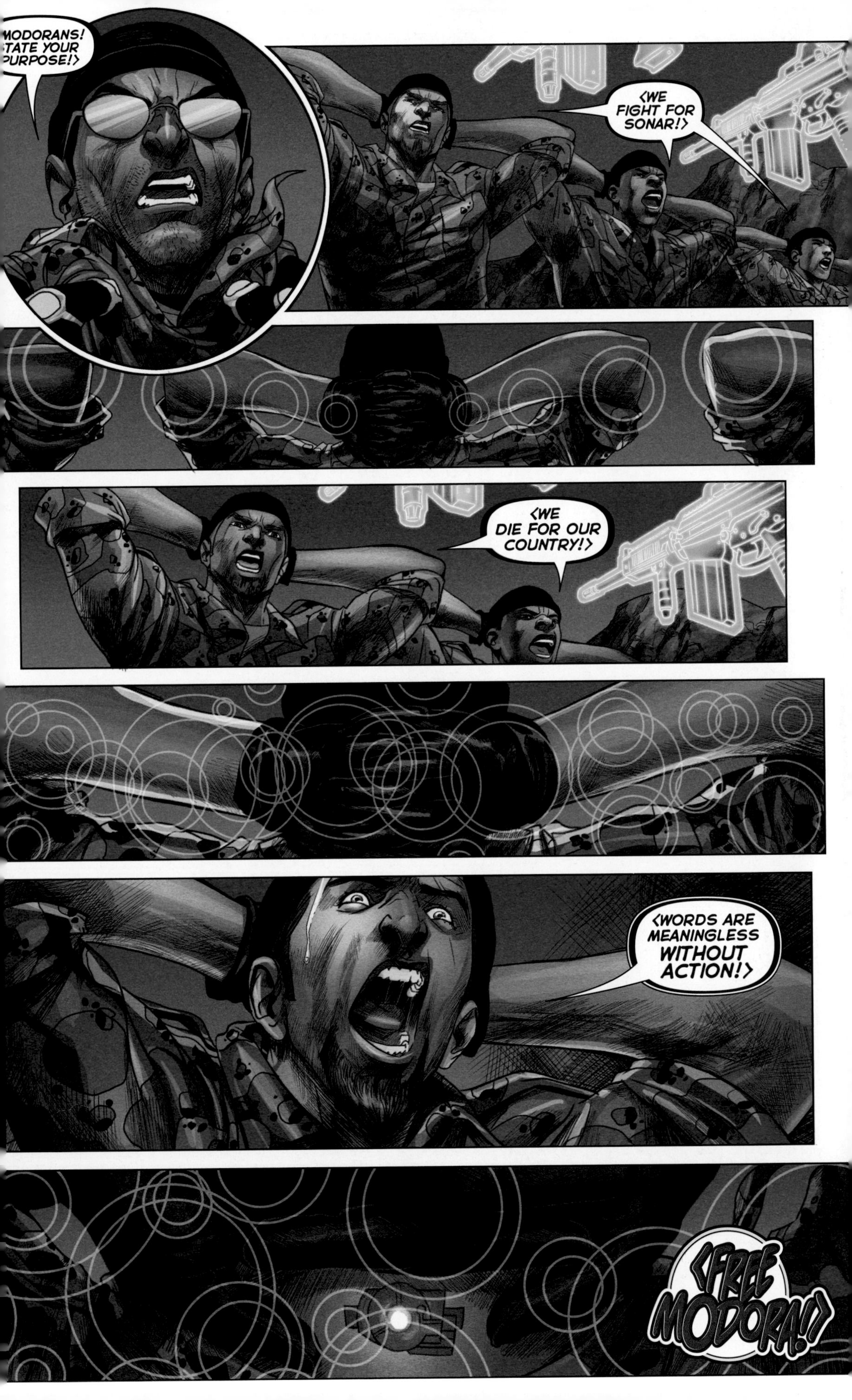
MODORANS! STATE YOUR PURPOSE!>
<WE FIGHT FOR SONAR!>
<WE DIE FOR OUR COUNTRY!>
<WORDS ARE MEANINGLESS WITHOUT ACTION!>
<FREE MODORA!>

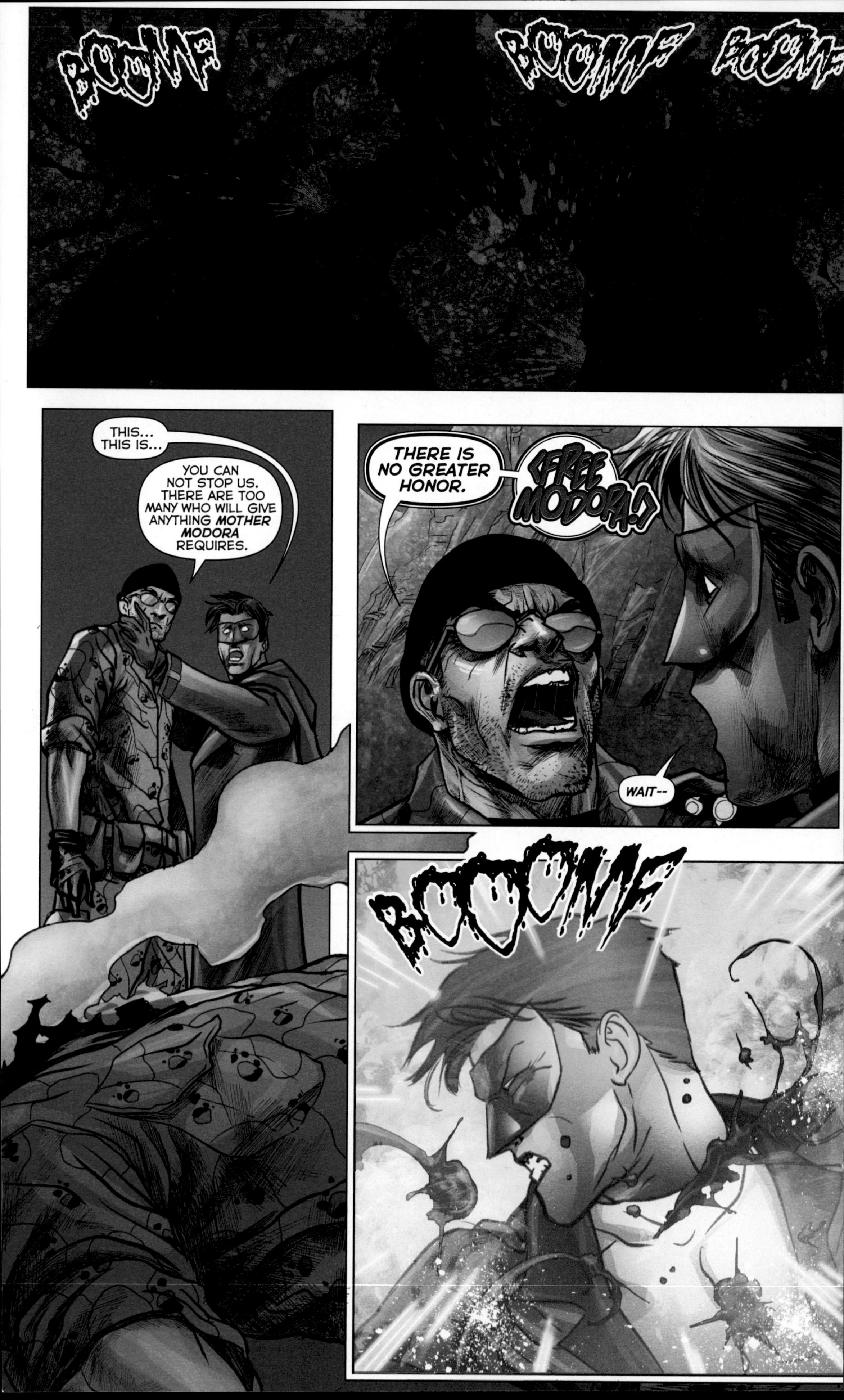
BOOMF
BOOMF
BOOMF
THIS... THIS IS...
YOU CAN NOT STOP US. THERE ARE TOO MANY WHO WILL GIVE ANYTHING *MOTHER MODORA* REQUIRES.
THERE IS NO GREATER HONOR.
<FREE MODORA!>
WAIT--
BOOOMF

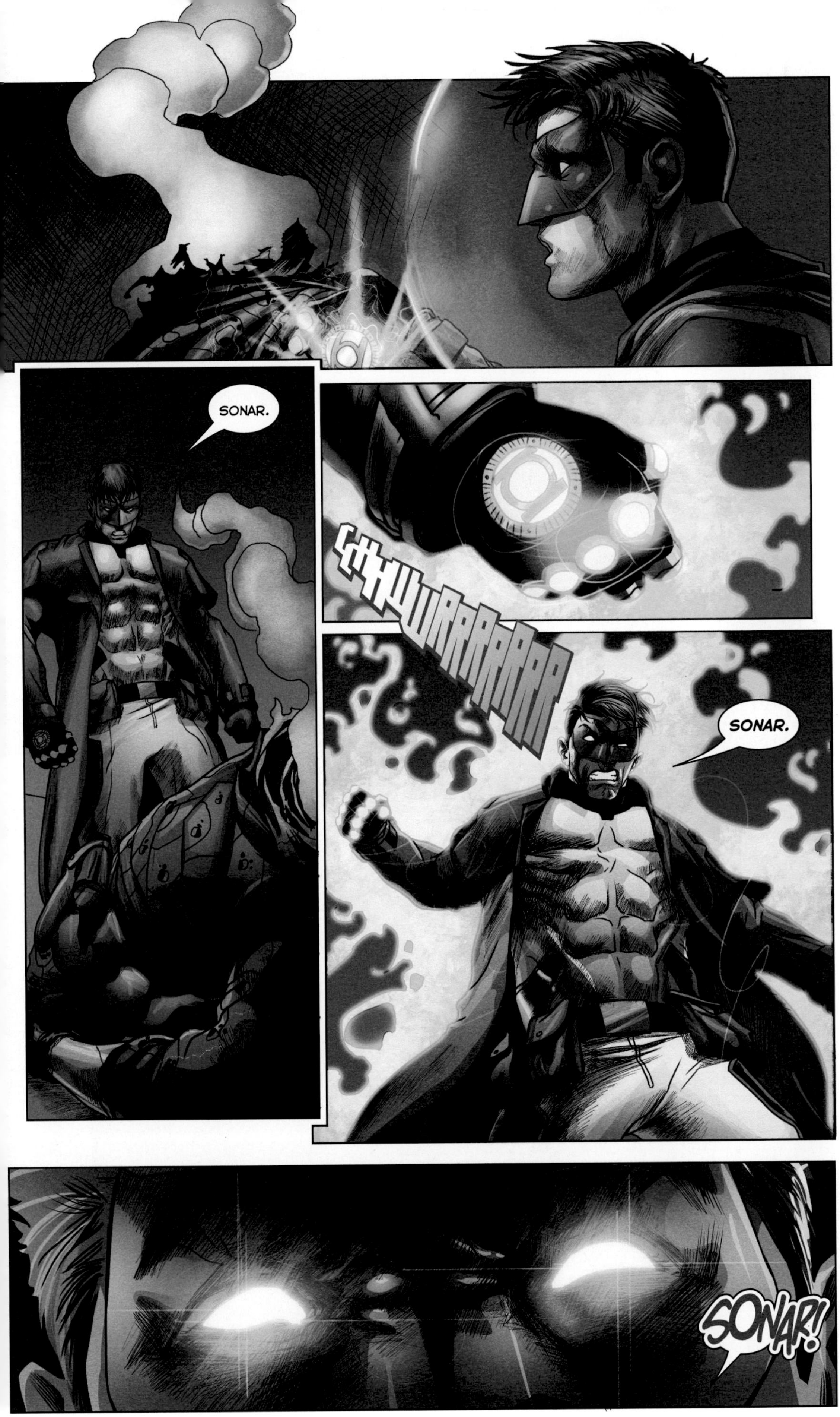
SONAR.
CHHWURRRRRRR
SONAR.
SONAR!

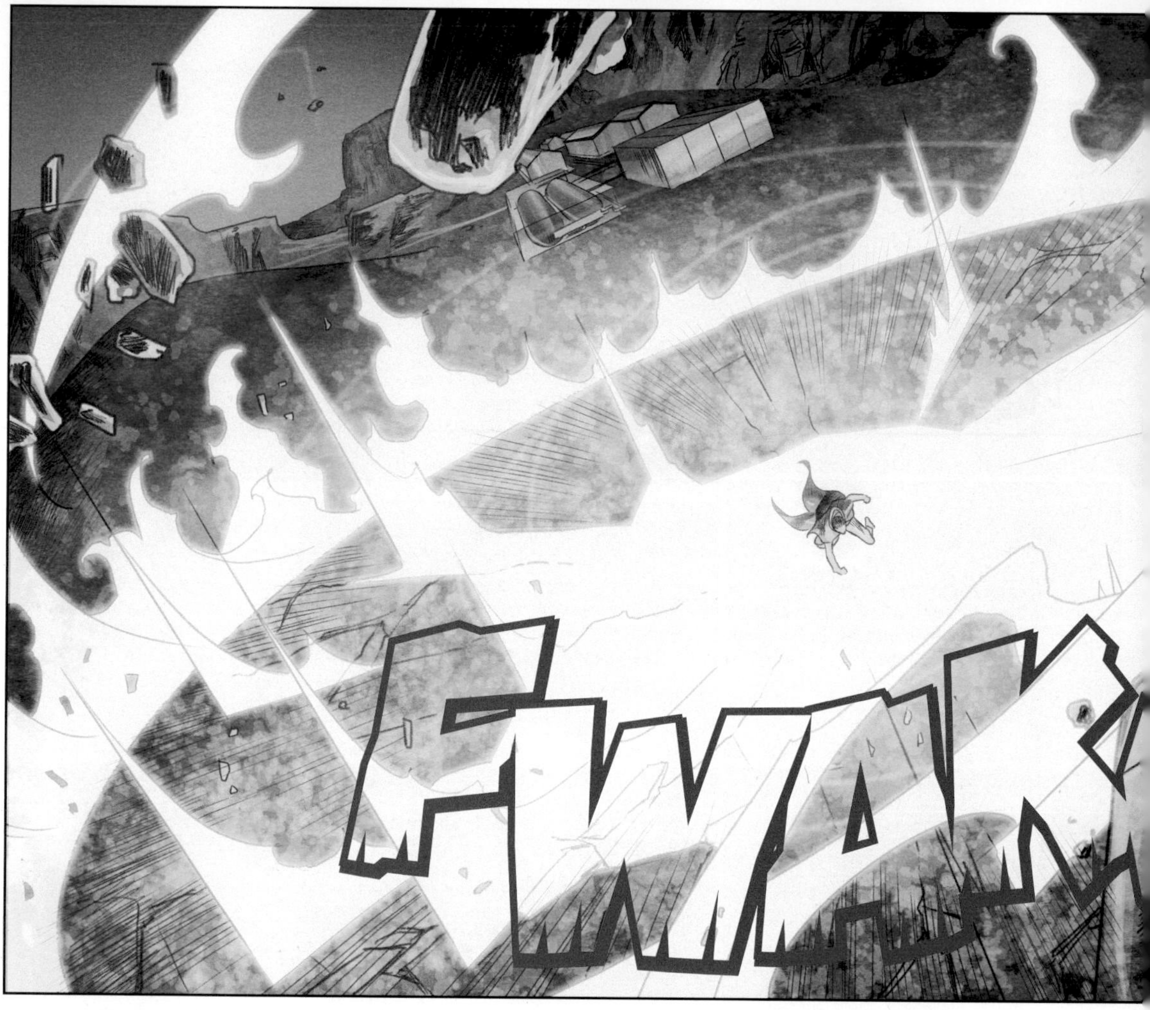
FWAK

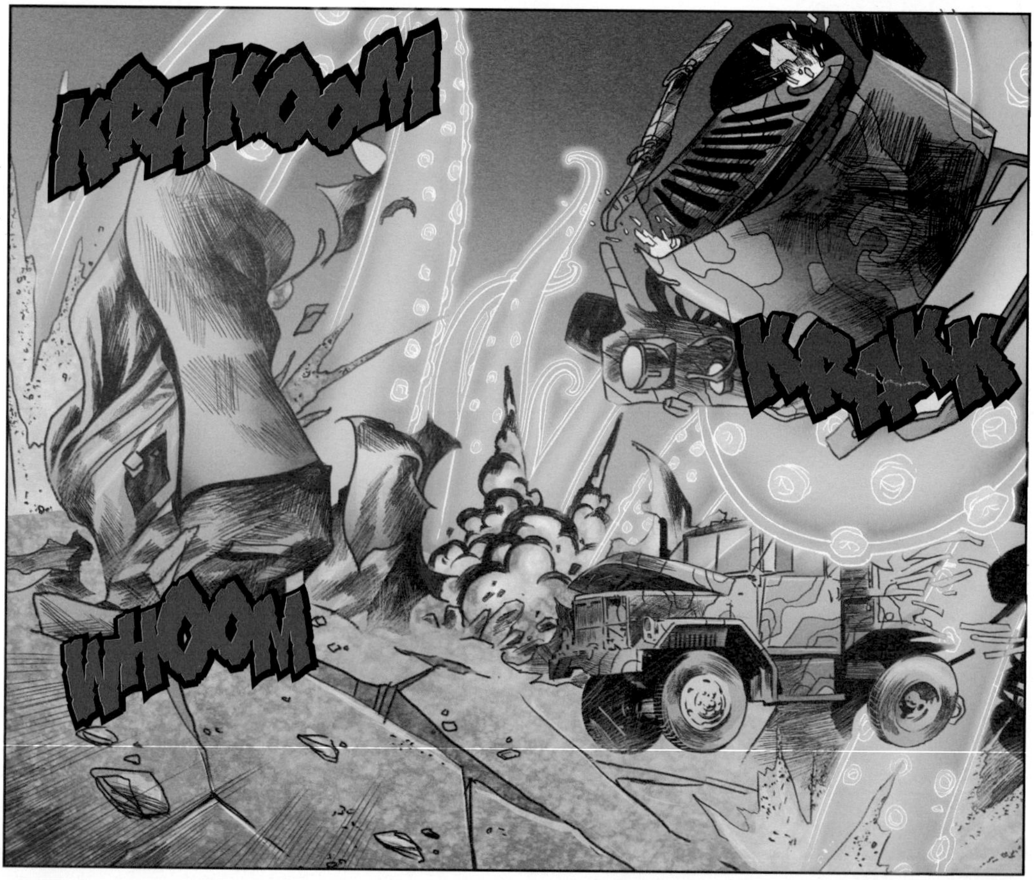
KRAKOOM
KRAKK
WHOOM

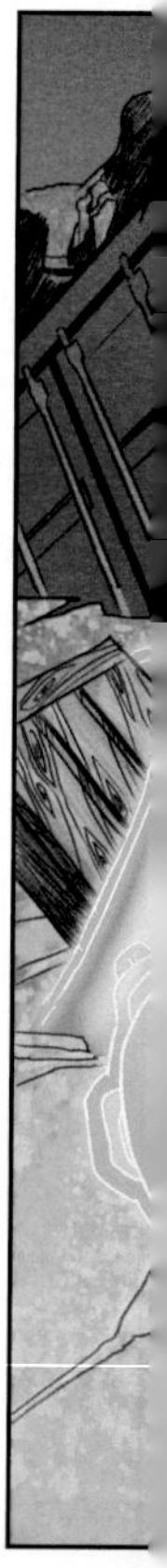

OOOOM

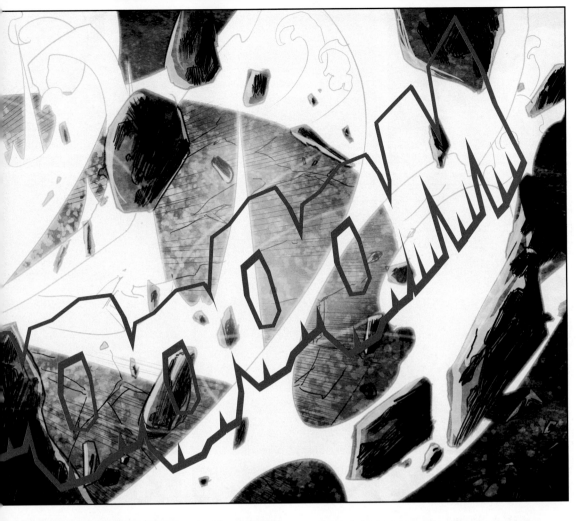

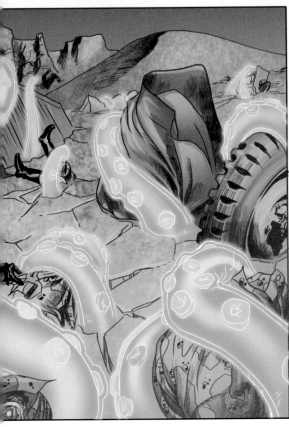

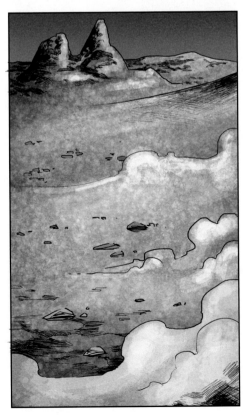

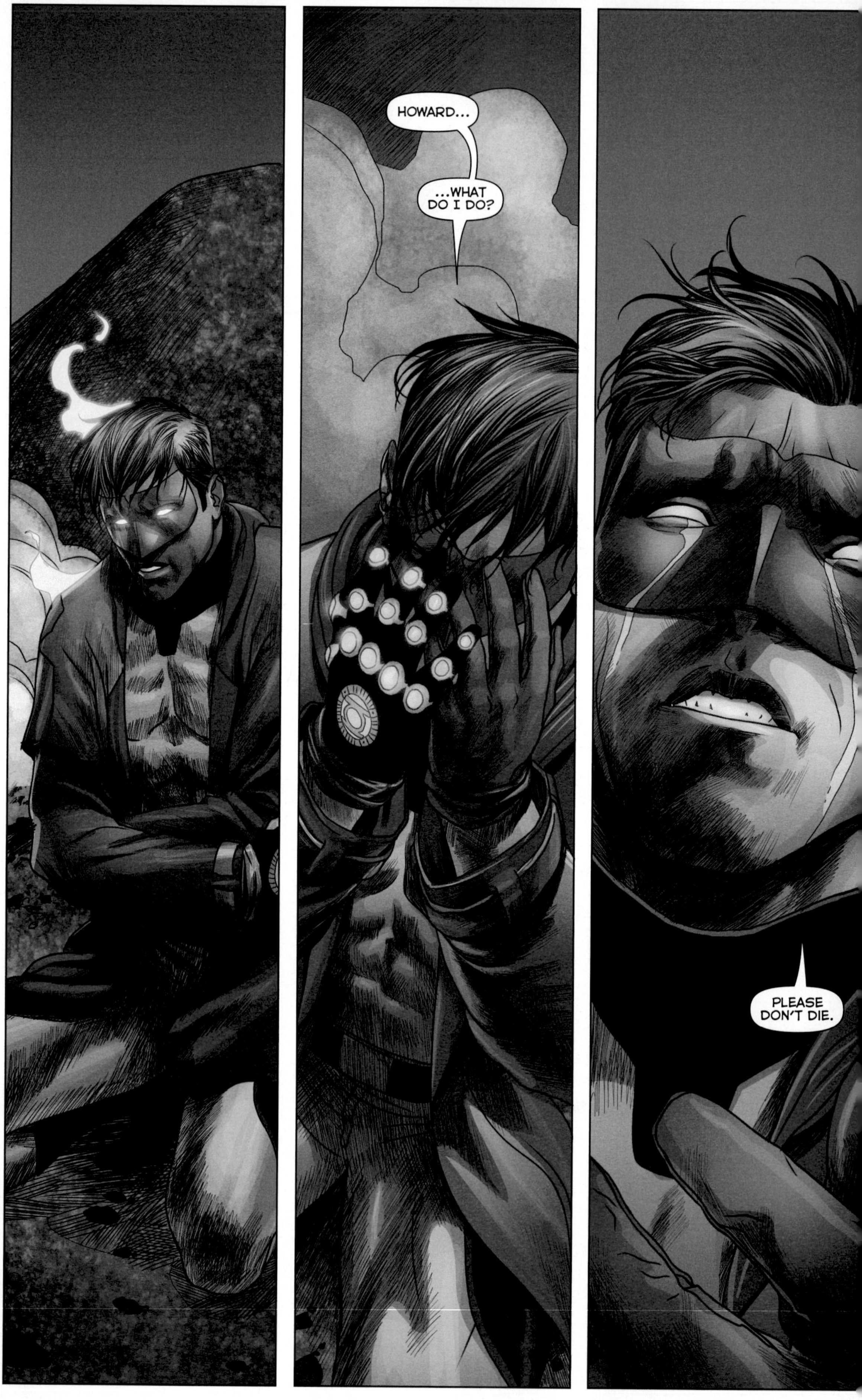
HOWARD...
...WHAT DO I DO?
PLEASE DON'T DIE.

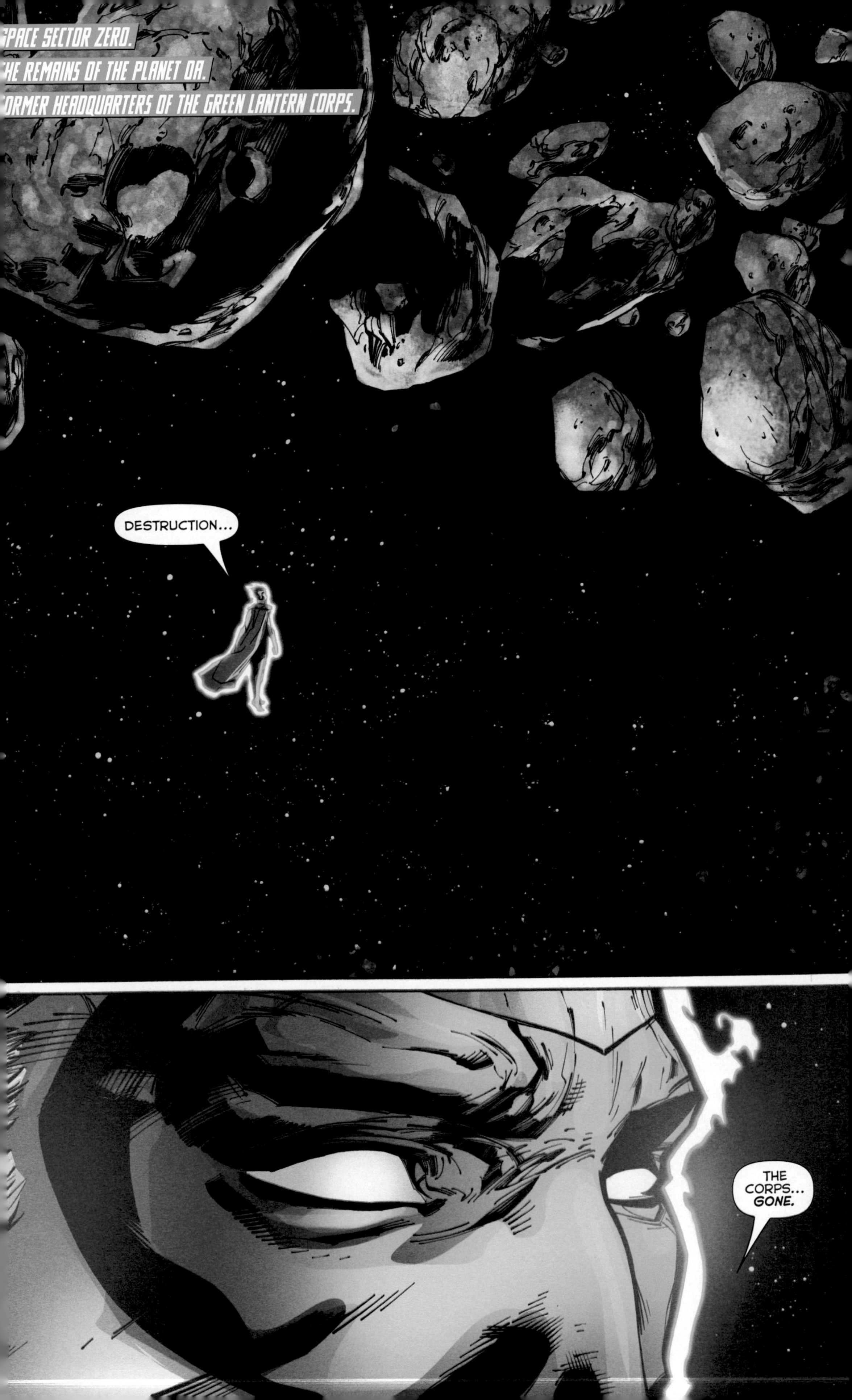
PACE SECTOR ZERO.
HE REMAINS OF THE PLANET OA.
ORMER HEADQUARTERS OF THE GREEN LANTERN CORPS.
DESTRUCTION...
THE CORPS... GONE.

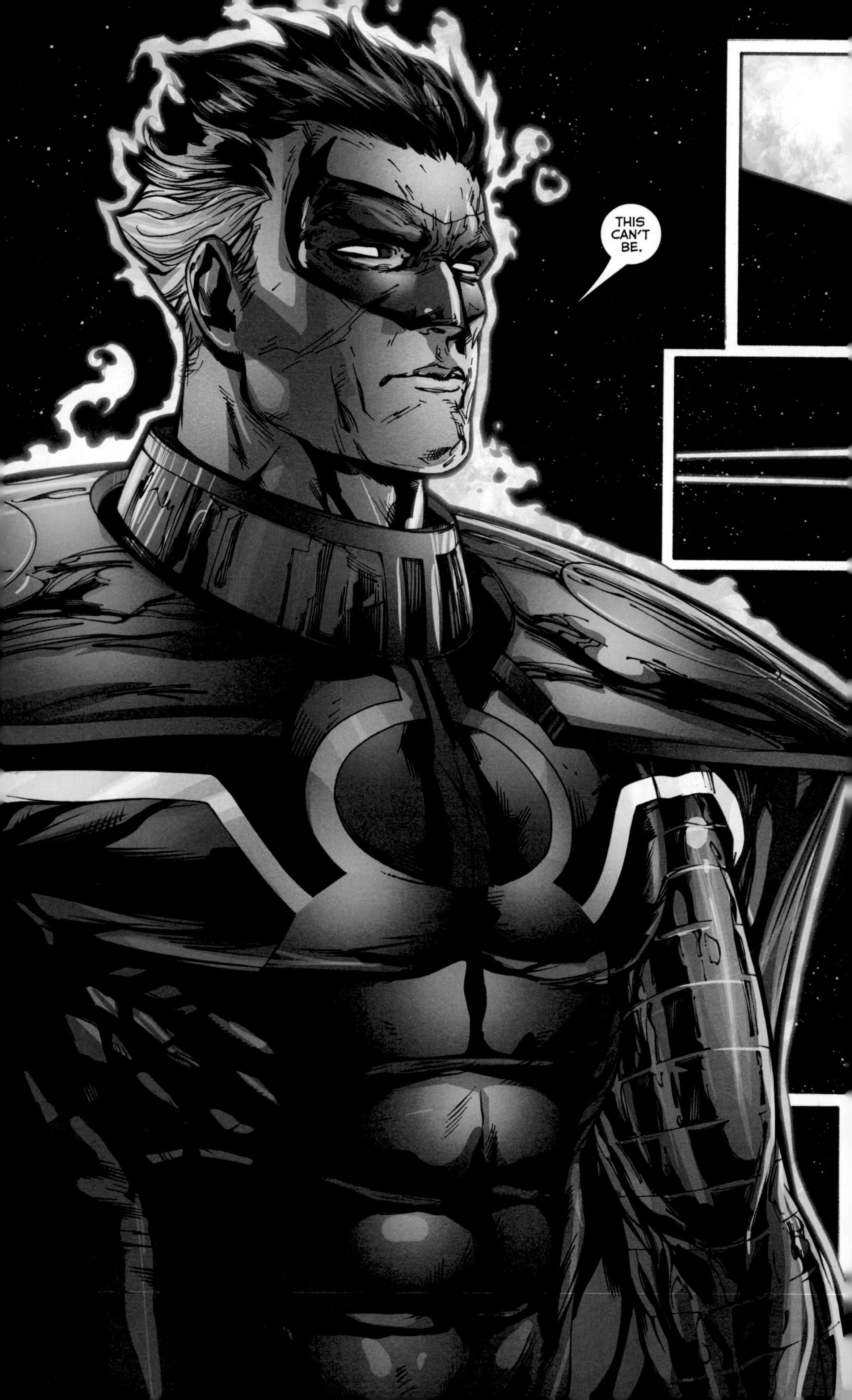
THIS CAN'T BE.

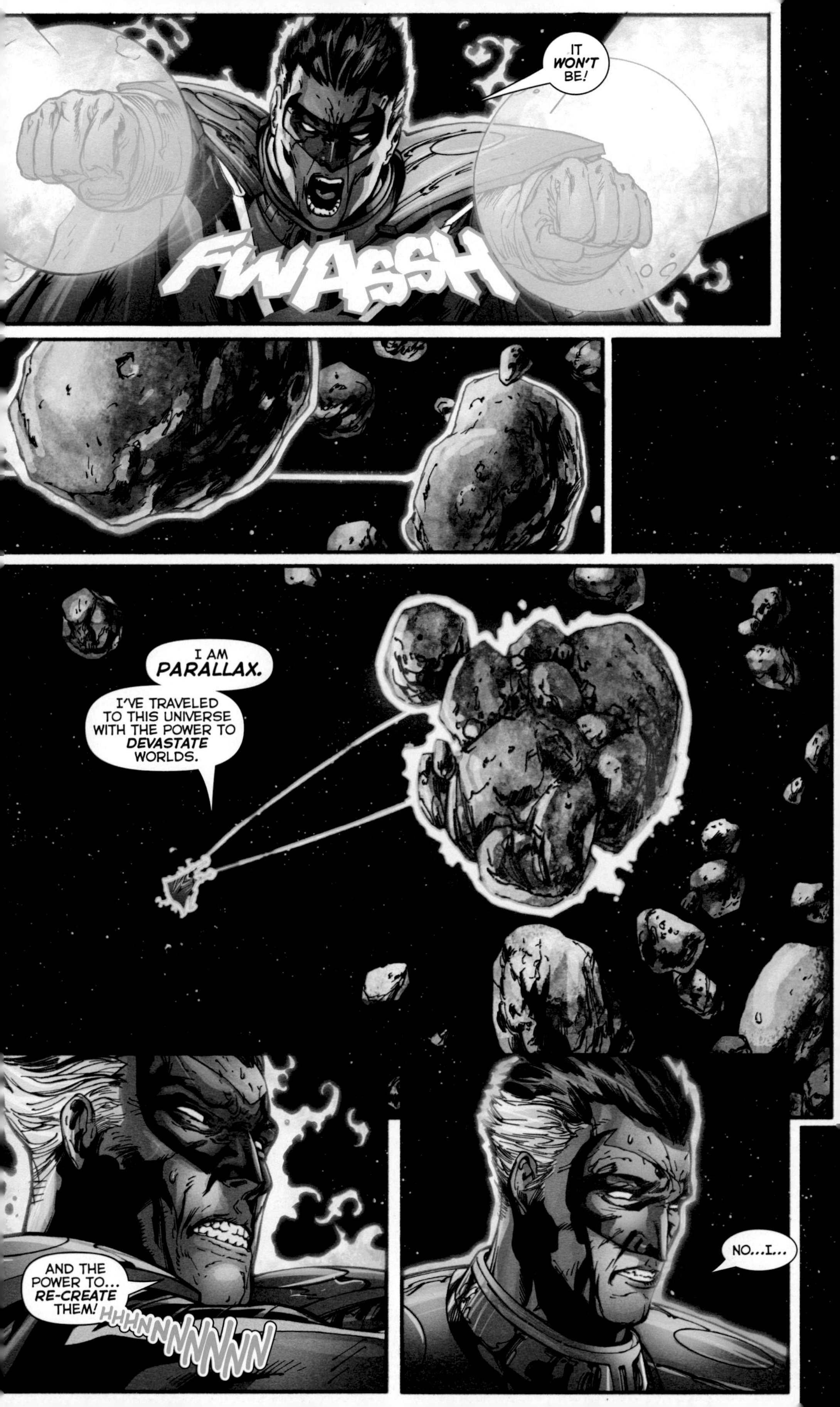
IT WON'T BE!
FWASSH
I AM PARALLAX.
I'VE TRAVELED TO THIS UNIVERSE WITH THE POWER TO DEVASTATE WORLDS.
AND THE POWER TO... RE-CREATE THEM!
HHHNNNNNNNN
NO...I...

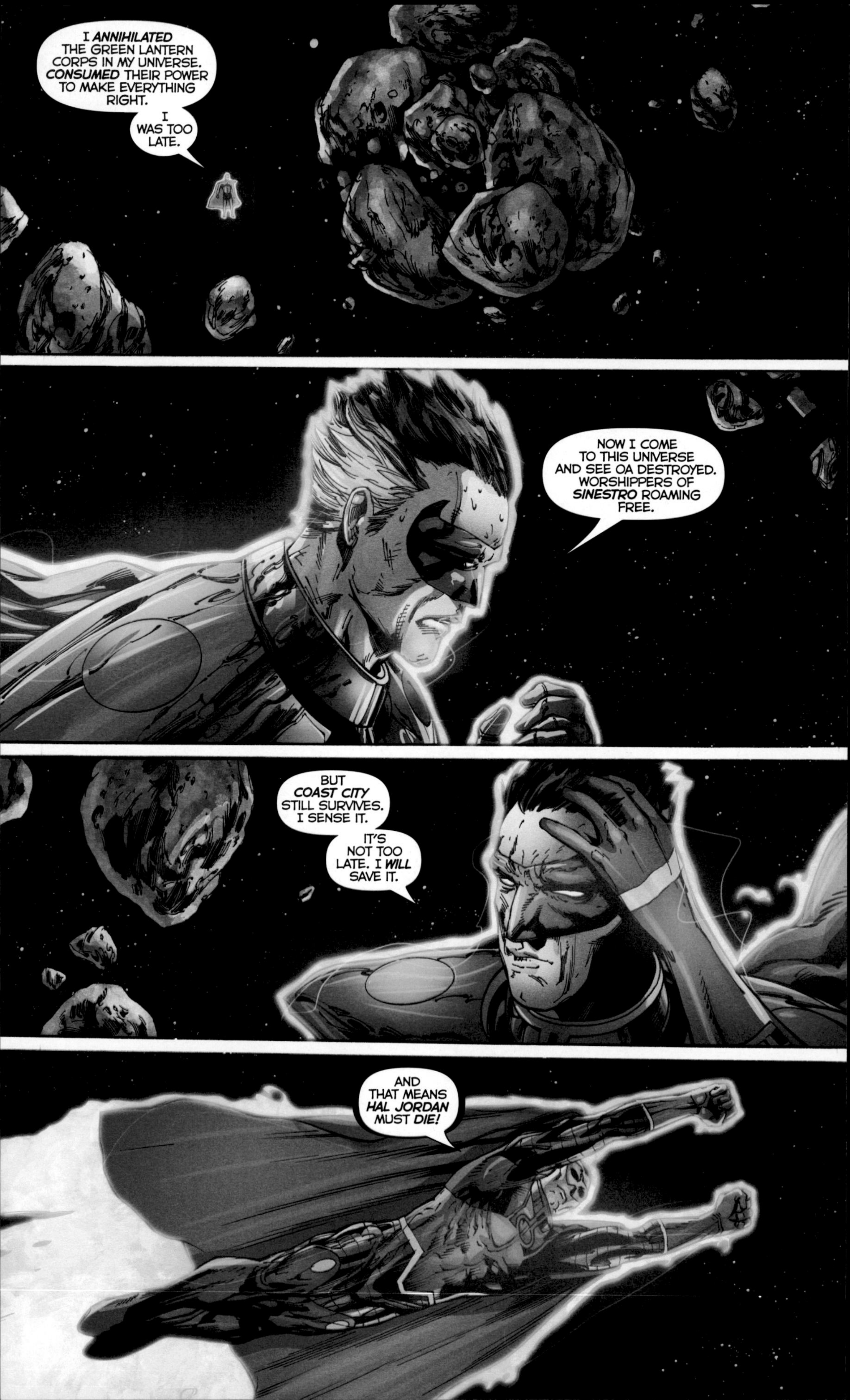
I ANNIHILATED THE GREEN LANTERN CORPS IN MY UNIVERSE. CONSUMED THEIR POWER TO MAKE EVERYTHING RIGHT.
I WAS TOO LATE.
NOW I COME TO THIS UNIVERSE AND SEE OA DESTROYED. WORSHIPPERS OF SINESTRO ROAMING FREE.
BUT COAST CITY STILL SURVIVES. I SENSE IT.
IT'S NOT TOO LATE. I WILL SAVE IT.
AND THAT MEANS HAL JORDAN MUST DIE!

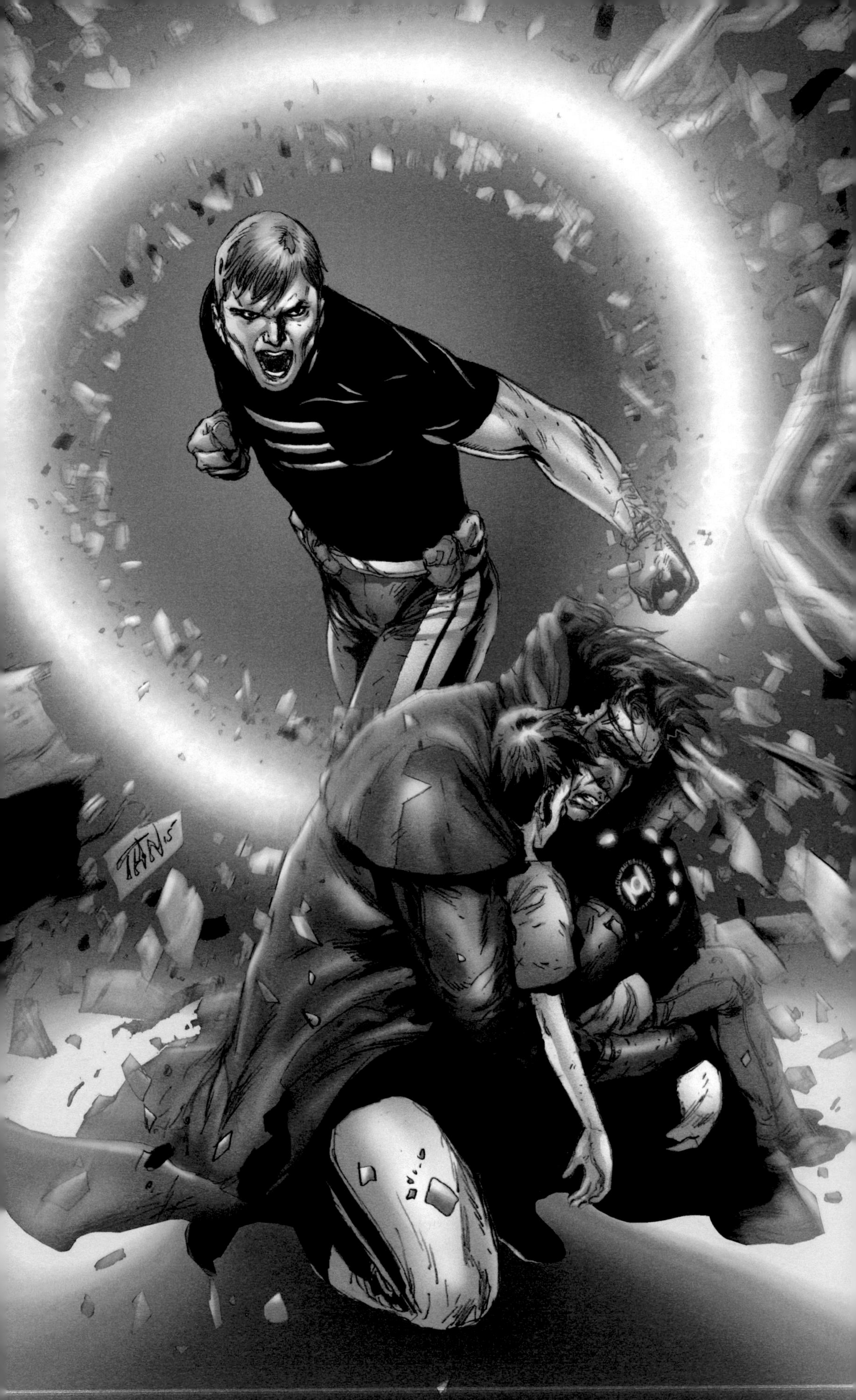

THE ROAR OF SILENCE

ROBERT VENDITTI writer MARTIN COCCOLO BILLY TAN pencillers MARK IRWIN inker TONY AVIÑA colorist DAVE SHARPE letterer BILLY TAN & PETE PANTAZIS cover

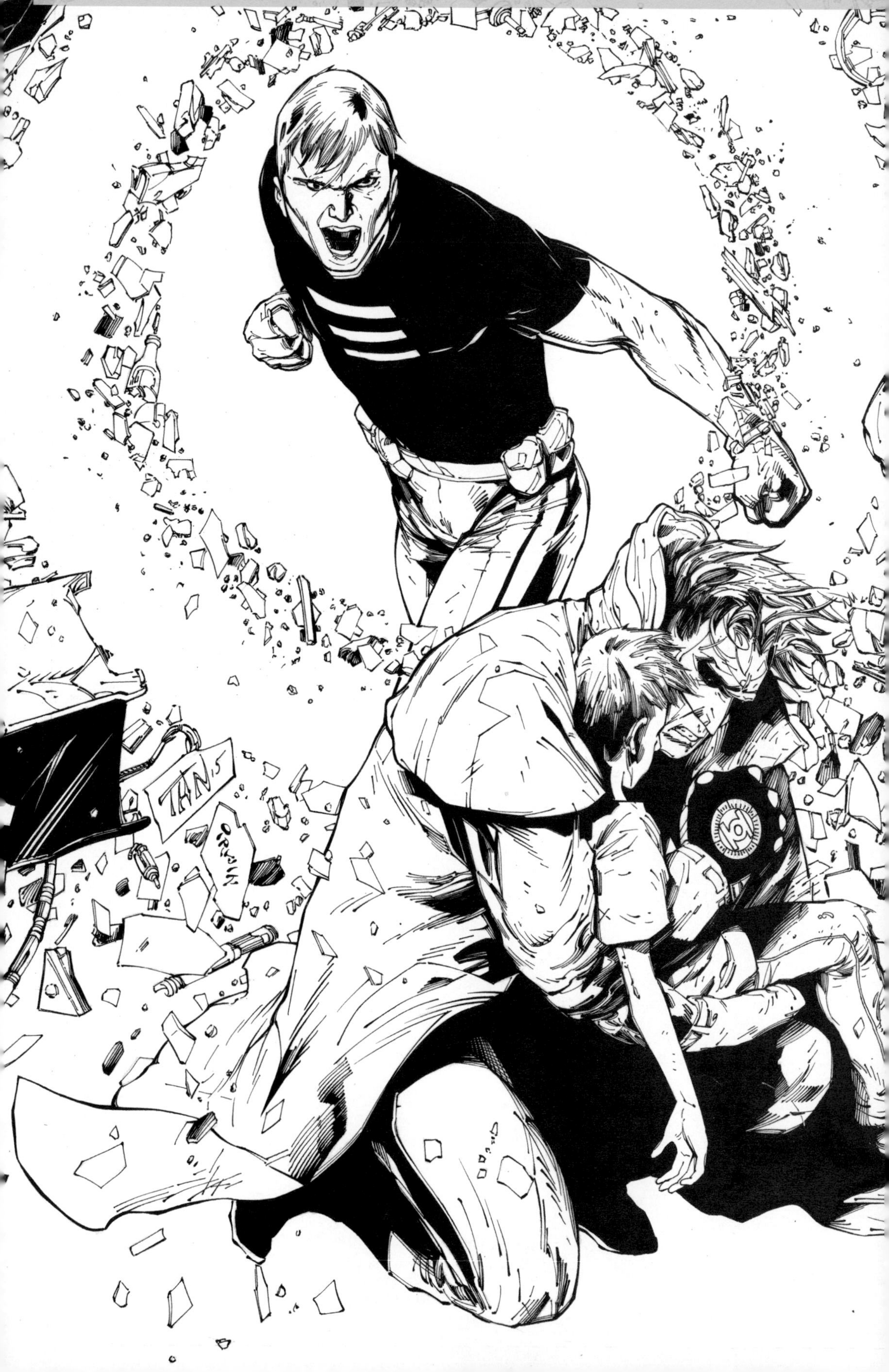

METROPOLIS.
AFTERNOON RUSH HOUR.

GOTHAM CITY.
HALF-PRICE MATINEE.

CENTRAL CITY.
SIXTH PERIOD.

STAR CITY.
THE LUNCH RUSH.

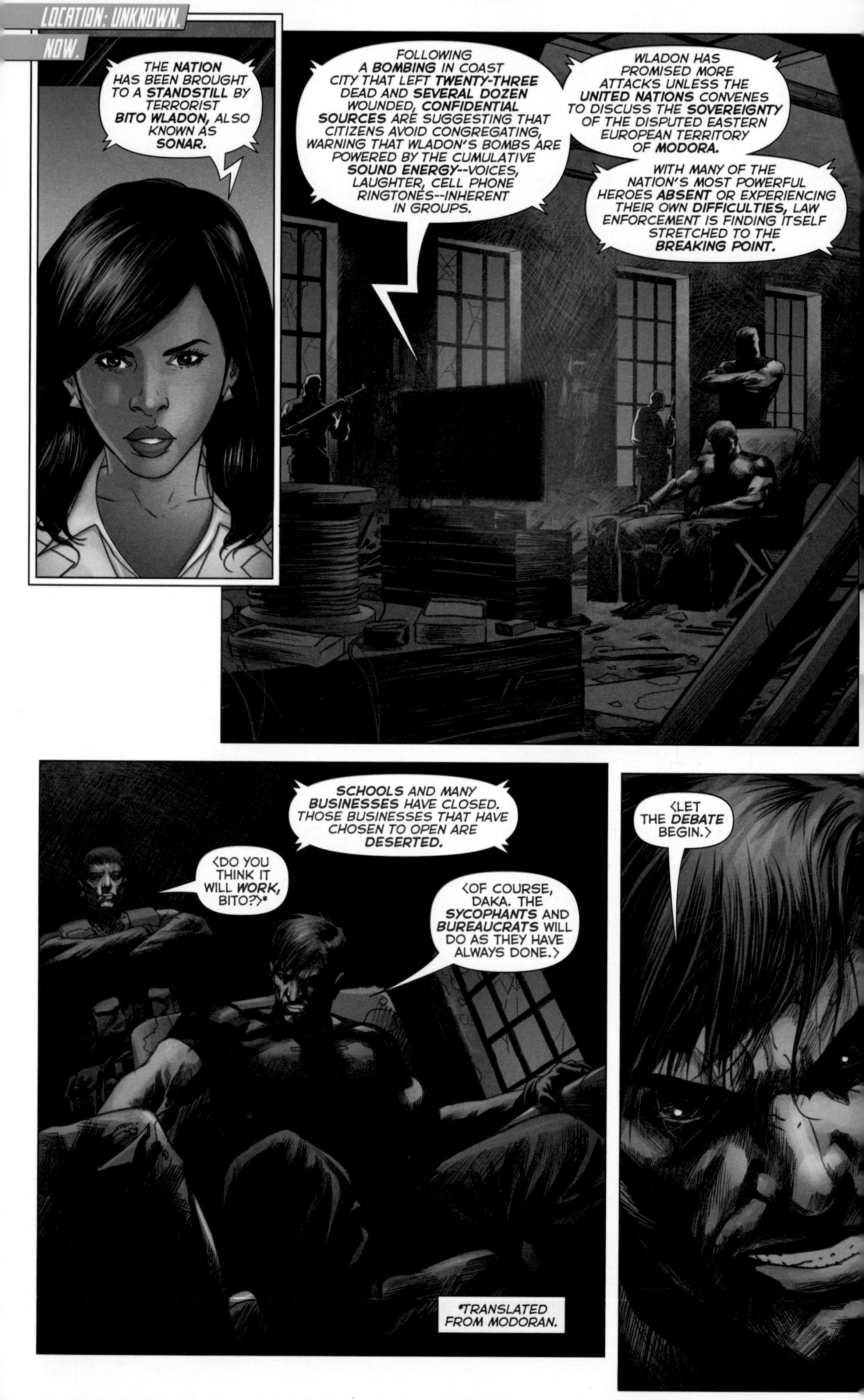
LOCATION: UNKNOWN.
NOW.
THE NATION HAS BEEN BROUGHT TO A STANDSTILL BY TERRORIST BITO WLADON, ALSO KNOWN AS SONAR.
FOLLOWING A BOMBING IN COAST CITY THAT LEFT TWENTY-THREE DEAD AND SEVERAL DOZEN WOUNDED, CONFIDENTIAL SOURCES ARE SUGGESTING THAT CITIZENS AVOID CONGREGATING, WARNING THAT WLADON'S BOMBS ARE POWERED BY THE CUMULATIVE SOUND ENERGY--VOICES, LAUGHTER, CELL PHONE RINGTONES--INHERENT IN GROUPS.
WLADON HAS PROMISED MORE ATTACKS UNLESS THE UNITED NATIONS CONVENES TO DISCUSS THE SOVEREIGNTY OF THE DISPUTED EASTERN EUROPEAN TERRITORY OF MODORA.
WITH MANY OF THE NATION'S MOST POWERFUL HEROES ABSENT OR EXPERIENCING THEIR OWN DIFFICULTIES, LAW ENFORCEMENT IS FINDING ITSELF STRETCHED TO THE BREAKING POINT.
SCHOOLS AND MANY BUSINESSES HAVE CLOSED. THOSE BUSINESSES THAT HAVE CHOSEN TO OPEN ARE DESERTED.
<DO YOU THINK IT WILL WORK, BITO?>*
<OF COURSE, DAKA. THE SYCOPHANTS AND BUREAUCRATS WILL DO AS THEY HAVE ALWAYS DONE.>
*TRANSLATED FROM MODORAN.
<LET THE DEBATE BEGIN.>

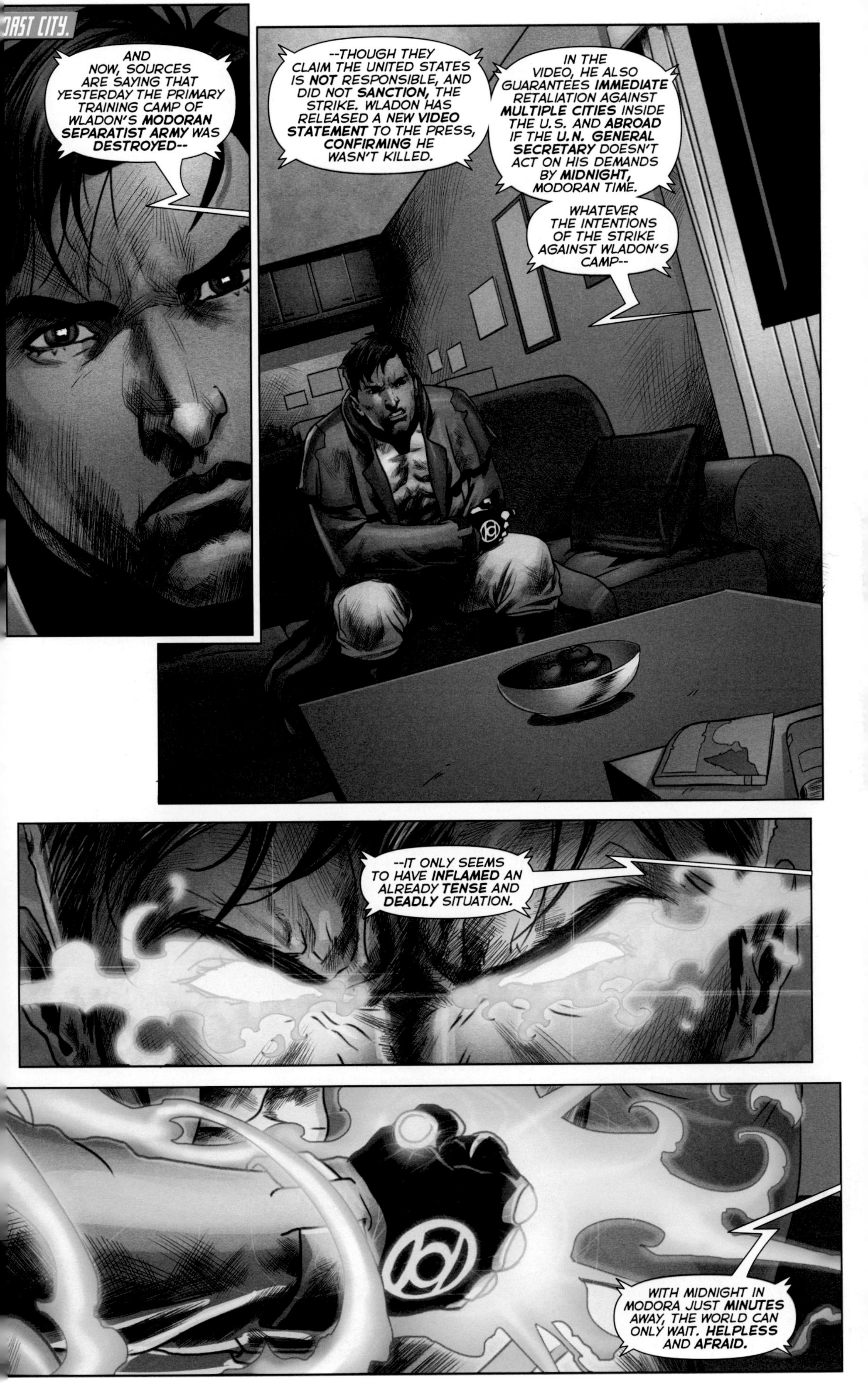

OAST CITY.
AND NOW, SOURCES ARE SAYING THAT YESTERDAY THE PRIMARY TRAINING CAMP OF WLADON'S MODORAN SEPARATIST ARMY WAS DESTROYED--
--THOUGH THEY CLAIM THE UNITED STATES IS NOT RESPONSIBLE, AND DID NOT SANCTION, THE STRIKE. WLADON HAS RELEASED A NEW VIDEO STATEMENT TO THE PRESS, CONFIRMING HE WASN'T KILLED.
IN THE VIDEO, HE ALSO GUARANTEES IMMEDIATE RETALIATION AGAINST MULTIPLE CITIES INSIDE THE U.S. AND ABROAD IF THE U.N. GENERAL SECRETARY DOESN'T ACT ON HIS DEMANDS BY MIDNIGHT, MODORAN TIME.
WHATEVER THE INTENTIONS OF THE STRIKE AGAINST WLADON'S CAMP--
--IT ONLY SEEMS TO HAVE INFLAMED AN ALREADY TENSE AND DEADLY SITUATION.
WITH MIDNIGHT IN MODORA JUST MINUTES AWAY, THE WORLD CAN ONLY WAIT. HELPLESS AND AFRAID.

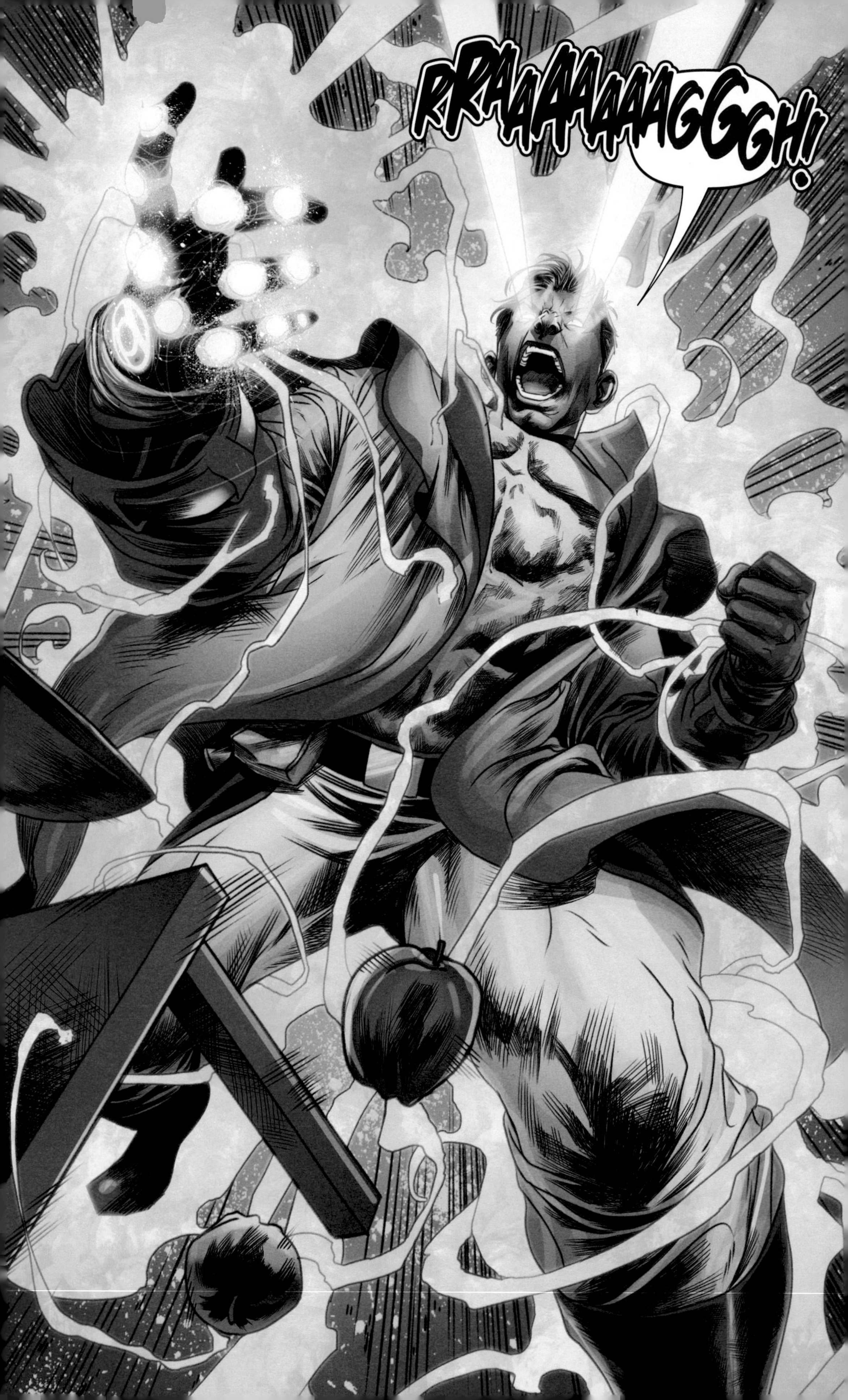
RRAAAAAAAAGGGH!

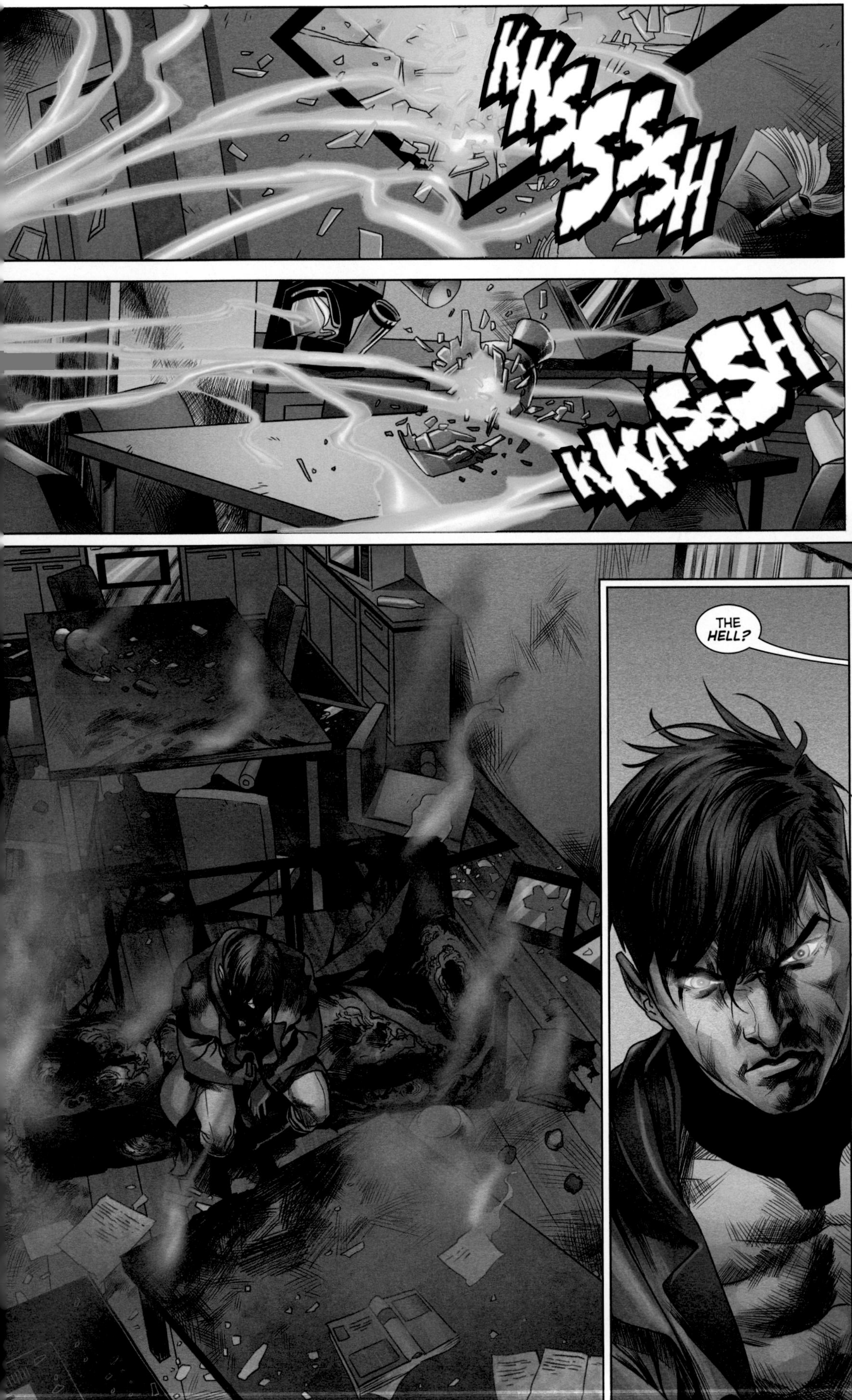
KKRSSSH
KKASSSH
THE HELL?

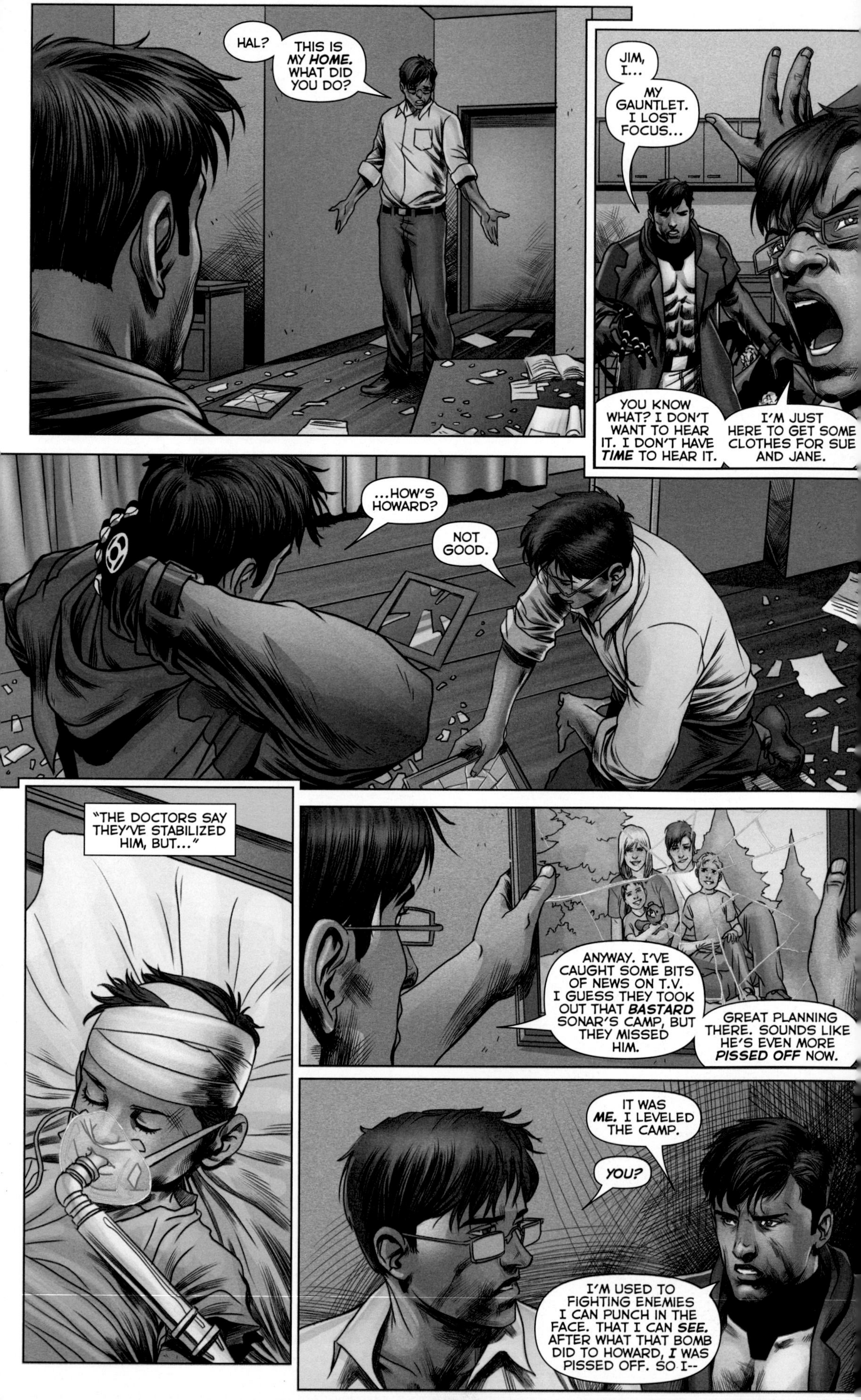
HAL?
THIS IS MY HOME. WHAT DID YOU DO?
JIM, I...
MY GAUNTLET. I LOST FOCUS...
YOU KNOW WHAT? I DON'T WANT TO HEAR IT. I DON'T HAVE TIME TO HEAR IT.
I'M JUST HERE TO GET SOME CLOTHES FOR SUE AND JANE.
...HOW'S HOWARD?
NOT GOOD.
"THE DOCTORS SAY THEY'VE STABILIZED HIM, BUT..."
ANYWAY. I'VE CAUGHT SOME BITS OF NEWS ON T.V. I GUESS THEY TOOK OUT THAT BASTARD SONAR'S CAMP, BUT THEY MISSED HIM.
GREAT PLANNING THERE. SOUNDS LIKE HE'S EVEN MORE PISSED OFF NOW.
IT WAS ME. I LEVELED THE CAMP.
YOU?
I'M USED TO FIGHTING ENEMIES I CAN PUNCH IN THE FACE. THAT I CAN SEE. AFTER WHAT THAT BOMB DID TO HOWARD, I WAS PISSED OFF. SO I--

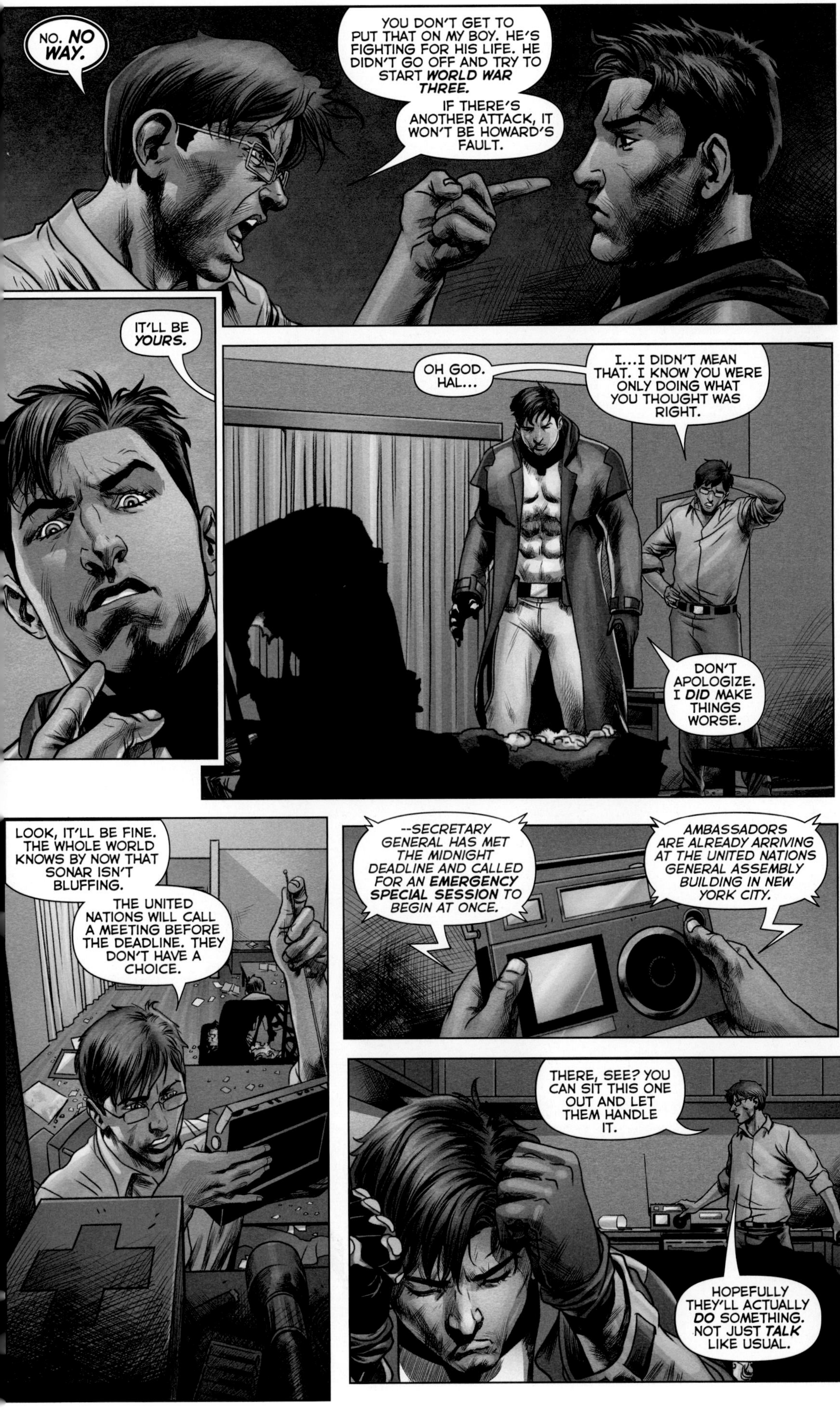
NO. NO WAY.
YOU DON'T GET TO PUT THAT ON MY BOY. HE'S FIGHTING FOR HIS LIFE. HE DIDN'T GO OFF AND TRY TO START WORLD WAR THREE.
IF THERE'S ANOTHER ATTACK, IT WON'T BE HOWARD'S FAULT.
IT'LL BE YOURS.
OH GOD. HAL...
I...I DIDN'T MEAN THAT. I KNOW YOU WERE ONLY DOING WHAT YOU THOUGHT WAS RIGHT.
DON'T APOLOGIZE. I DID MAKE THINGS WORSE.
LOOK, IT'LL BE FINE. THE WHOLE WORLD KNOWS BY NOW THAT SONAR ISN'T BLUFFING.
THE UNITED NATIONS WILL CALL A MEETING BEFORE THE DEADLINE. THEY DON'T HAVE A CHOICE.
--SECRETARY GENERAL HAS MET THE MIDNIGHT DEADLINE AND CALLED FOR AN EMERGENCY SPECIAL SESSION TO BEGIN AT ONCE.
AMBASSADORS ARE ALREADY ARRIVING AT THE UNITED NATIONS GENERAL ASSEMBLY BUILDING IN NEW YORK CITY.
THERE, SEE? YOU CAN SIT THIS ONE OUT AND LET THEM HANDLE IT.
HOPEFULLY THEY'LL ACTUALLY DO SOMETHING. NOT JUST TALK LIKE USUAL.

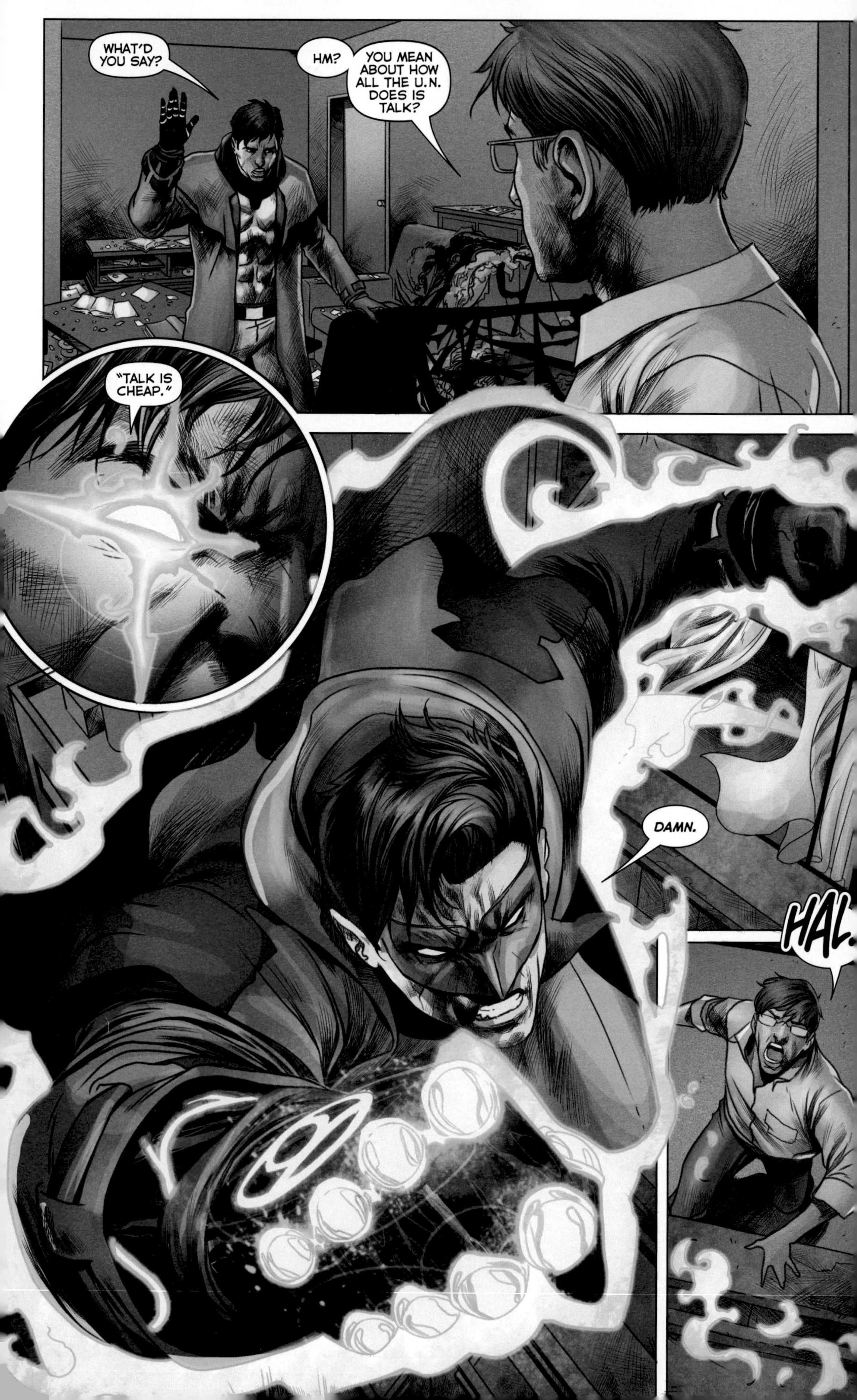
WHAT'D YOU SAY?
HM?
YOU MEAN ABOUT HOW ALL THE U.N. DOES IS TALK?
"TALK IS CHEAP."
DAMN.
HAL

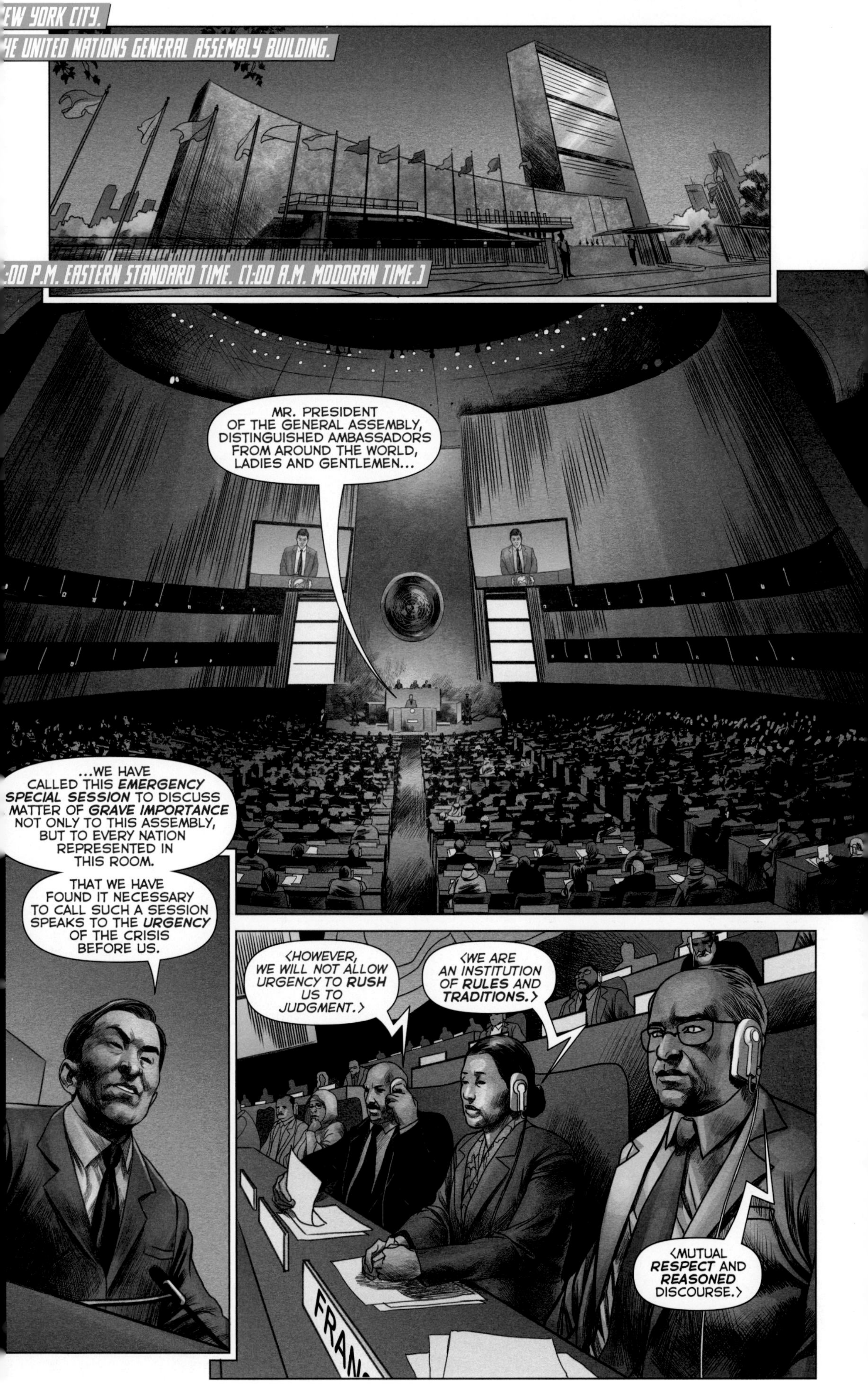
EW YORK CITY.
HE UNITED NATIONS GENERAL ASSEMBLY BUILDING.
:00 P.M. EASTERN STANDARD TIME. (1:00 A.M. MODORAN TIME.)
MR. PRESIDENT OF THE GENERAL ASSEMBLY, DISTINGUISHED AMBASSADORS FROM AROUND THE WORLD, LADIES AND GENTLEMEN...
...WE HAVE CALLED THIS **EMERGENCY SPECIAL SESSION** TO DISCUSS MATTER OF **GRAVE IMPORTANCE** NOT ONLY TO THIS ASSEMBLY, BUT TO EVERY NATION REPRESENTED IN THIS ROOM.
THAT WE HAVE FOUND IT NECESSARY TO CALL SUCH A SESSION SPEAKS TO THE **URGENCY** OF THE CRISIS BEFORE US.
‹HOWEVER, WE WILL NOT ALLOW URGENCY TO **RUSH** US TO JUDGMENT.›
‹WE ARE AN INSTITUTION OF **RULES** AND **TRADITIONS.**›
‹MUTUAL **RESPECT** AND **REASONED** DISCOURSE.›
FRAN

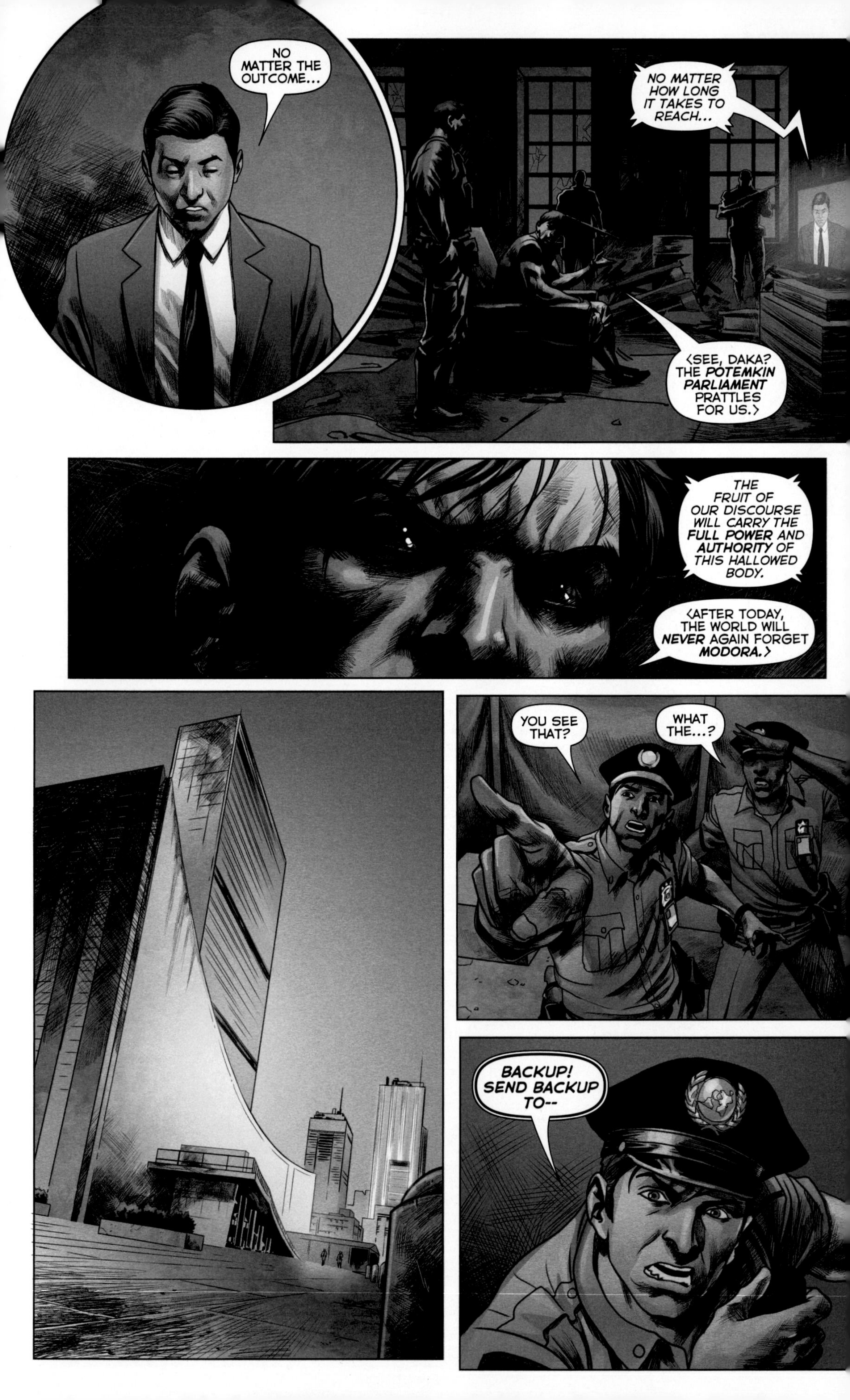
NO MATTER THE OUTCOME...
NO MATTER HOW LONG IT TAKES TO REACH...
<SEE, DAKA? THE POTEMKIN PARLIAMENT PRATTLES FOR US.>
THE FRUIT OF OUR DISCOURSE WILL CARRY THE FULL POWER AND AUTHORITY OF THIS HALLOWED BODY.
<AFTER TODAY, THE WORLD WILL NEVER AGAIN FORGET MODORA.>
YOU SEE THAT?
WHAT THE...?
BACKUP! SEND BACKUP TO--

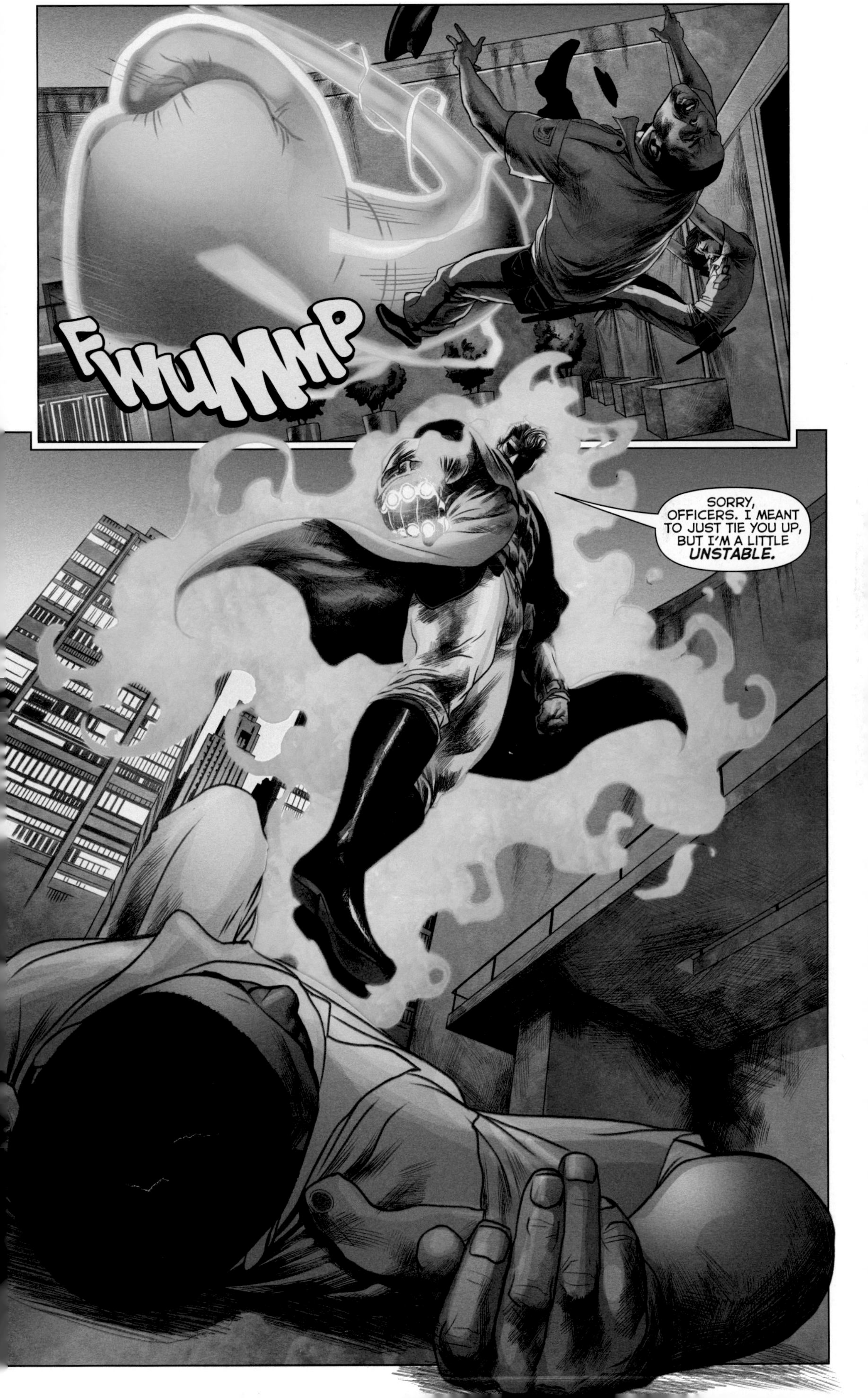
FWUMMP
SORRY, OFFICERS. I MEANT TO JUST TIE YOU UP, BUT I'M A LITTLE UNSTABLE.

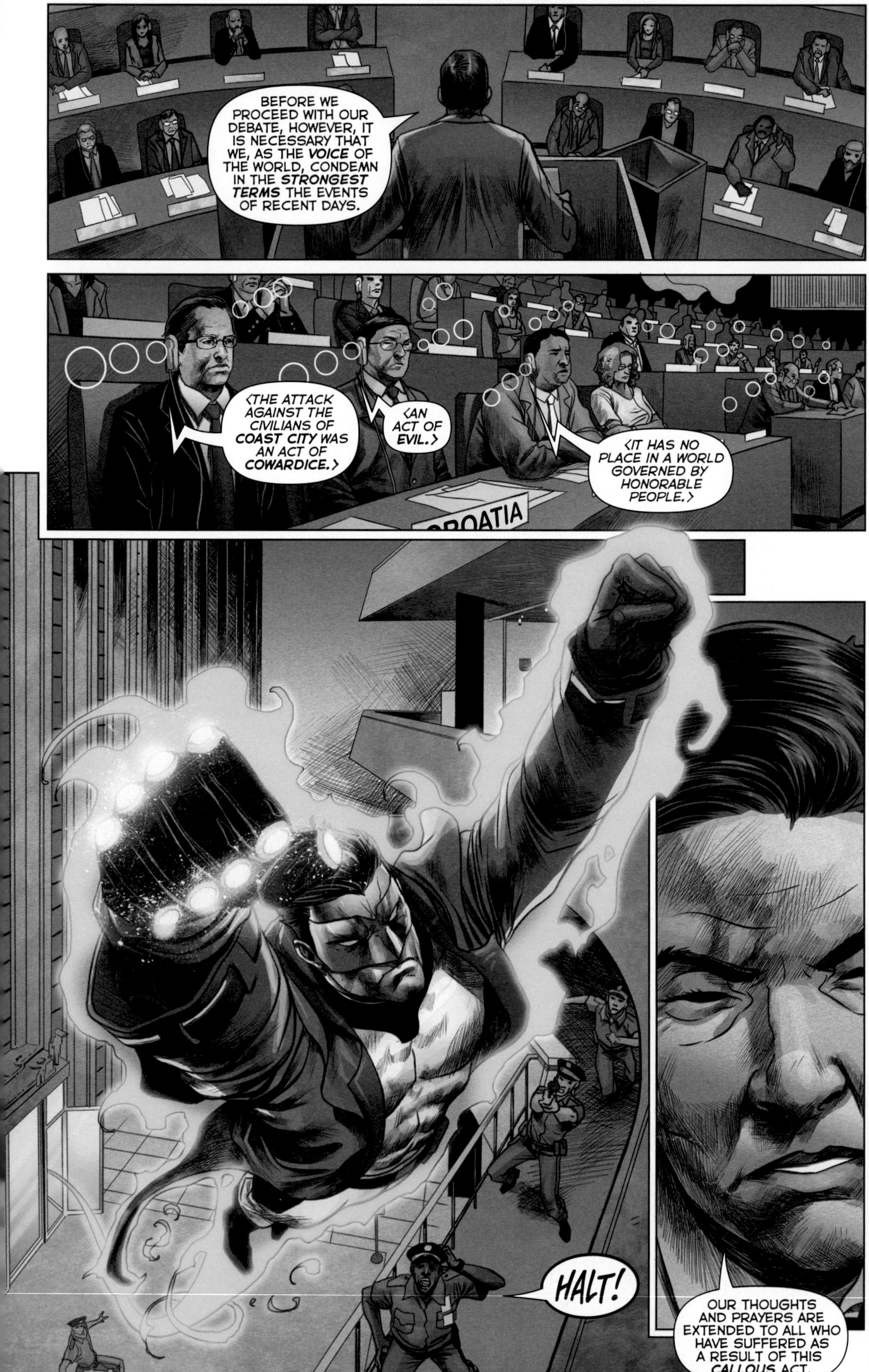
BEFORE WE PROCEED WITH OUR DEBATE, HOWEVER, IT IS NECESSARY THAT WE, AS THE VOICE OF THE WORLD, CONDEMN IN THE STRONGEST TERMS THE EVENTS OF RECENT DAYS.
<THE ATTACK AGAINST THE CIVILIANS OF COAST CITY WAS AN ACT OF COWARDICE.>
<AN ACT OF EVIL.>
<IT HAS NO PLACE IN A WORLD GOVERNED BY HONORABLE PEOPLE.>
ROATIA
HALT!
OUR THOUGHTS AND PRAYERS ARE EXTENDED TO ALL WHO HAVE SUFFERED AS A RESULT OF THIS CALLOUS ACT.

‹BUT WE MUST MOVE FORWARD.›

SSHINNK

THE TASK BEFORE US IS *DIFFICULT*, BUT NECESSARY. *ARDUOUS*, BUT VITAL. AND IF WE TRUST OURSELVES AND OUR PROCESS--

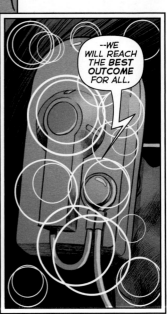

--WE WILL REACH THE *BEST* OUTCOME FOR ALL.

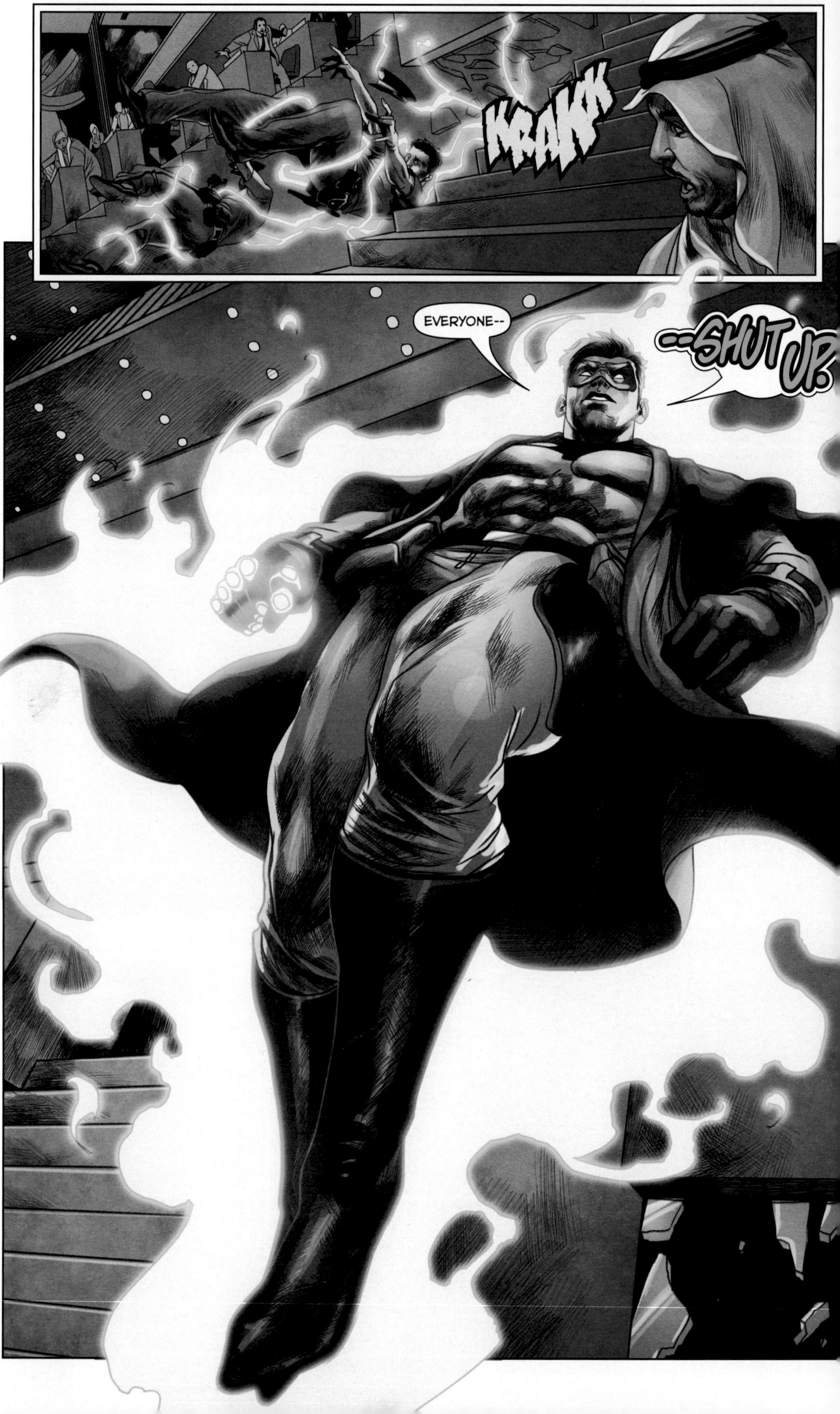
KRAKK
EVERYONE--
--SHUT UP.

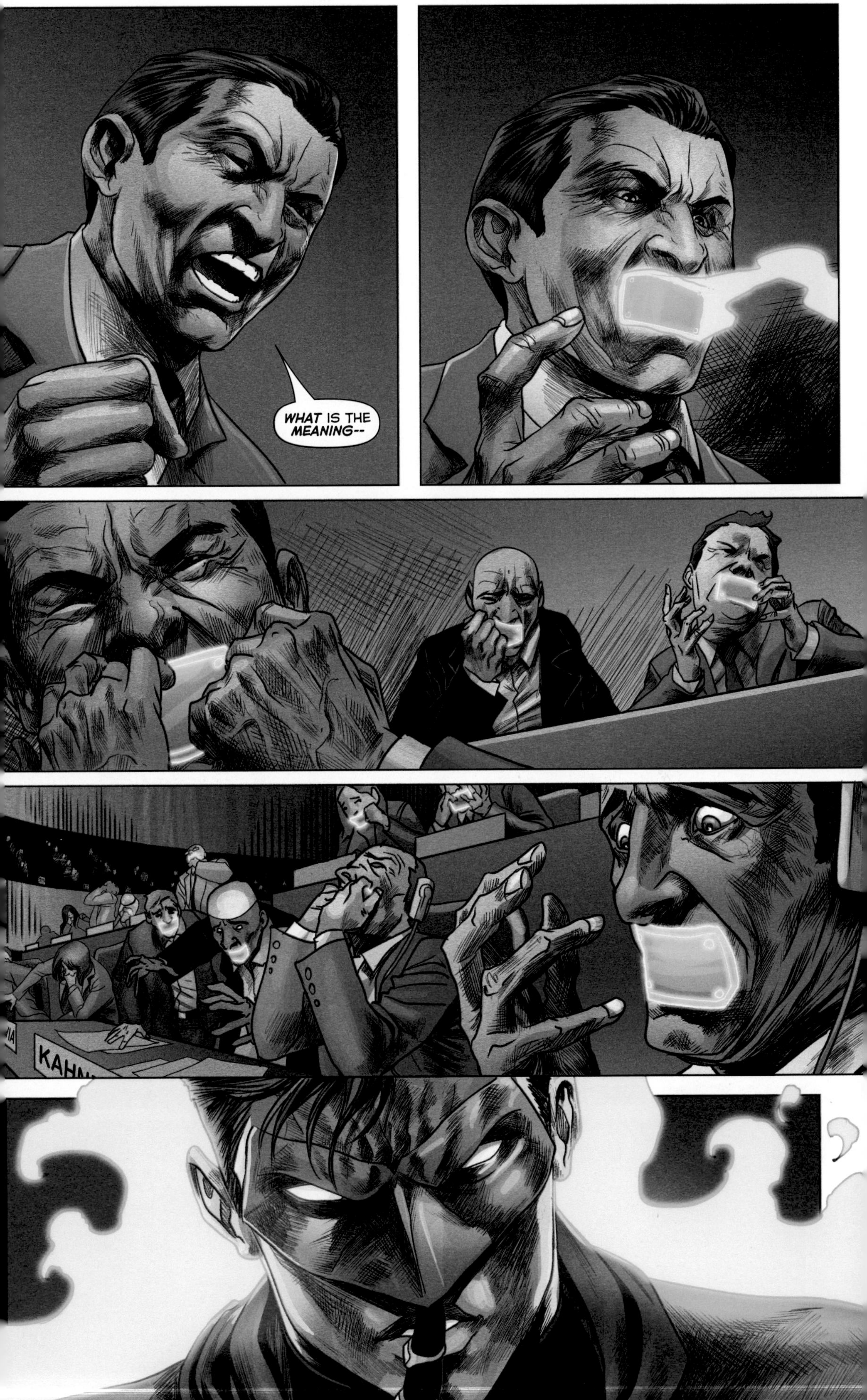
WHAT IS THE MEANING--
KAHN

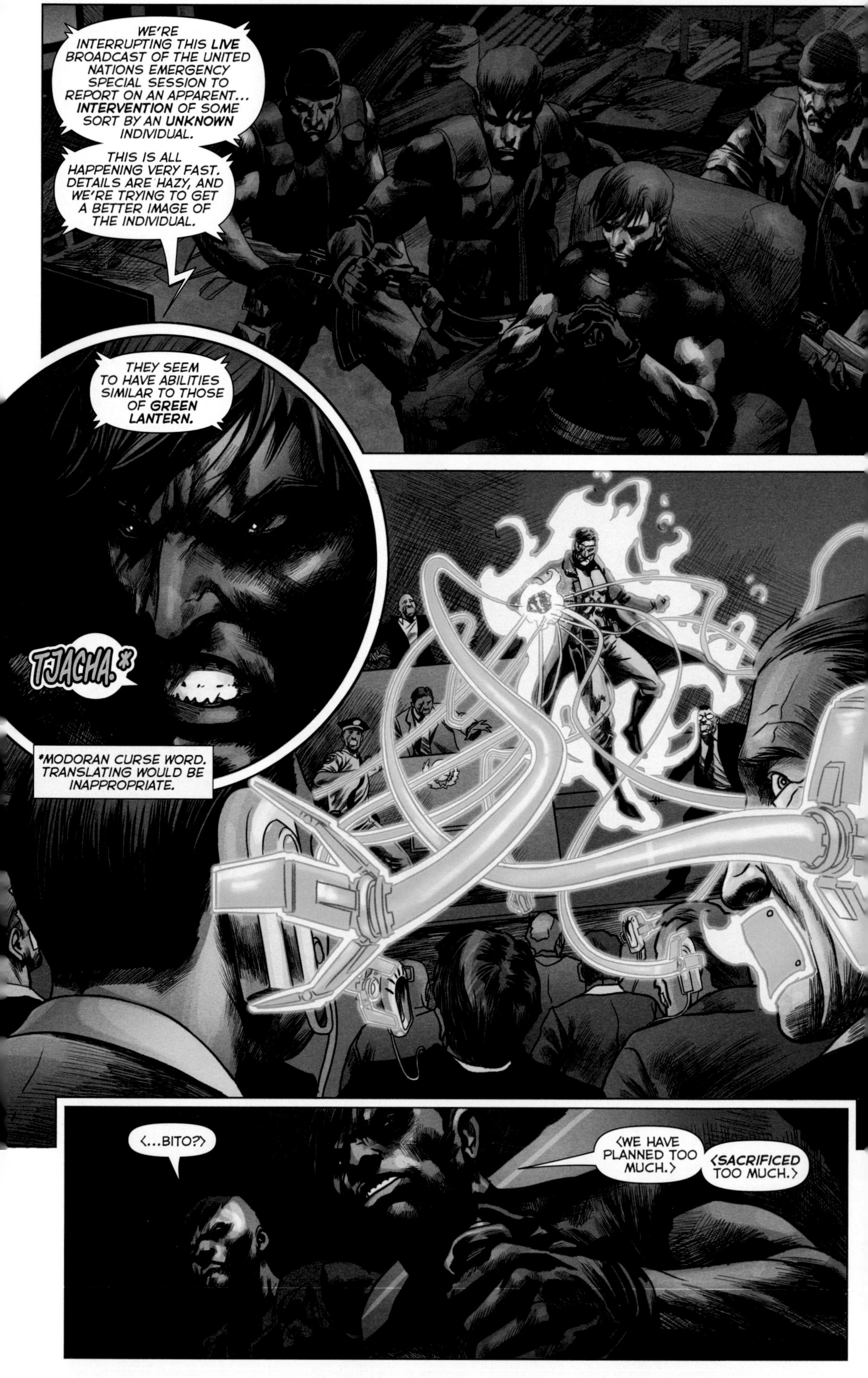
WE'RE INTERRUPTING THIS LIVE BROADCAST OF THE UNITED NATIONS EMERGENCY SPECIAL SESSION TO REPORT ON AN APPARENT... INTERVENTION OF SOME SORT BY AN UNKNOWN INDIVIDUAL.
THIS IS ALL HAPPENING VERY FAST. DETAILS ARE HAZY, AND WE'RE TRYING TO GET A BETTER IMAGE OF THE INDIVIDUAL.
THEY SEEM TO HAVE ABILITIES SIMILAR TO THOSE OF GREEN LANTERN.
TJACHA.*
*MODORAN CURSE WORD. TRANSLATING WOULD BE INAPPROPRIATE.
<...BITO?>
<WE HAVE PLANNED TOO MUCH.>
<SACRIFICED TOO MUCH.>

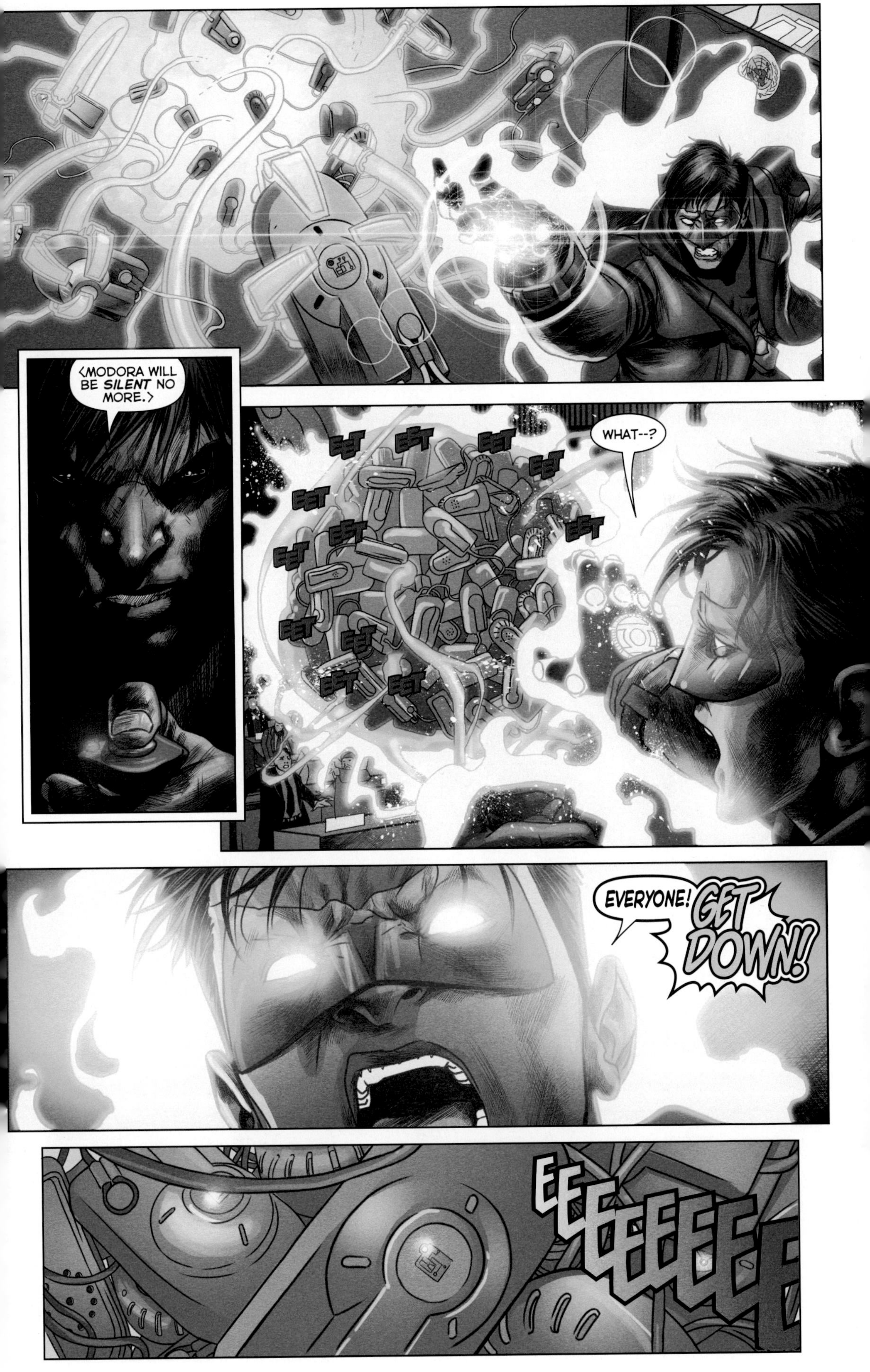
<MODORA WILL BE *SILENT* NO MORE.>
EEET
WHAT--?
EVERYONE! GET DOWN!
EEEEEEEEE

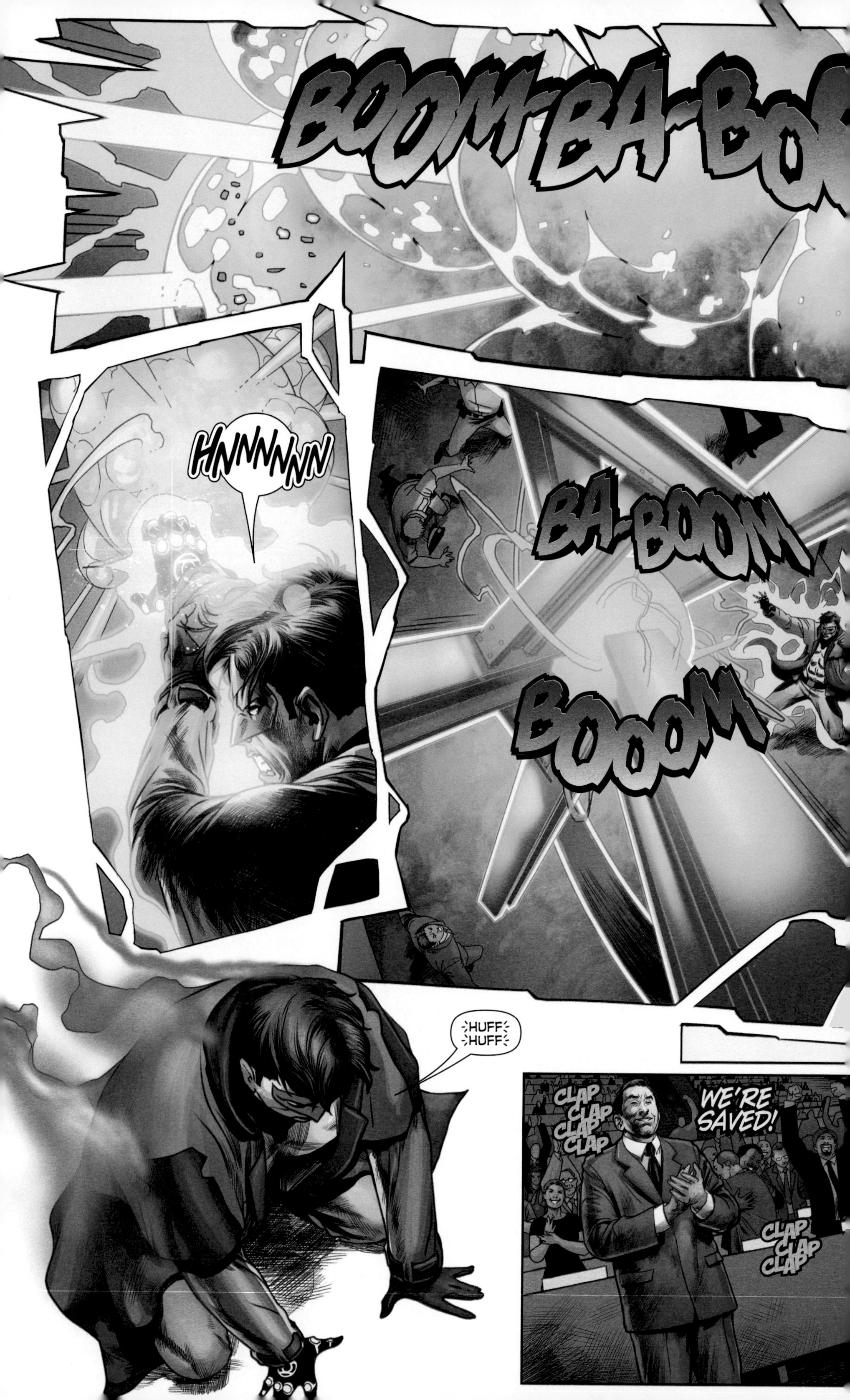
BOOM-BA-BO
HNNNNNN
BA-BOOM
BOOOM
HUFF HUFF
CLAP CLAP CLAP CLAP
WE'RE SAVED!
CLAP CLAP CLAP

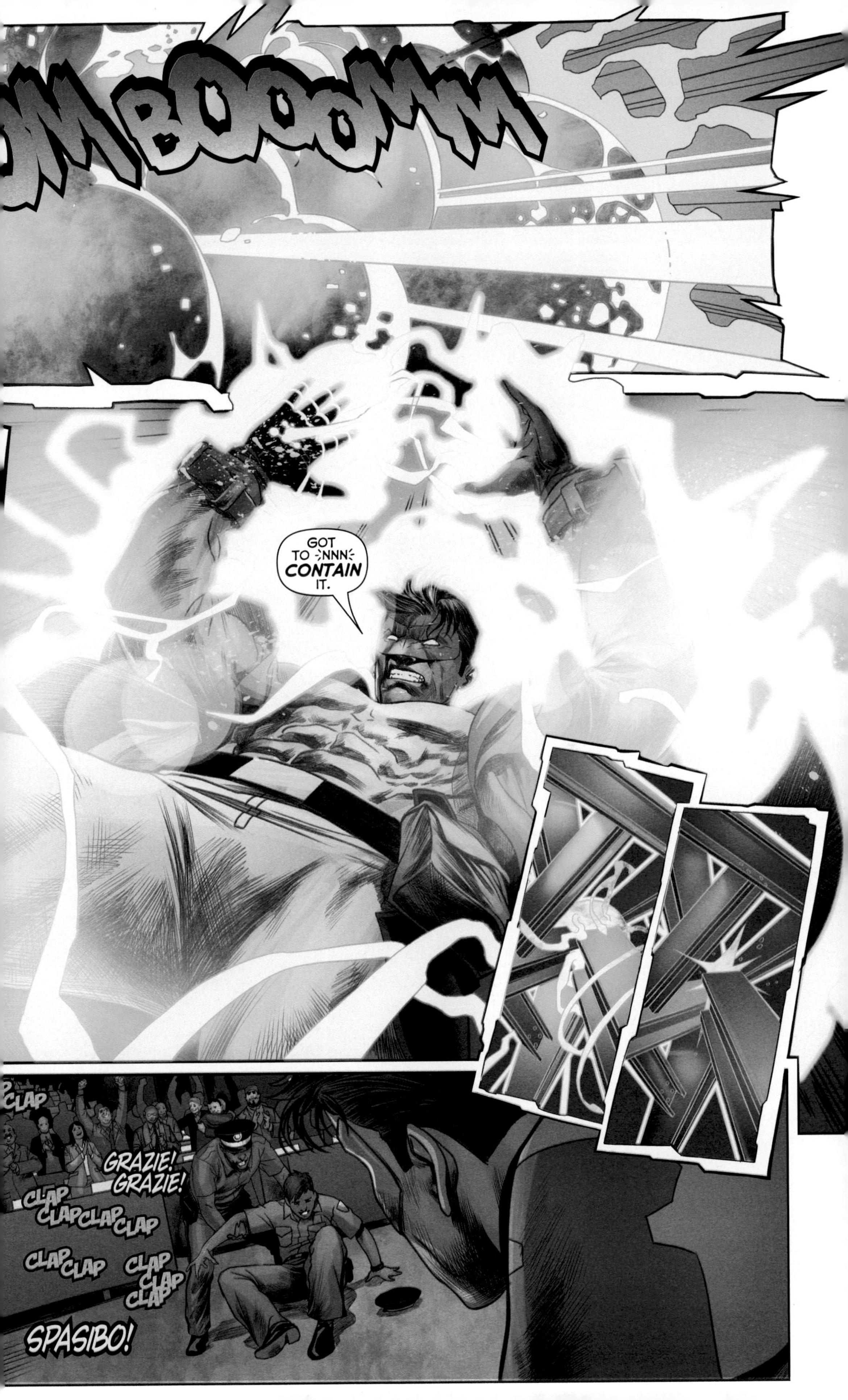

MMBOOOMMM
GOT TO -NNN- CONTAIN IT.
CLAP
GRAZIE! GRAZIE!
CLAP CLAP CLAP CLAP
CLAP CLAP
CLAP CLAP CLAP
SPASIBO!

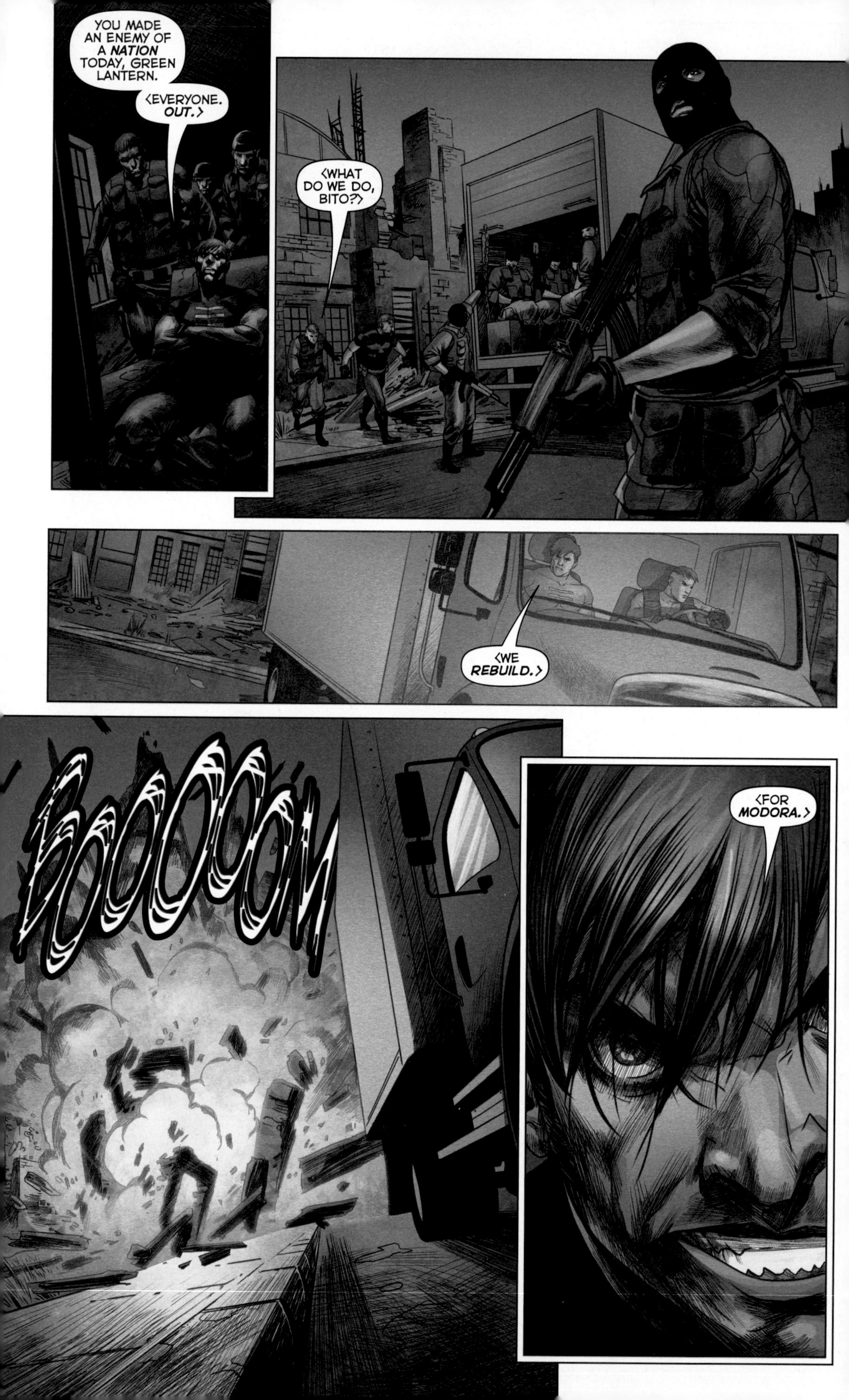
YOU MADE AN ENEMY OF A NATION TODAY, GREEN LANTERN.
<EVERYONE. OUT.>
<WHAT DO WE DO, BITO?>
<WE REBUILD.>
BOOOOOM
<FOR MODORA.>

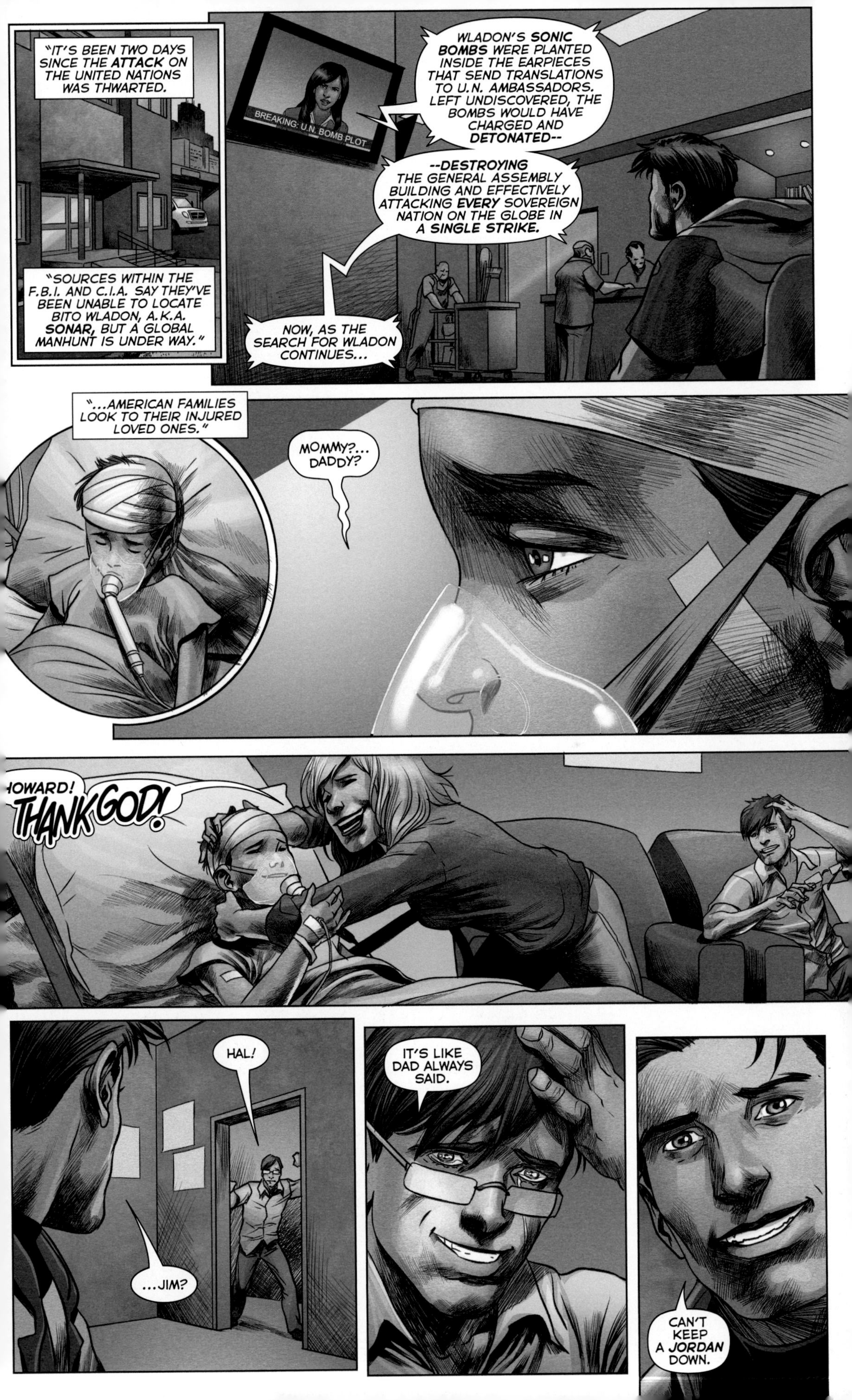

"IT'S BEEN TWO DAYS SINCE THE ATTACK ON THE UNITED NATIONS WAS THWARTED.
"SOURCES WITHIN THE F.B.I. AND C.I.A. SAY THEY'VE BEEN UNABLE TO LOCATE BITO WLADON, A.K.A. SONAR, BUT A GLOBAL MANHUNT IS UNDER WAY."
BREAKING: U.N. BOMB PLOT
WLADON'S SONIC BOMBS WERE PLANTED INSIDE THE EARPIECES THAT SEND TRANSLATIONS TO U.N. AMBASSADORS. LEFT UNDISCOVERED, THE BOMBS WOULD HAVE CHARGED AND DETONATED--
--DESTROYING THE GENERAL ASSEMBLY BUILDING AND EFFECTIVELY ATTACKING EVERY SOVEREIGN NATION ON THE GLOBE IN A SINGLE STRIKE.
NOW, AS THE SEARCH FOR WLADON CONTINUES...
"...AMERICAN FAMILIES LOOK TO THEIR INJURED LOVED ONES."
MOMMY?... DADDY?
HOWARD! THANK GOD!
HAL!
...JIM?
IT'S LIKE DAD ALWAYS SAID.
CAN'T KEEP A JORDAN DOWN.

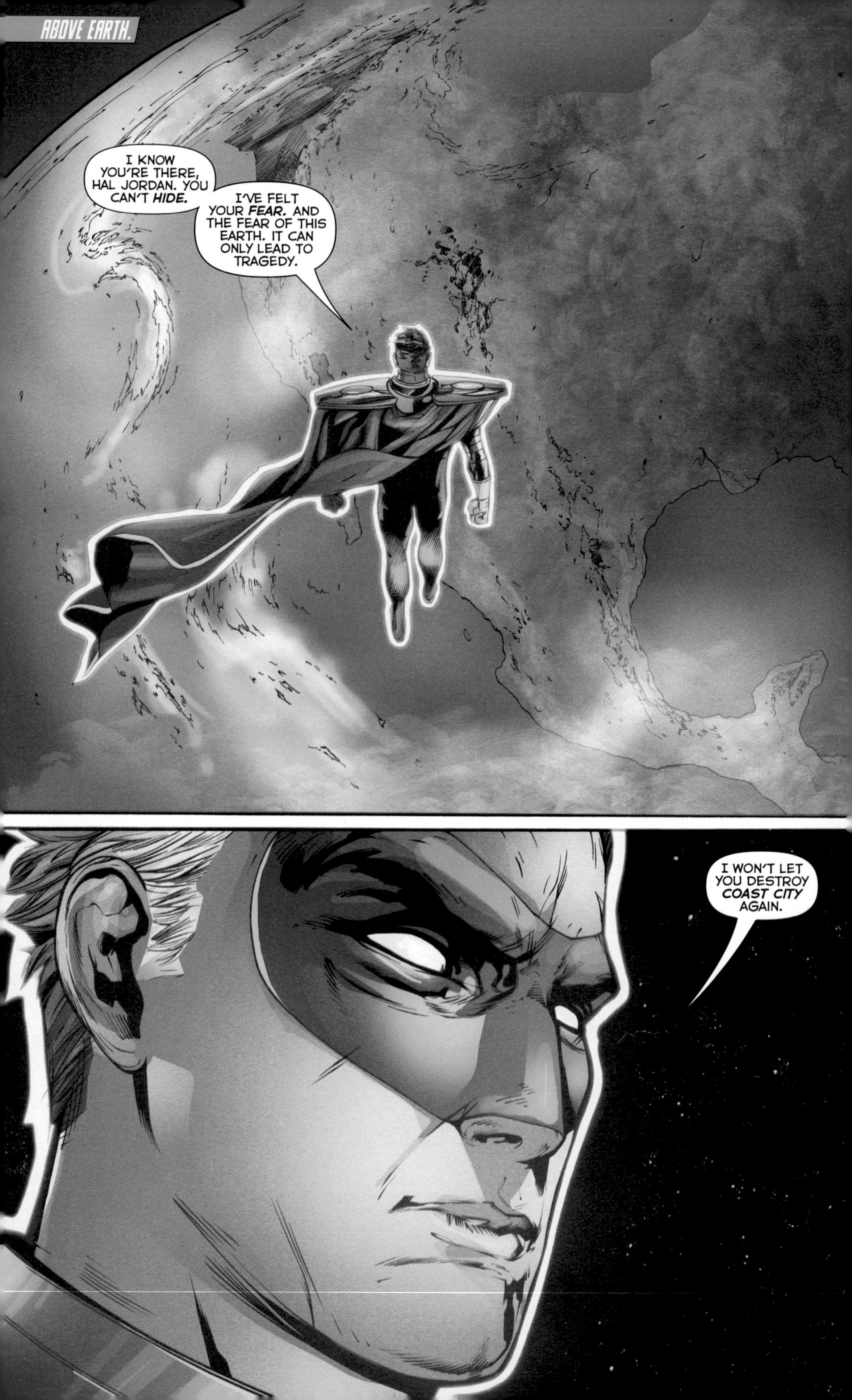
ABOVE EARTH.
I KNOW YOU'RE THERE, HAL JORDAN. YOU CAN'T HIDE.
I'VE FELT YOUR FEAR. AND THE FEAR OF THIS EARTH. IT CAN ONLY LEAD TO TRAGEDY.
I WON'T LET YOU DESTROY COAST CITY AGAIN.

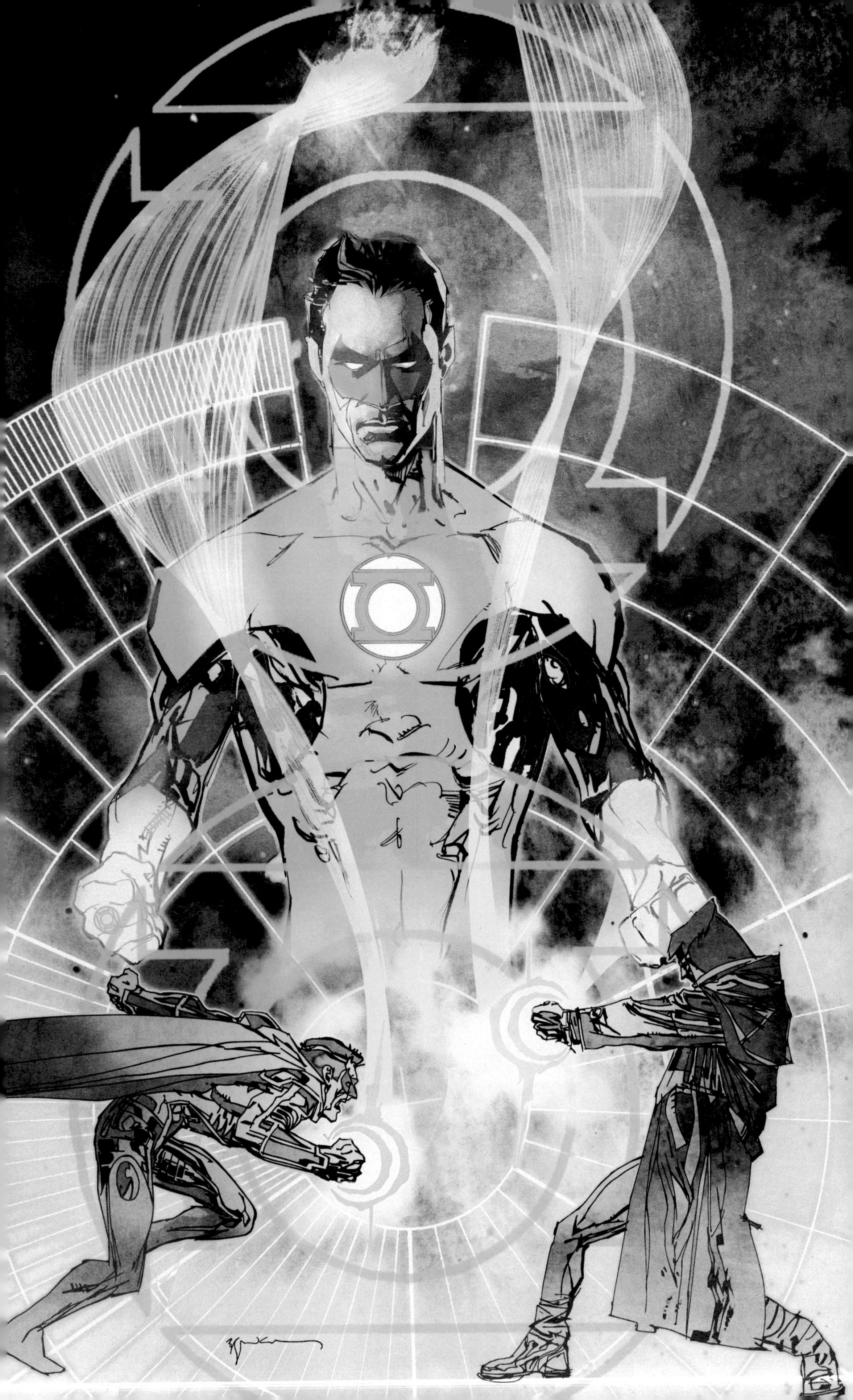

REFLECTIONS

ROBERT VENDITTI writer BILLY TAN VICENTE CIFUENTES pencillers MARK IRWIN JOHN LIVESAY VICENTE CIFUENTES inkers ALEX SINCLAIR TONY AVIÑA colorists DAVE SHARPE letterer BILL SIENKIEWICZ cover

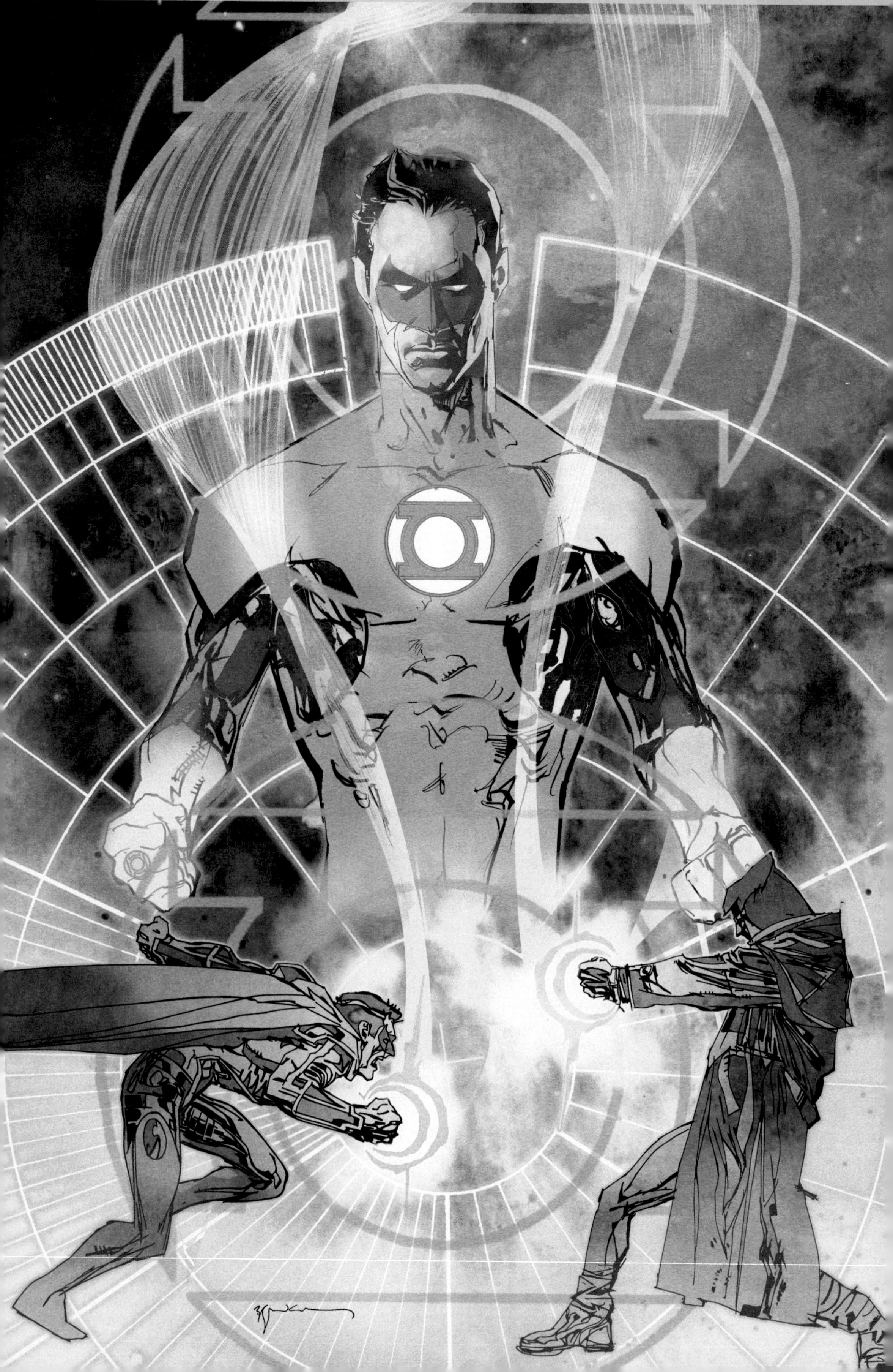

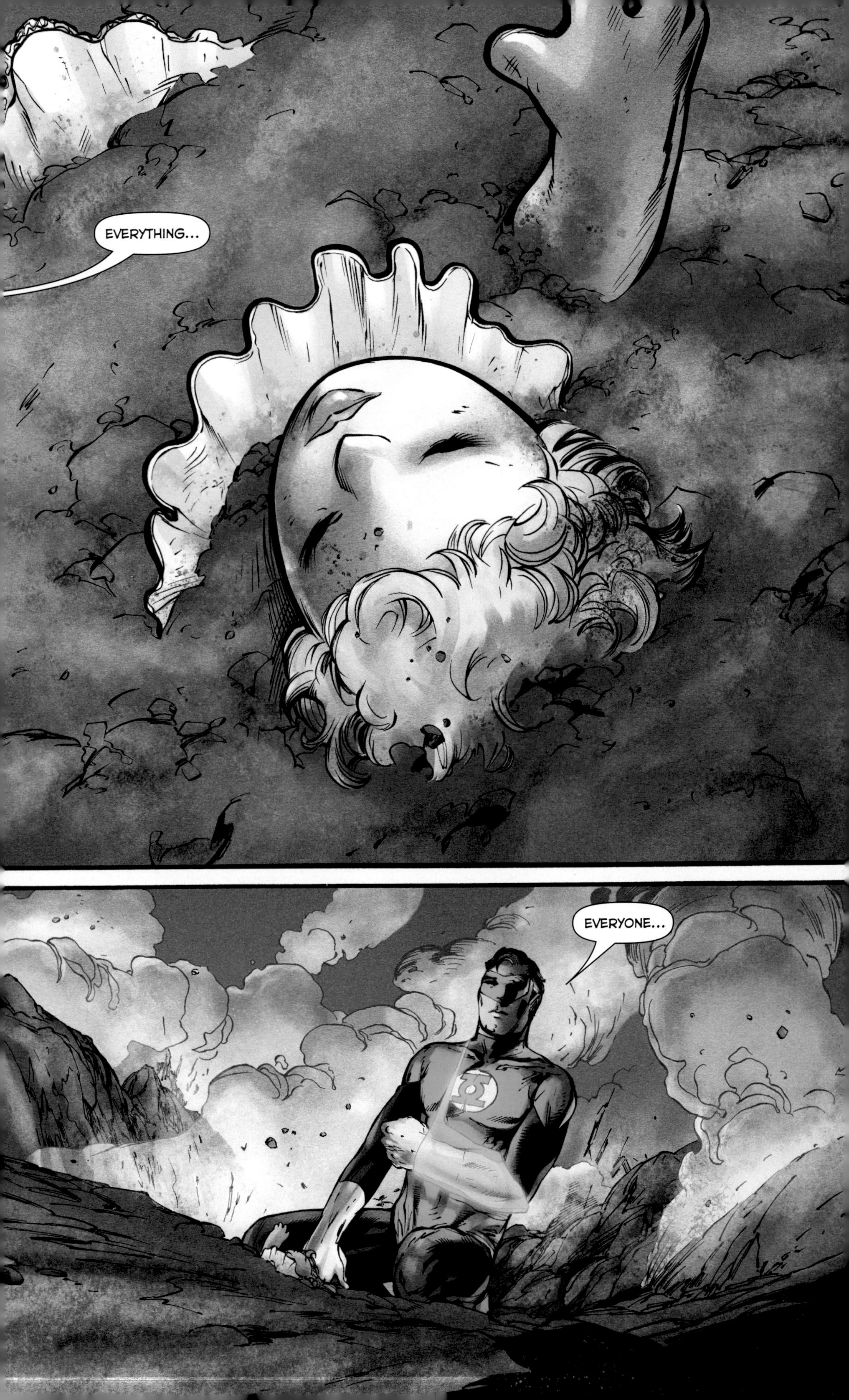
EVERYTHING...
EVERYONE...

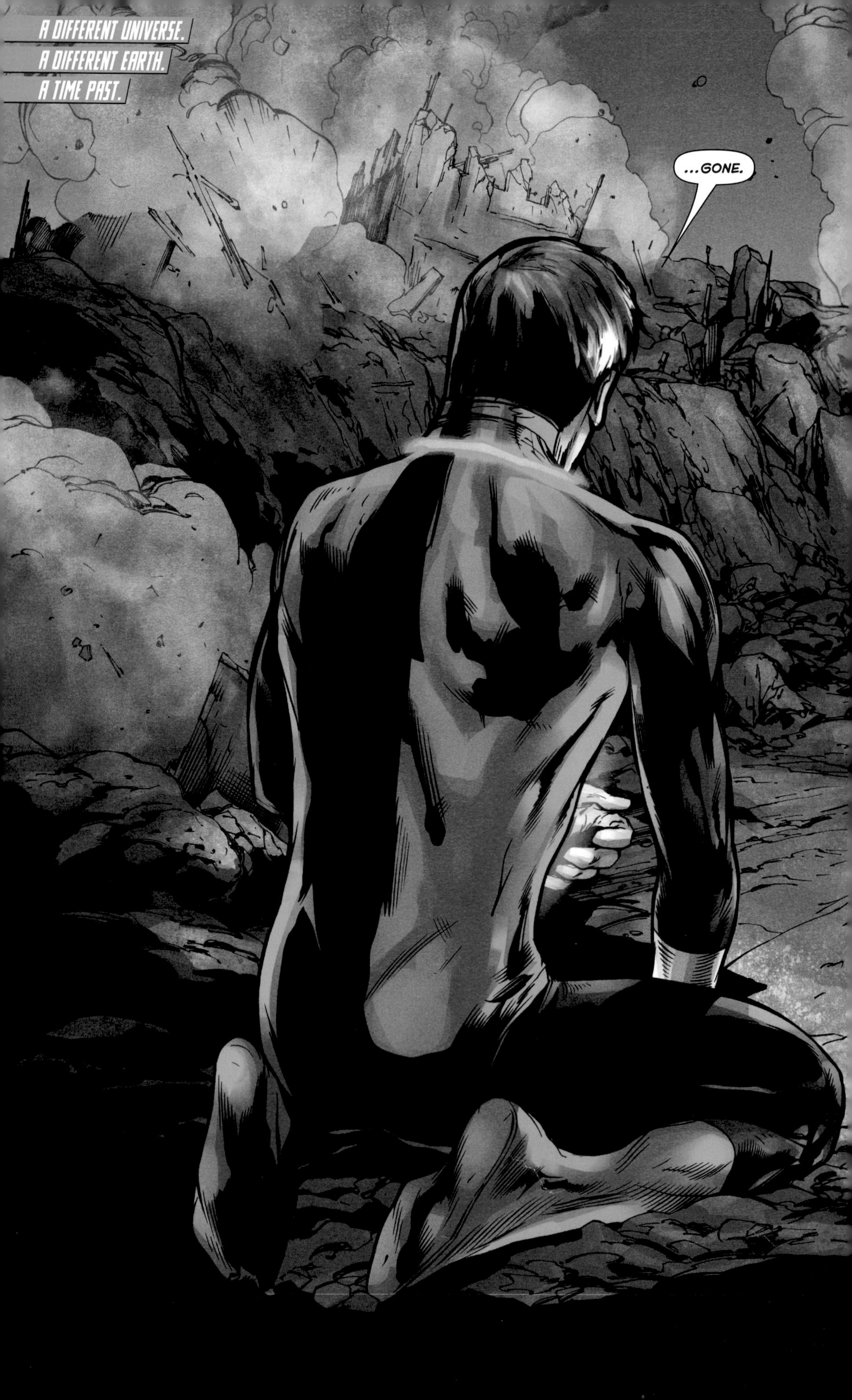
A DIFFERENT UNIVERSE.
A DIFFERENT EARTH.
A TIME PAST.
...GONE.

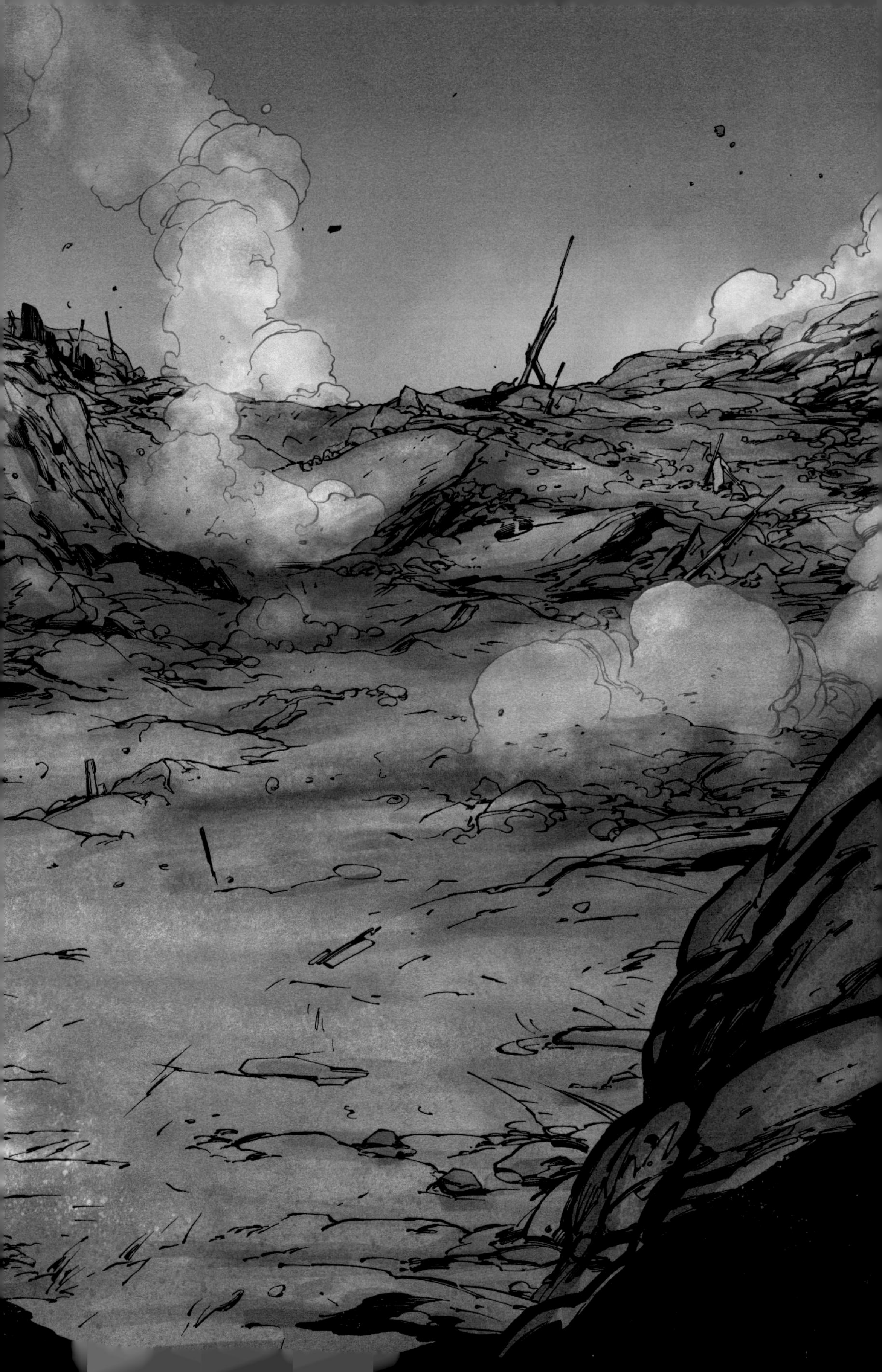

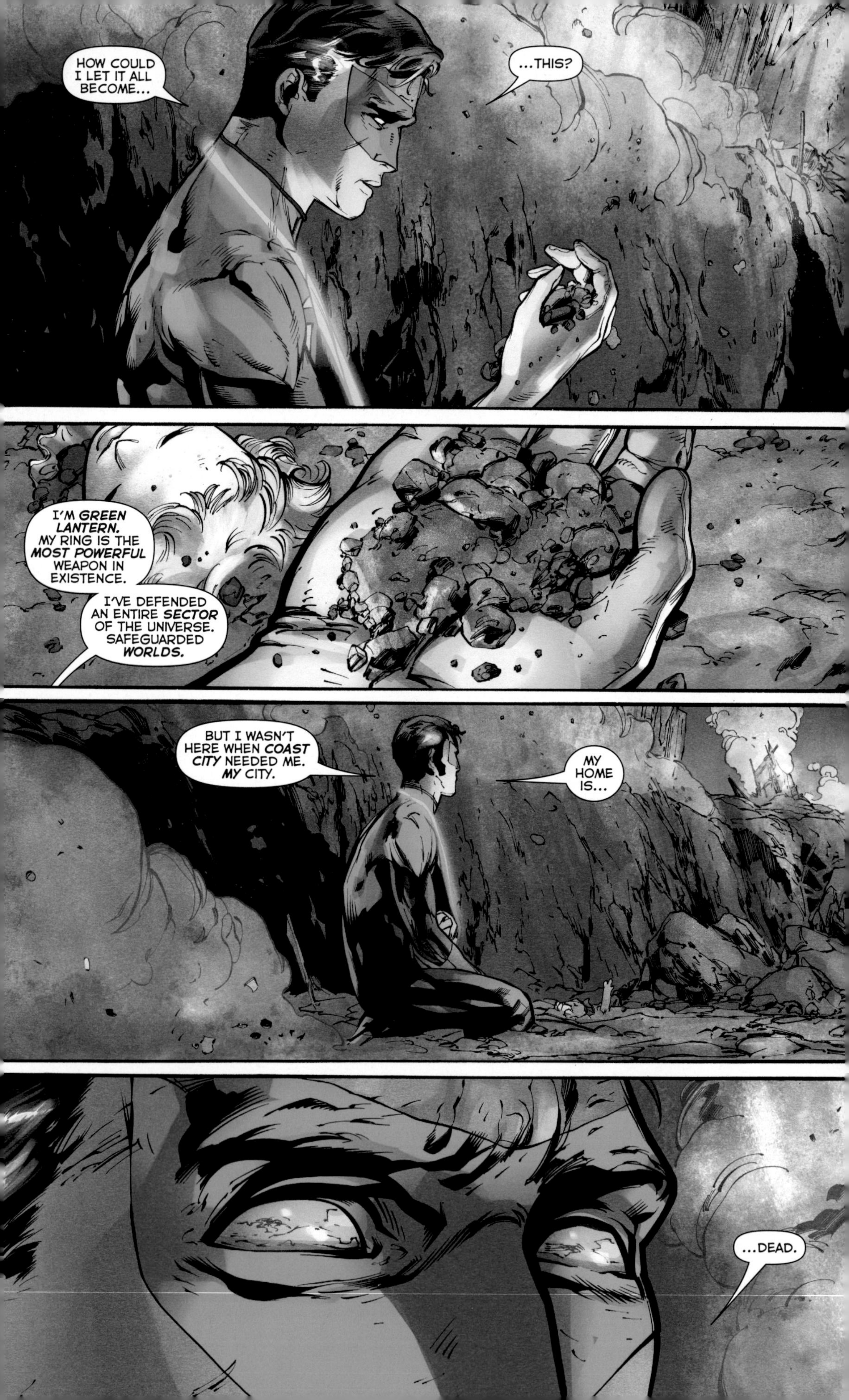
HOW COULD I LET IT ALL BECOME...
...THIS?
I'M GREEN LANTERN. MY RING IS THE MOST POWERFUL WEAPON IN EXISTENCE.
I'VE DEFENDED AN ENTIRE SECTOR OF THE UNIVERSE. SAFEGUARDED WORLDS.
BUT I WASN'T HERE WHEN COAST CITY NEEDED ME. MY CITY.
MY HOME IS...
...DEAD.

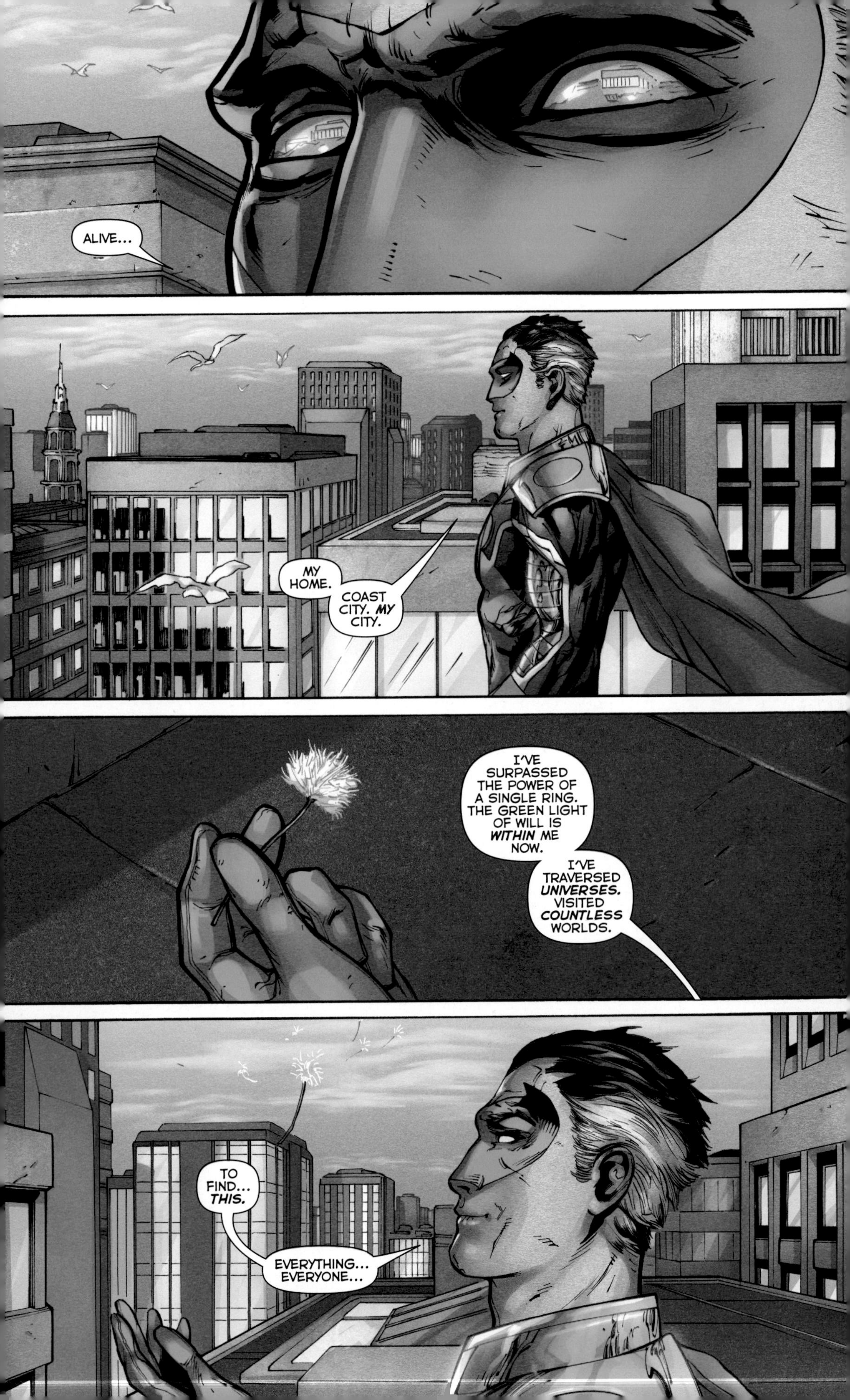

ALIVE...
MY HOME.
COAST CITY. *MY* CITY.
I'VE SURPASSED THE POWER OF A SINGLE RING. THE GREEN LIGHT OF WILL IS *WITHIN* ME NOW.
I'VE TRAVERSED *UNIVERSES.* VISITED *COUNTLESS* WORLDS.
TO FIND... *THIS.*
EVERYTHING... EVERYONE...

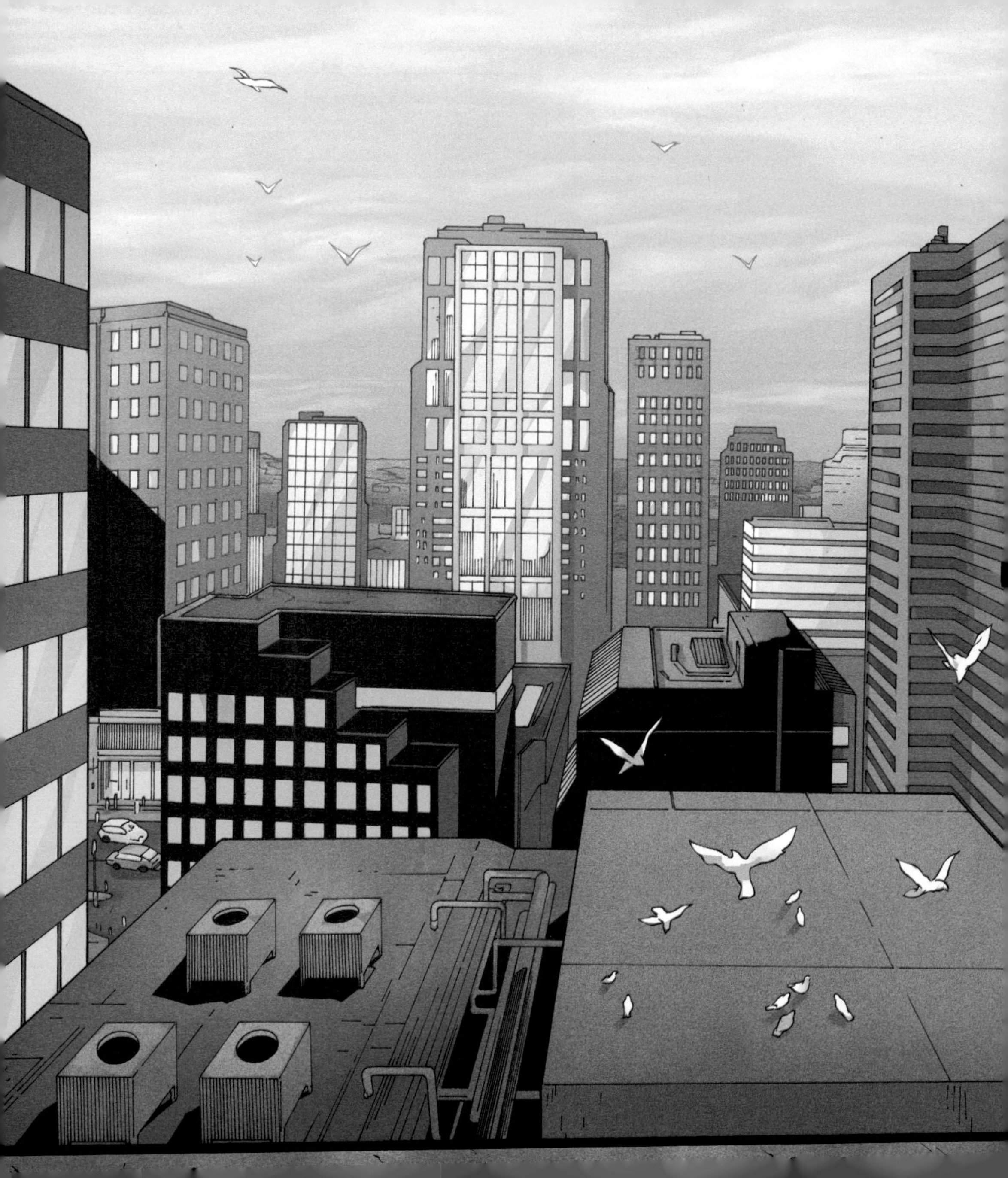

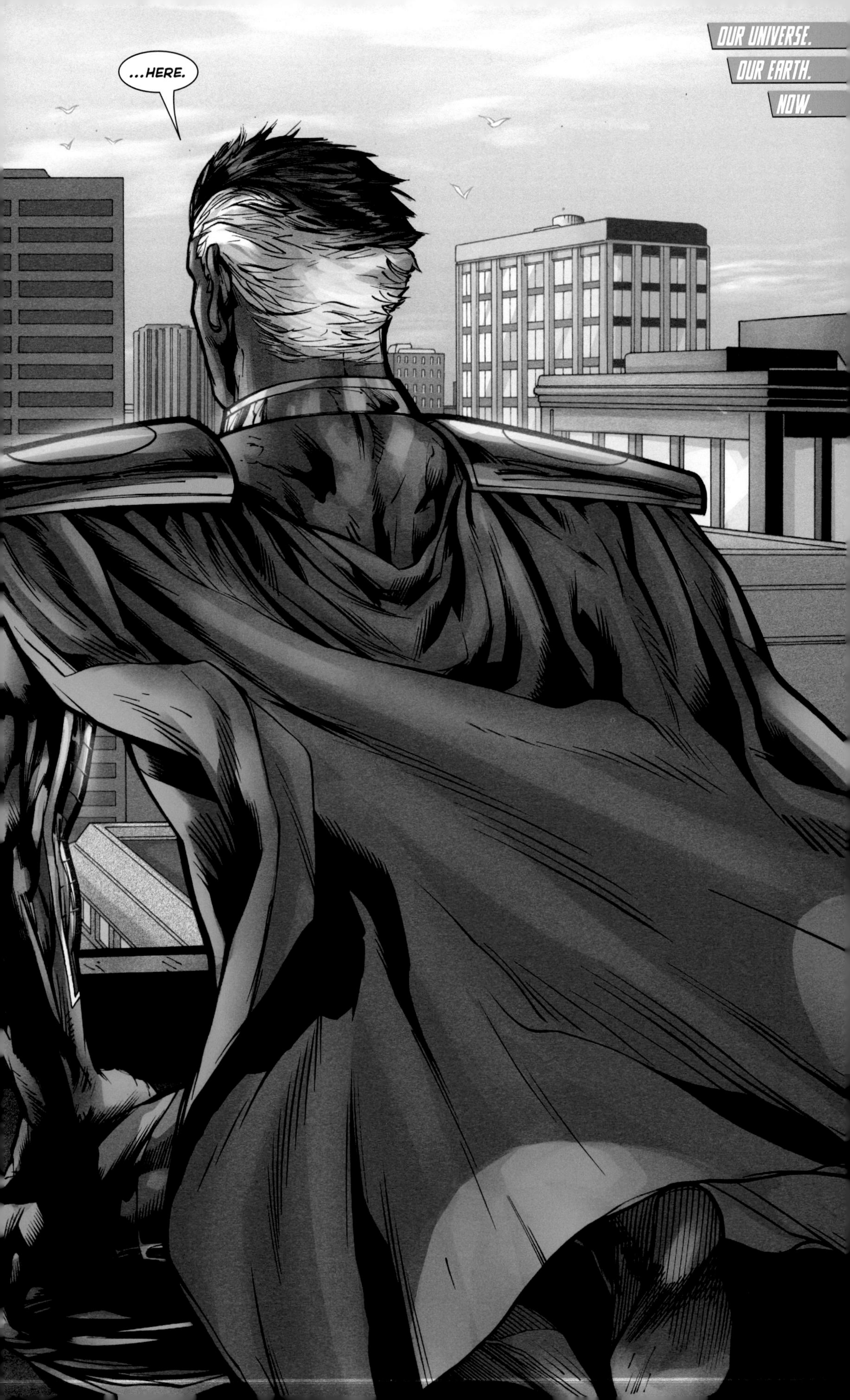

...HERE.
OUR UNIVERSE.
OUR EARTH.
NOW.

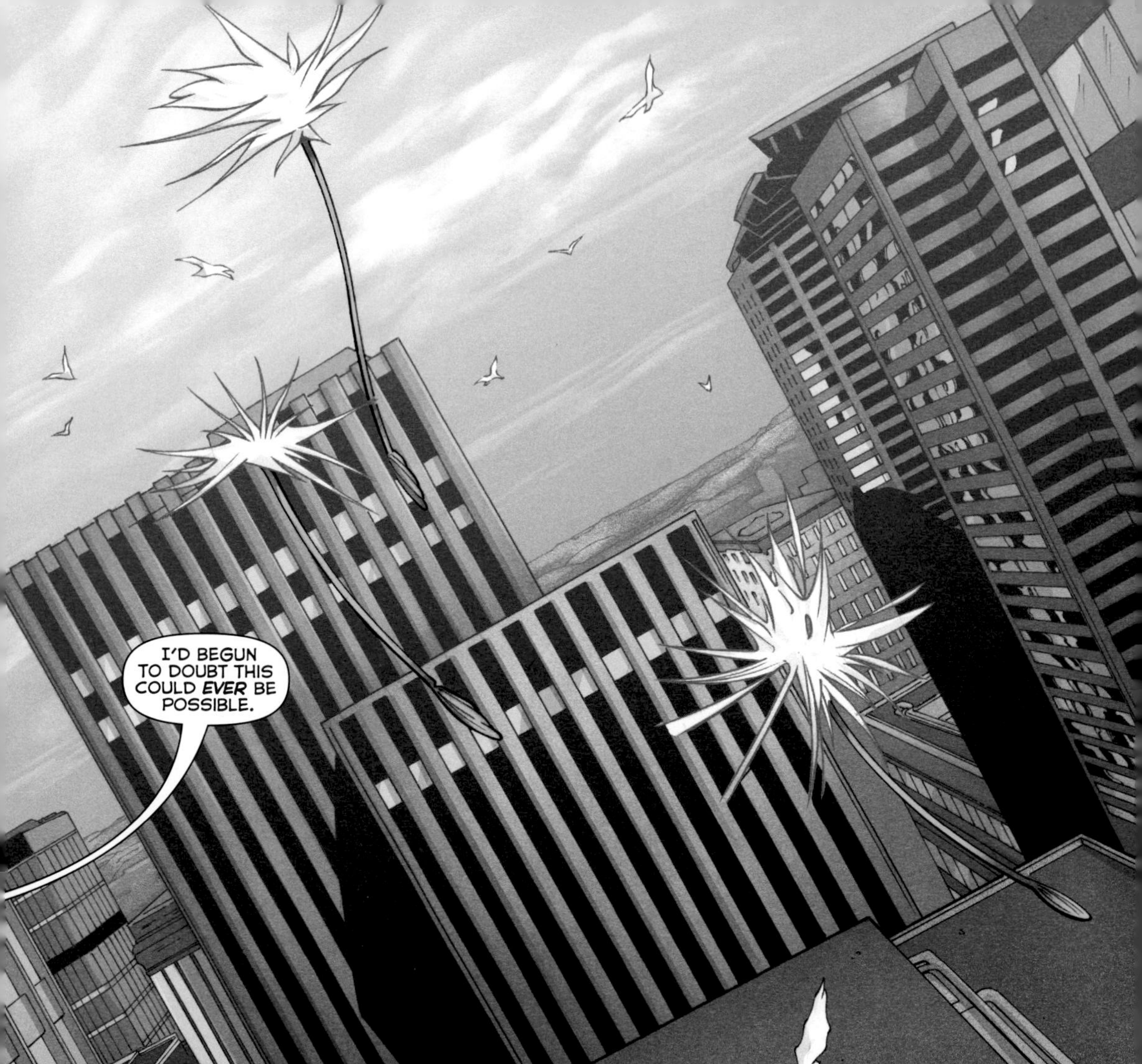
I'D BEGUN TO DOUBT THIS COULD EVER BE POSSIBLE.

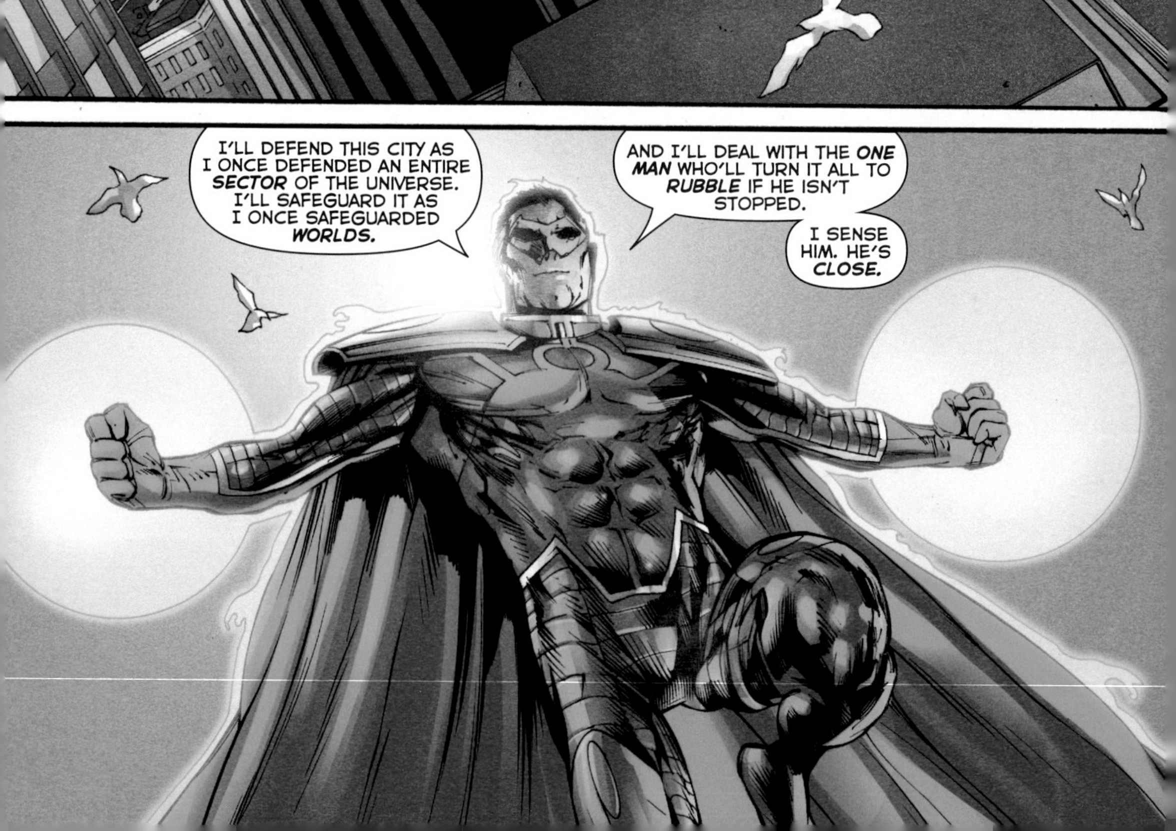
I'LL DEFEND THIS CITY AS I ONCE DEFENDED AN ENTIRE SECTOR OF THE UNIVERSE. I'LL SAFEGUARD IT AS I ONCE SAFEGUARDED WORLDS.
AND I'LL DEAL WITH THE ONE MAN WHO'LL TURN IT ALL TO RUBBLE IF HE ISN'T STOPPED.
I SENSE HIM. HE'S CLOSE.

"HAL JORDAN."

YOU HAVE TO MAKE IT UP TO HIM, HAL.

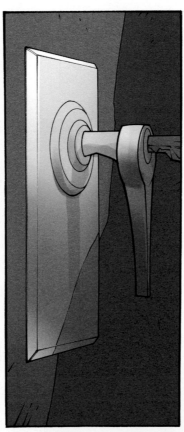

DON'T SCREW IT UP.

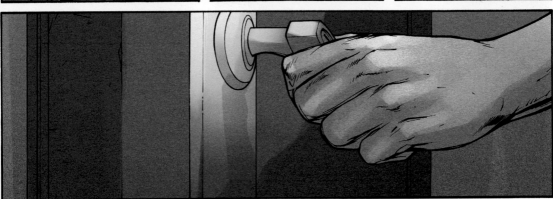

HAL?

WHAT--?

YOU'RE EARLY!

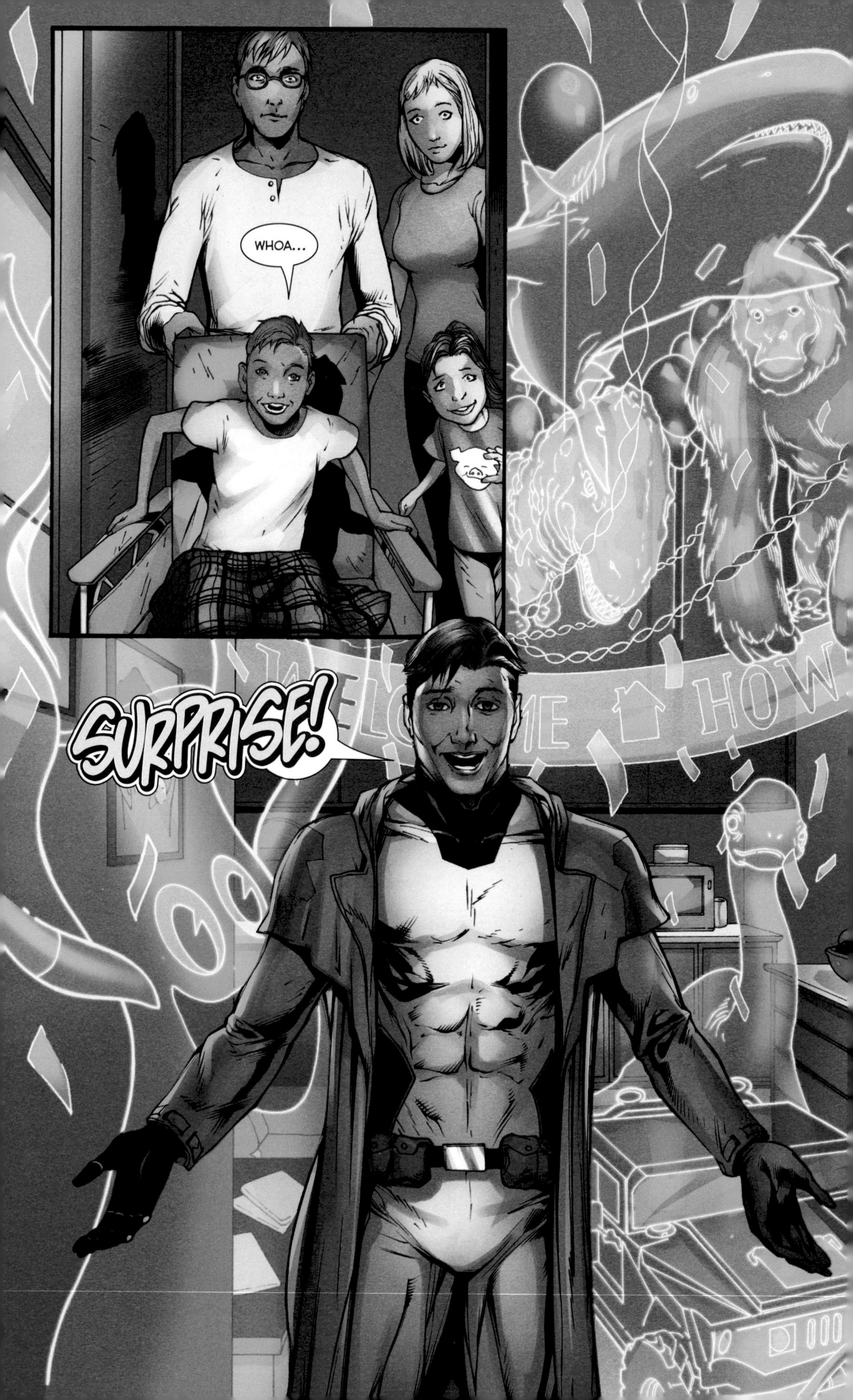
WHOA...
SURPRISE!

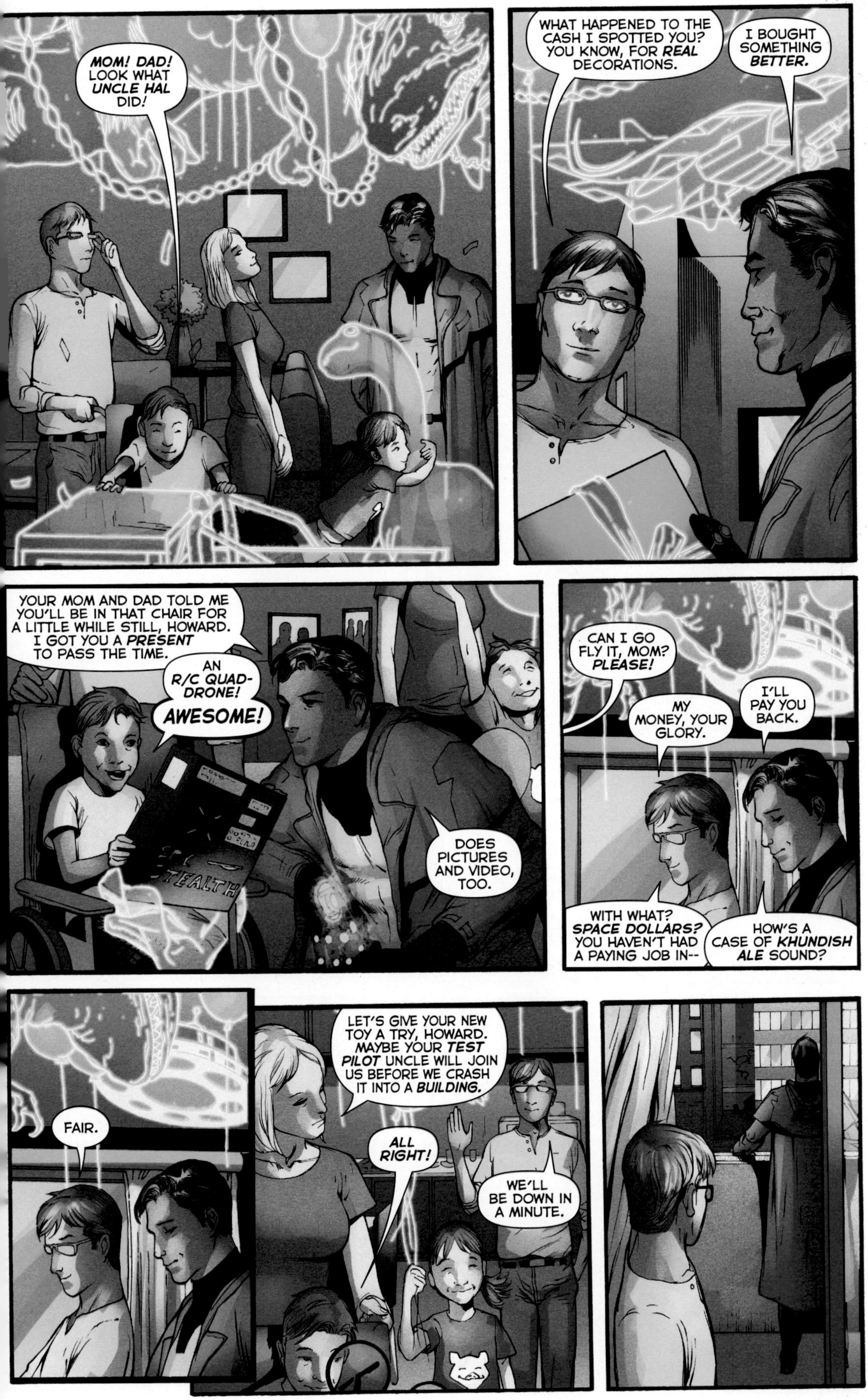

MOM! DAD! LOOK WHAT UNCLE HAL DID!
WHAT HAPPENED TO THE CASH I SPOTTED YOU? YOU KNOW, FOR REAL DECORATIONS.
I BOUGHT SOMETHING BETTER.
YOUR MOM AND DAD TOLD ME YOU'LL BE IN THAT CHAIR FOR A LITTLE WHILE STILL, HOWARD. I GOT YOU A PRESENT TO PASS THE TIME.
AN R/C QUAD-DRONE! AWESOME!
STEALTH
DOES PICTURES AND VIDEO, TOO.
CAN I GO FLY IT, MOM? PLEASE!
MY MONEY, YOUR GLORY.
I'LL PAY YOU BACK.
WITH WHAT? SPACE DOLLARS? YOU HAVEN'T HAD A PAYING JOB IN--
HOW'S A CASE OF KHUNDISH ALE SOUND?
FAIR.
LET'S GIVE YOUR NEW TOY A TRY, HOWARD. MAYBE YOUR TEST PILOT UNCLE WILL JOIN US BEFORE WE CRASH IT INTO A BUILDING.
ALL RIGHT!
WE'LL BE DOWN IN A MINUTE.

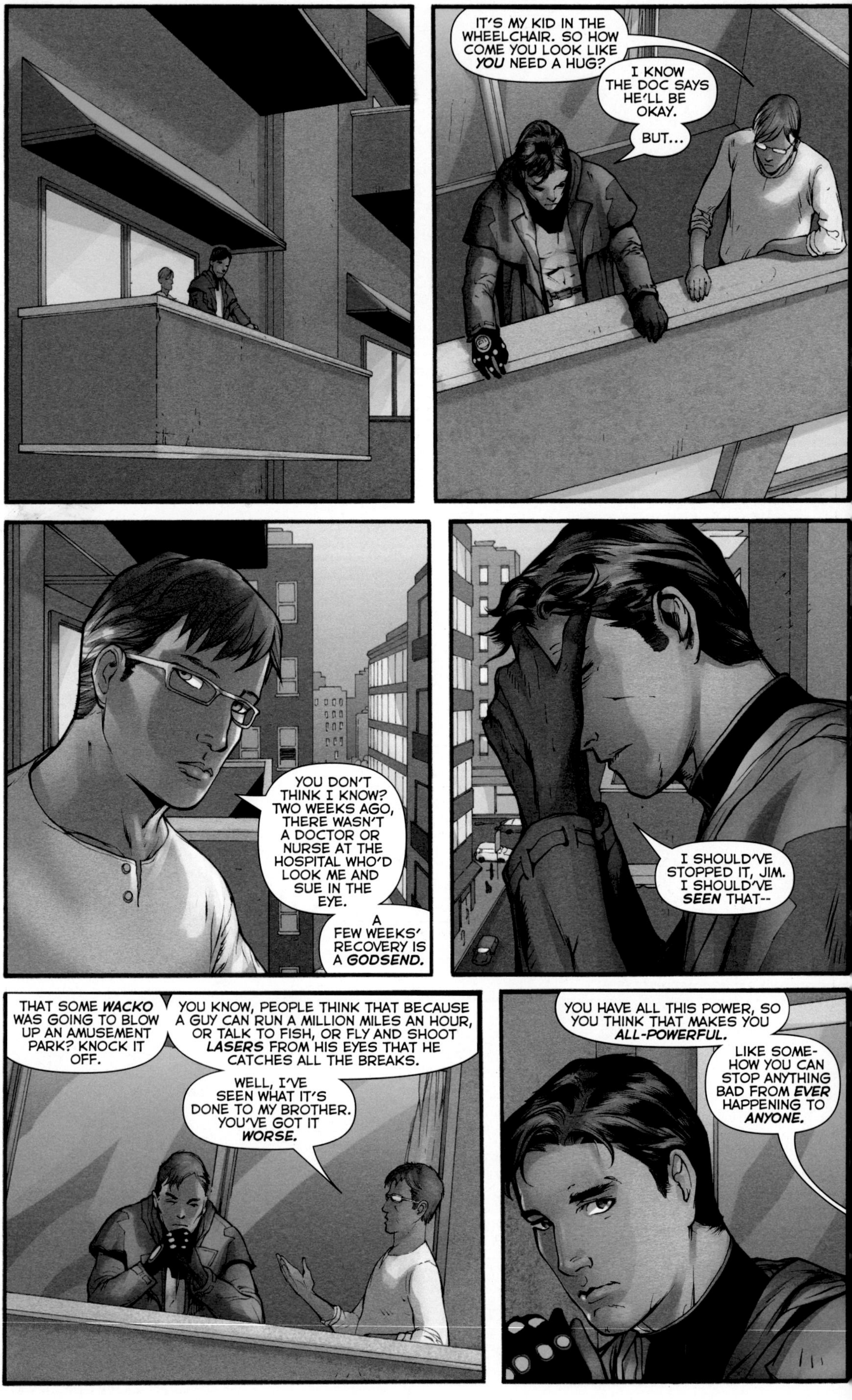
IT'S MY KID IN THE WHEELCHAIR. SO HOW COME YOU LOOK LIKE *YOU* NEED A HUG?
I KNOW THE DOC SAYS HE'LL BE OKAY.
BUT...
YOU DON'T THINK I KNOW? TWO WEEKS AGO, THERE WASN'T A DOCTOR OR NURSE AT THE HOSPITAL WHO'D LOOK ME AND SUE IN THE EYE.
A FEW WEEKS' RECOVERY IS A *GODSEND.*
I SHOULD'VE STOPPED IT, JIM. I SHOULD'VE *SEEN* THAT--
THAT SOME *WACKO* WAS GOING TO BLOW UP AN AMUSEMENT PARK? KNOCK IT OFF.
YOU KNOW, PEOPLE THINK THAT BECAUSE A GUY CAN RUN A MILLION MILES AN HOUR, OR TALK TO FISH, OR FLY AND SHOOT *LASERS* FROM HIS EYES THAT HE CATCHES ALL THE BREAKS.
WELL, I'VE SEEN WHAT IT'S DONE TO MY BROTHER. YOU'VE GOT IT *WORSE.*
YOU HAVE ALL THIS POWER, SO YOU THINK THAT MAKES YOU *ALL-POWERFUL.*
LIKE SOME-HOW YOU CAN STOP ANYTHING BAD FROM *EVER* HAPPENING TO *ANYONE.*

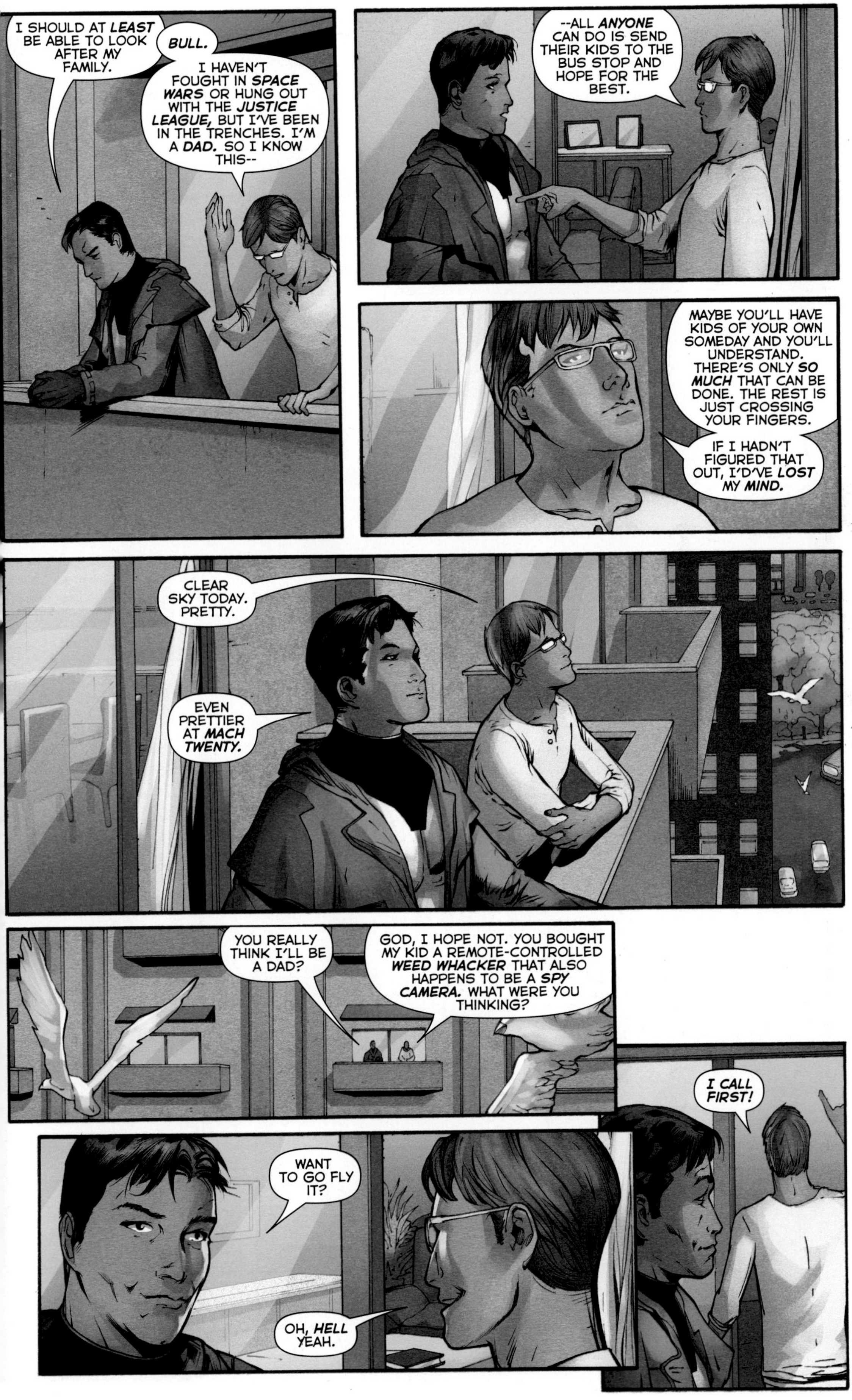

I SHOULD AT LEAST BE ABLE TO LOOK AFTER MY FAMILY.
BULL.
I HAVEN'T FOUGHT IN SPACE WARS OR HUNG OUT WITH THE JUSTICE LEAGUE, BUT I'VE BEEN IN THE TRENCHES. I'M A DAD. SO I KNOW THIS--
--ALL ANYONE CAN DO IS SEND THEIR KIDS TO THE BUS STOP AND HOPE FOR THE BEST.
MAYBE YOU'LL HAVE KIDS OF YOUR OWN SOMEDAY AND YOU'LL UNDERSTAND. THERE'S ONLY SO MUCH THAT CAN BE DONE. THE REST IS JUST CROSSING YOUR FINGERS.
IF I HADN'T FIGURED THAT OUT, I'D'VE LOST MY MIND.
CLEAR SKY TODAY. PRETTY.
EVEN PRETTIER AT MACH TWENTY.
YOU REALLY THINK I'LL BE A DAD?
GOD, I HOPE NOT. YOU BOUGHT MY KID A REMOTE-CONTROLLED WEED WHACKER THAT ALSO HAPPENS TO BE A SPY CAMERA. WHAT WERE YOU THINKING?
WANT TO GO FLY IT?
OH, HELL YEAH.
I CALL FIRST!

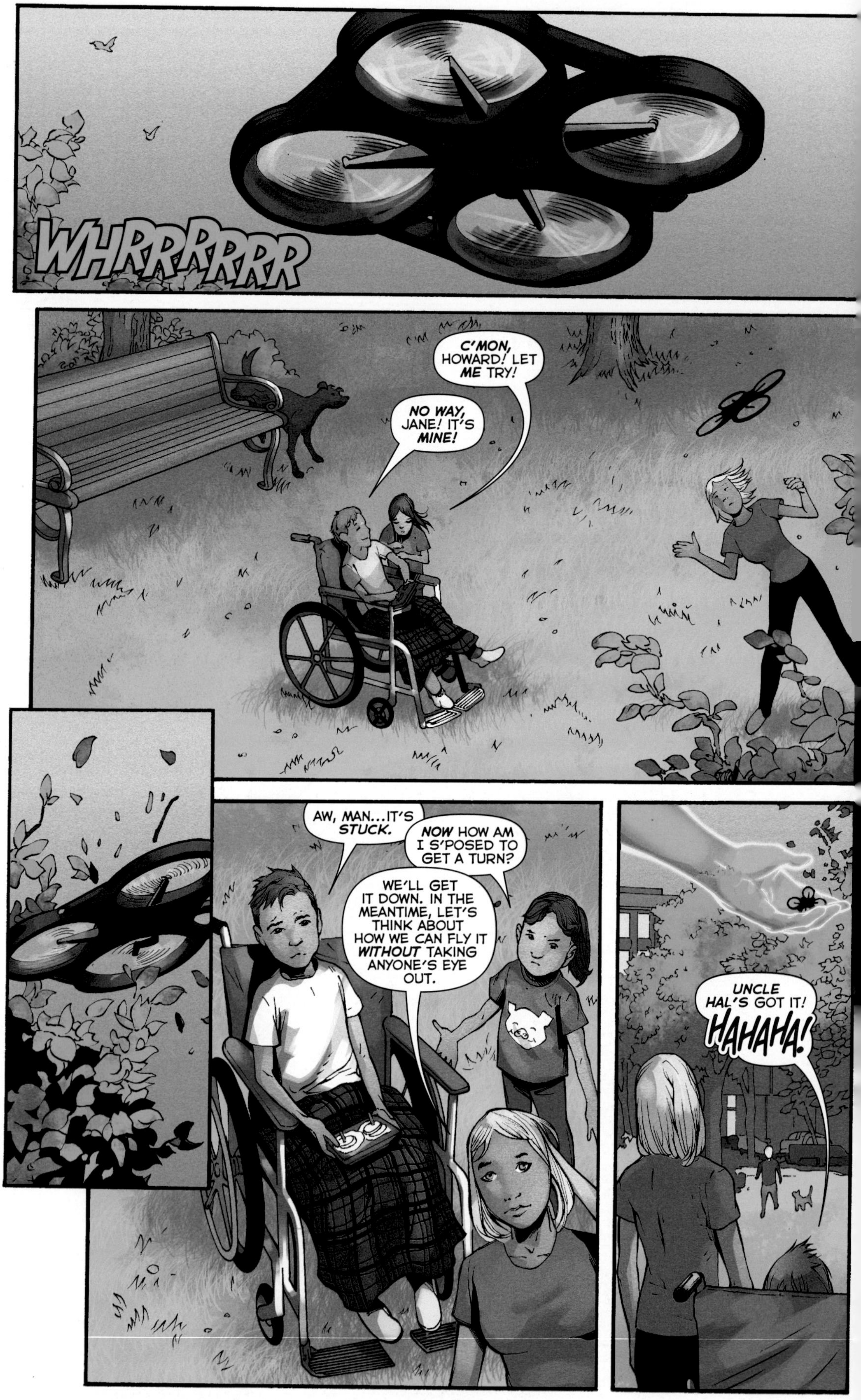
WHRRRRRR
C'MON, HOWARD! LET ME TRY!
NO WAY, JANE! IT'S MINE!
AW, MAN...IT'S STUCK.
NOW HOW AM I S'POSED TO GET A TURN?
WE'LL GET IT DOWN. IN THE MEANTIME, LET'S THINK ABOUT HOW WE CAN FLY IT WITHOUT TAKING ANYONE'S EYE OUT.
UNCLE HAL'S GOT IT!
HAHAHA!

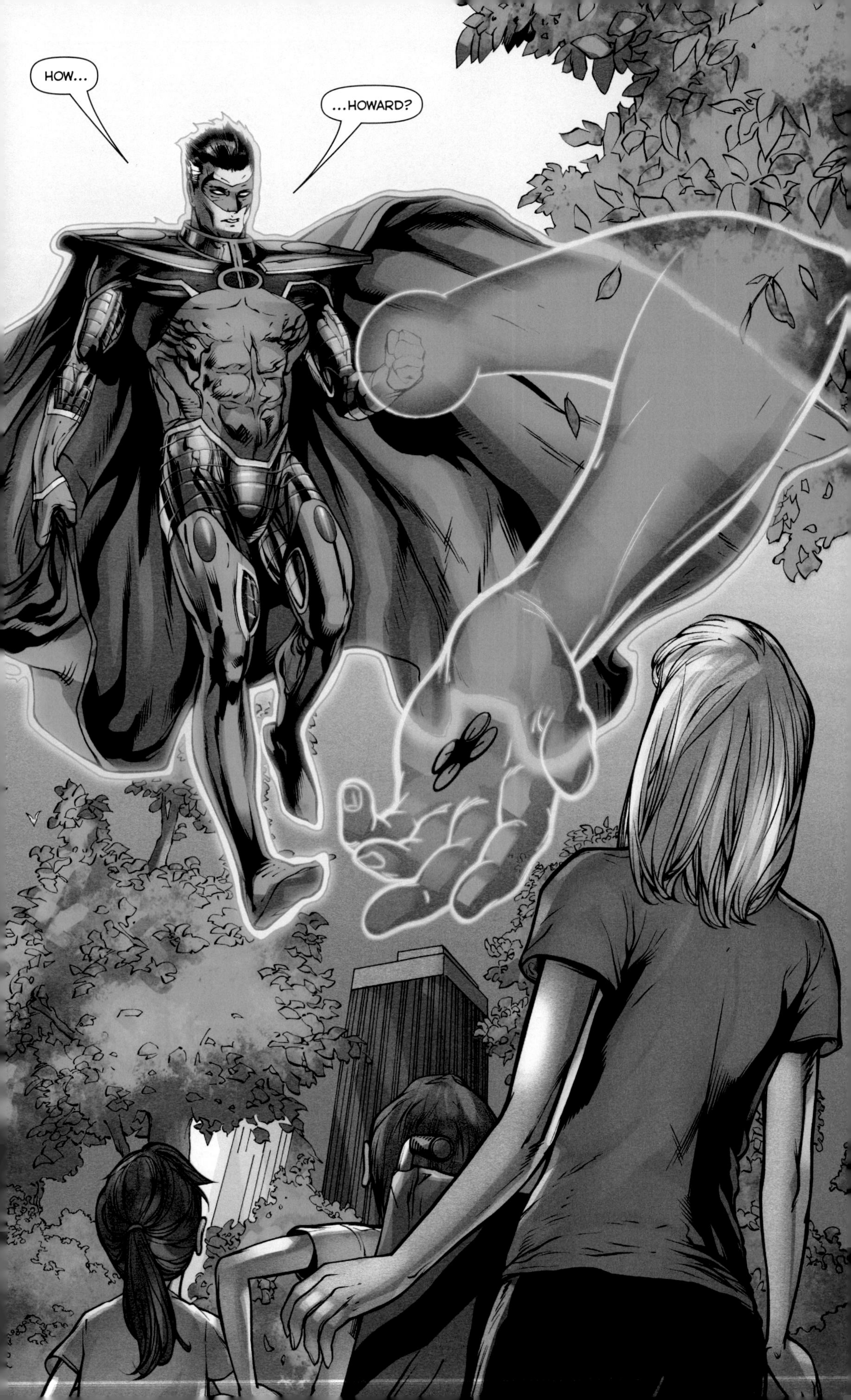
HOW...
...HOWARD?

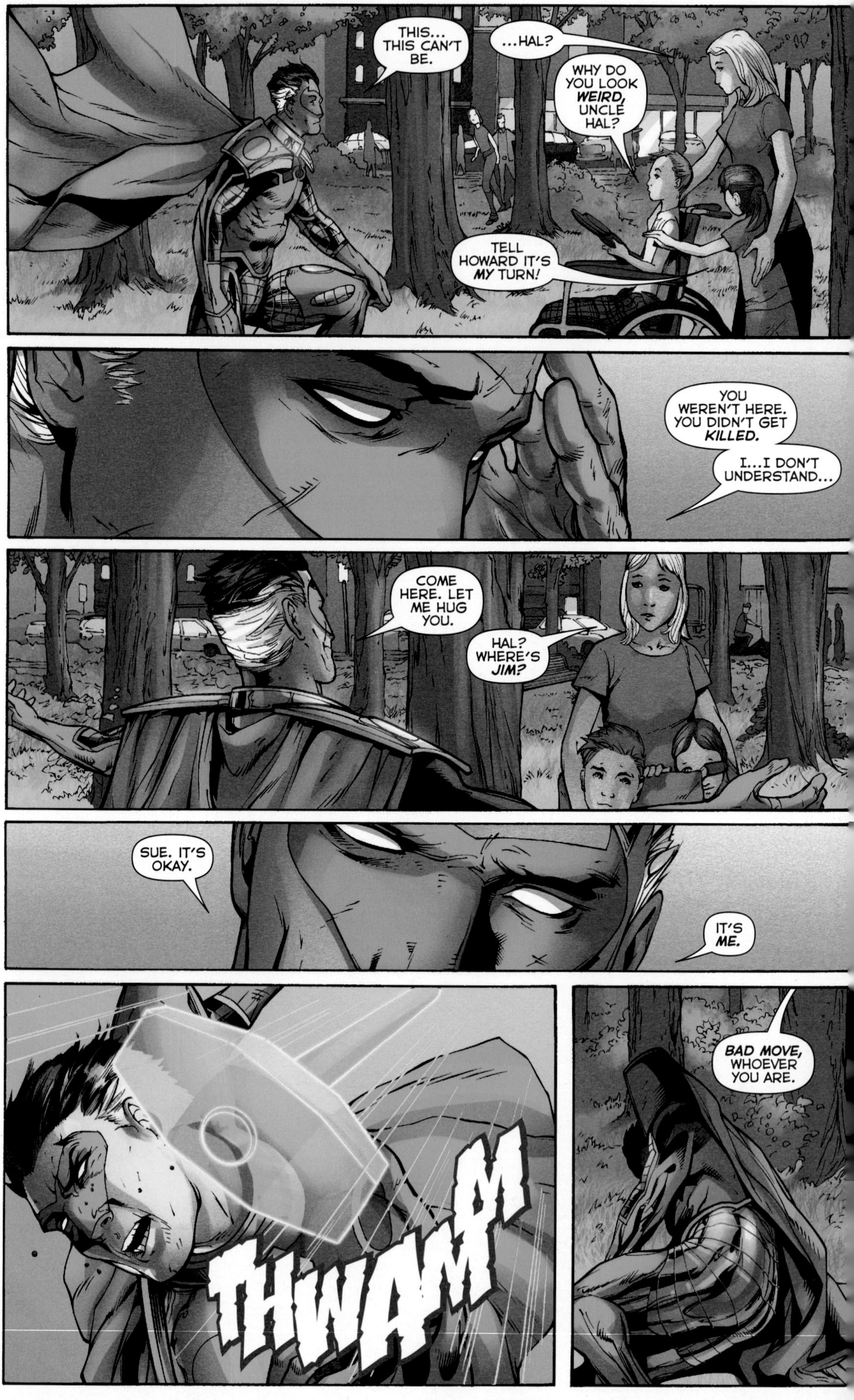
THIS... THIS CAN'T BE.
...HAL?
WHY DO YOU LOOK WEIRD, UNCLE HAL?
TELL HOWARD IT'S MY TURN!
YOU WEREN'T HERE. YOU DIDN'T GET KILLED.
I...I DON'T UNDERSTAND...
COME HERE. LET ME HUG YOU.
HAL? WHERE'S JIM?
SUE. IT'S OKAY.
IT'S ME.
THWAMM
BAD MOVE, WHOEVER YOU ARE.

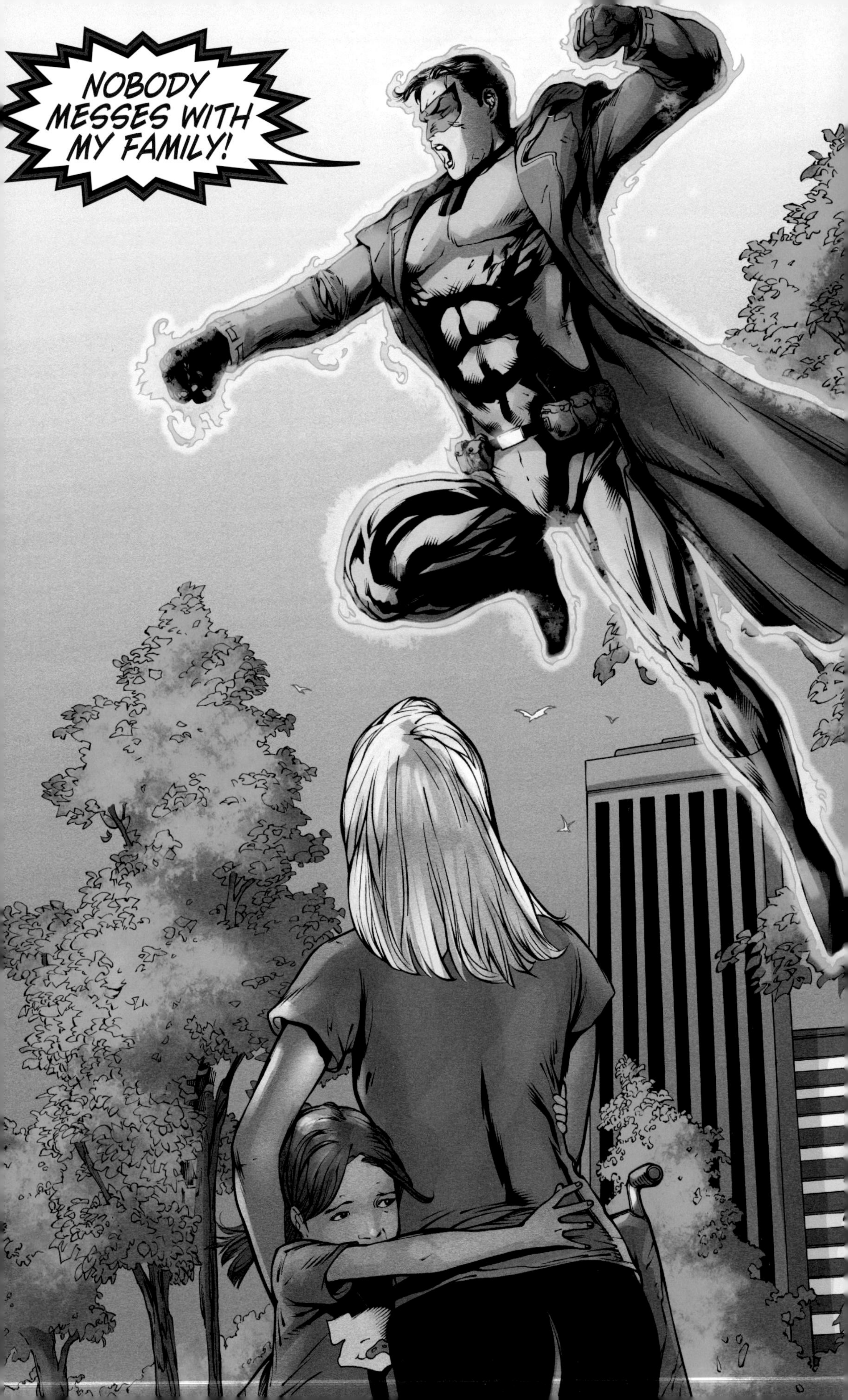
NOBODY MESSES WITH MY FAMILY!

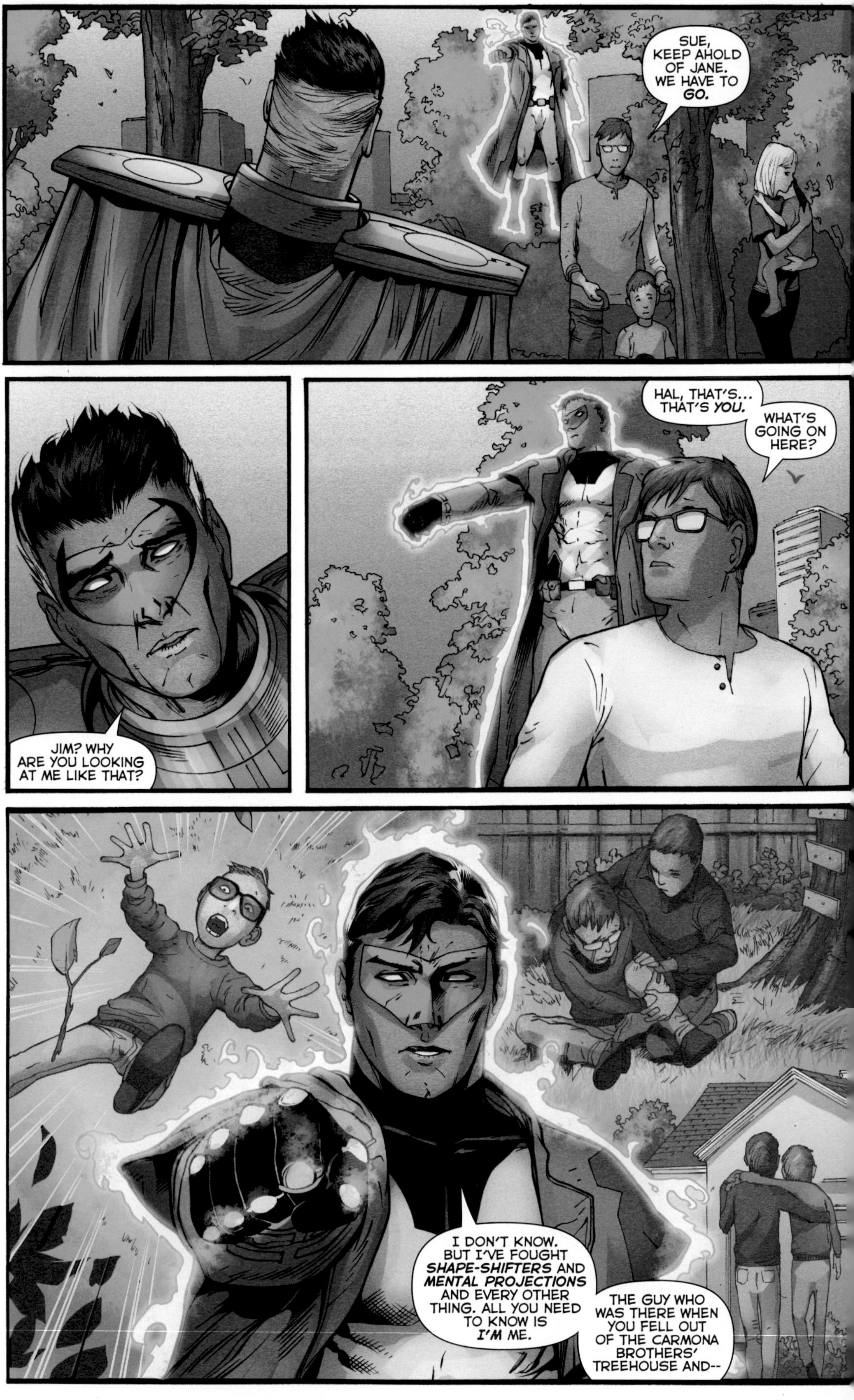
SUE, KEEP AHOLD OF JANE. WE HAVE TO GO.
JIM? WHY ARE YOU LOOKING AT ME LIKE THAT?
HAL, THAT'S... THAT'S YOU.
WHAT'S GOING ON HERE?
I DON'T KNOW. BUT I'VE FOUGHT SHAPE-SHIFTERS AND MENTAL PROJECTIONS AND EVERY OTHER THING. ALL YOU NEED TO KNOW IS I'M ME.
THE GUY WHO WAS THERE WHEN YOU FELL OUT OF THE CARMONA BROTHERS' TREEHOUSE AND--

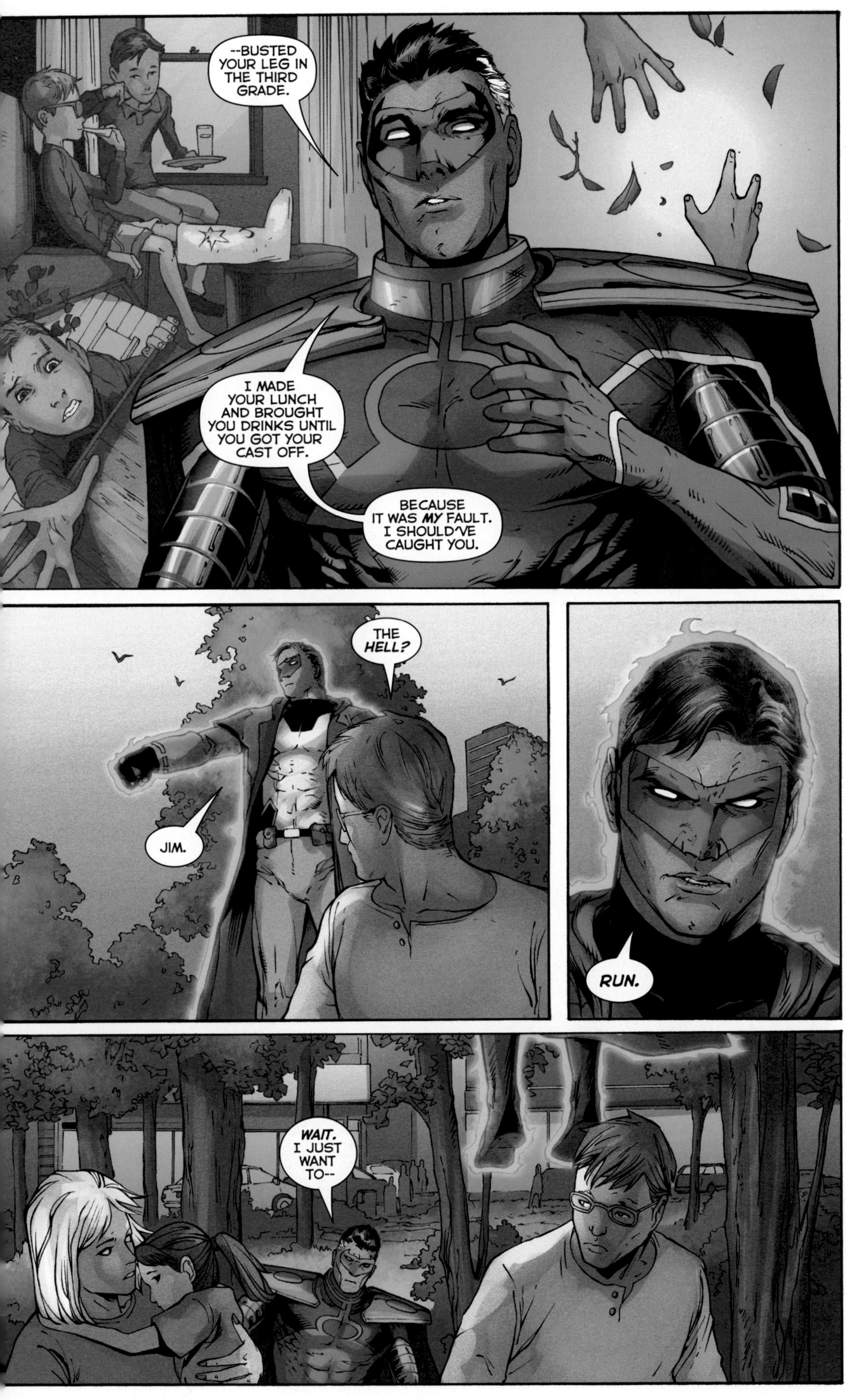
--BUSTED YOUR LEG IN THE THIRD GRADE.
I MADE YOUR LUNCH AND BROUGHT YOU DRINKS UNTIL YOU GOT YOUR CAST OFF.
BECAUSE IT WAS *MY* FAULT. I SHOULD'VE CAUGHT YOU.
THE *HELL?*
JIM.
RUN.
WAIT. I JUST WANT TO--

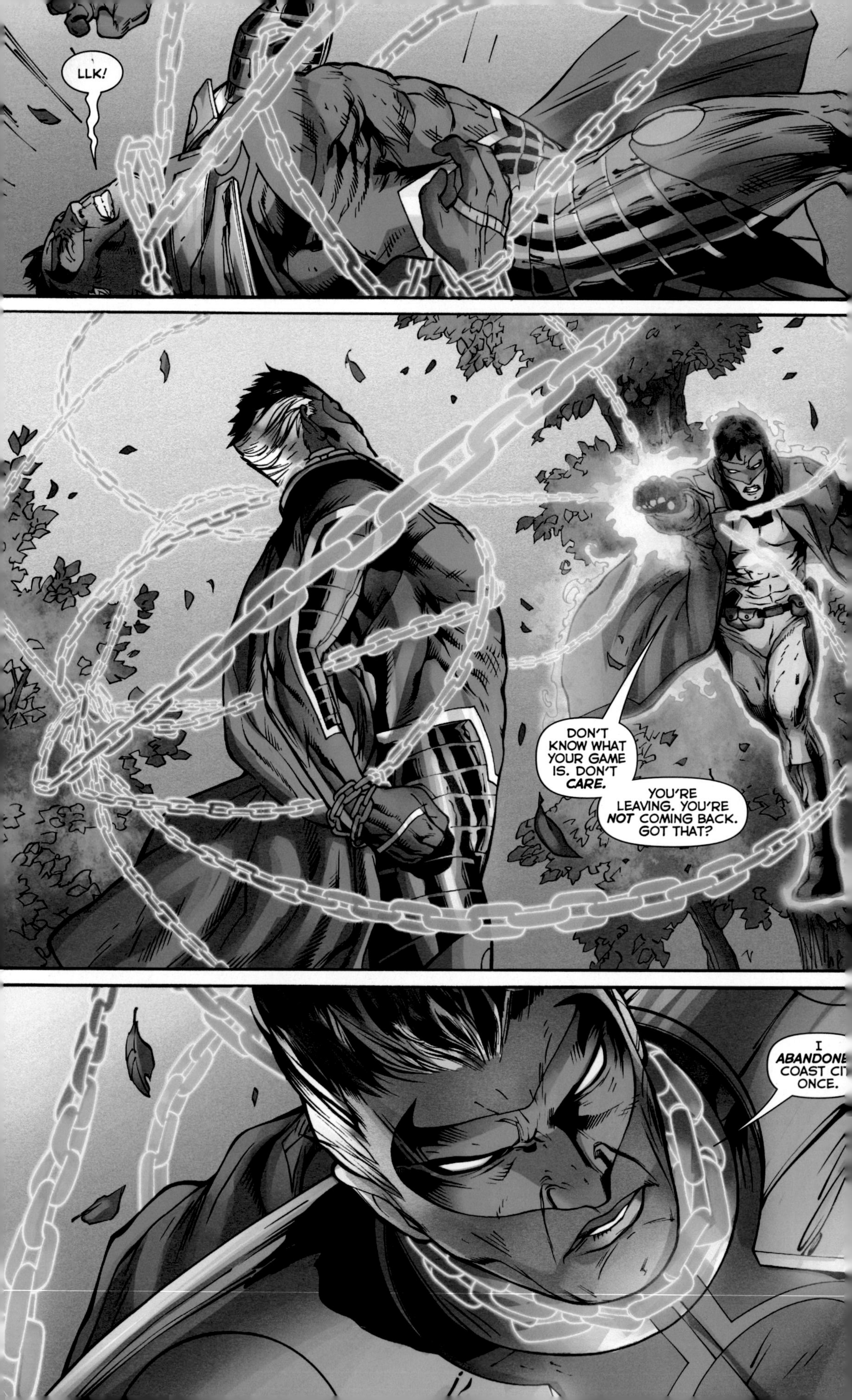
LLK!
DON'T KNOW WHAT YOUR GAME IS. DON'T CARE.
YOU'RE LEAVING. YOU'RE NOT COMING BACK. GOT THAT?
I ABANDONE COAST CIT ONCE.

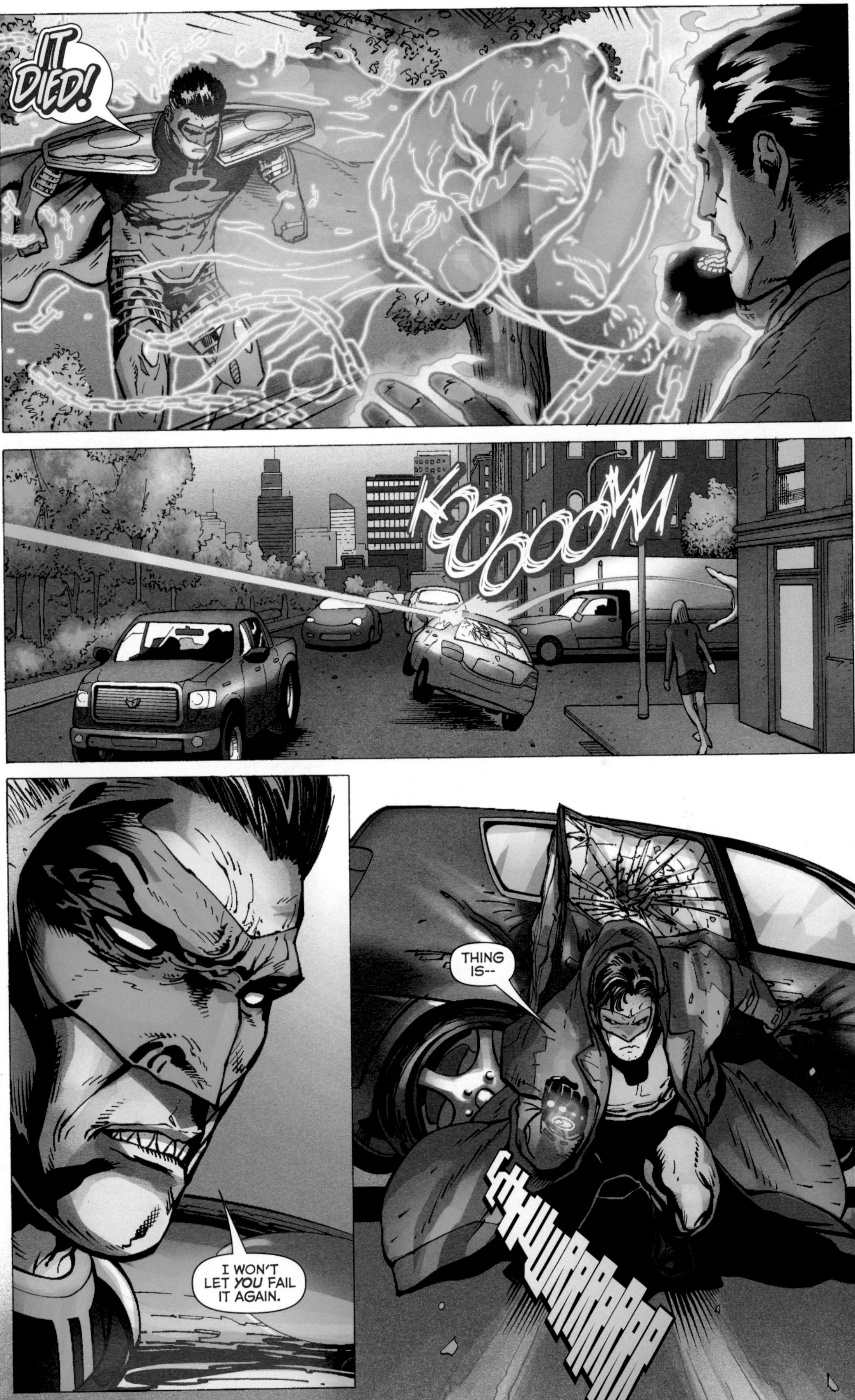
IT DIED!
KOOOOOM
I WON'T LET YOU FAIL IT AGAIN.
THING IS--
SCHWRRRRRR

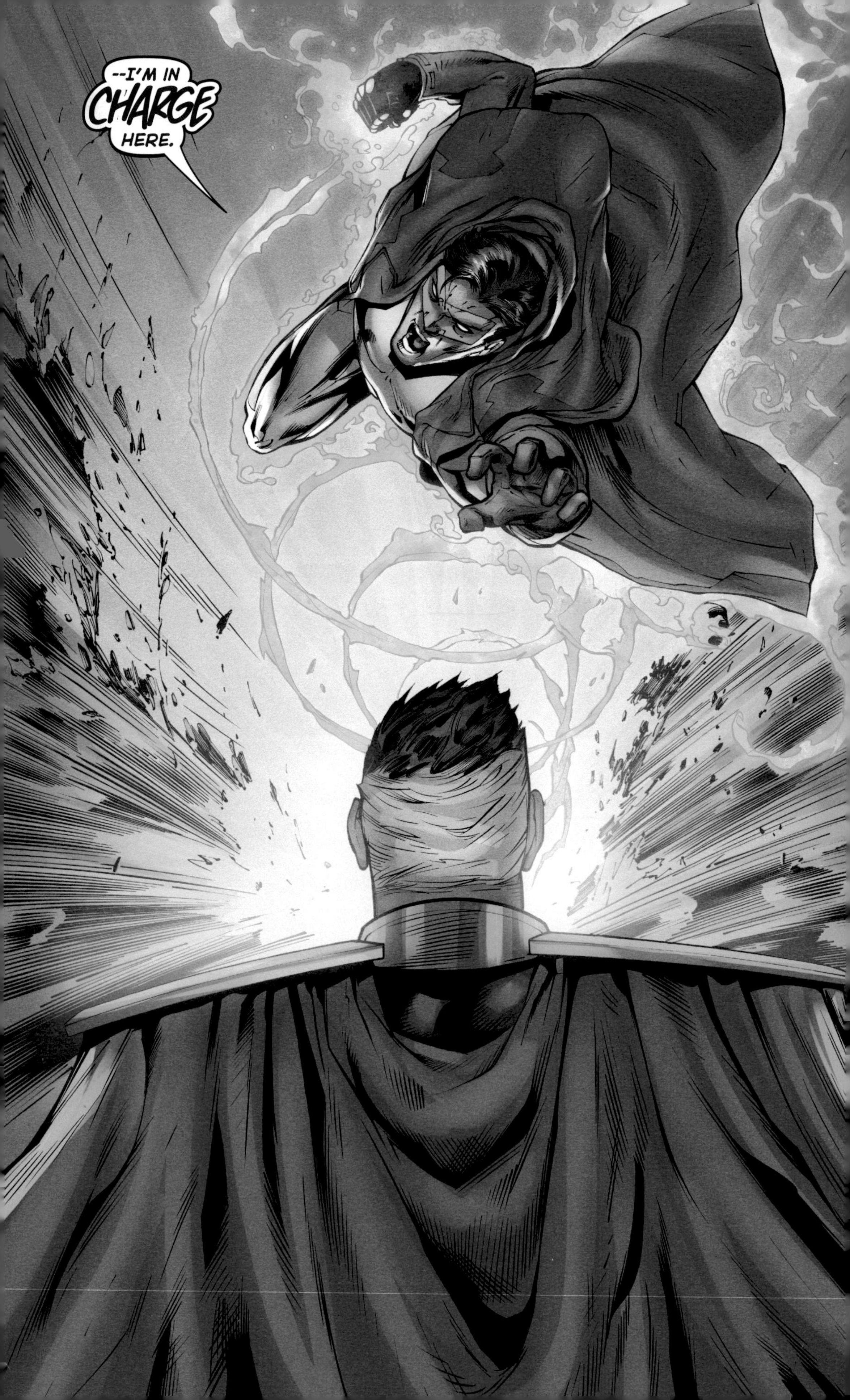
--I'M IN CHARGE HERE.

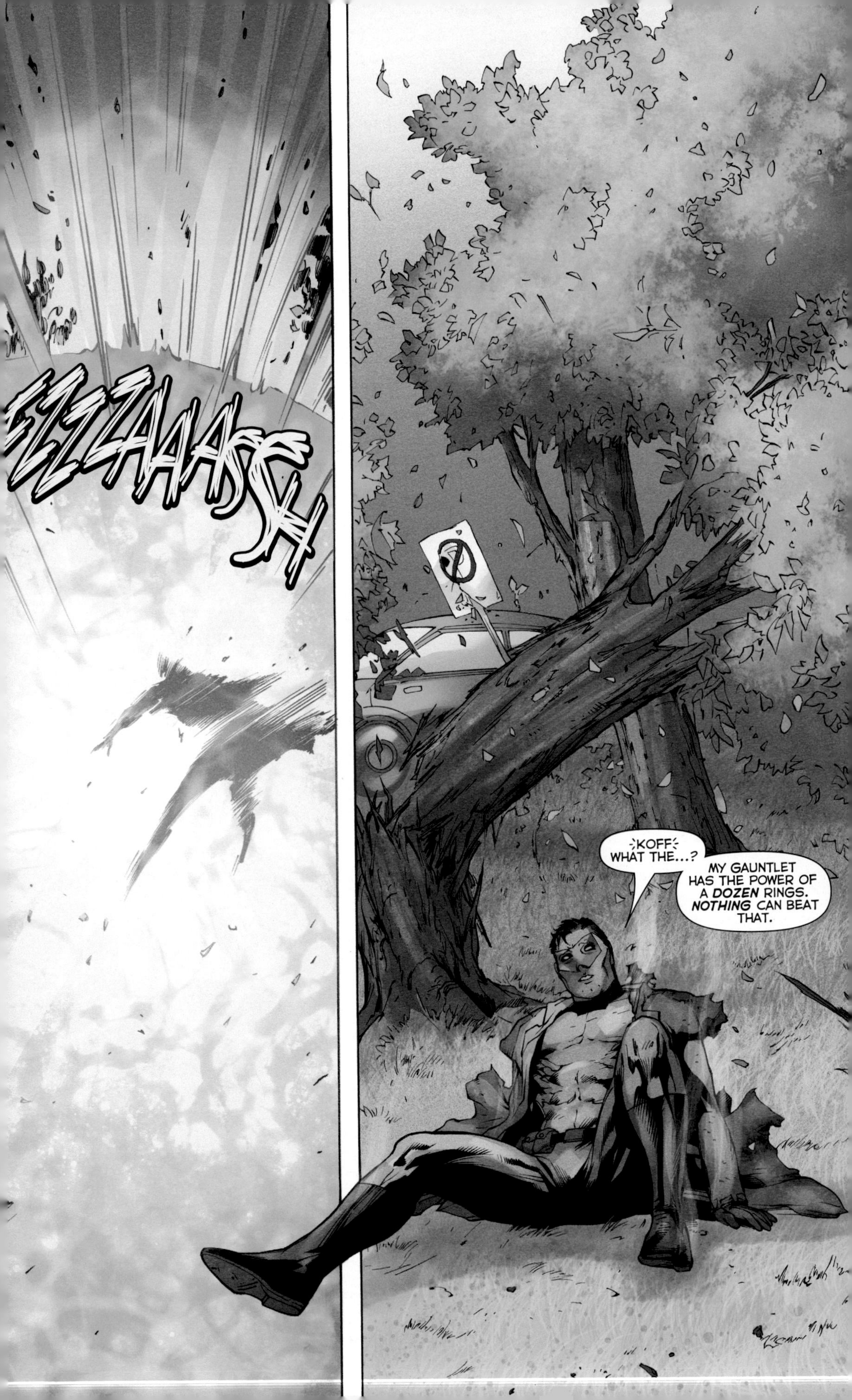
FZZZAAAASSH
KOFF WHAT THE...?
MY GAUNTLET HAS THE POWER OF A DOZEN RINGS. NOTHING CAN BEAT THAT.

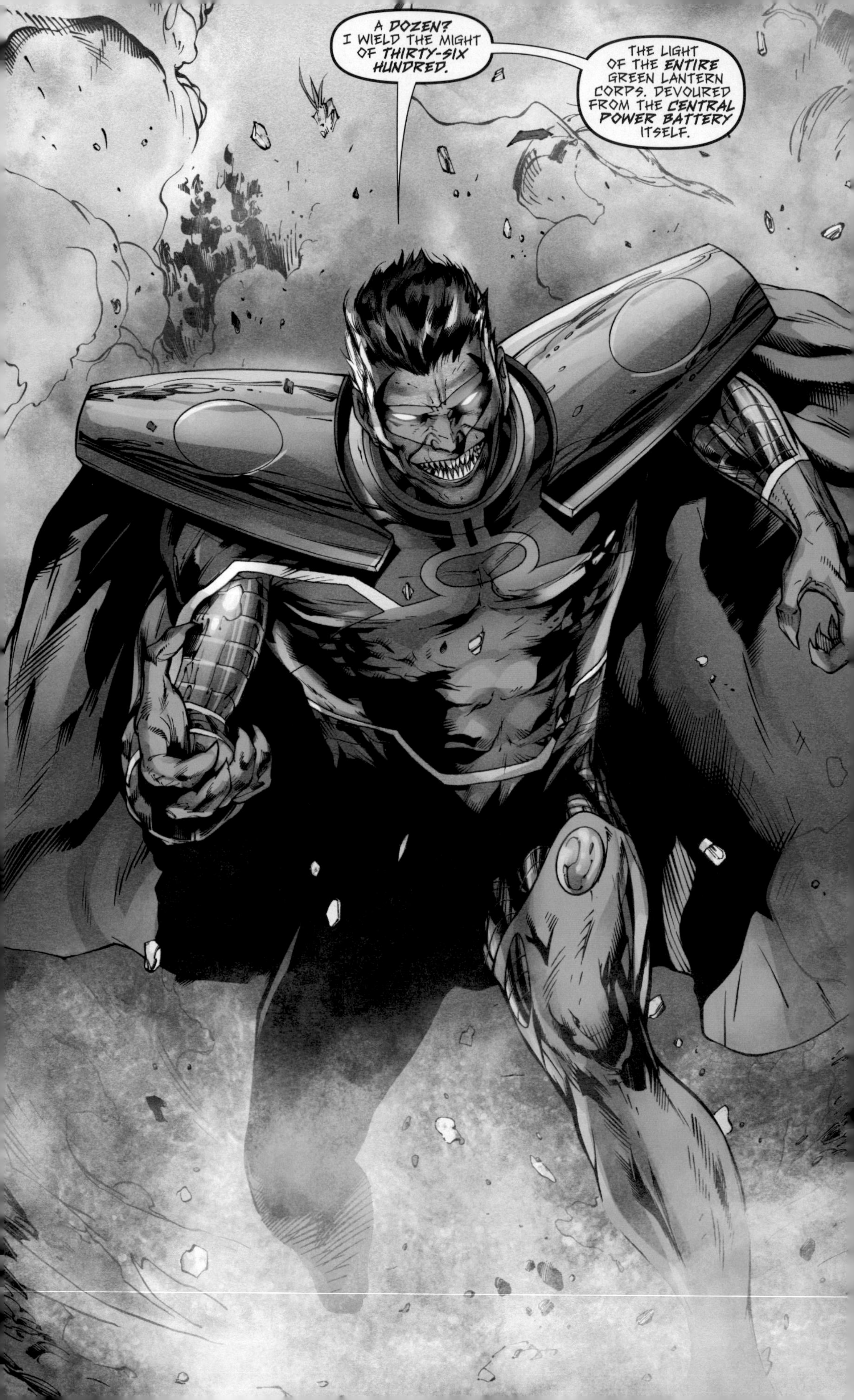
A DOZEN? I WIELD THE MIGHT OF THIRTY-SIX HUNDRED.
THE LIGHT OF THE ENTIRE GREEN LANTERN CORPS. DEVOURED FROM THE CENTRAL POWER BATTERY ITSELF.

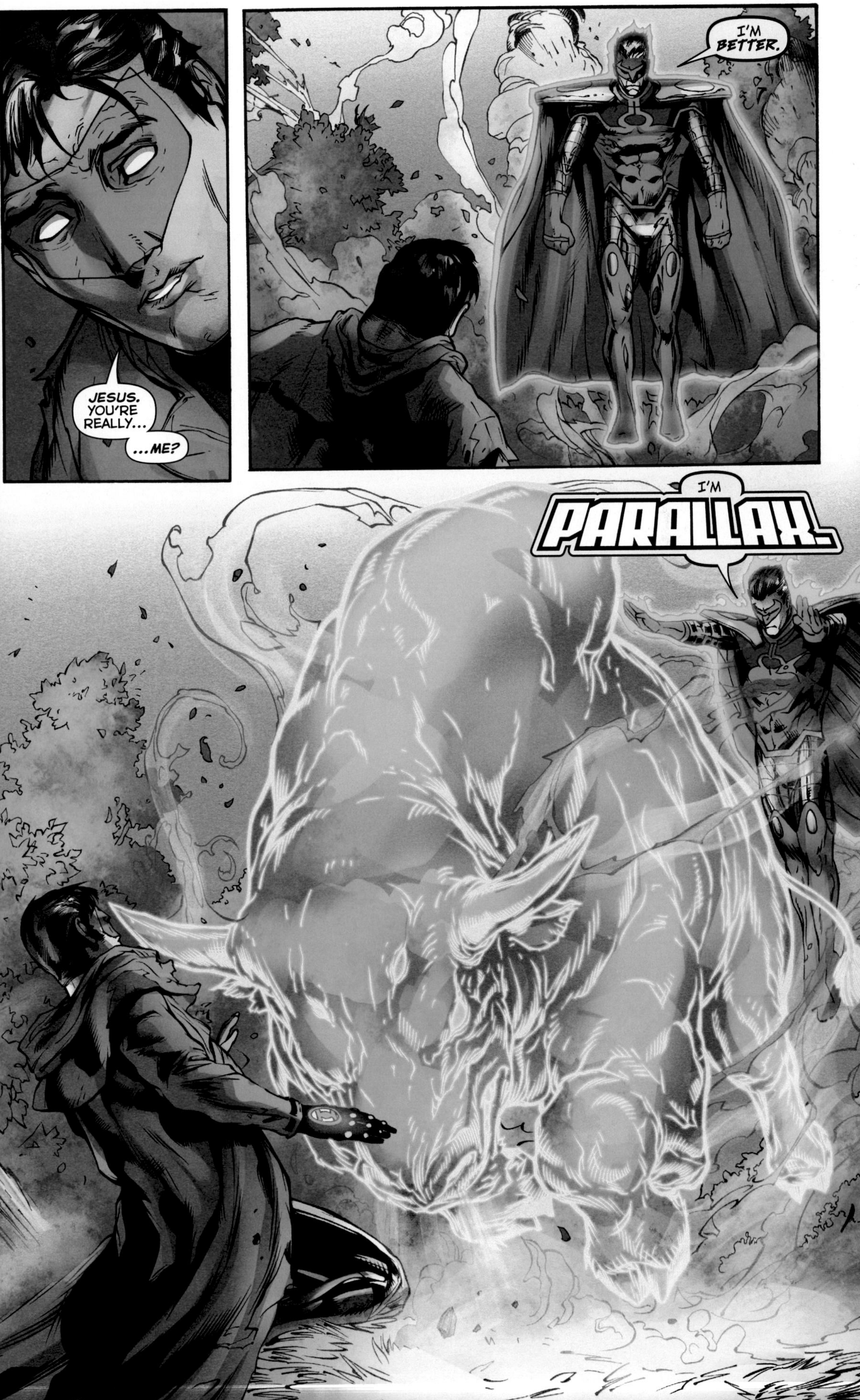
JESUS. YOU'RE REALLY...
...ME?
I'M BETTER.
I'M
PARALLAX.

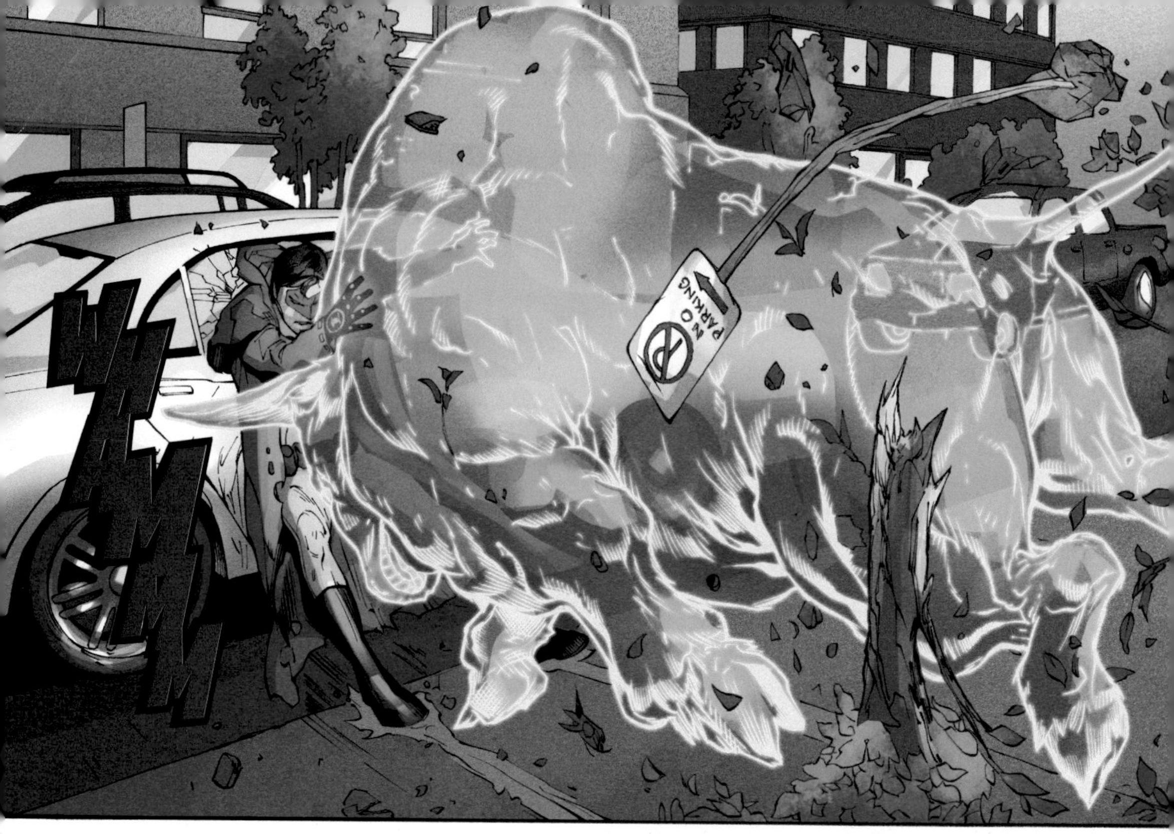
WHAMMM
NO PARKING

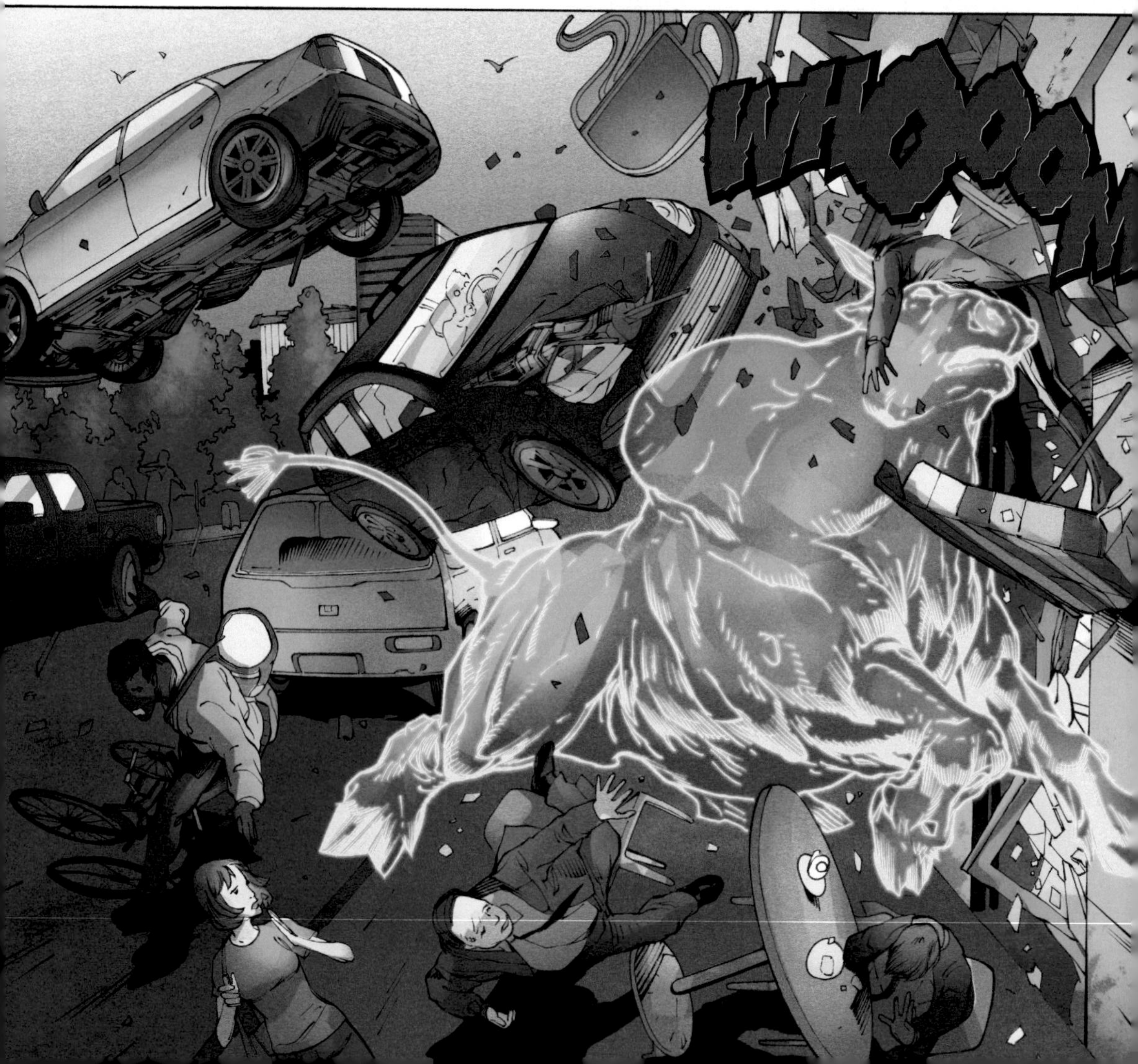
WHOOOM

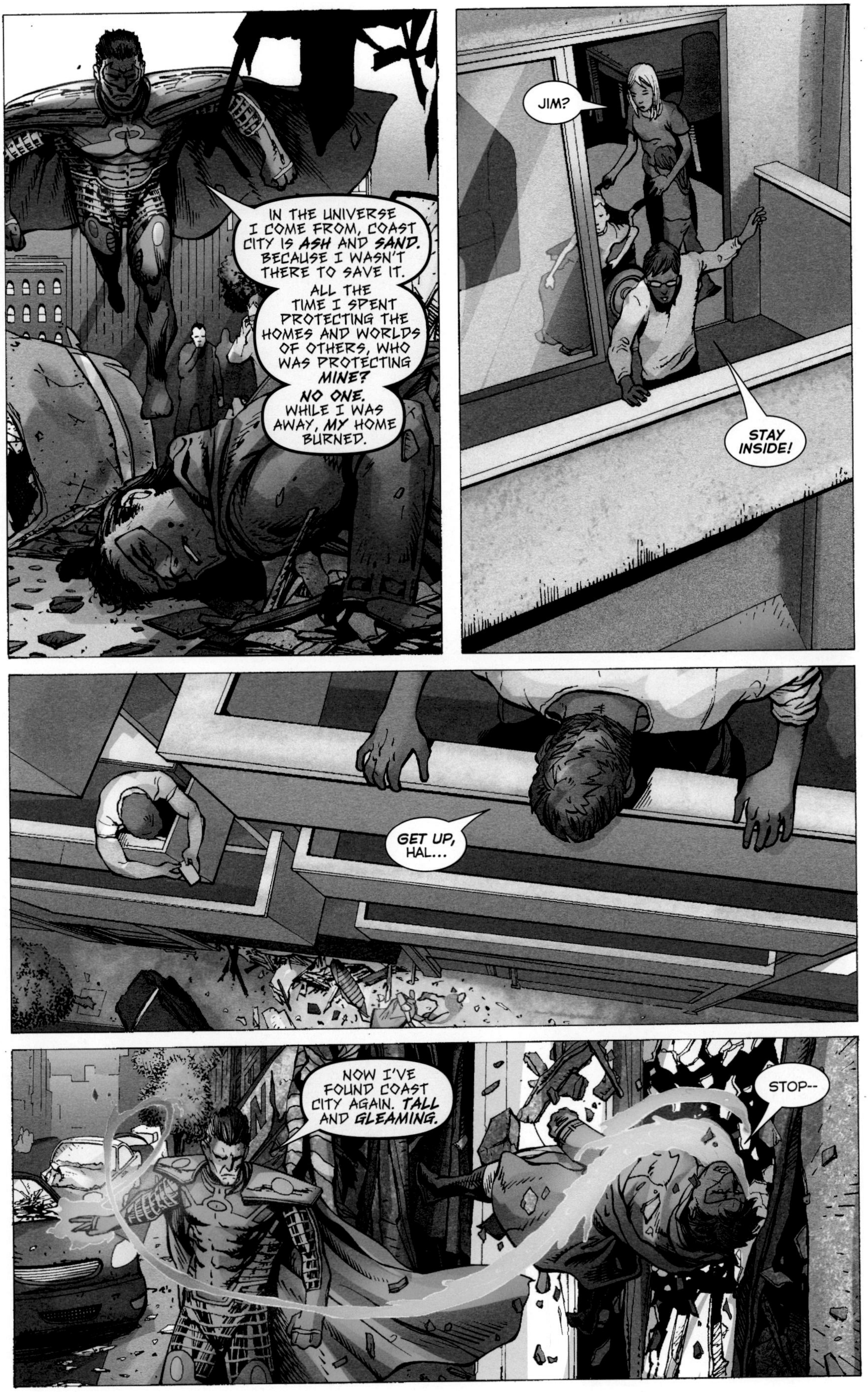
IN THE UNIVERSE I COME FROM, COAST CITY IS ASH AND SAND. BECAUSE I WASN'T THERE TO SAVE IT.
ALL THE TIME I SPENT PROTECTING THE HOMES AND WORLDS OF OTHERS, WHO WAS PROTECTING MINE?
NO ONE. WHILE I WAS AWAY, MY HOME BURNED.
JIM?
STAY INSIDE!
GET UP, HAL...
NOW I'VE FOUND COAST CITY AGAIN. TALL AND GLEAMING.
STOP--

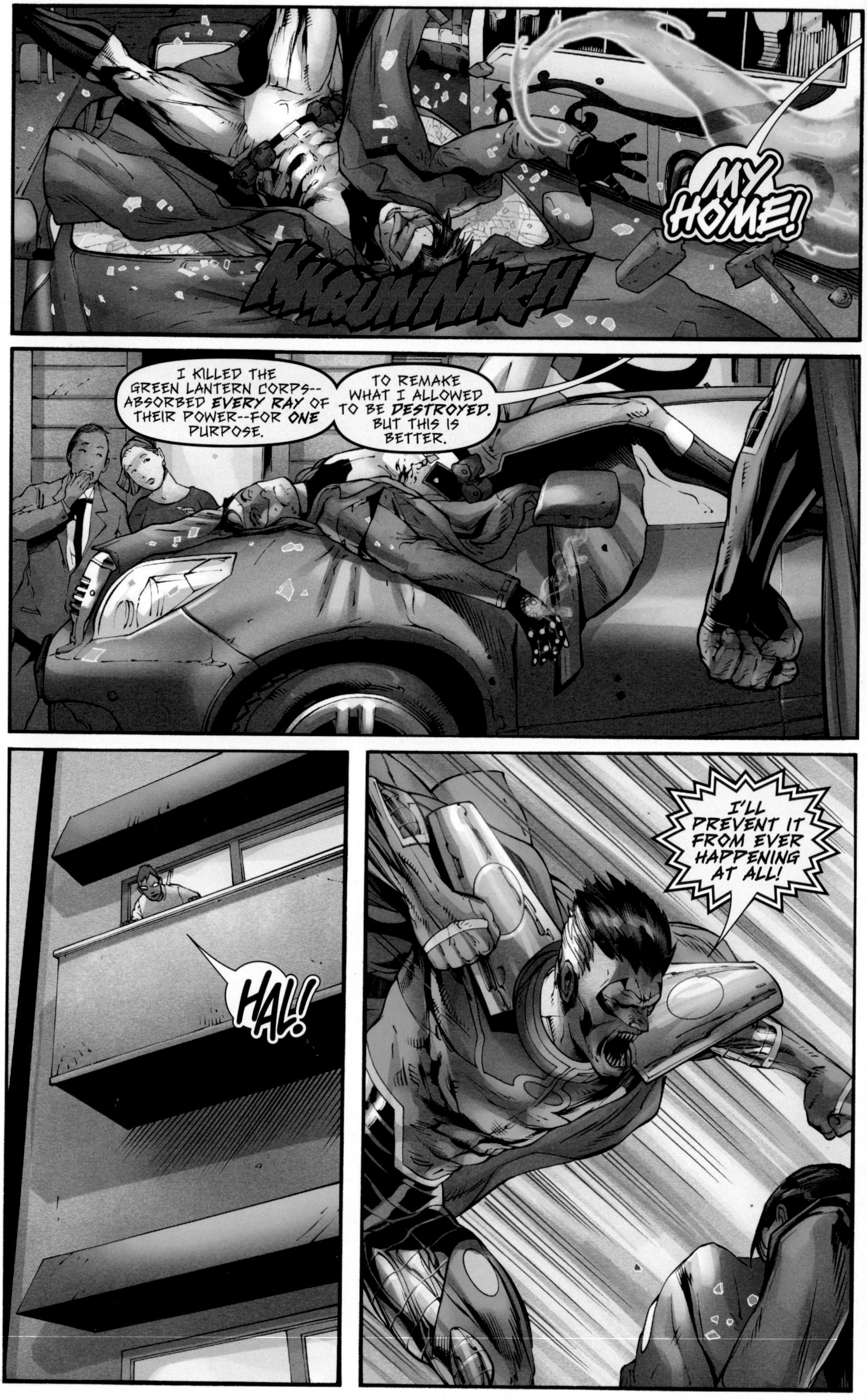
MY HOME!
KKRUNNNKH
I KILLED THE GREEN LANTERN CORPS--ABSORBED EVERY RAY OF THEIR POWER--FOR ONE PURPOSE.
TO REMAKE WHAT I ALLOWED TO BE DESTROYED. BUT THIS IS BETTER.
HAL!
I'LL PREVENT IT FROM EVER HAPPENING AT ALL!

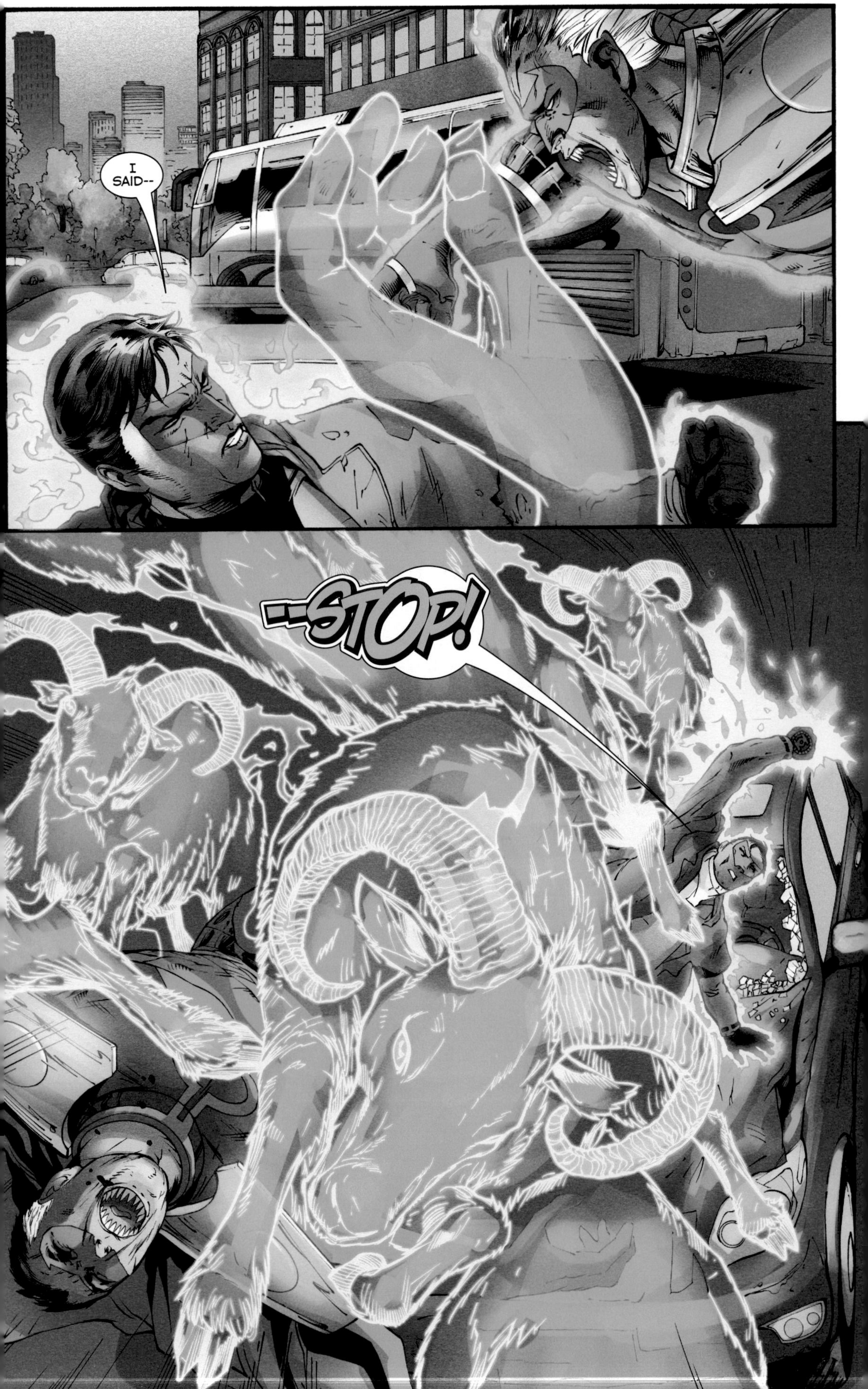
I SAID--
--STOP!

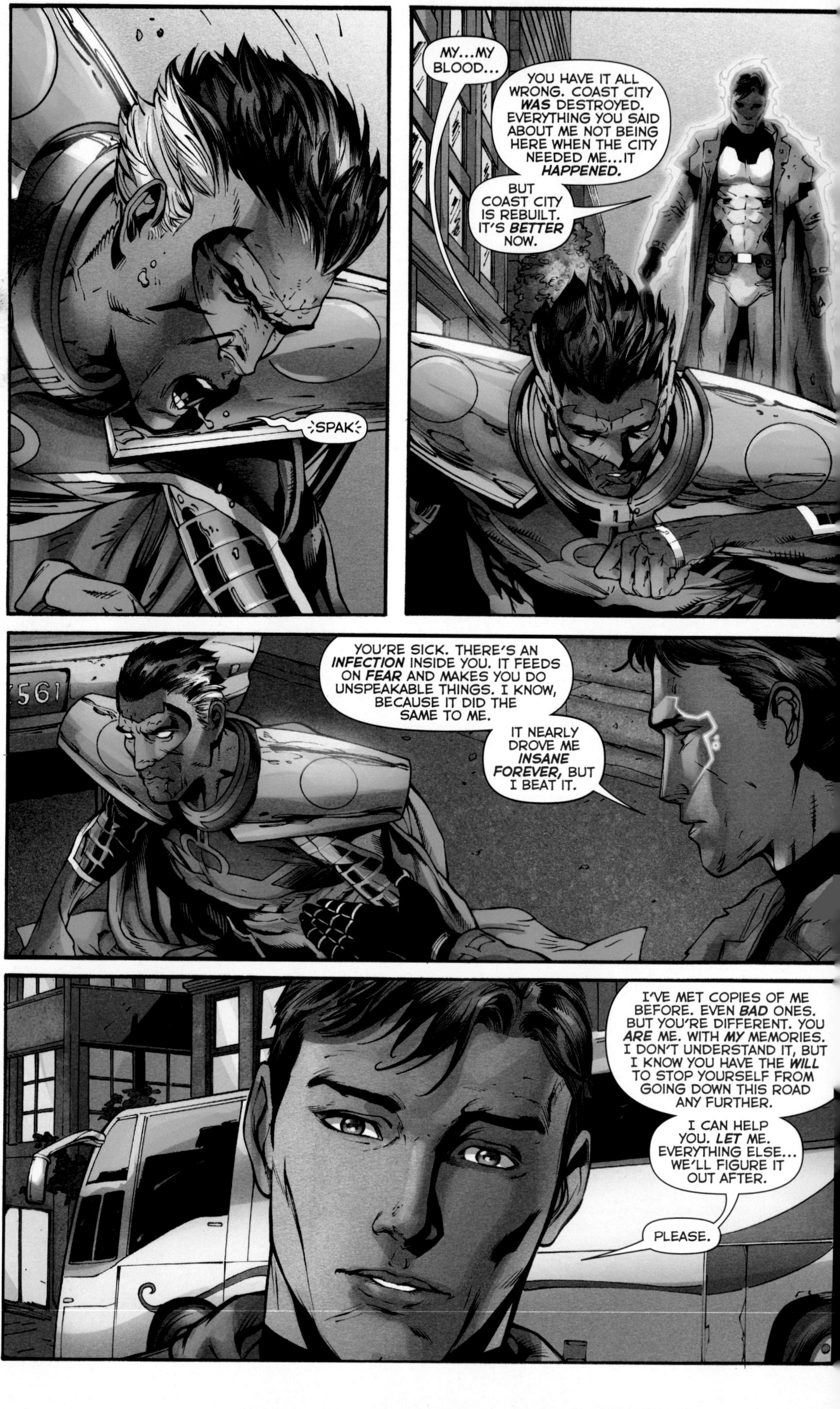
SPAK
MY...MY BLOOD...
YOU HAVE IT ALL WRONG. COAST CITY WAS DESTROYED. EVERYTHING YOU SAID ABOUT ME NOT BEING HERE WHEN THE CITY NEEDED ME...IT HAPPENED.
BUT COAST CITY IS REBUILT. IT'S BETTER NOW.
YOU'RE SICK. THERE'S AN INFECTION INSIDE YOU. IT FEEDS ON FEAR AND MAKES YOU DO UNSPEAKABLE THINGS. I KNOW, BECAUSE IT DID THE SAME TO ME.
IT NEARLY DROVE ME INSANE FOREVER, BUT I BEAT IT.
I'VE MET COPIES OF ME BEFORE. EVEN BAD ONES. BUT YOU'RE DIFFERENT. YOU ARE ME. WITH MY MEMORIES. I DON'T UNDERSTAND IT, BUT I KNOW YOU HAVE THE WILL TO STOP YOURSELF FROM GOING DOWN THIS ROAD ANY FURTHER.
I CAN HELP YOU. LET ME. EVERYTHING ELSE... WE'LL FIGURE IT OUT AFTER.
PLEASE.

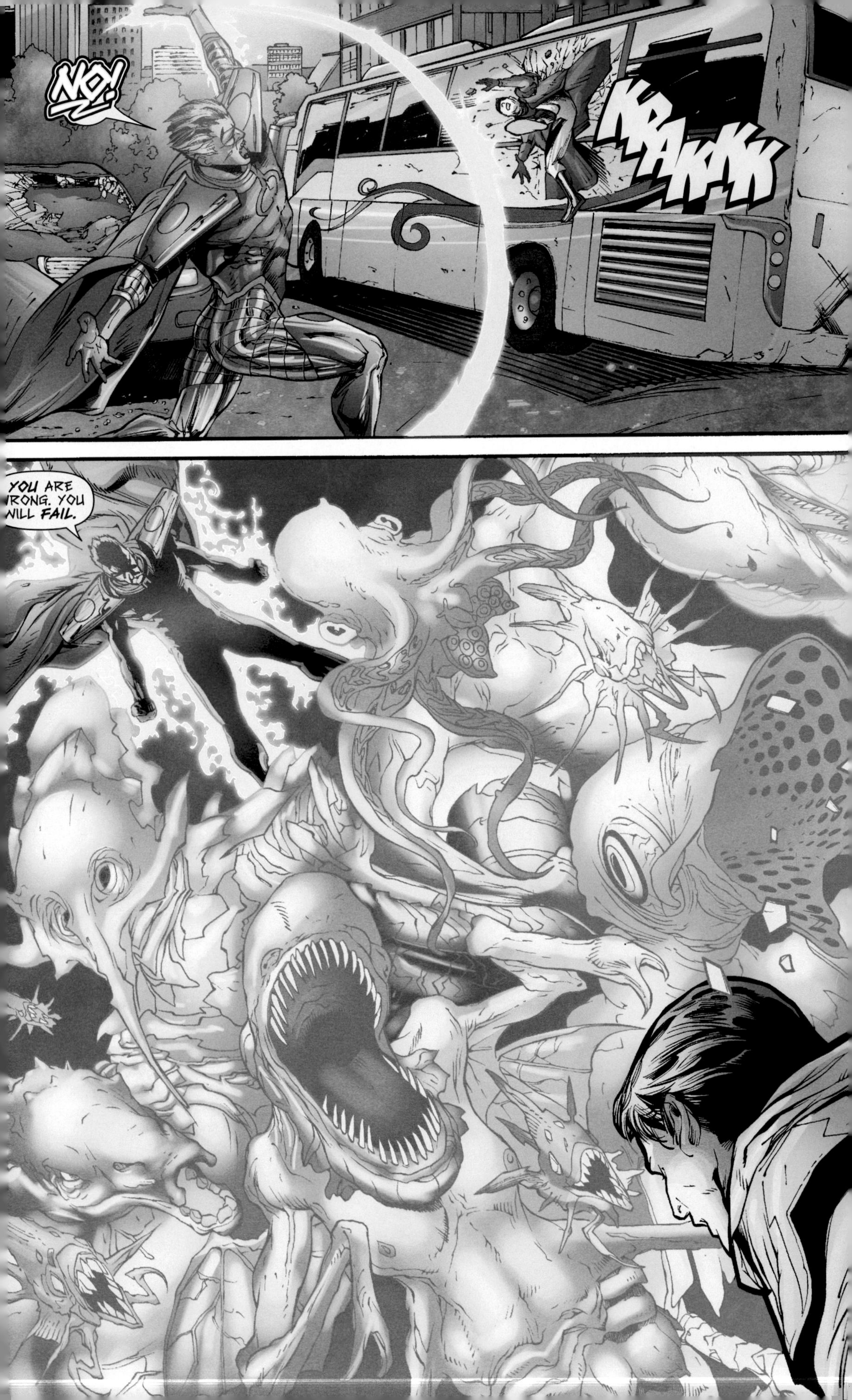
NO!
KRAKKK
YOU ARE WRONG. YOU WILL FAIL.

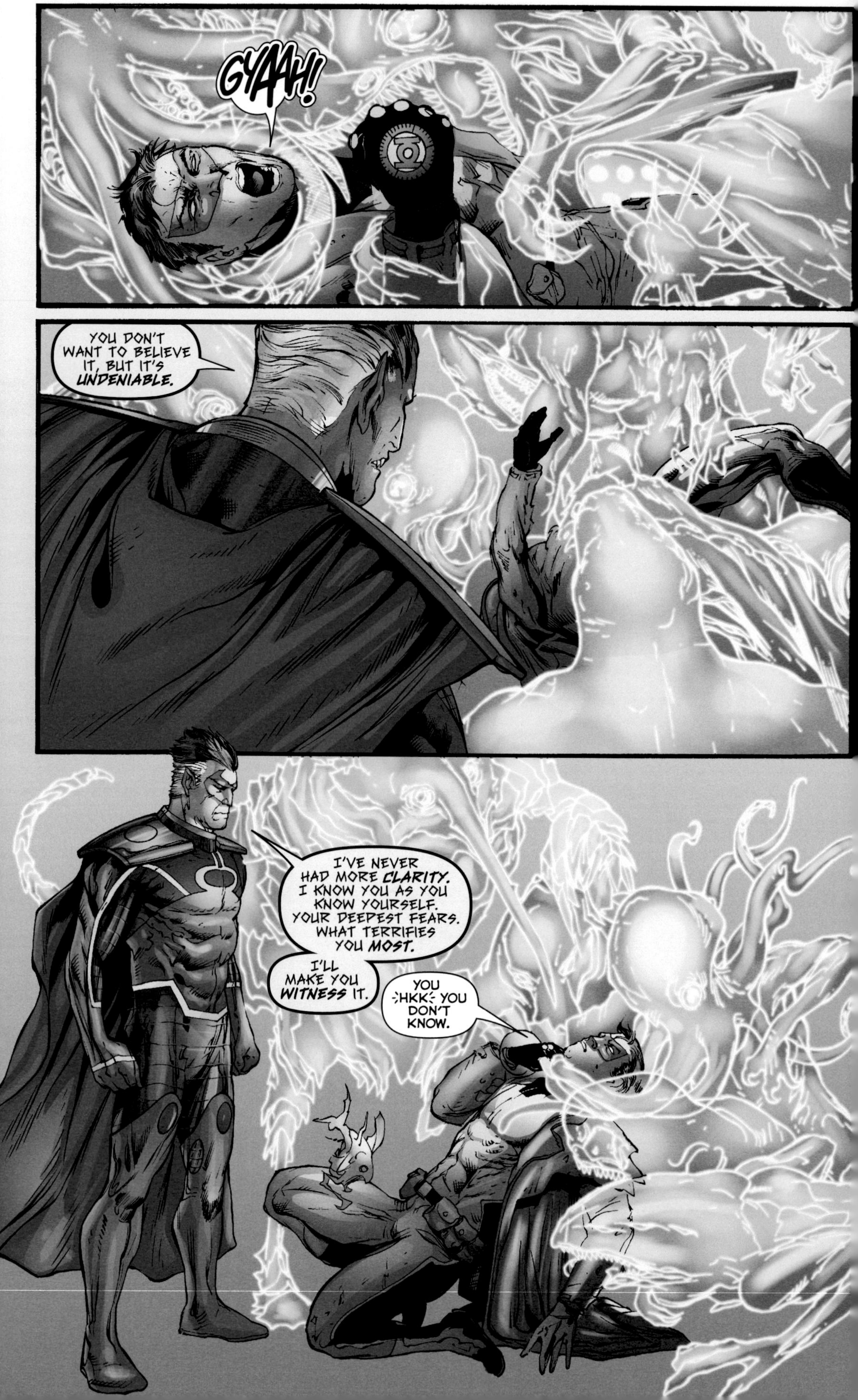
GYAAH!
YOU DON'T WANT TO BELIEVE IT, BUT IT'S UNDENIABLE.
I'VE NEVER HAD MORE CLARITY. I KNOW YOU AS YOU KNOW YOURSELF. YOUR DEEPEST FEARS. WHAT TERRIFIES YOU MOST.
I'LL MAKE YOU WITNESS IT.
YOU -HKK- YOU DON'T KNOW.

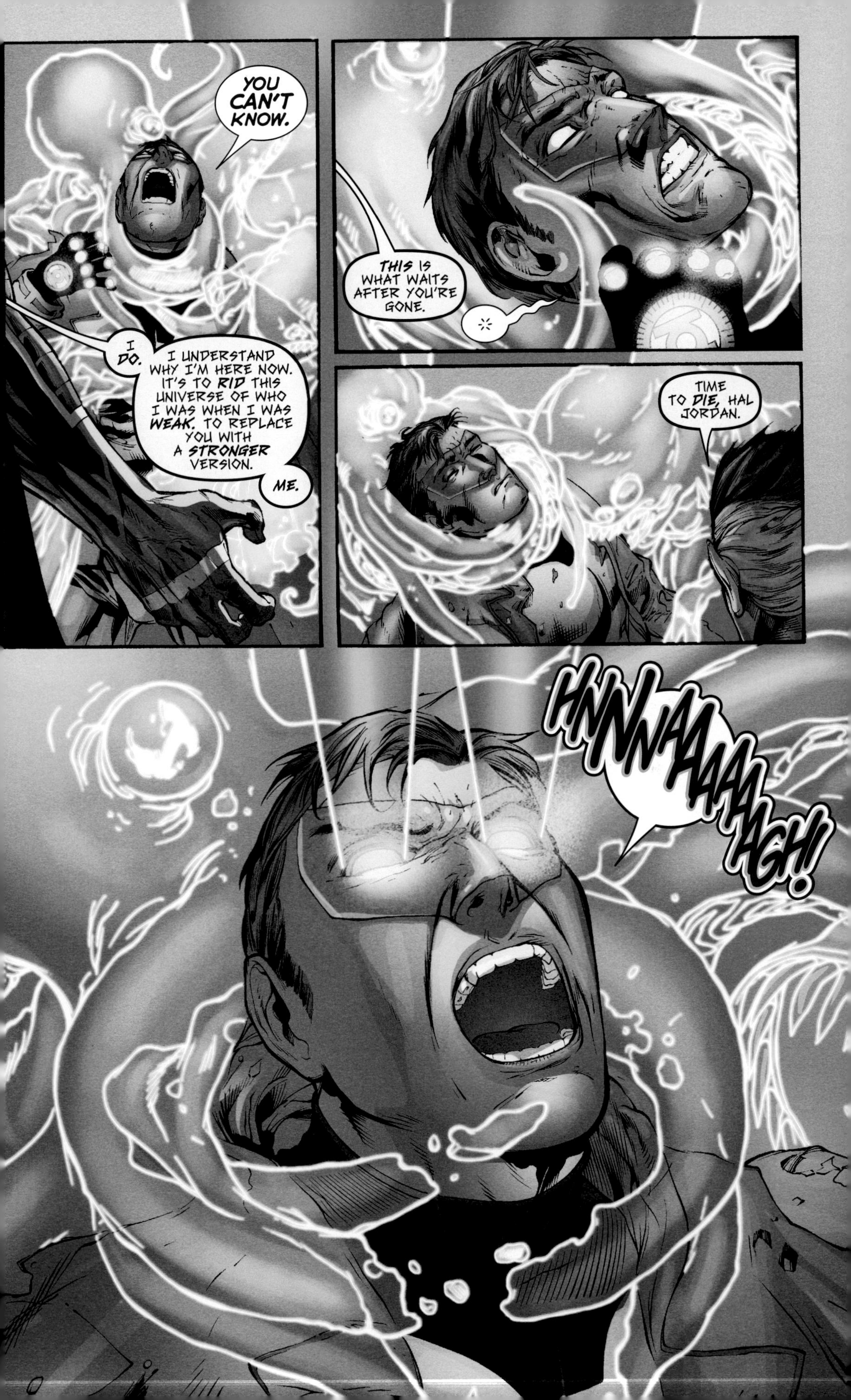

YOU CAN'T KNOW.
THIS IS WHAT WAITS AFTER YOU'RE GONE.
I DO.
I UNDERSTAND WHY I'M HERE NOW. IT'S TO RID THIS UNIVERSE OF WHO I WAS WHEN I WAS WEAK. TO REPLACE YOU WITH A STRONGER VERSION.
ME.
TIME TO DIE, HAL JORDAN.
HNNNAAAAAAAGH!

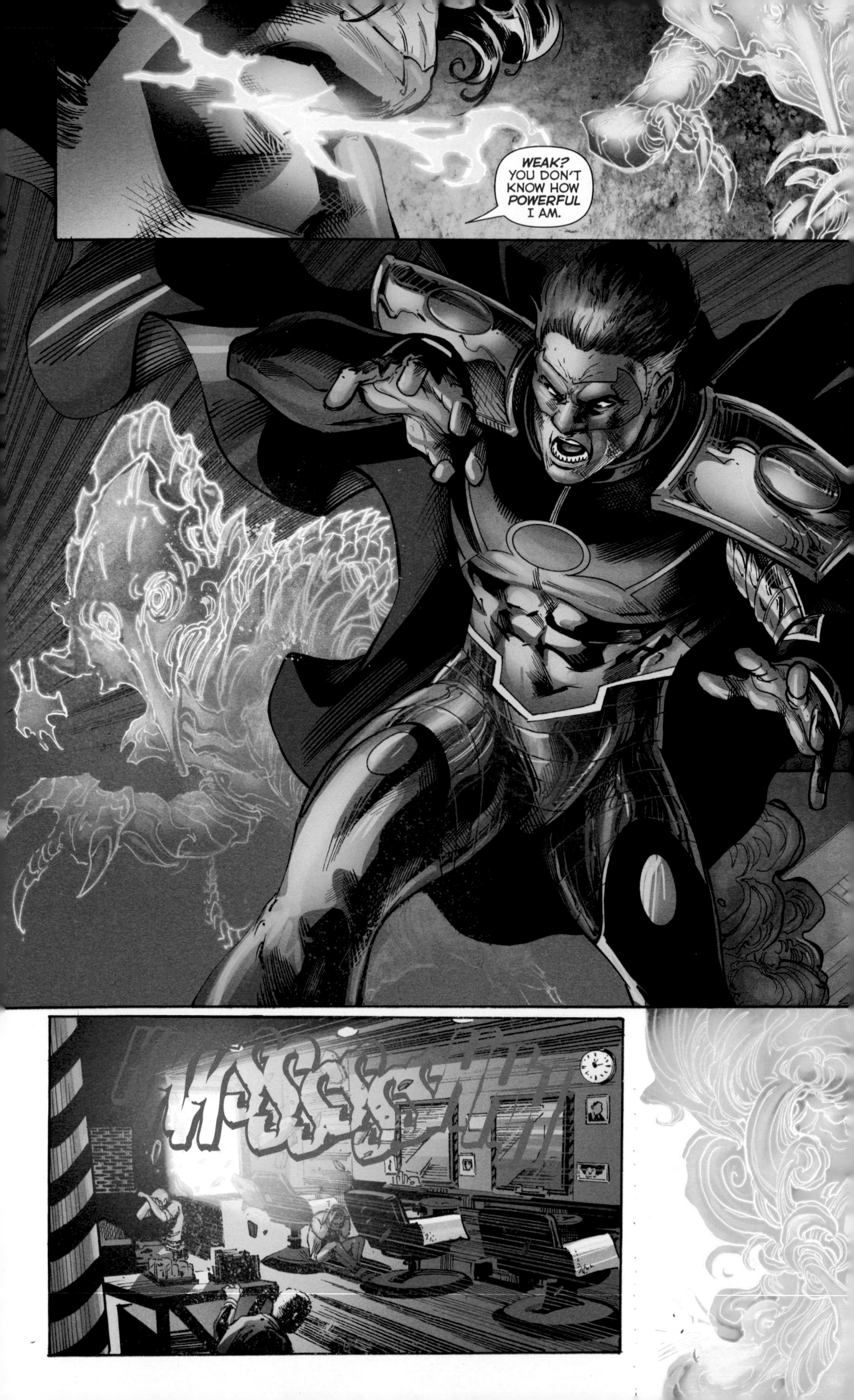
WEAK? YOU DON'T KNOW HOW POWERFUL I AM.

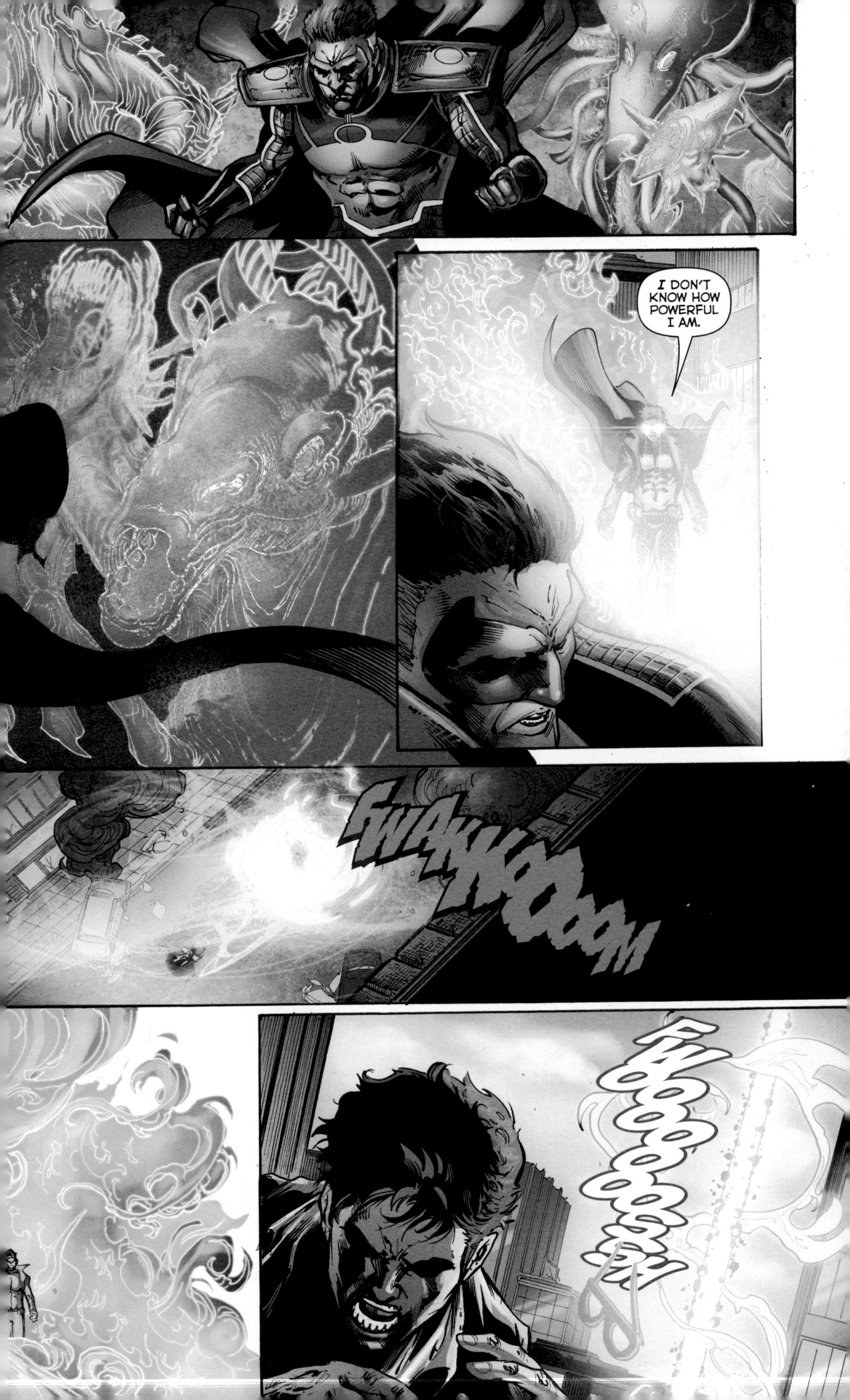
I DON'T KNOW HOW POWERFUL I AM.

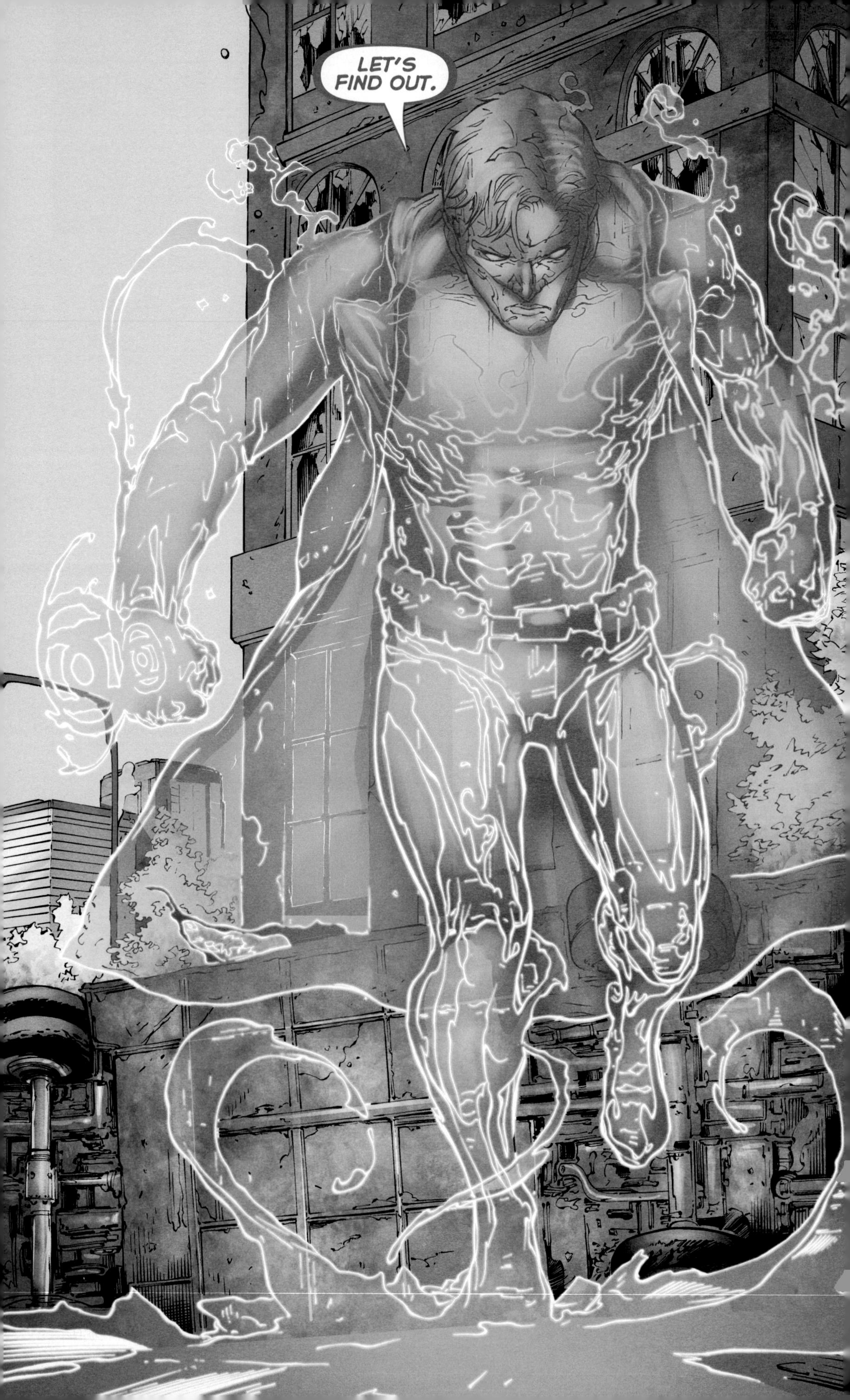
LET'S FIND OUT.

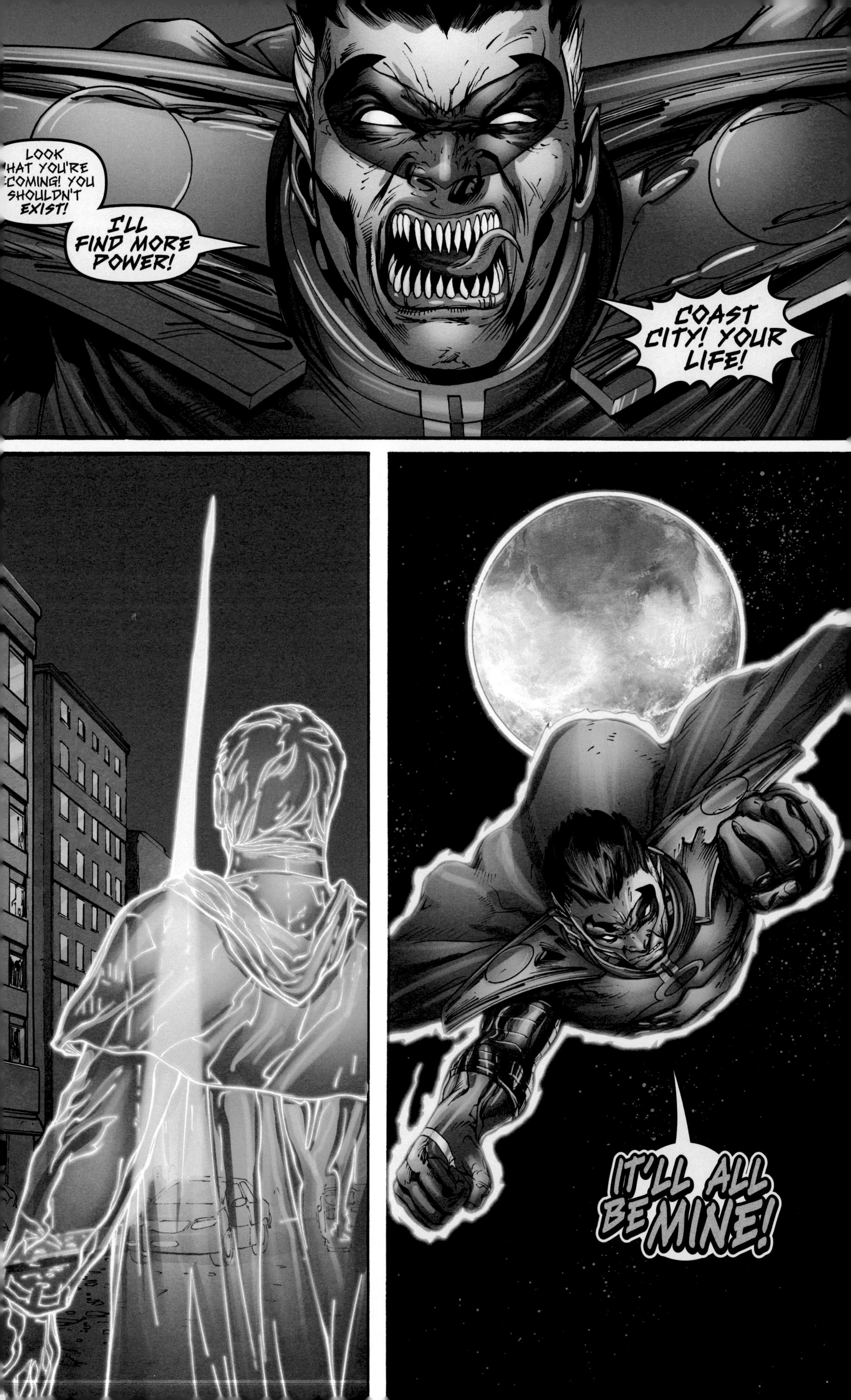
LOOK HAT YOU'RE ECOMING! YOU SHOULDN'T EXIST!
I'LL FIND MORE POWER!
COAST CITY! YOUR LIFE!
IT'LL ALL BE MINE!

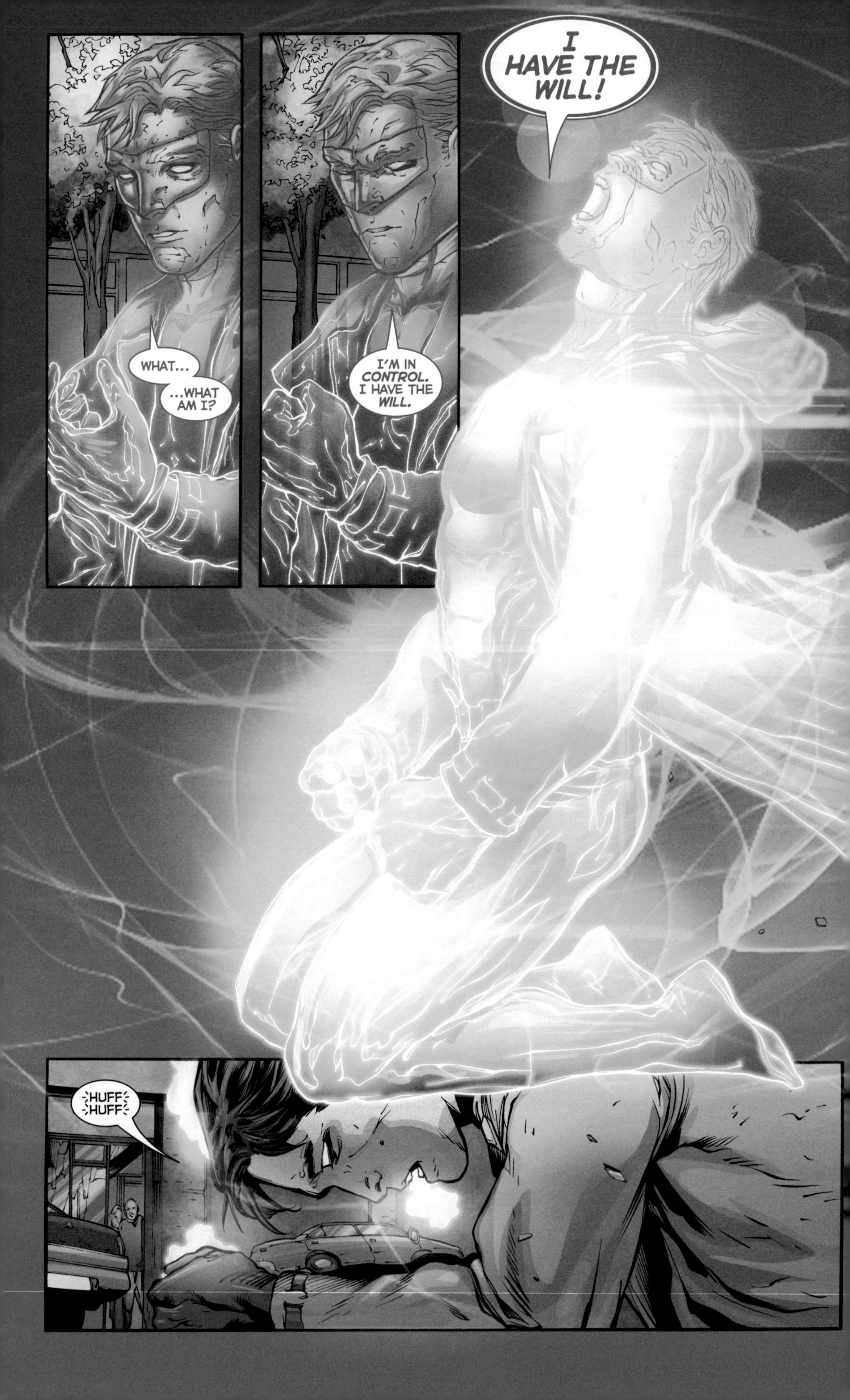
WHAT...
...WHAT AM I?
I'M IN CONTROL. I HAVE THE WILL.
I HAVE THE WILL!
HUFF HUFF

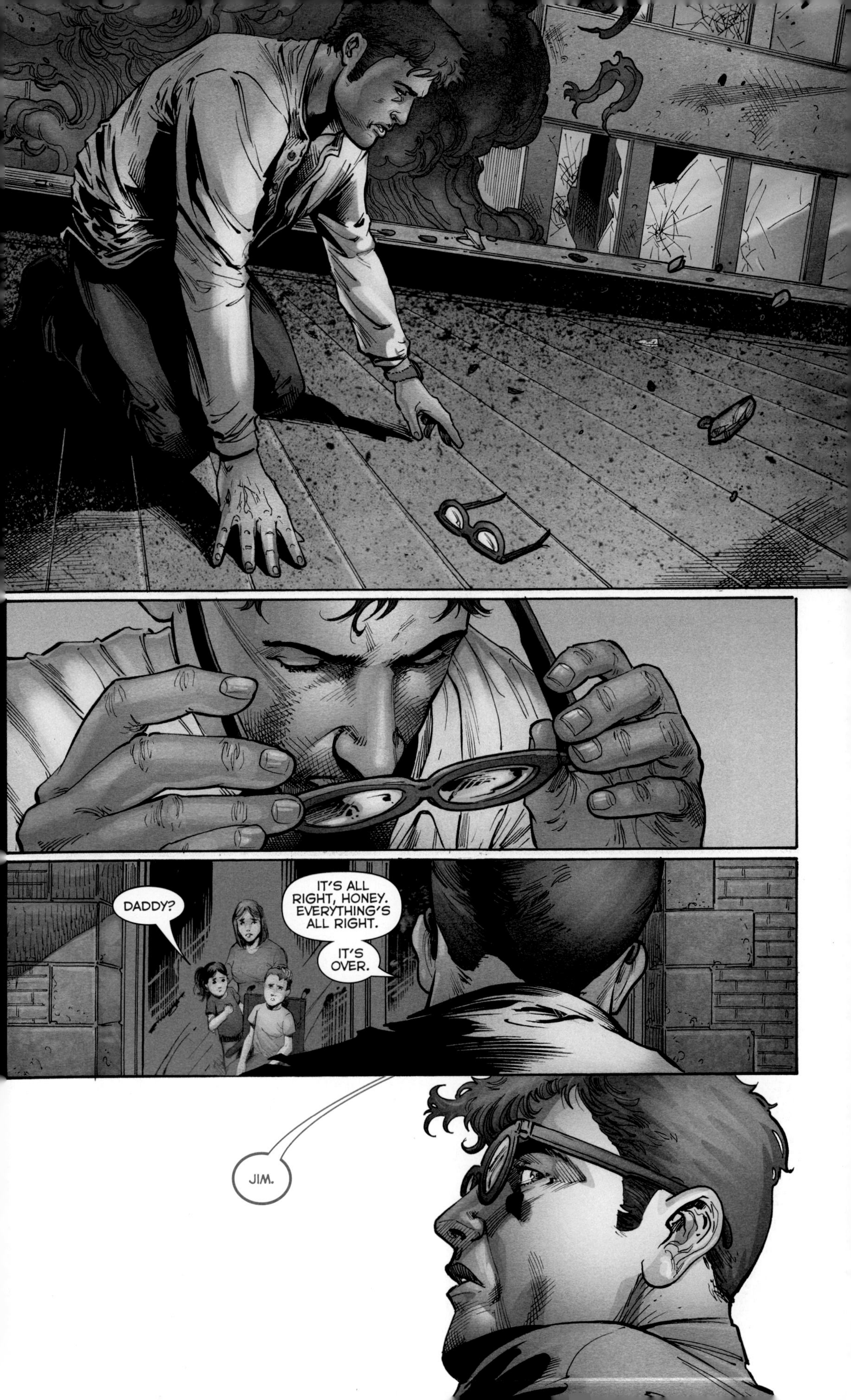
DADDY?
IT'S ALL RIGHT, HONEY. EVERYTHING'S ALL RIGHT.
IT'S OVER.
JIM.

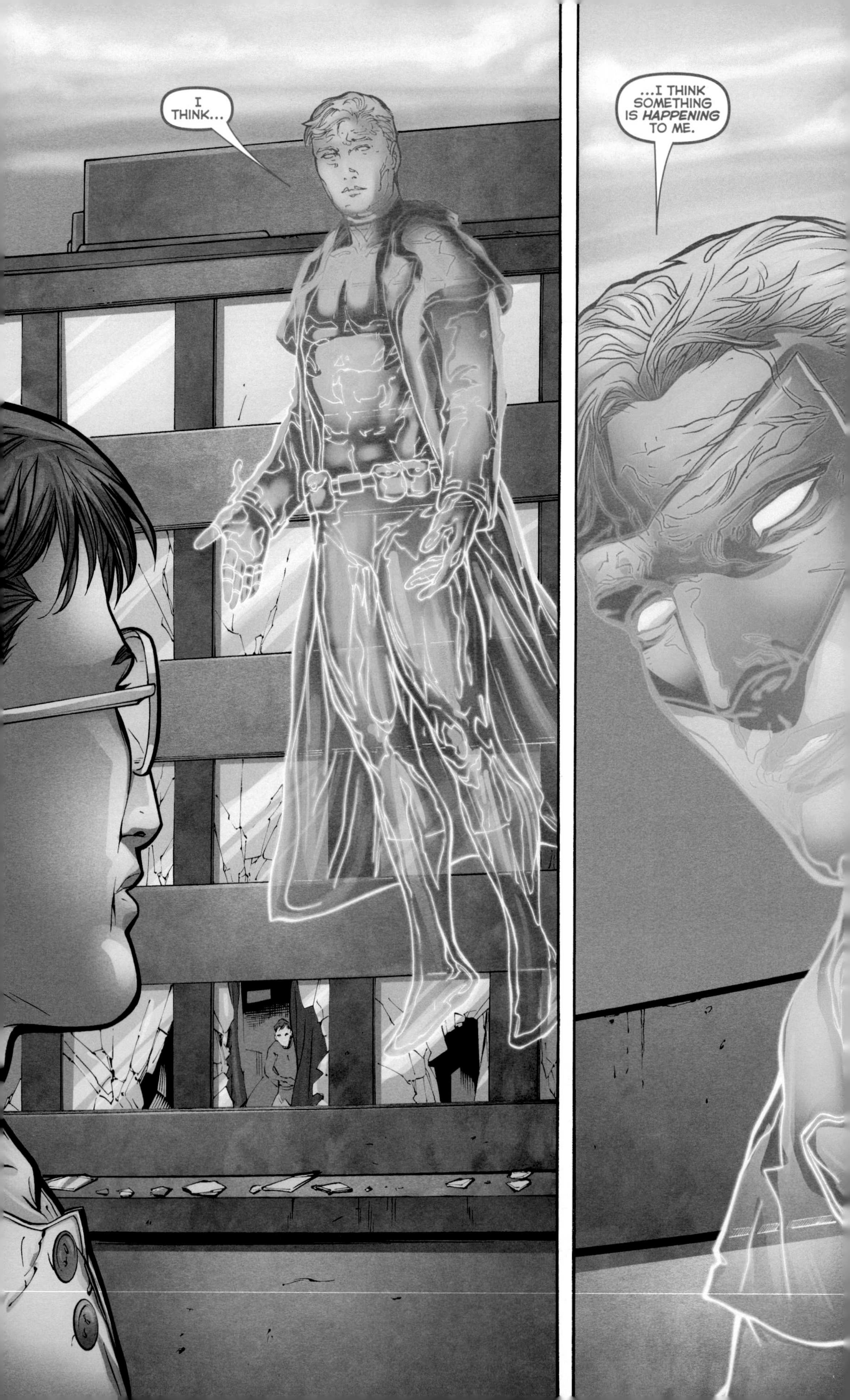
I THINK...
...I THINK SOMETHING IS *HAPPENING* TO ME.

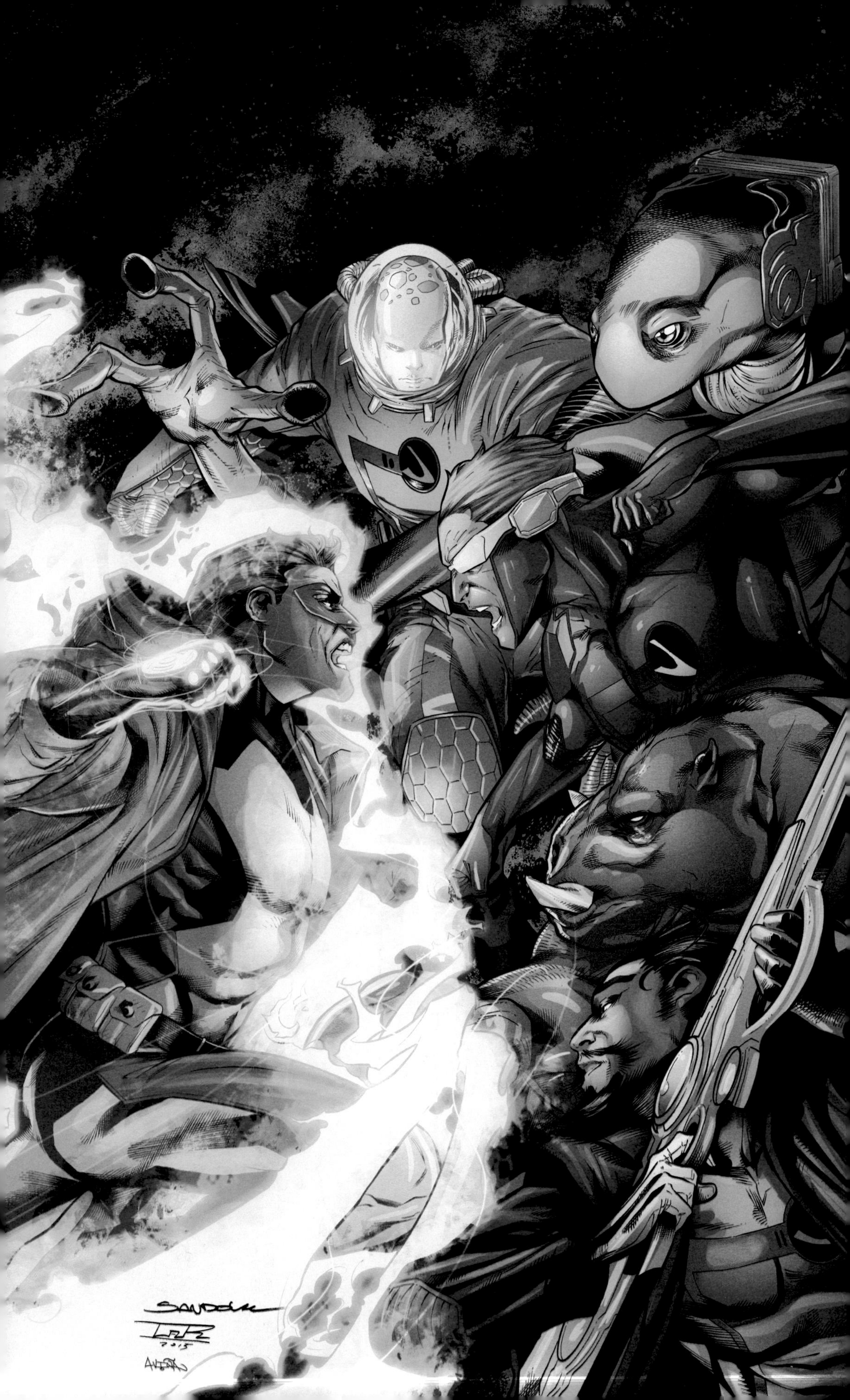

STATE OF TRANSFORMATION

ROBERT VENDITTI writer **RAFA SANDOVAL** penciller **JORDI TARRAGONA** inker **TONY AVIÑA** colorist **DAVE SHARPE** letterer **RAFA SANDOVAL & JORDI TARRAGONA** cover

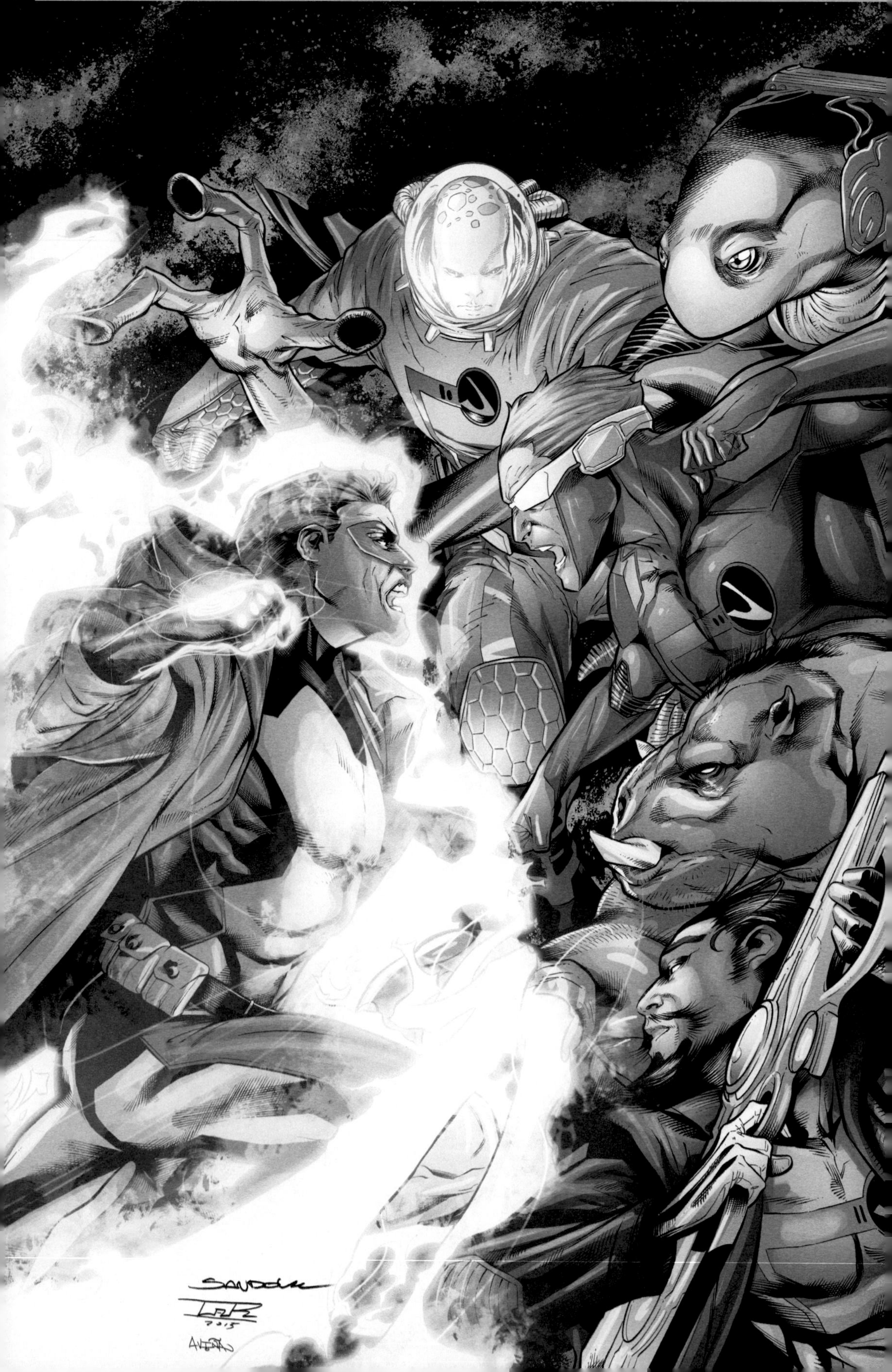

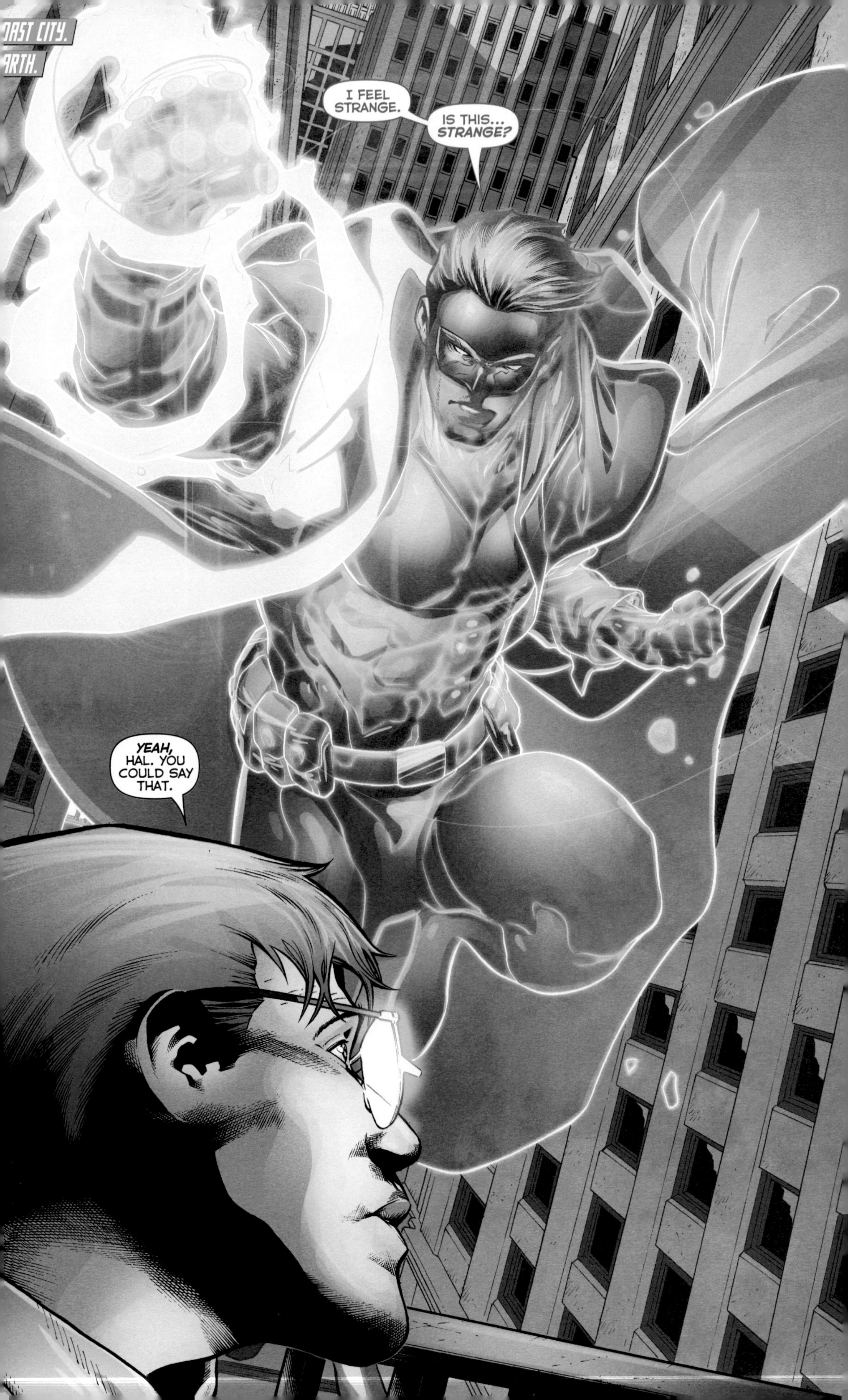
OAST CITY.
ARTH.
I FEEL STRANGE.
IS THIS... STRANGE?
YEAH, HAL. YOU COULD SAY THAT.

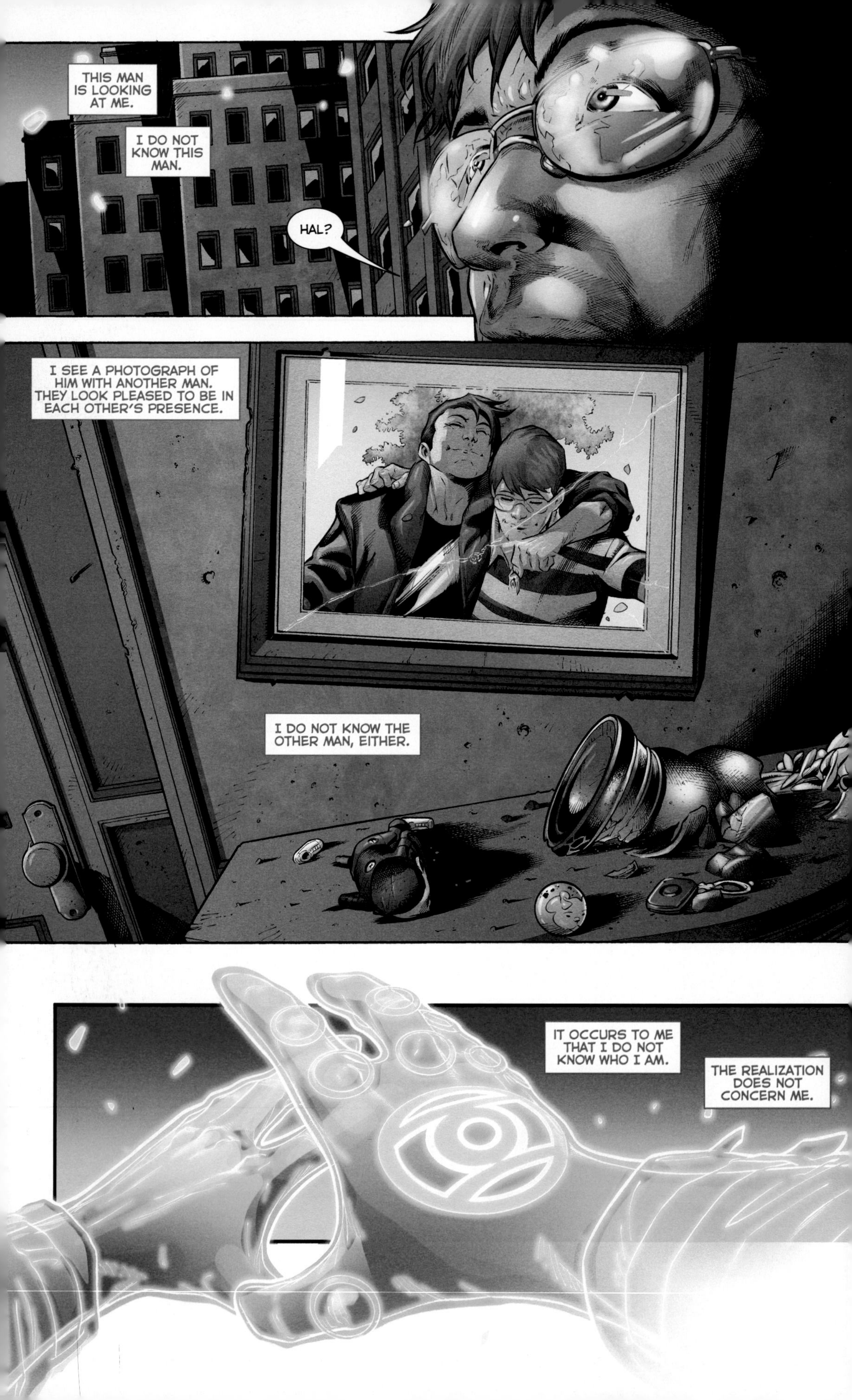
THIS MAN IS LOOKING AT ME.
I DO NOT KNOW THIS MAN.
HAL?
I SEE A PHOTOGRAPH OF HIM WITH ANOTHER MAN. THEY LOOK PLEASED TO BE IN EACH OTHER'S PRESENCE.
I DO NOT KNOW THE OTHER MAN, EITHER.
IT OCCURS TO ME THAT I DO NOT KNOW WHO I AM.
THE REALIZATION DOES NOT CONCERN ME.

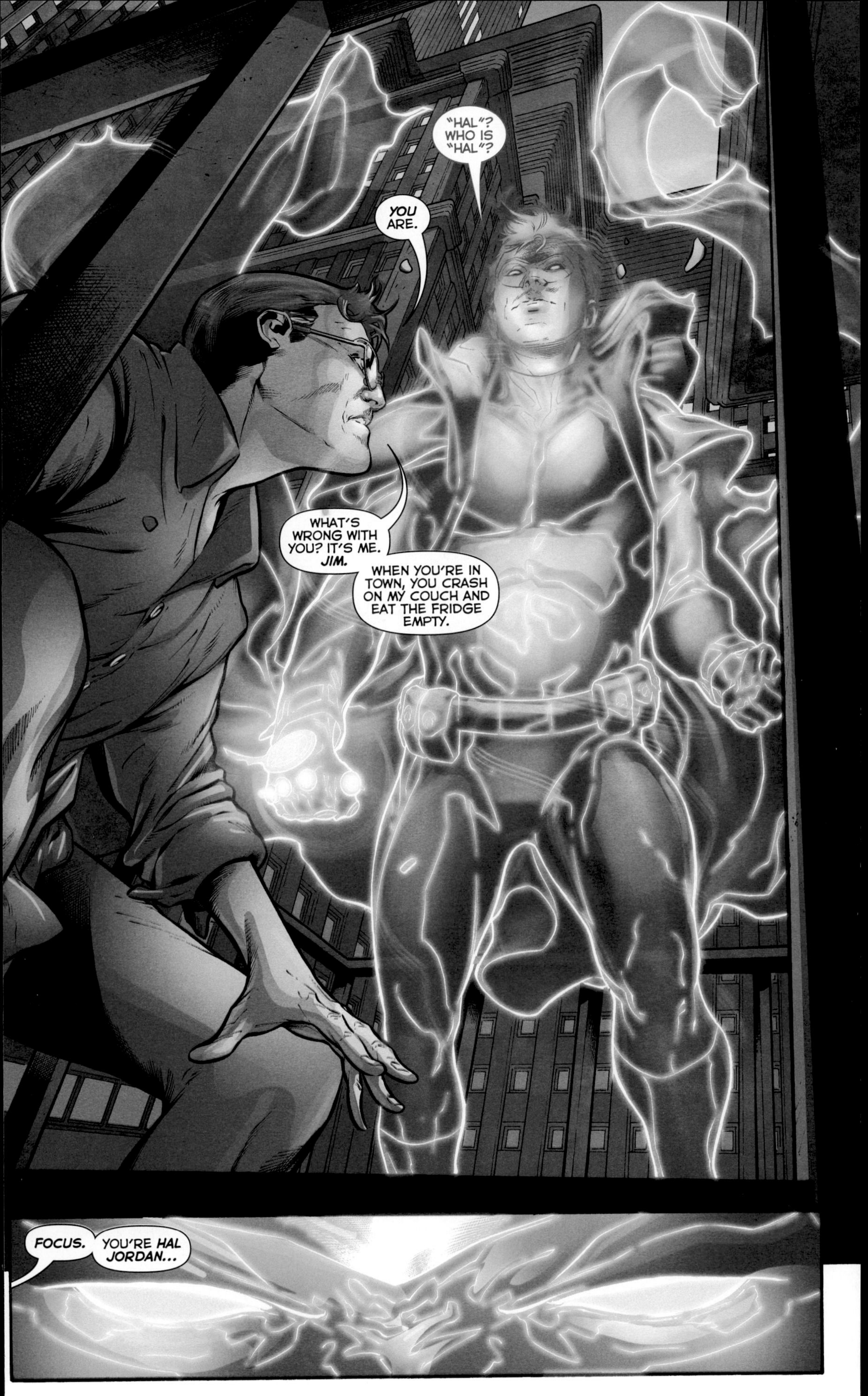
"HAL"? WHO IS "HAL"?
YOU ARE.
WHAT'S WRONG WITH YOU? IT'S ME. JIM.
WHEN YOU'RE IN TOWN, YOU CRASH ON MY COUCH AND EAT THE FRIDGE EMPTY.
FOCUS.
YOU'RE HAL JORDAN...

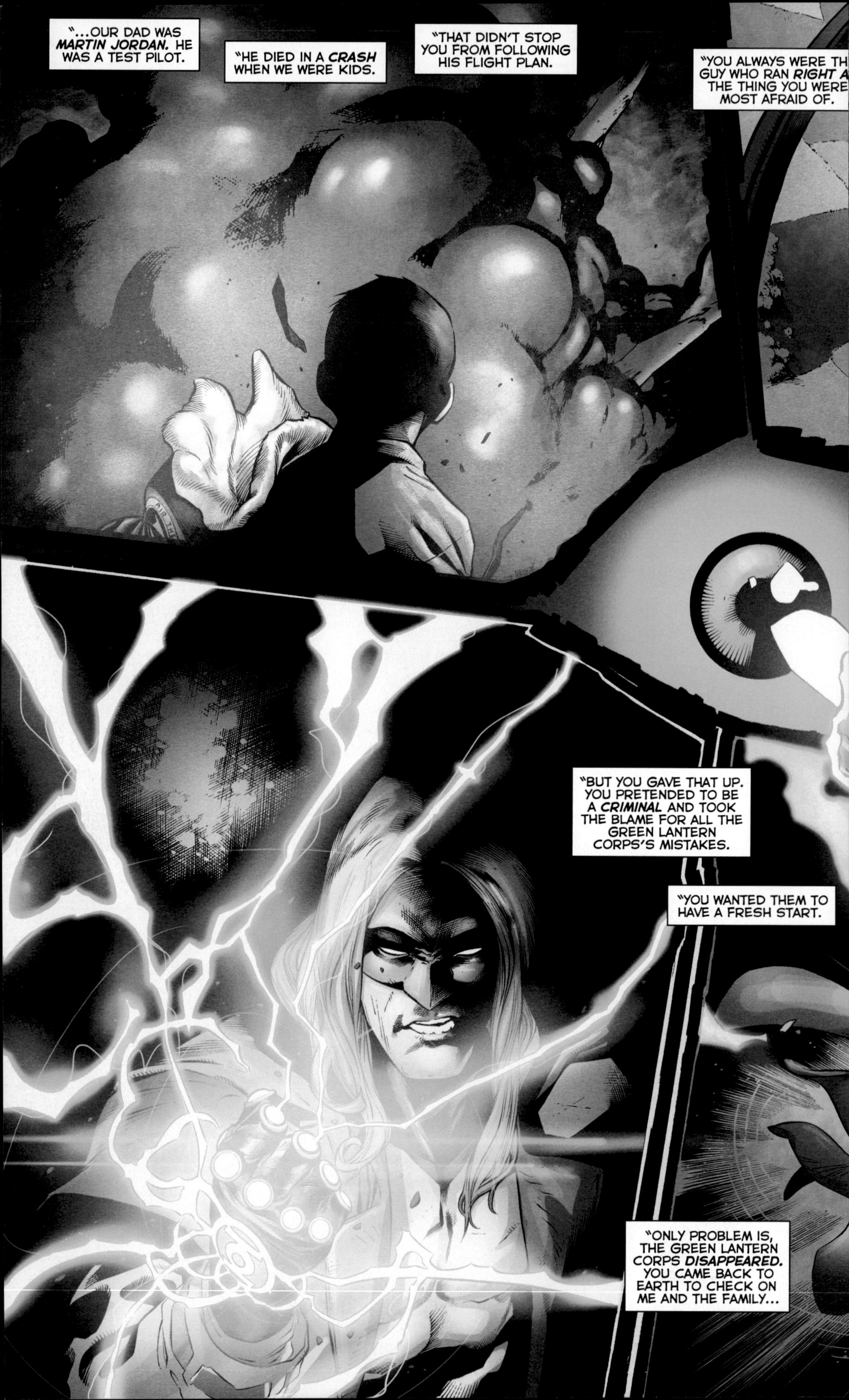
"...OUR DAD WAS MARTIN JORDAN. HE WAS A TEST PILOT.
"HE DIED IN A CRASH WHEN WE WERE KIDS.
"THAT DIDN'T STOP YOU FROM FOLLOWING HIS FLIGHT PLAN.
"YOU ALWAYS WERE TH GUY WHO RAN RIGHT A THE THING YOU WERE MOST AFRAID OF.
"BUT YOU GAVE THAT UP. YOU PRETENDED TO BE A CRIMINAL AND TOOK THE BLAME FOR ALL THE GREEN LANTERN CORPS'S MISTAKES.
"YOU WANTED THEM TO HAVE A FRESH START.
"ONLY PROBLEM IS, THE GREEN LANTERN CORPS DISAPPEARED. YOU CAME BACK TO EARTH TO CHECK ON ME AND THE FAMILY...

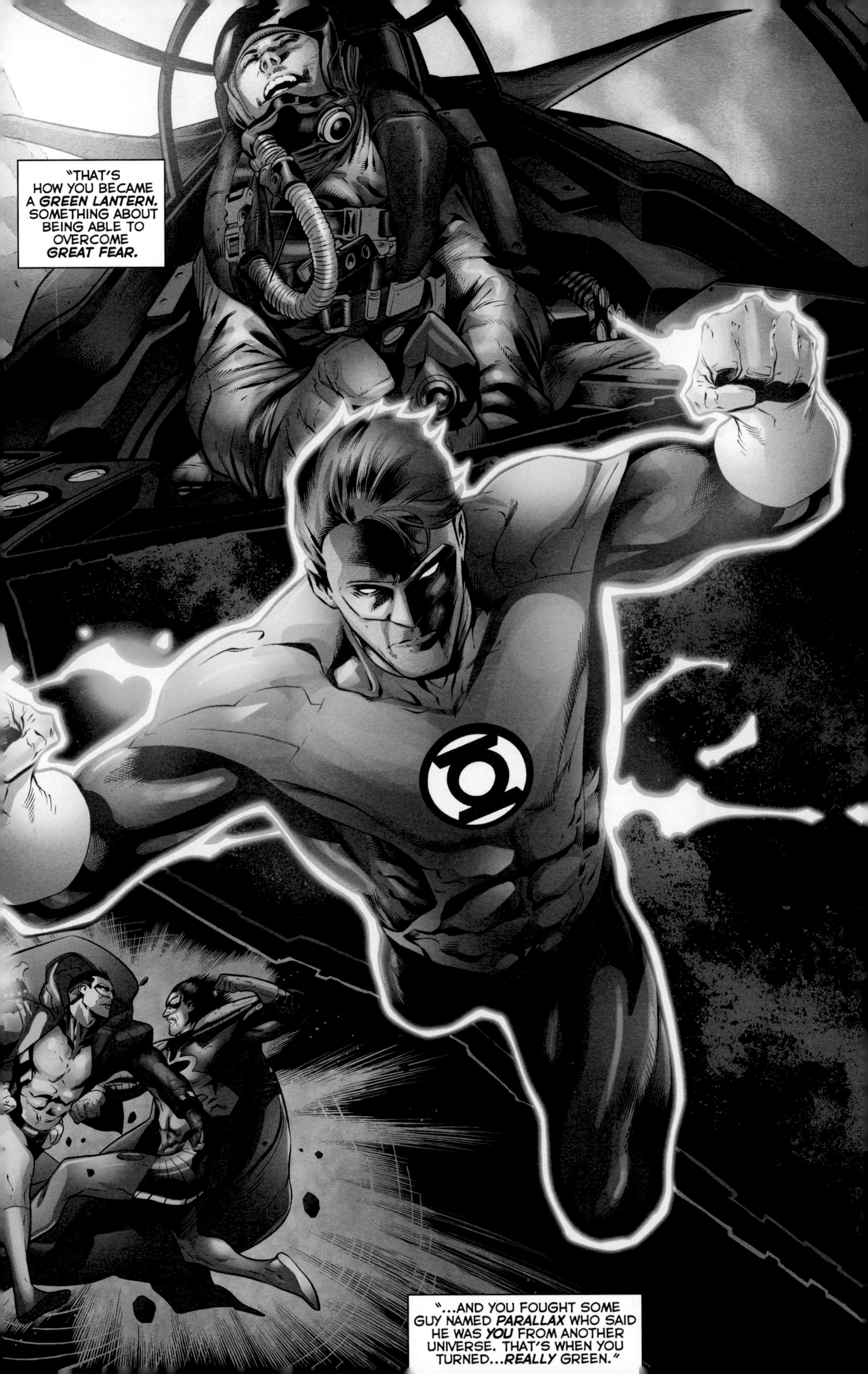
"THAT'S HOW YOU BECAME A ***GREEN LANTERN.*** SOMETHING ABOUT BEING ABLE TO OVERCOME ***GREAT FEAR.***
"...AND YOU FOUGHT SOME GUY NAMED ***PARALLAX*** WHO SAID HE WAS ***YOU*** FROM ANOTHER UNIVERSE. THAT'S WHEN YOU TURNED...***REALLY*** GREEN."

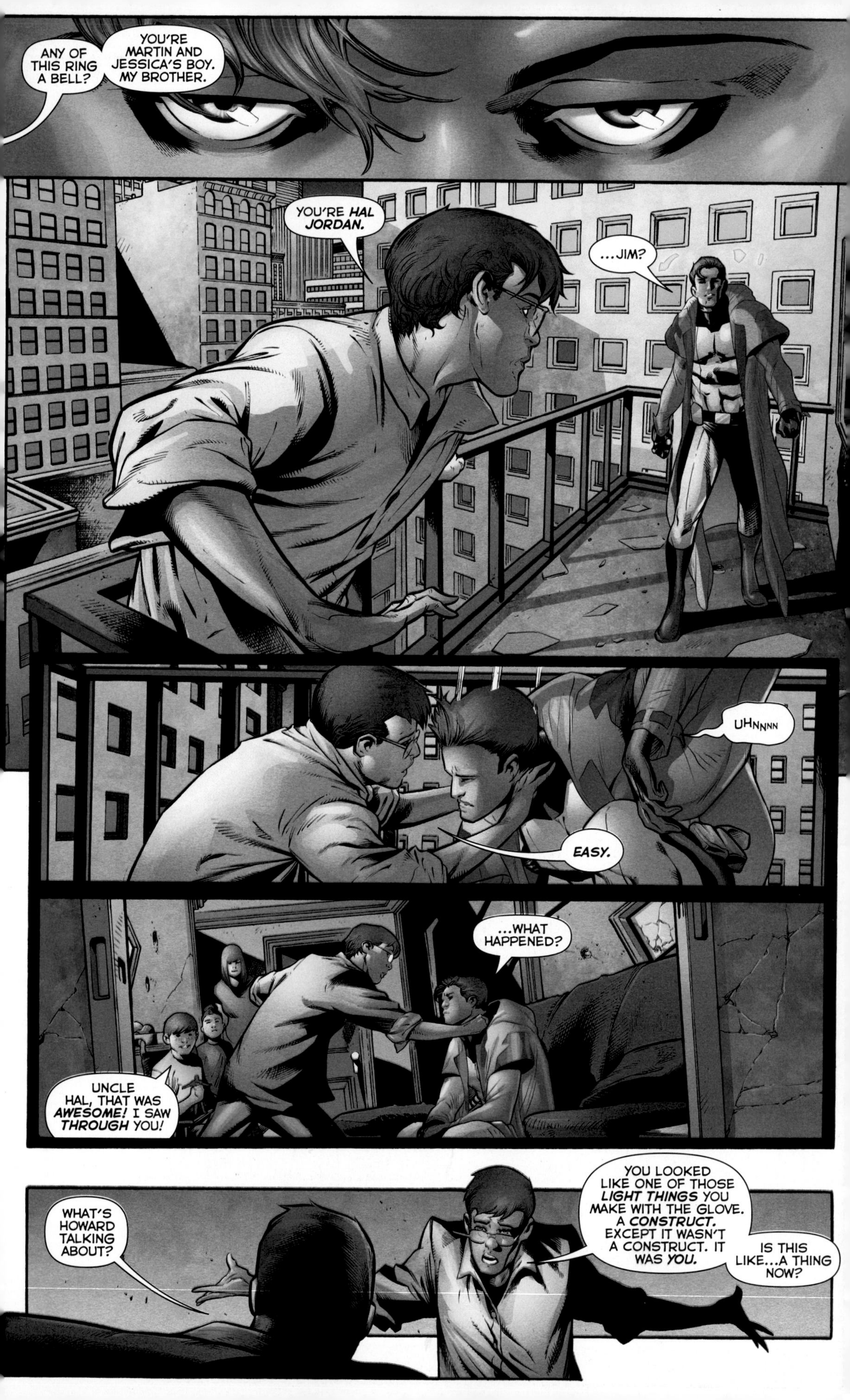

ANY OF THIS RING A BELL?
YOU'RE MARTIN AND JESSICA'S BOY. MY BROTHER.
YOU'RE *HAL JORDAN.*
...JIM?
UHNNNN
EASY.
...WHAT HAPPENED?
UNCLE HAL, THAT WAS *AWESOME!* I SAW *THROUGH* YOU!
WHAT'S HOWARD TALKING ABOUT?
YOU LOOKED LIKE ONE OF THOSE *LIGHT THINGS* YOU MAKE WITH THE GLOVE. A *CONSTRUCT.* EXCEPT IT WASN'T A CONSTRUCT. IT WAS *YOU.*
IS THIS LIKE...A THING NOW?

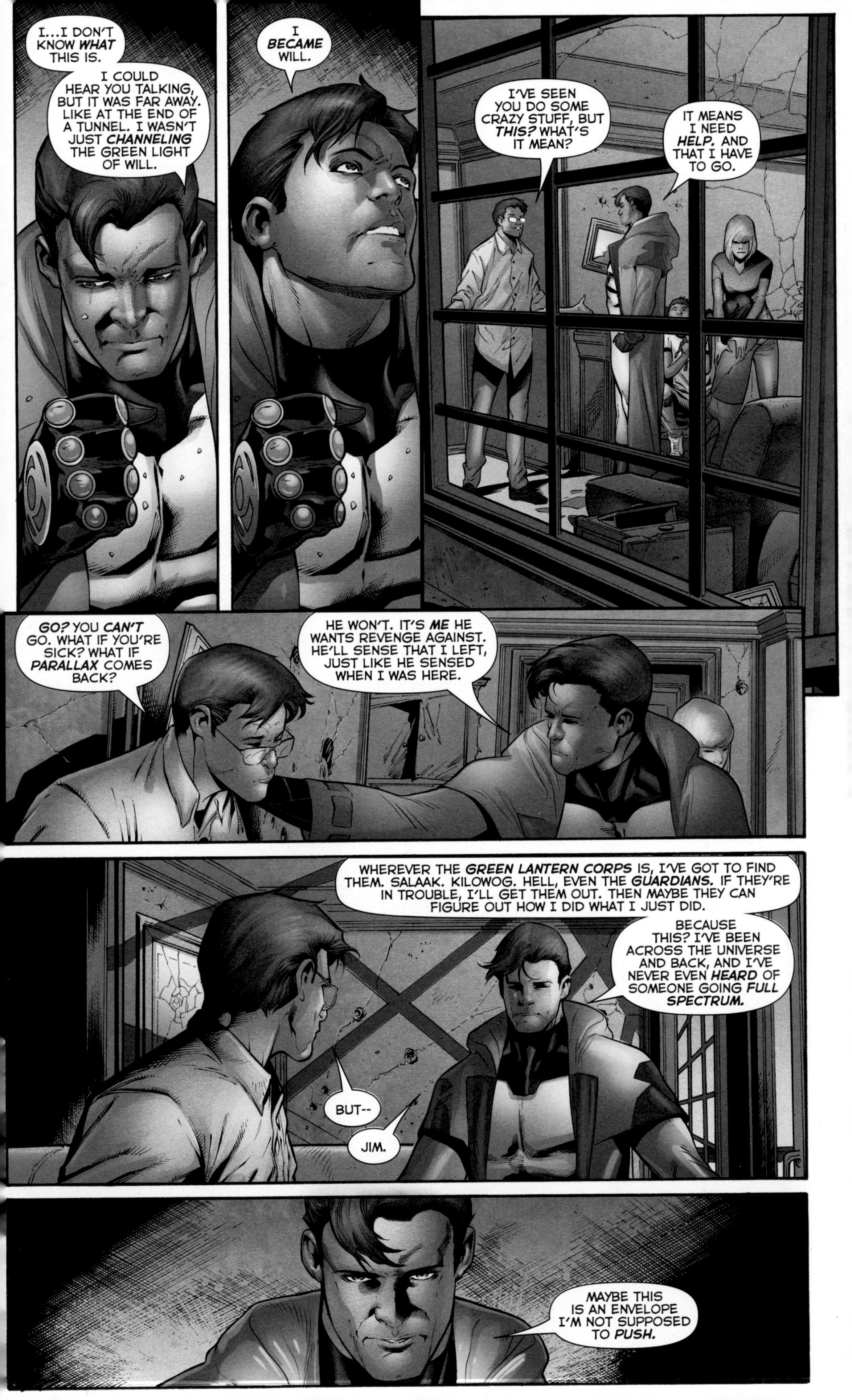
I...I DON'T KNOW *WHAT* THIS IS.
I COULD HEAR YOU TALKING, BUT IT WAS FAR AWAY. LIKE AT THE END OF A TUNNEL. I WASN'T JUST *CHANNELING* THE GREEN LIGHT OF WILL.
I *BECAME* WILL.
I'VE SEEN YOU DO SOME CRAZY STUFF, BUT *THIS?* WHAT'S IT MEAN?
IT MEANS I NEED *HELP.* AND THAT I HAVE TO GO.
GO? YOU *CAN'T* GO. WHAT IF YOU'RE SICK? WHAT IF *PARALLAX* COMES BACK?
HE WON'T. IT'S *ME* HE WANTS REVENGE AGAINST. HE'LL SENSE THAT I LEFT, JUST LIKE HE SENSED WHEN I WAS HERE.
WHEREVER THE *GREEN LANTERN CORPS* IS, I'VE GOT TO FIND THEM. SALAAK. KILOWOG. HELL, EVEN THE *GUARDIANS.* IF THEY'RE IN TROUBLE, I'LL GET THEM OUT. THEN MAYBE THEY CAN FIGURE OUT HOW I DID WHAT I JUST DID.
BECAUSE THIS? I'VE BEEN ACROSS THE UNIVERSE AND BACK, AND I'VE NEVER EVEN *HEARD* OF SOMEONE GOING *FULL SPECTRUM.*
BUT--
JIM.
MAYBE THIS IS AN ENVELOPE I'M NOT SUPPOSED TO *PUSH.*

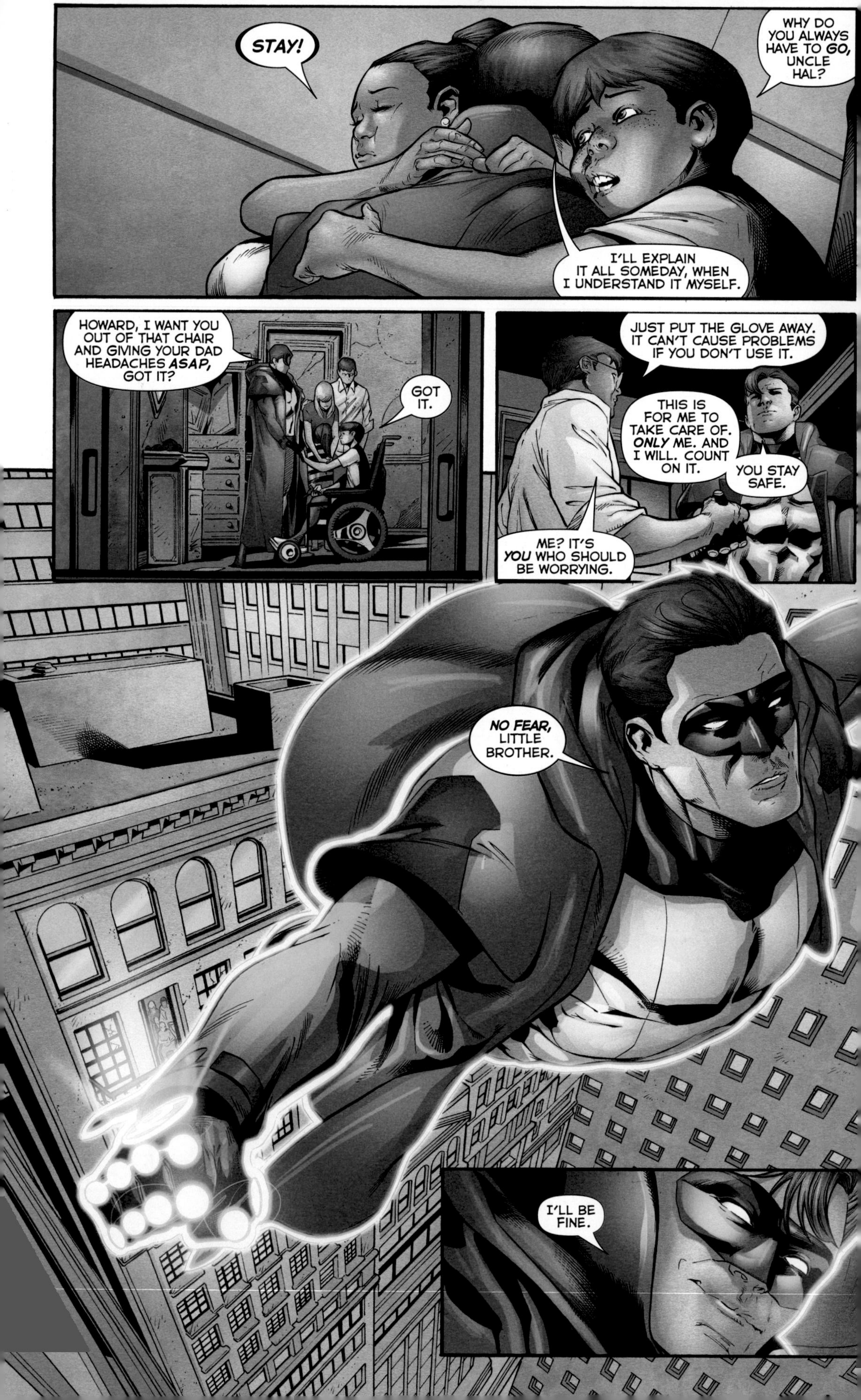
STAY!
WHY DO YOU ALWAYS HAVE TO GO, UNCLE HAL?
I'LL EXPLAIN IT ALL SOMEDAY, WHEN I UNDERSTAND IT MYSELF.
HOWARD, I WANT YOU OUT OF THAT CHAIR AND GIVING YOUR DAD HEADACHES ASAP, GOT IT?
GOT IT.
JUST PUT THE GLOVE AWAY. IT CAN'T CAUSE PROBLEMS IF YOU DON'T USE IT.
THIS IS FOR ME TO TAKE CARE OF. ONLY ME. AND I WILL. COUNT ON IT.
YOU STAY SAFE.
ME? IT'S YOU WHO SHOULD BE WORRYING.
NO FEAR, LITTLE BROTHER.
I'LL BE FINE.

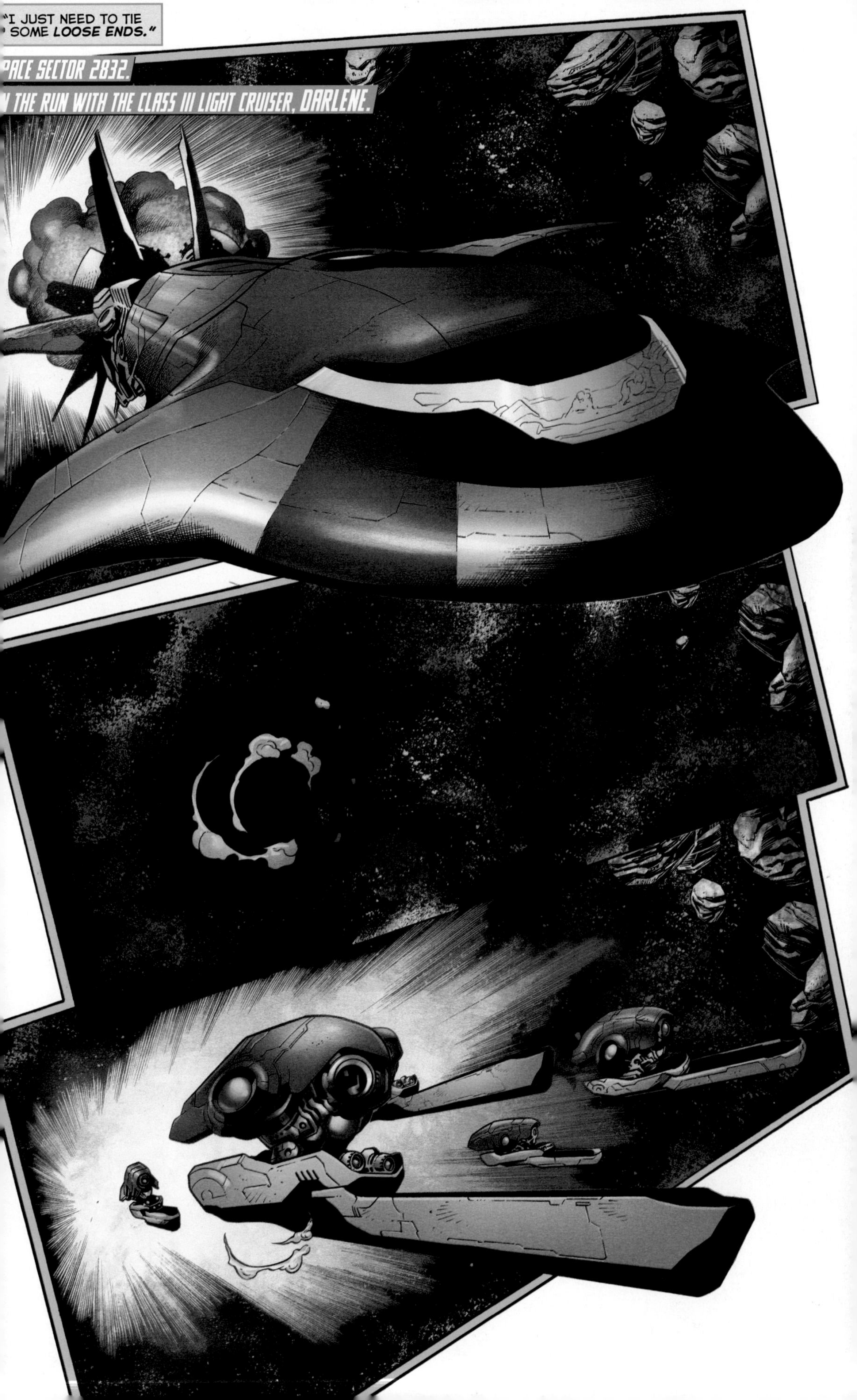
"I JUST NEED TO TIE
SOME LOOSE ENDS."
PACE SECTOR 2832.
THE RUN WITH THE CLASS III LIGHT CRUISER, DARLENE.

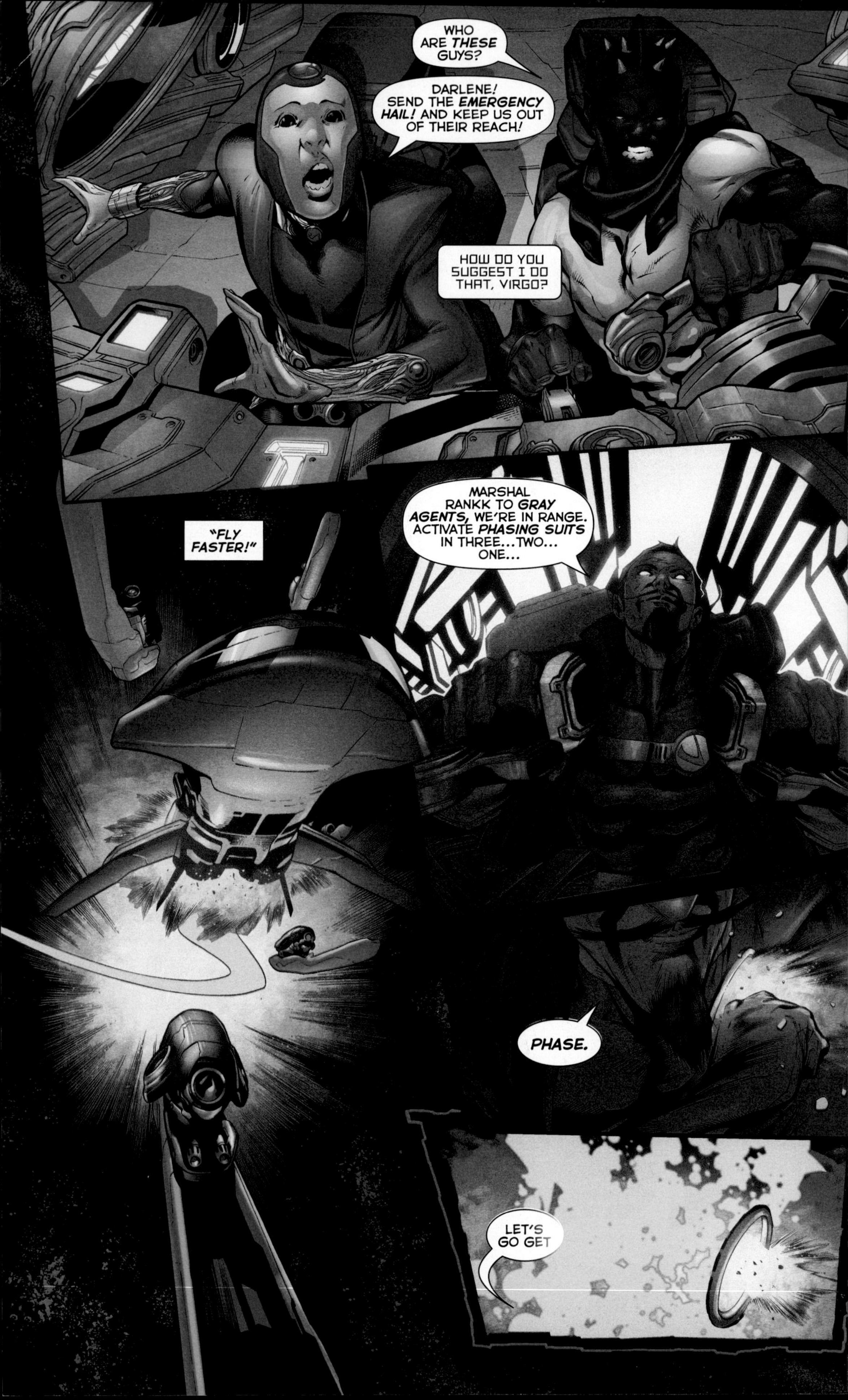

WHO ARE *THESE* GUYS?
DARLENE! SEND THE *EMERGENCY HAIL!* AND KEEP US OUT OF THEIR REACH!
HOW DO YOU SUGGEST I DO THAT, VIRGO?
"FLY FASTER!"
MARSHAL RANKK TO *GRAY AGENTS,* WE'RE IN RANGE. ACTIVATE *PHASING SUITS* IN THREE... TWO... ONE...
PHASE.
LET'S GO GET

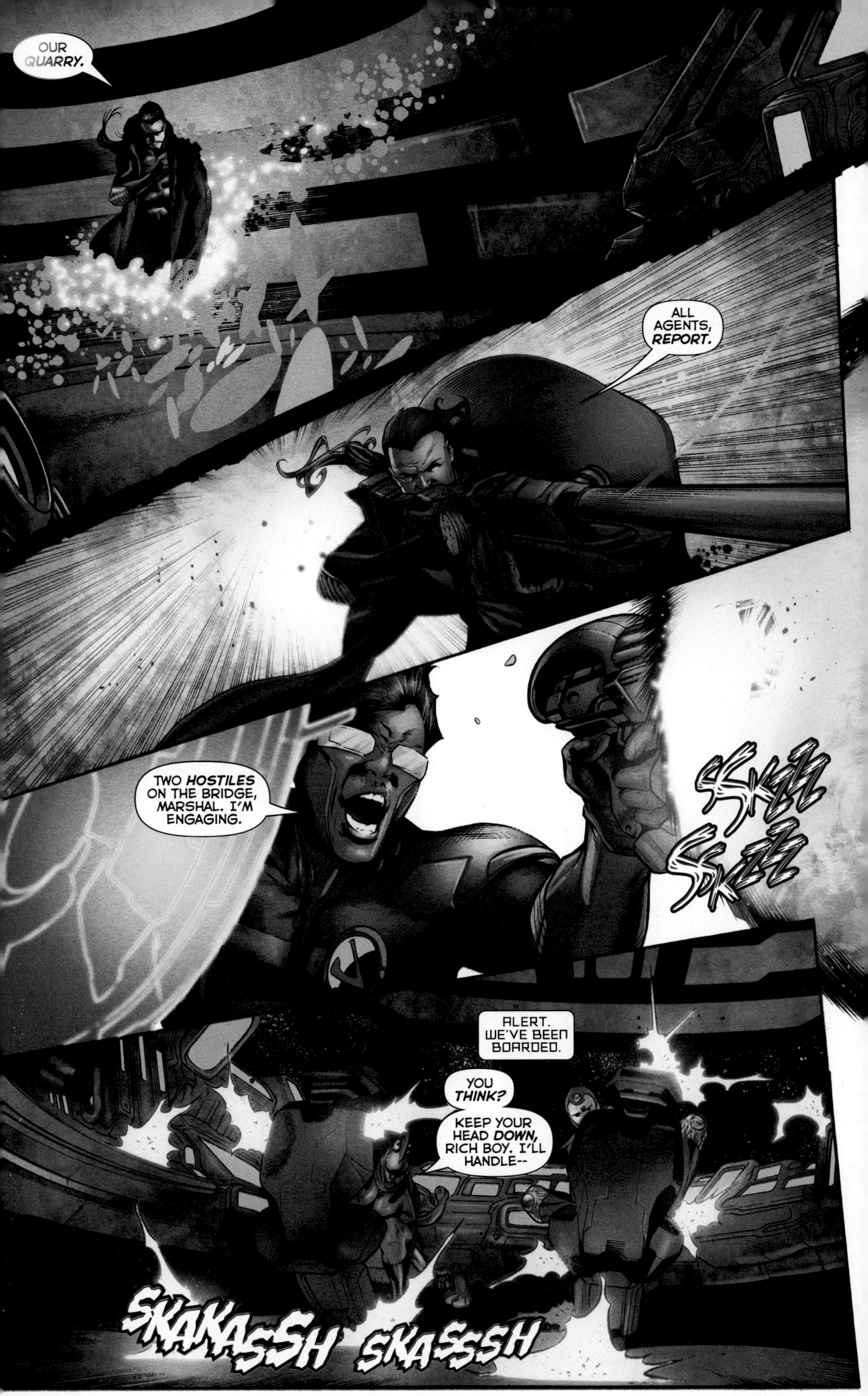
OUR QUARRY.
ALL AGENTS, REPORT.
TWO HOSTILES ON THE BRIDGE, MARSHAL. I'M ENGAGING.
SSKZZZ
SSKZZZ
ALERT. WE'VE BEEN BOARDED.
YOU THINK?
KEEP YOUR HEAD DOWN, RICH BOY. I'LL HANDLE--
SKAKASSH SKASSSH

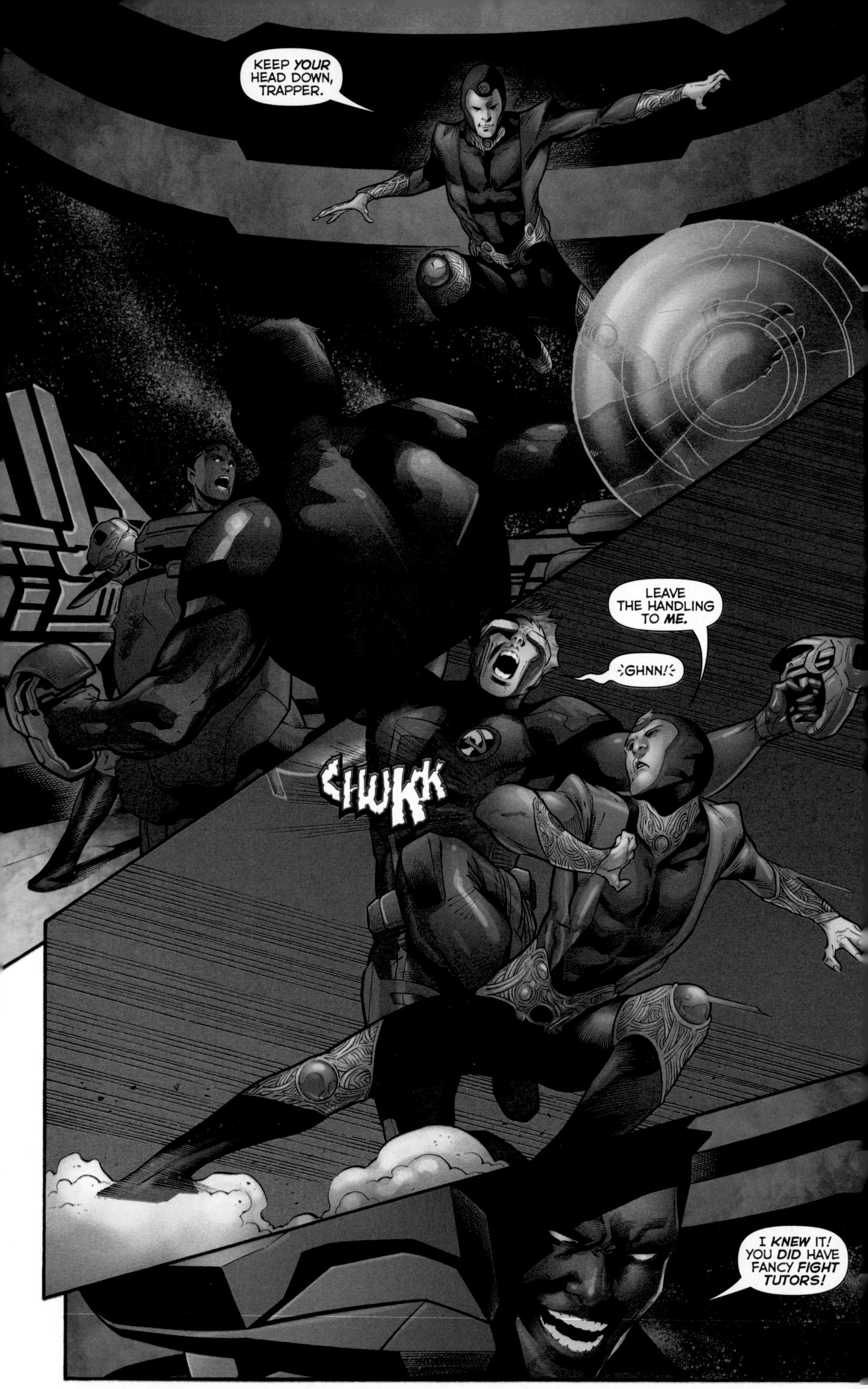
KEEP *YOUR* HEAD DOWN, TRAPPER.
LEAVE THE HANDLING TO *ME.*
GHNN!
CHUKK
I *KNEW* IT! YOU *DID* HAVE FANCY *FIGHT TUTORS!*

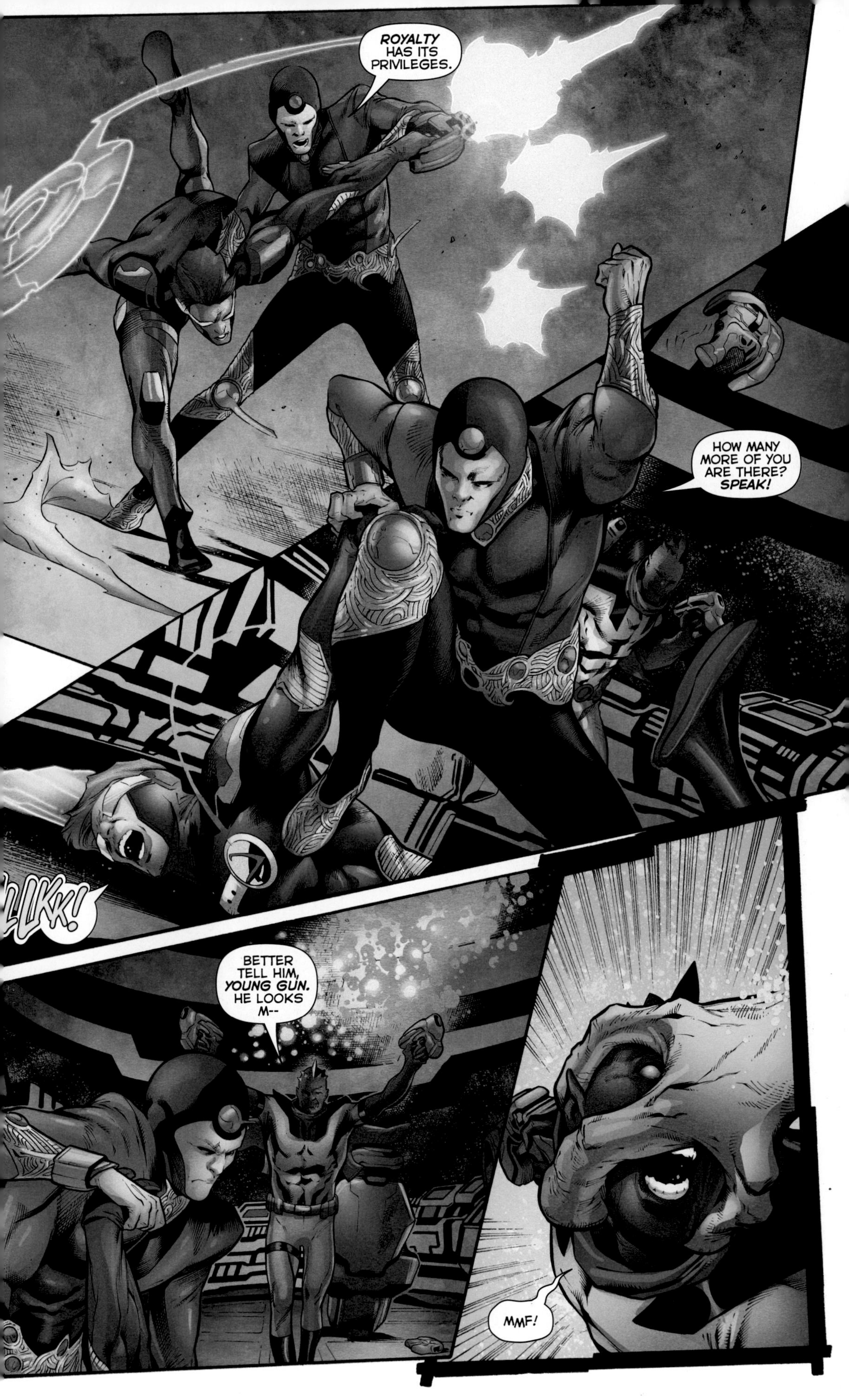
ROYALTY HAS ITS PRIVILEGES.
HOW MANY MORE OF YOU ARE THERE? SPEAK!
LKK!
BETTER TELL HIM, YOUNG GUN. HE LOOKS M--
MMF!

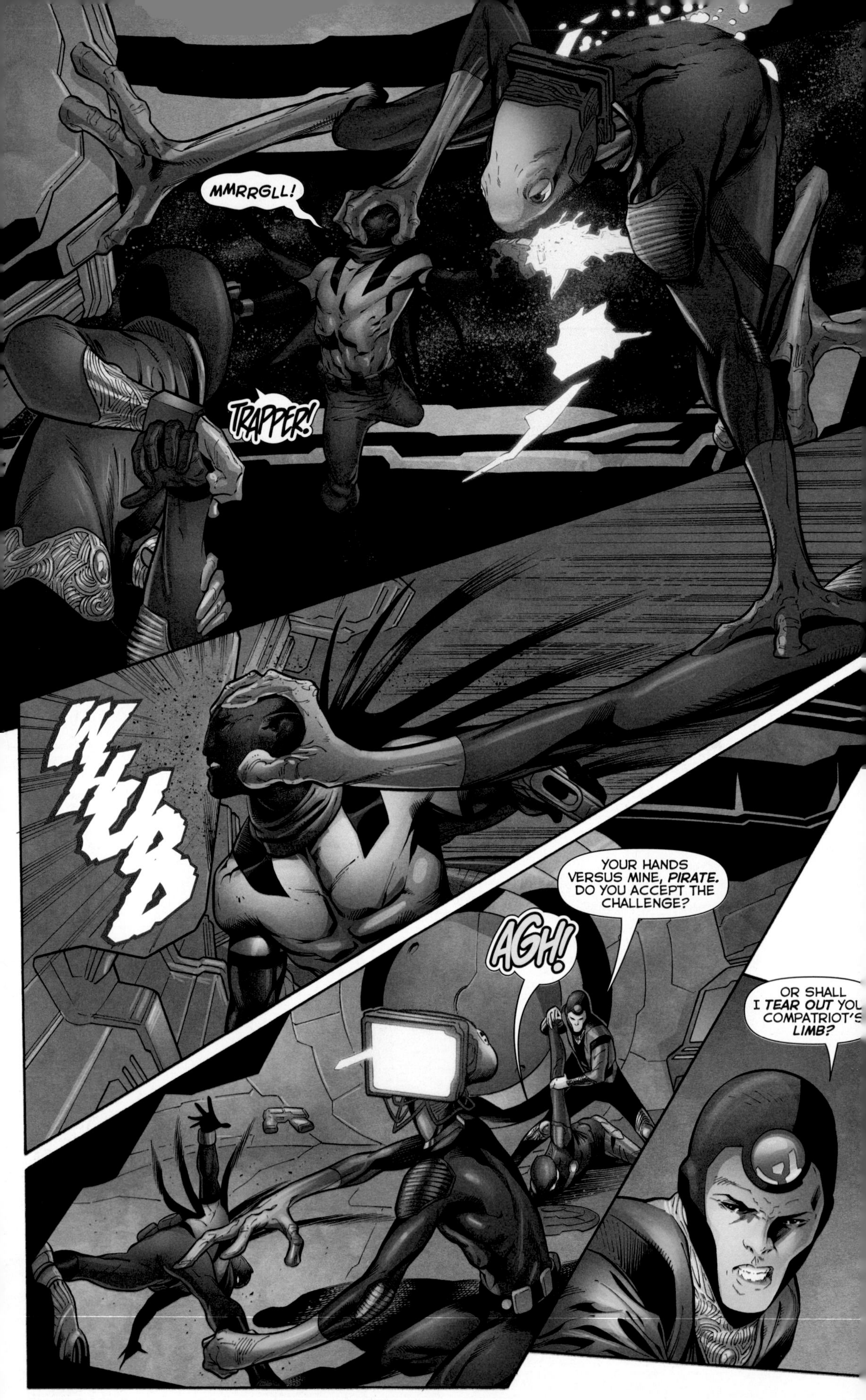
MMRRGLL!
TRAPPER!
WUB
YOUR HANDS VERSUS MINE, PIRATE. DO YOU ACCEPT THE CHALLENGE?
AGH!
OR SHALL I TEAR OUT YOU COMPATRIOT'S LIMB?

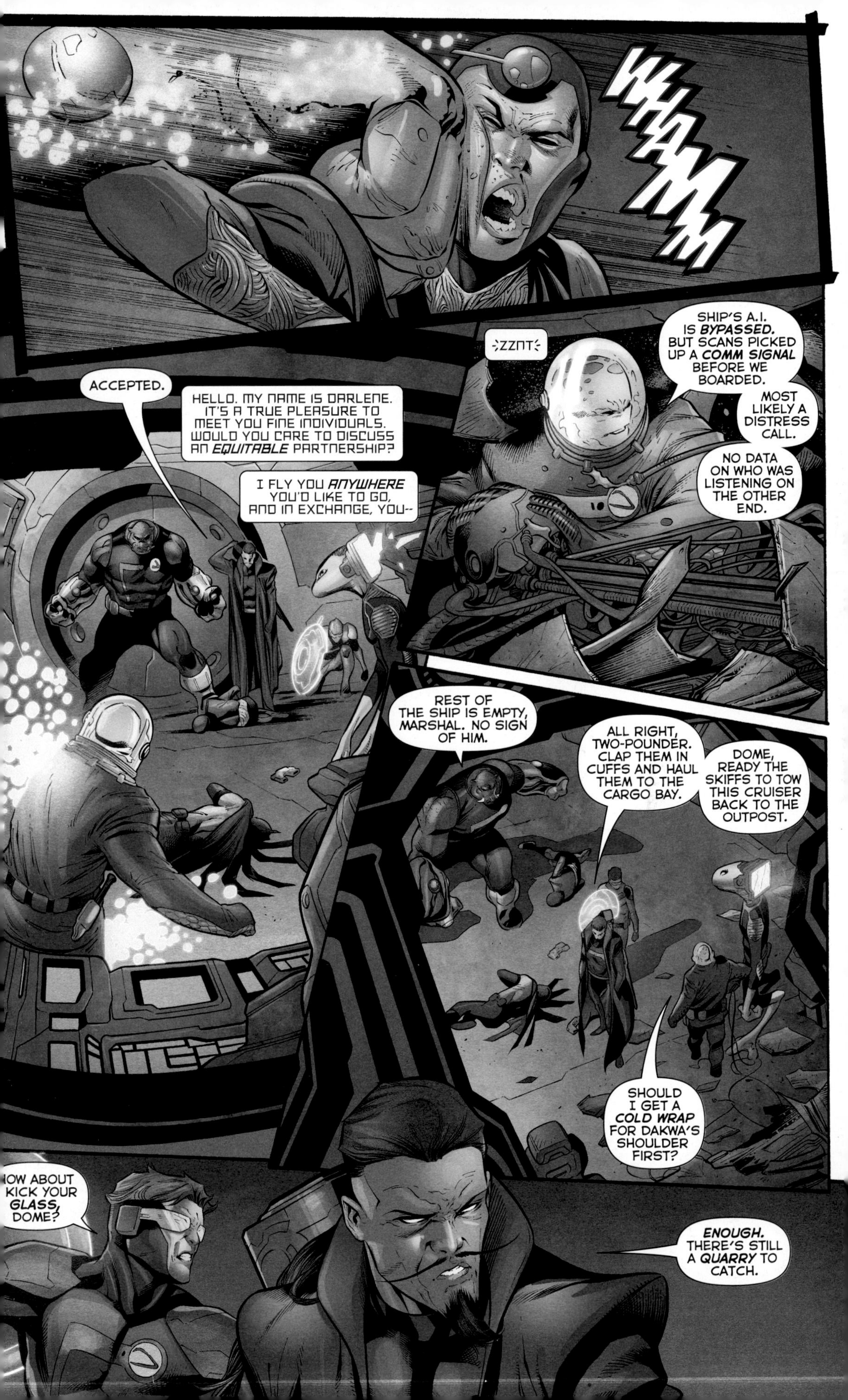
WHAMM
ACCEPTED.
HELLO. MY NAME IS DARLENE. IT'S A TRUE PLEASURE TO MEET YOU FINE INDIVIDUALS. WOULD YOU CARE TO DISCUSS AN EQUITABLE PARTNERSHIP?
I FLY YOU ANYWHERE YOU'D LIKE TO GO, AND IN EXCHANGE, YOU--
ZZNT
SHIP'S A.I. IS BYPASSED. BUT SCANS PICKED UP A COMM SIGNAL BEFORE WE BOARDED.
MOST LIKELY A DISTRESS CALL.
NO DATA ON WHO WAS LISTENING ON THE OTHER END.
REST OF THE SHIP IS EMPTY, MARSHAL. NO SIGN OF HIM.
ALL RIGHT, TWO-POUNDER. CLAP THEM IN CUFFS AND HAUL THEM TO THE CARGO BAY.
DOME, READY THE SKIFFS TO TOW THIS CRUISER BACK TO THE OUTPOST.
SHOULD I GET A COLD WRAP FOR DAKWA'S SHOULDER FIRST?
OW ABOUT KICK YOUR GLASS, DOME?
ENOUGH. THERE'S STILL A QUARRY TO CATCH.

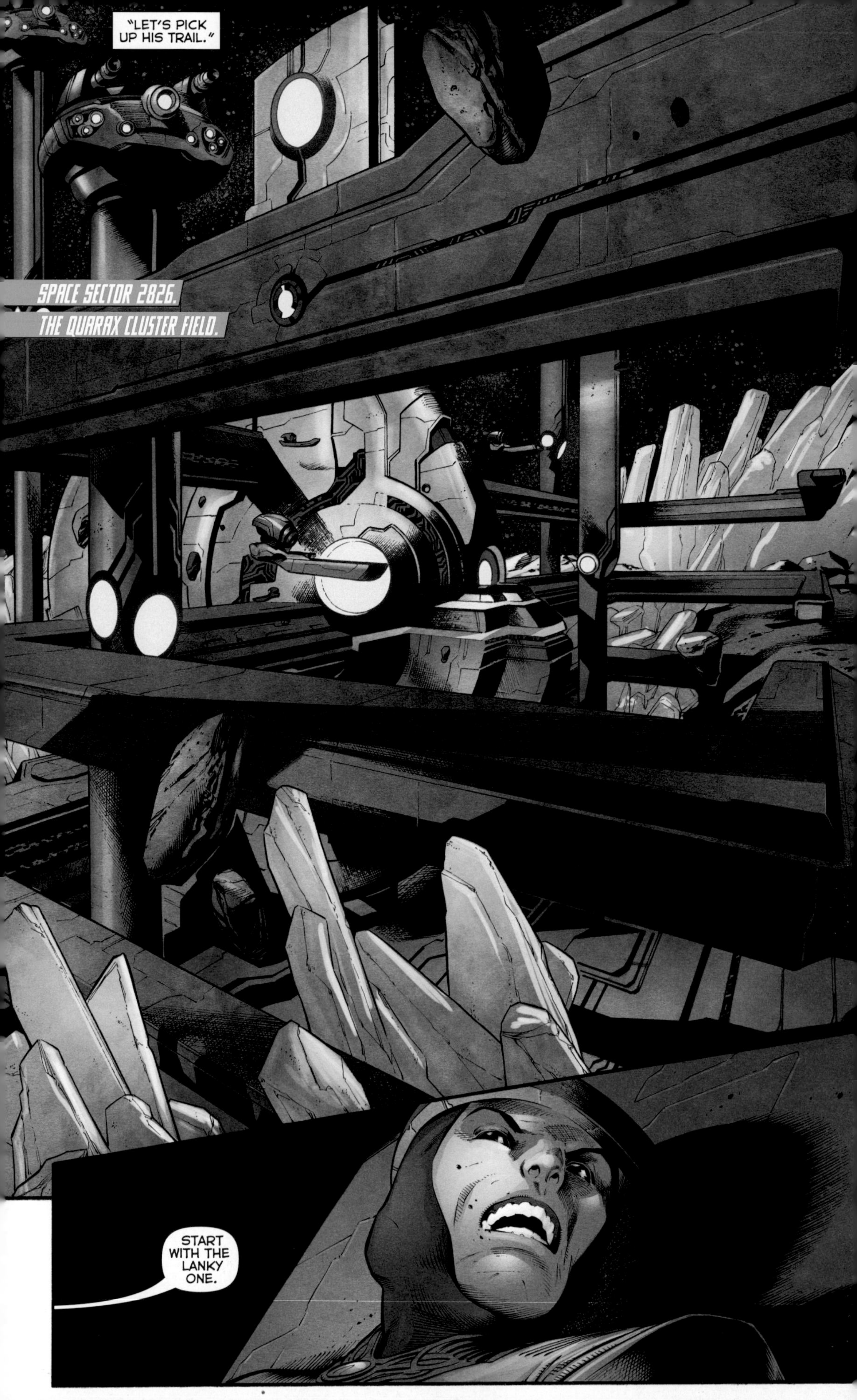
"LET'S PICK UP HIS TRAIL."
SPACE SECTOR 2826.
THE QUARAX CLUSTER FIELD.
START WITH THE LANKY ONE.

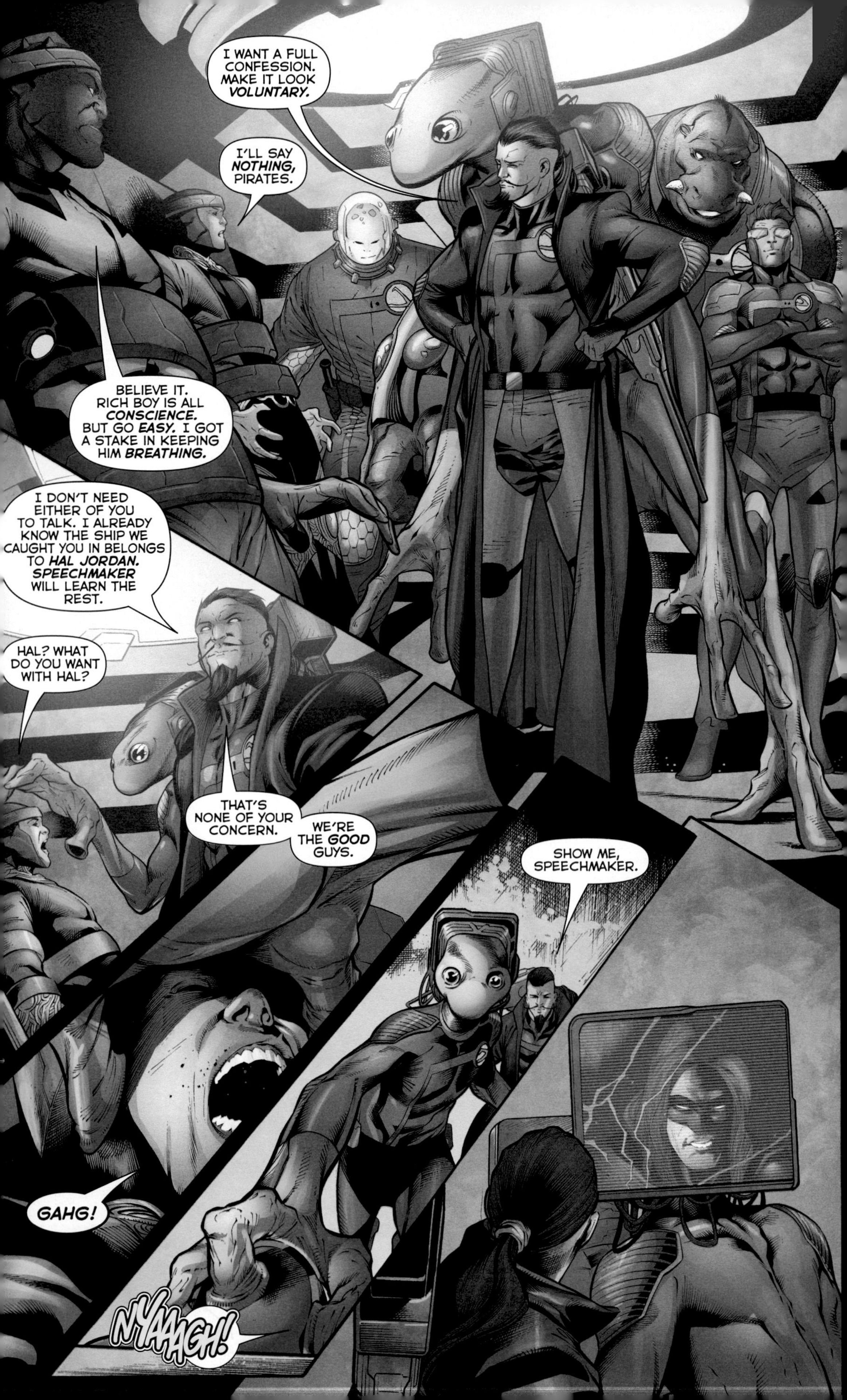
I WANT A FULL CONFESSION. MAKE IT LOOK VOLUNTARY.
I'LL SAY NOTHING, PIRATES.
BELIEVE IT. RICH BOY IS ALL CONSCIENCE. BUT GO EASY. I GOT A STAKE IN KEEPING HIM BREATHING.
I DON'T NEED EITHER OF YOU TO TALK. I ALREADY KNOW THE SHIP WE CAUGHT YOU IN BELONGS TO HAL JORDAN. SPEECHMAKER WILL LEARN THE REST.
HAL? WHAT DO YOU WANT WITH HAL?
THAT'S NONE OF YOUR CONCERN.
WE'RE THE GOOD GUYS.
SHOW ME, SPEECHMAKER.
GAHG!
NYAAAGH!

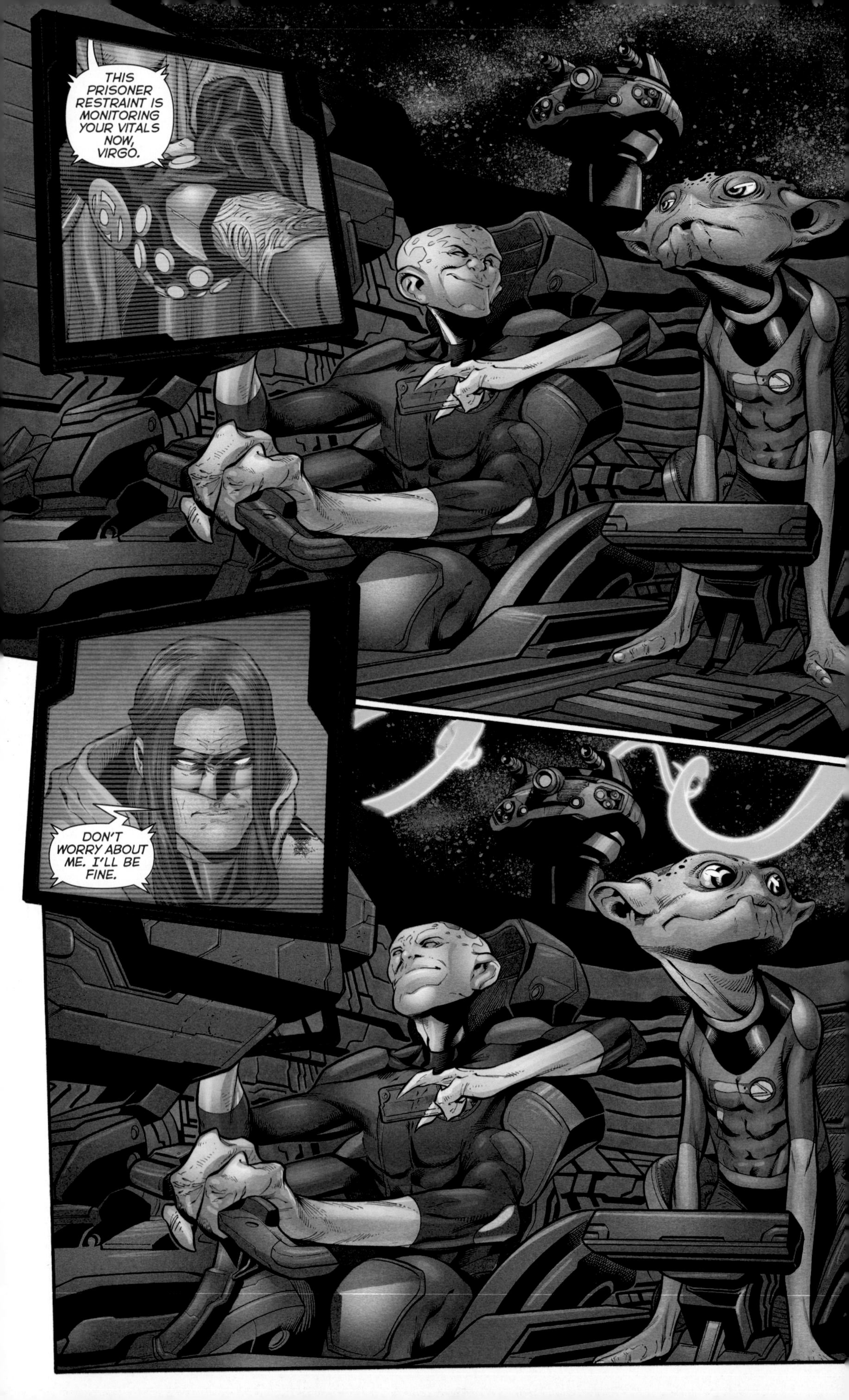
THIS PRISONER RESTRAINT IS MONITORING YOUR VITALS NOW, VIRGO.
DON'T WORRY ABOUT ME. I'LL BE FINE.

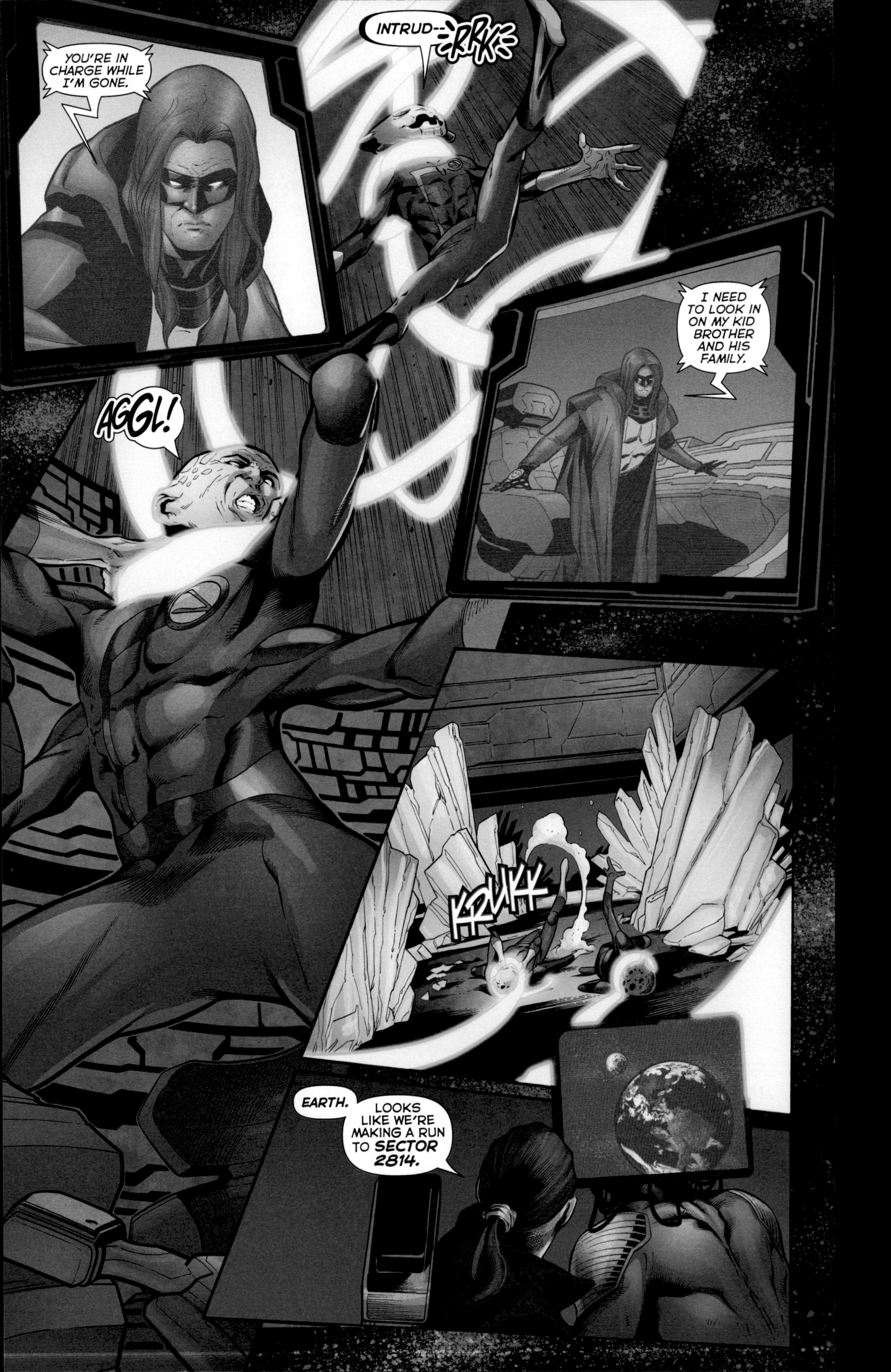
YOU'RE IN CHARGE WHILE I'M GONE.
INTRUD--
RRK
AGGL!
I NEED TO LOOK IN ON MY KID BROTHER AND HIS FAMILY.
KRUKK
EARTH.
LOOKS LIKE WE'RE MAKING A RUN TO SECTOR 2814.

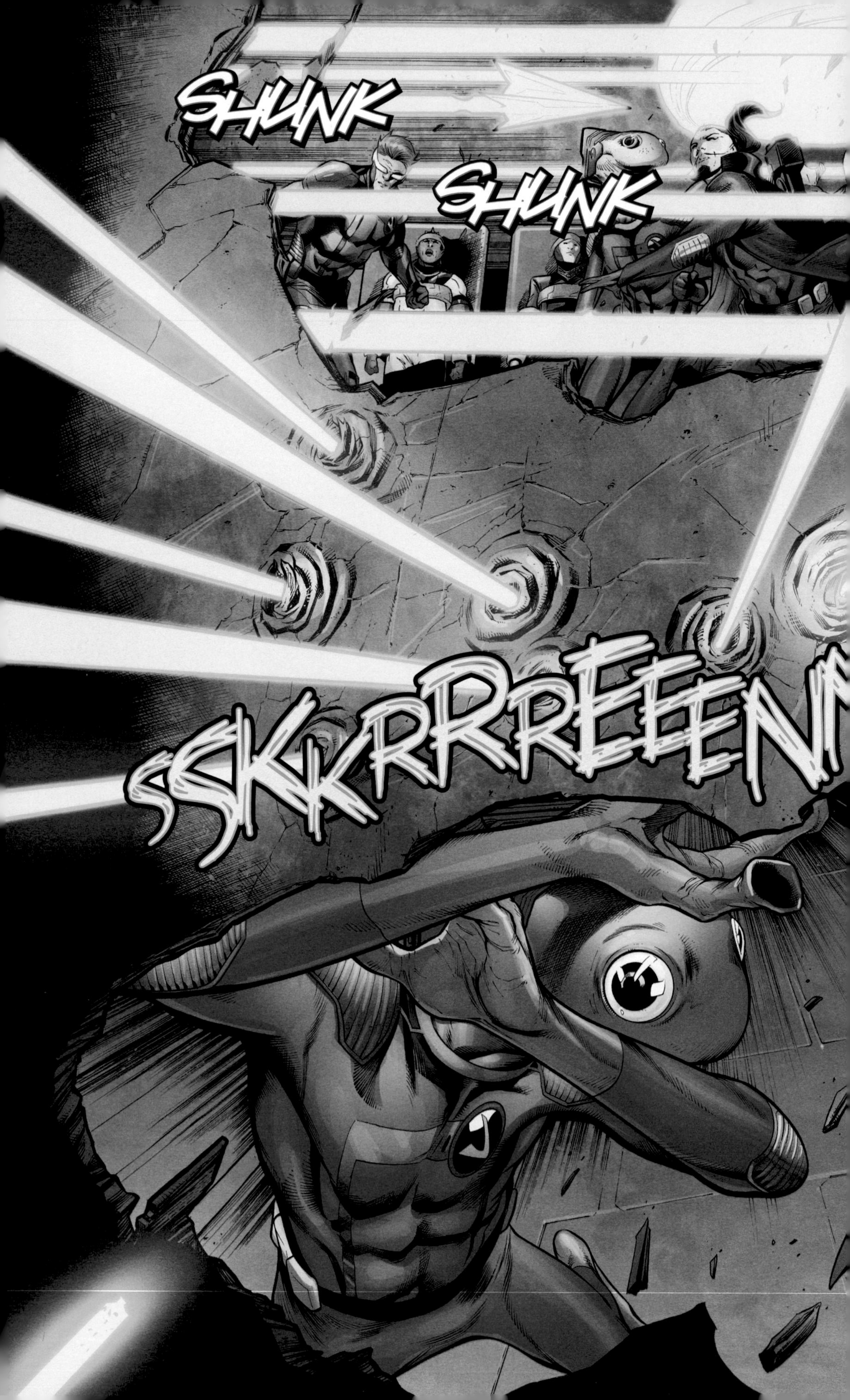
SHUNK
SHUNK
SKRRREEEN

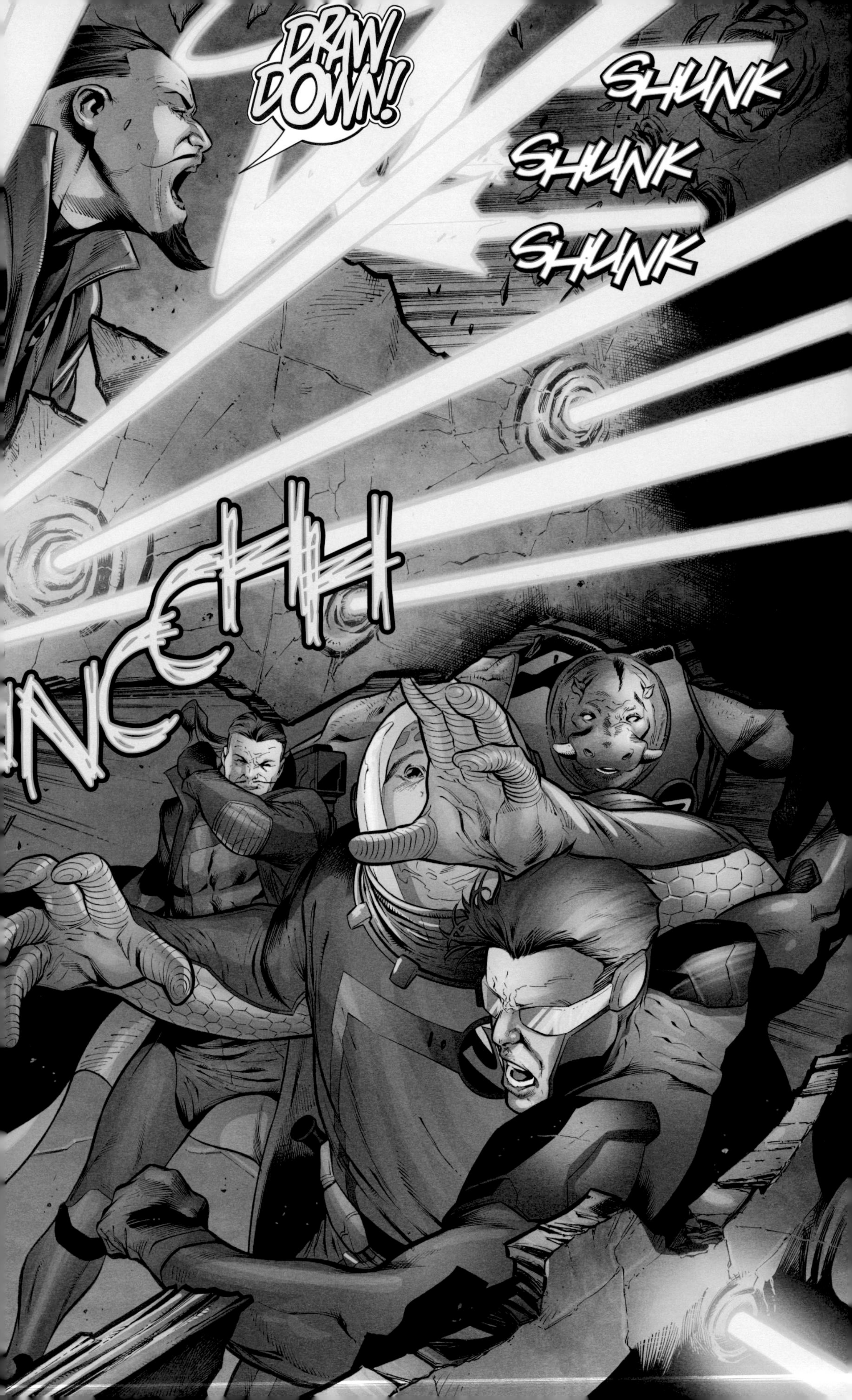
DRAW DOWN!
SHUNK
SHUNK
SHUNK
NCHH

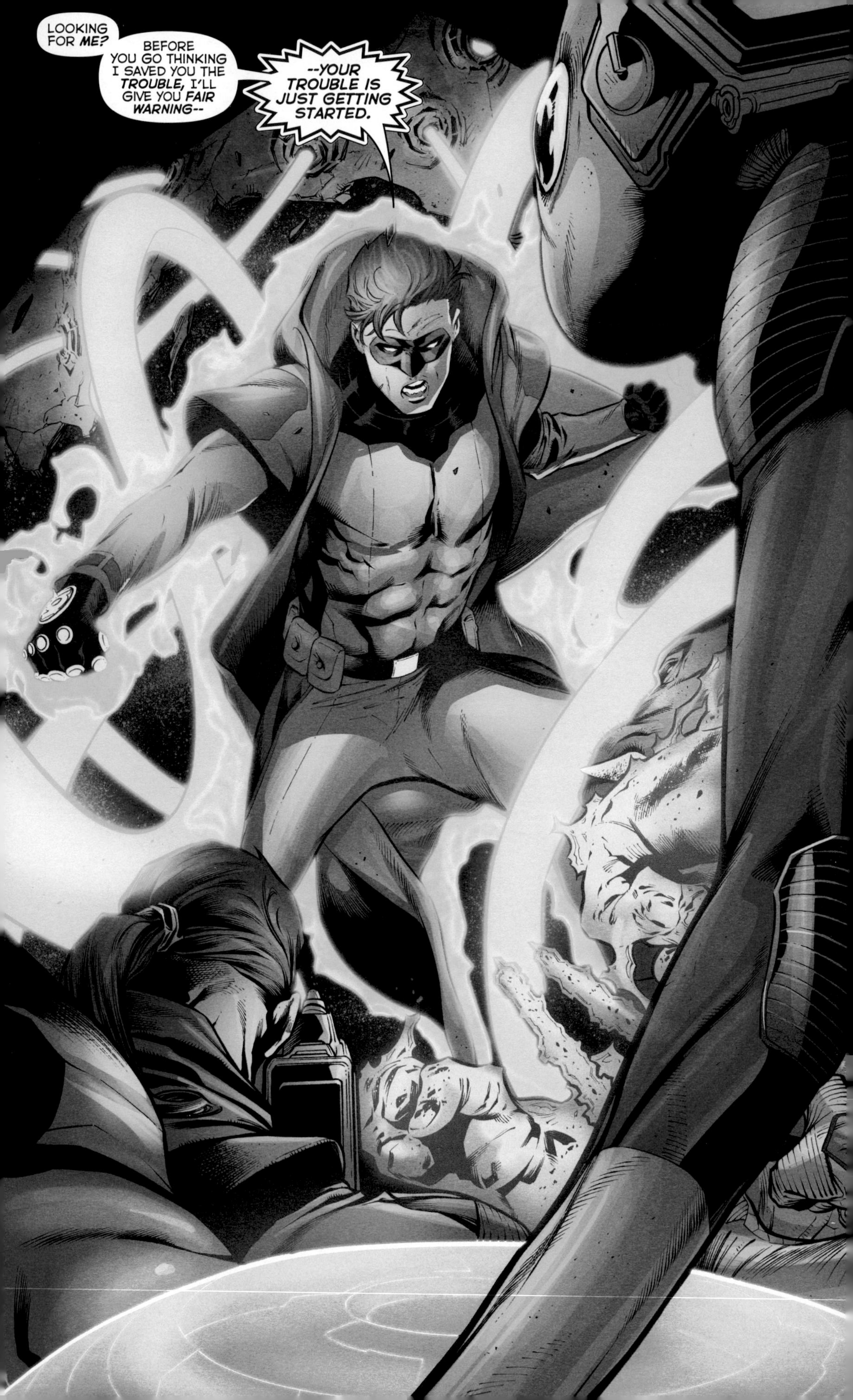

LOOKING FOR ME?
BEFORE YOU GO THINKING I SAVED YOU THE TROUBLE, I'LL GIVE YOU FAIR WARNING--
--YOUR TROUBLE IS JUST GETTING STARTED.

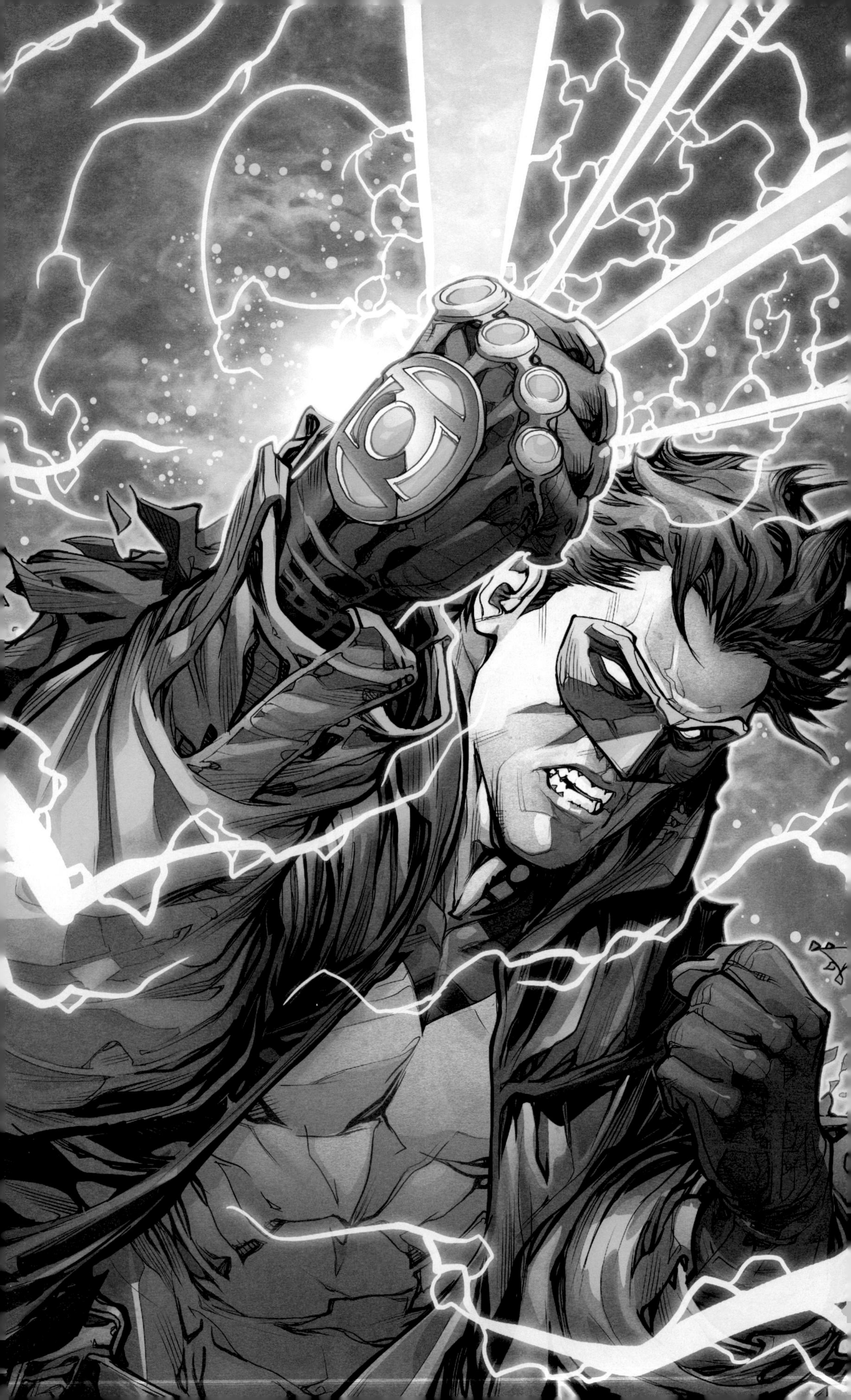

AGENTS OF GLORY

ROBERT VENDITTI writer **BILLY TAN** penciller **MARK IRWIN JOHN LIVESAY** inkers **ALEX SINCLAIR** colorist **DAVE SHARPE** letterer **HOWARD PORTER & HI-FI** cover

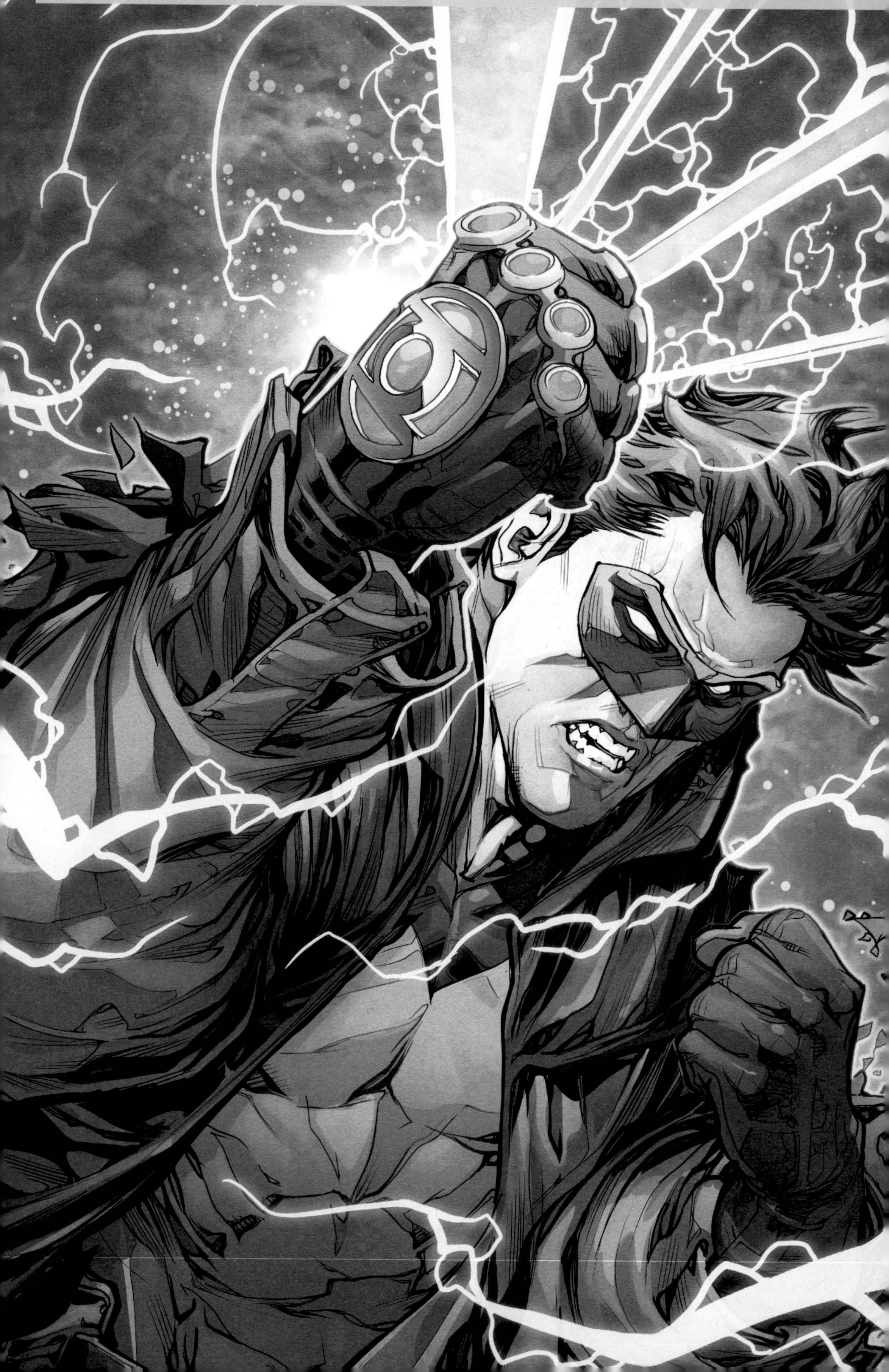

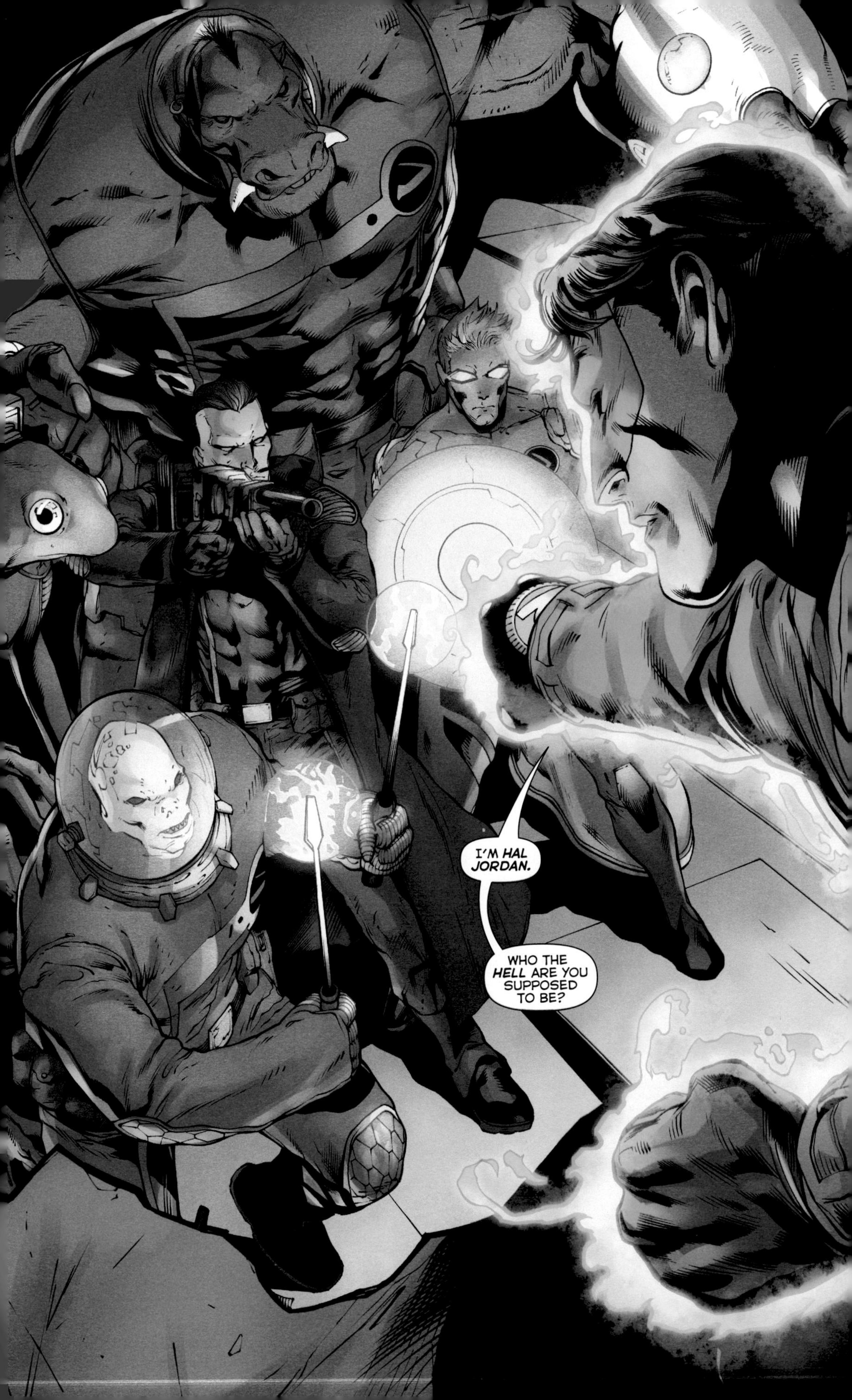
I'M HAL JORDAN.
WHO THE HELL ARE YOU SUPPOSED TO BE?

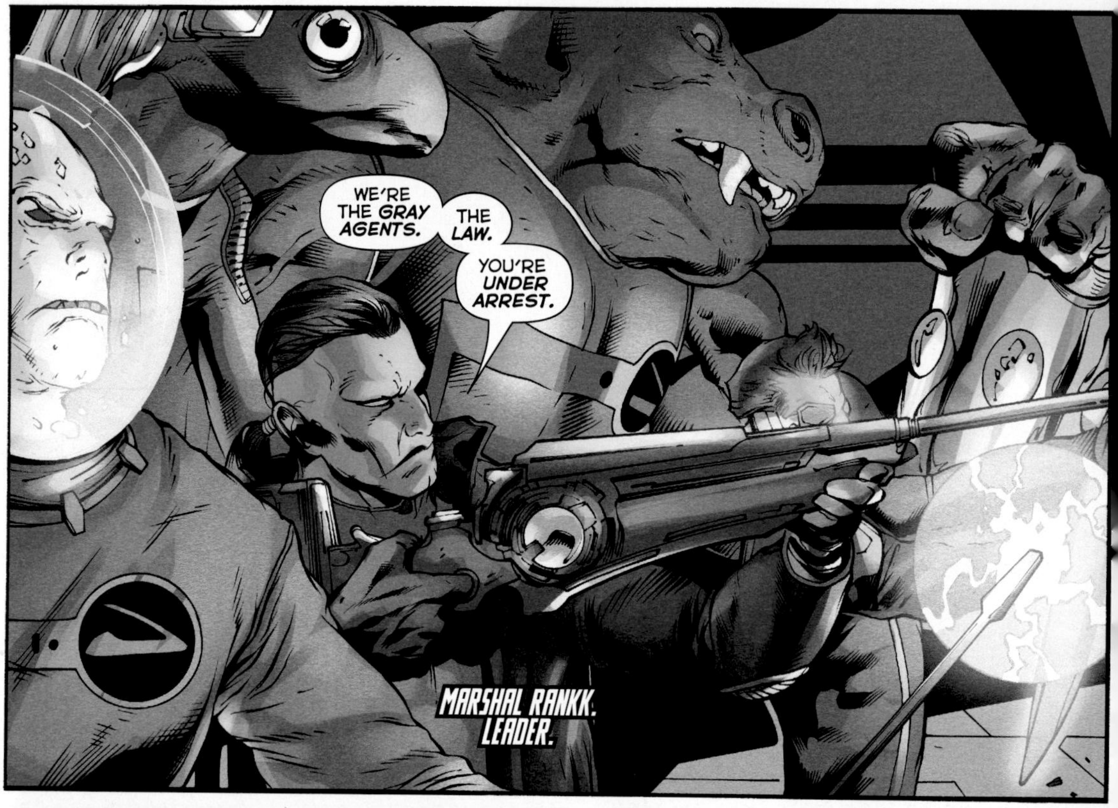
WE'RE THE GRAY AGENTS.
THE LAW.
YOU'RE UNDER ARREST.
MARSHAL RANKK. LEADER.

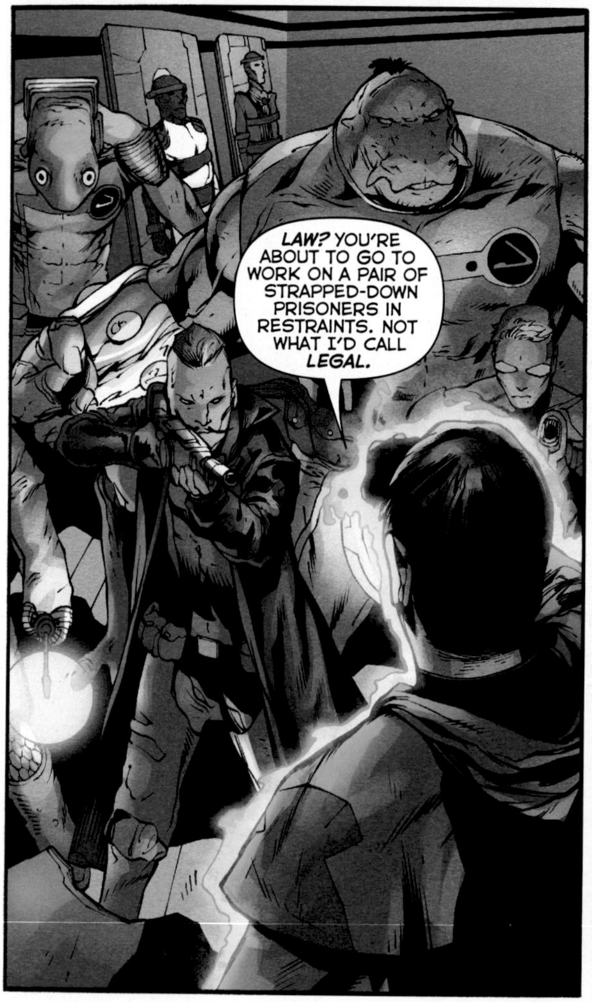
LAW? YOU'RE ABOUT TO GO TO WORK ON A PAIR OF STRAPPED-DOWN PRISONERS IN RESTRAINTS. NOT WHAT I'D CALL LEGAL.

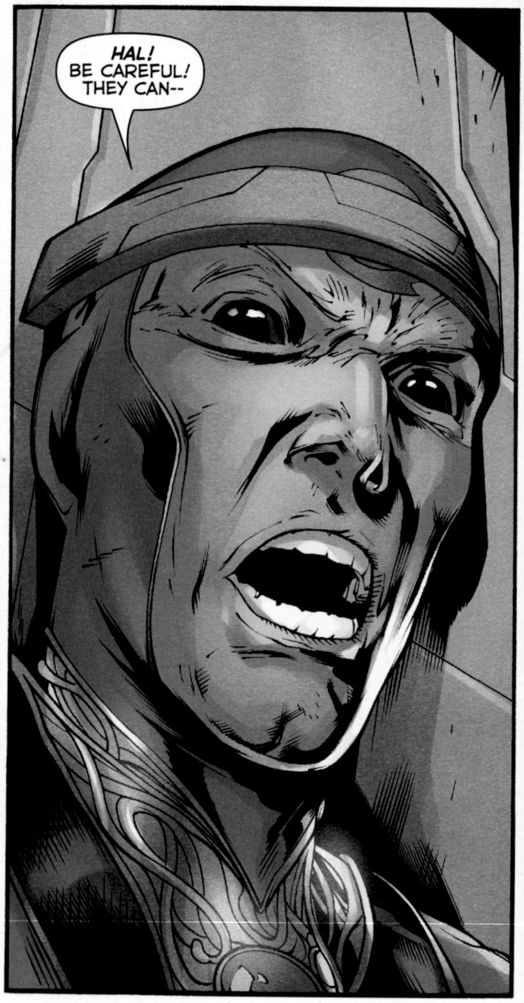
HAL! BE CAREFUL! THEY CAN--

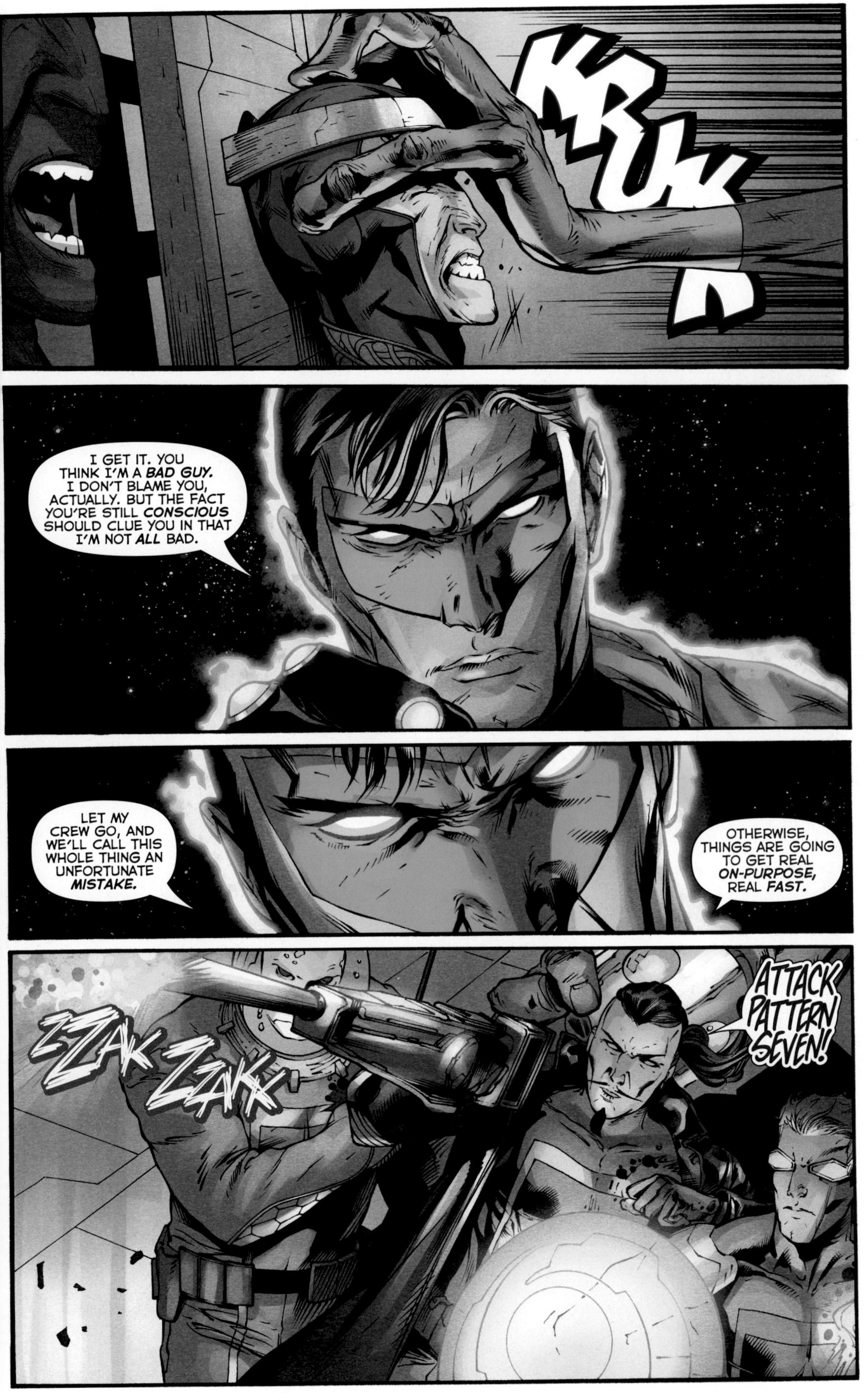
KRUNK
I GET IT. YOU THINK I'M A BAD GUY. I DON'T BLAME YOU, ACTUALLY. BUT THE FACT YOU'RE STILL CONSCIOUS SHOULD CLUE YOU IN THAT I'M NOT ALL BAD.
LET MY CREW GO, AND WE'LL CALL THIS WHOLE THING AN UNFORTUNATE MISTAKE.
OTHERWISE, THINGS ARE GOING TO GET REAL ON-PURPOSE, REAL FAST.
ZZAK ZZAKK
ATTACK PATTERN SEVEN!

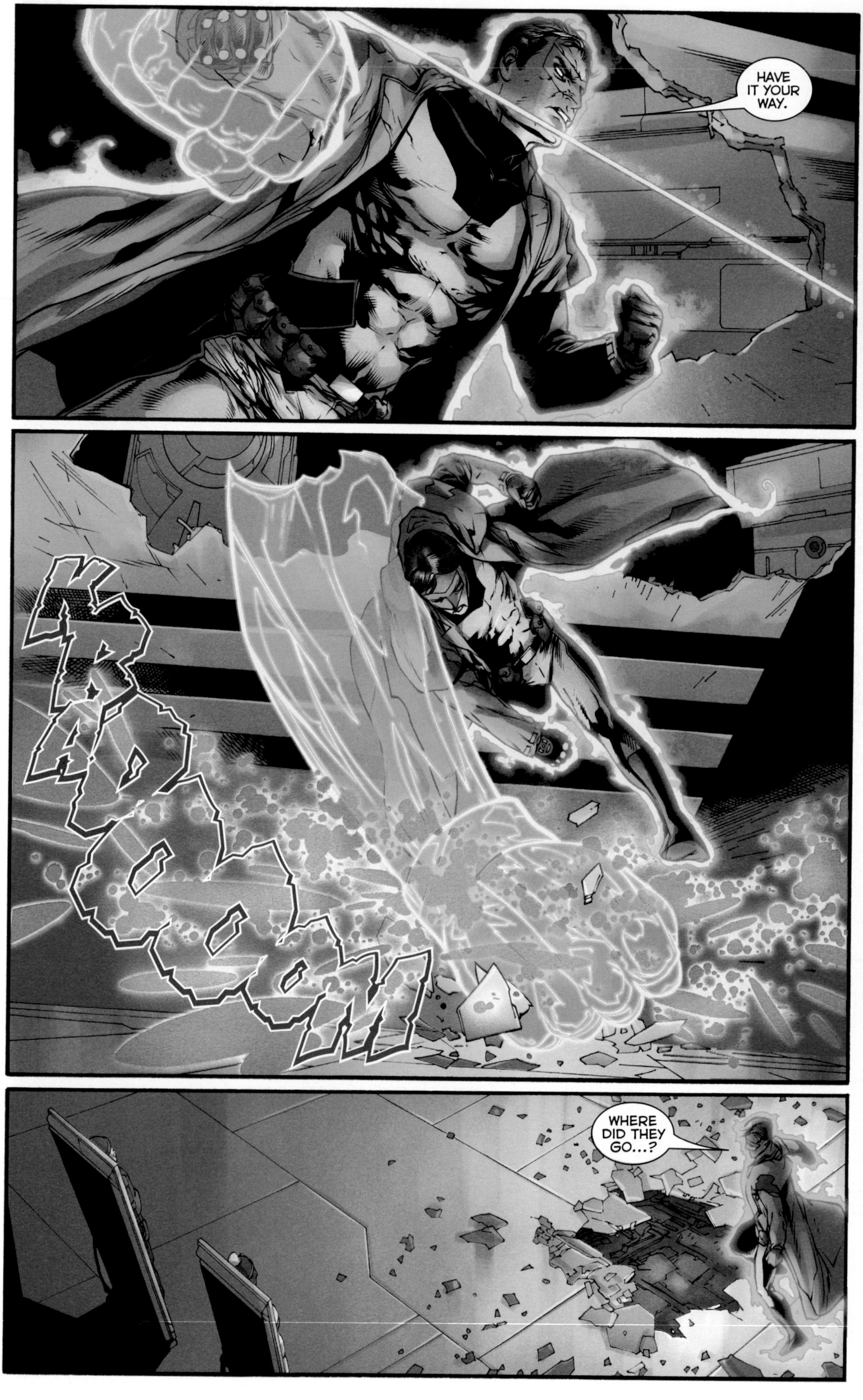
HAVE IT YOUR WAY.
KRAAAM
WHERE DID THEY GO...?

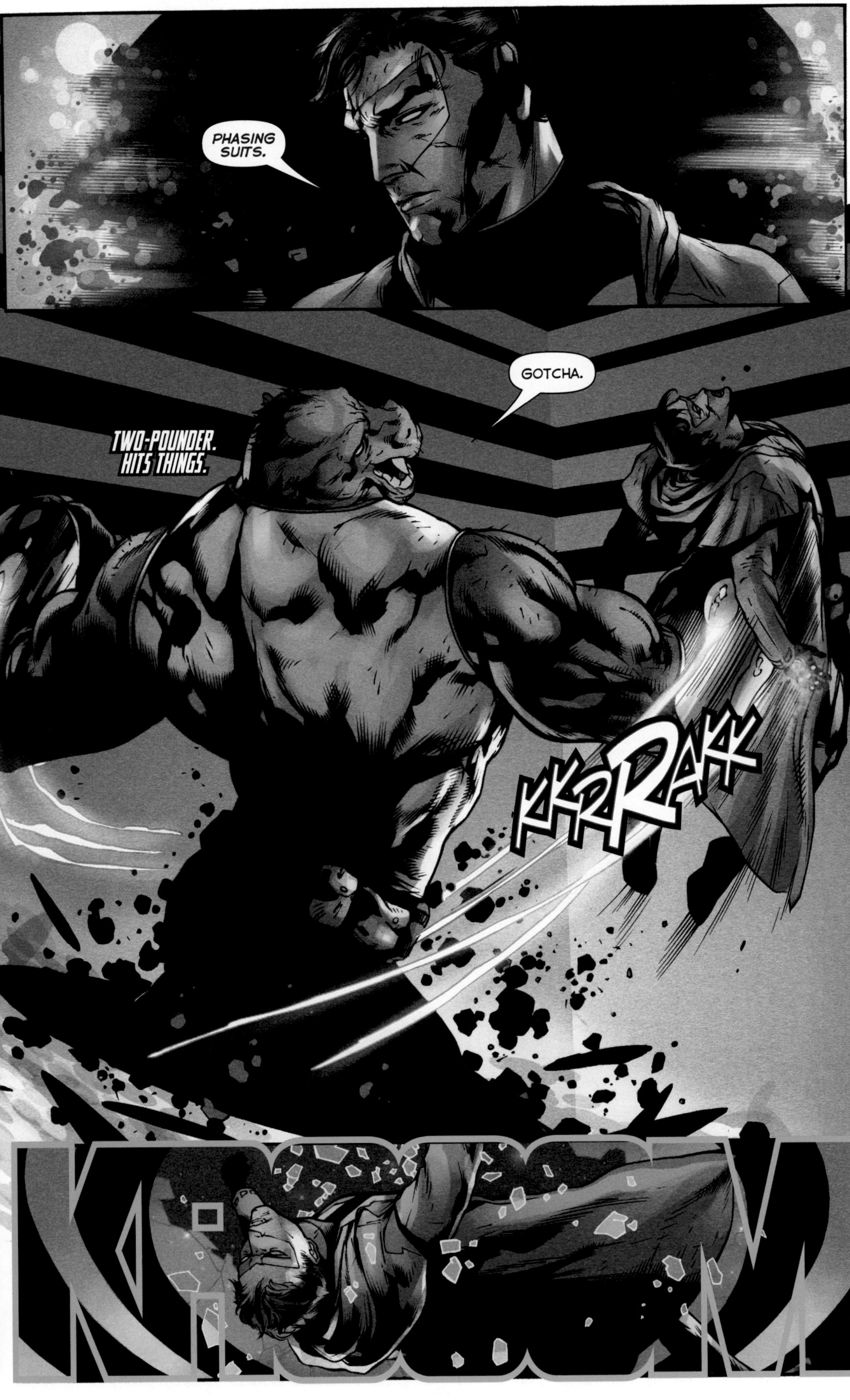
PHASING SUITS.
GOTCHA.
TWO-POUNDER. HITS THINGS.
KKRRAKK
KROOM

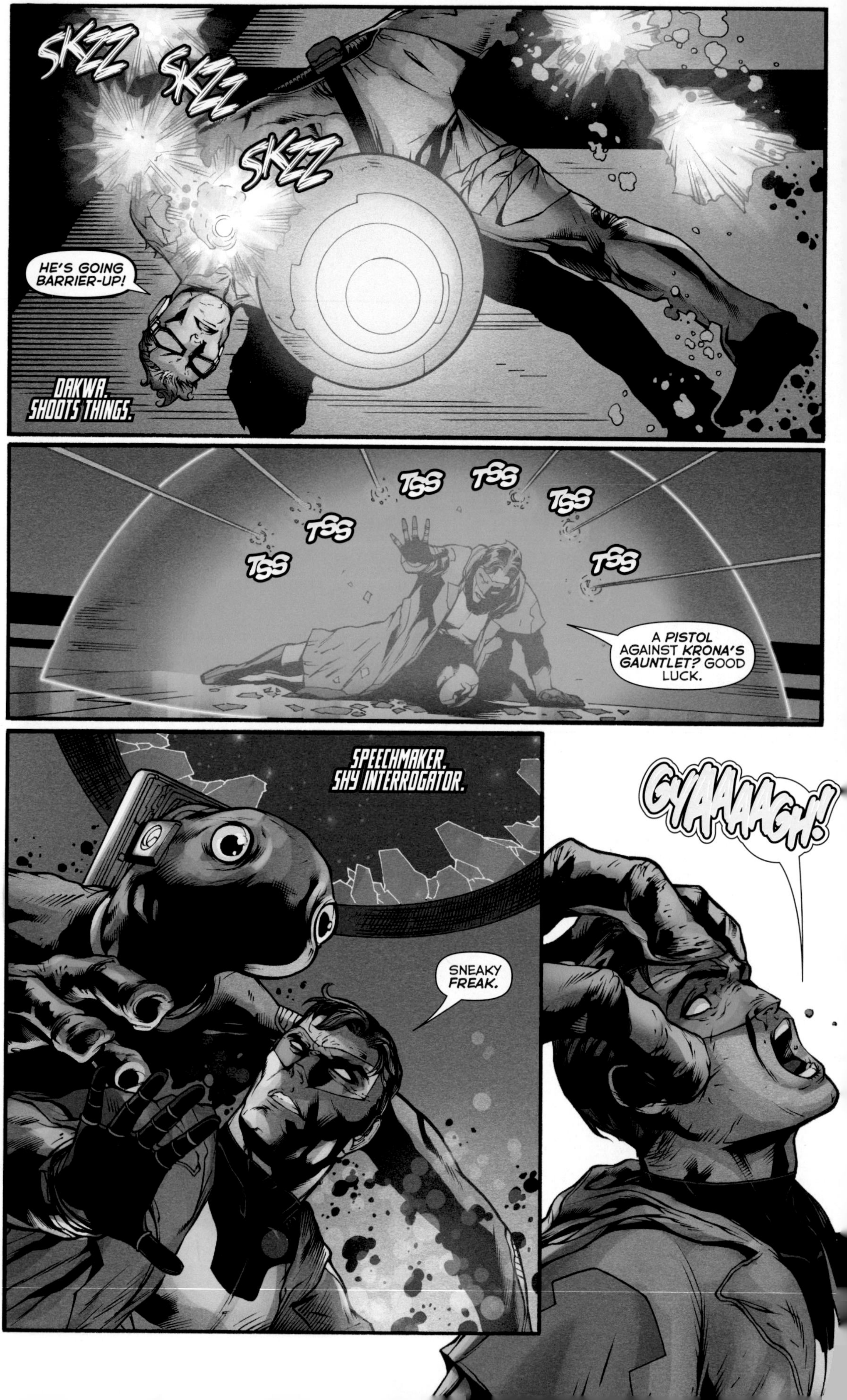
SKZZ
SKZZ
SKZZ
HE'S GOING BARRIER-UP!
DAKWA. SHOOTS THINGS.
TSS
TSS
TSS
TSS
TSS
TSS
A PISTOL AGAINST KRONA'S GAUNTLET? GOOD LUCK.
SPEECHMAKER. SHY INTERROGATOR.
SNEAKY FREAK.
GYAAAAGH!

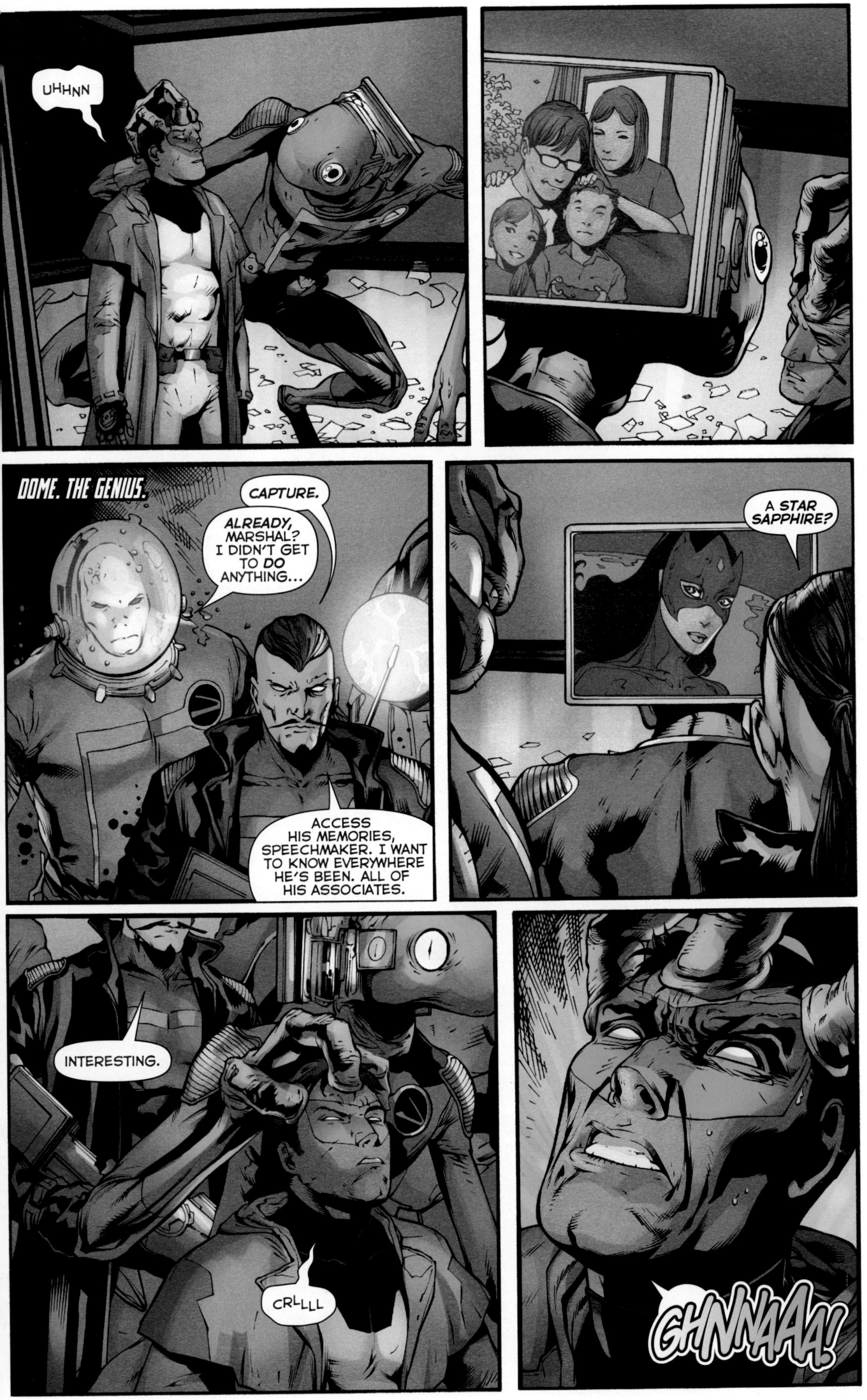
UHHNN
DOME. THE GENIUS.
CAPTURE.
ALREADY, MARSHAL? I DIDN'T GET TO DO ANYTHING...
ACCESS HIS MEMORIES, SPEECHMAKER. I WANT TO KNOW EVERYWHERE HE'S BEEN. ALL OF HIS ASSOCIATES.
A STAR SAPPHIRE?
INTERESTING.
CRLLLL
GHNNAAA!

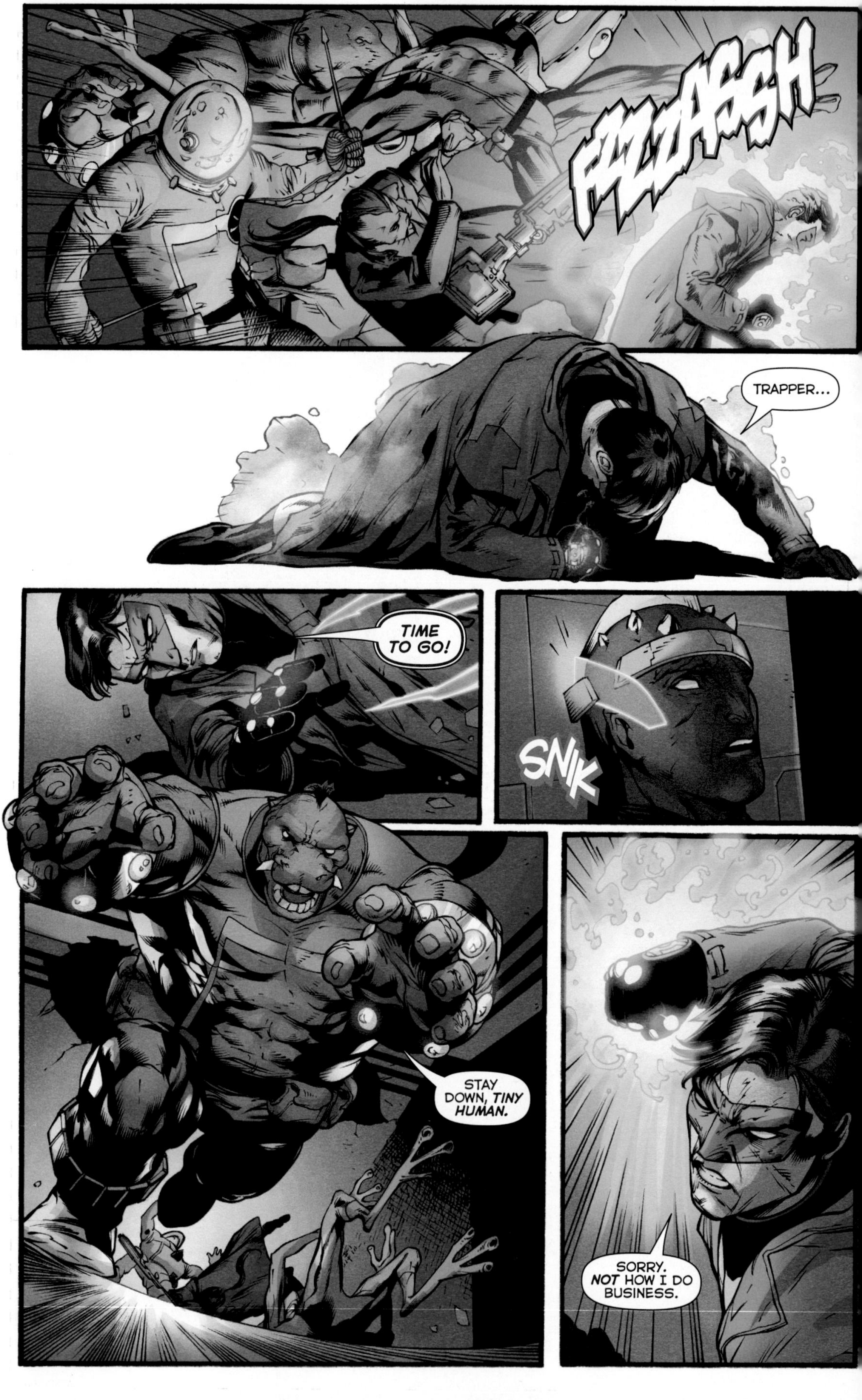
FZZZASSH
TRAPPER...
TIME TO GO!
SNIK
STAY DOWN, *TINY HUMAN.*
SORRY. ***NOT*** HOW I DO BUSINESS.

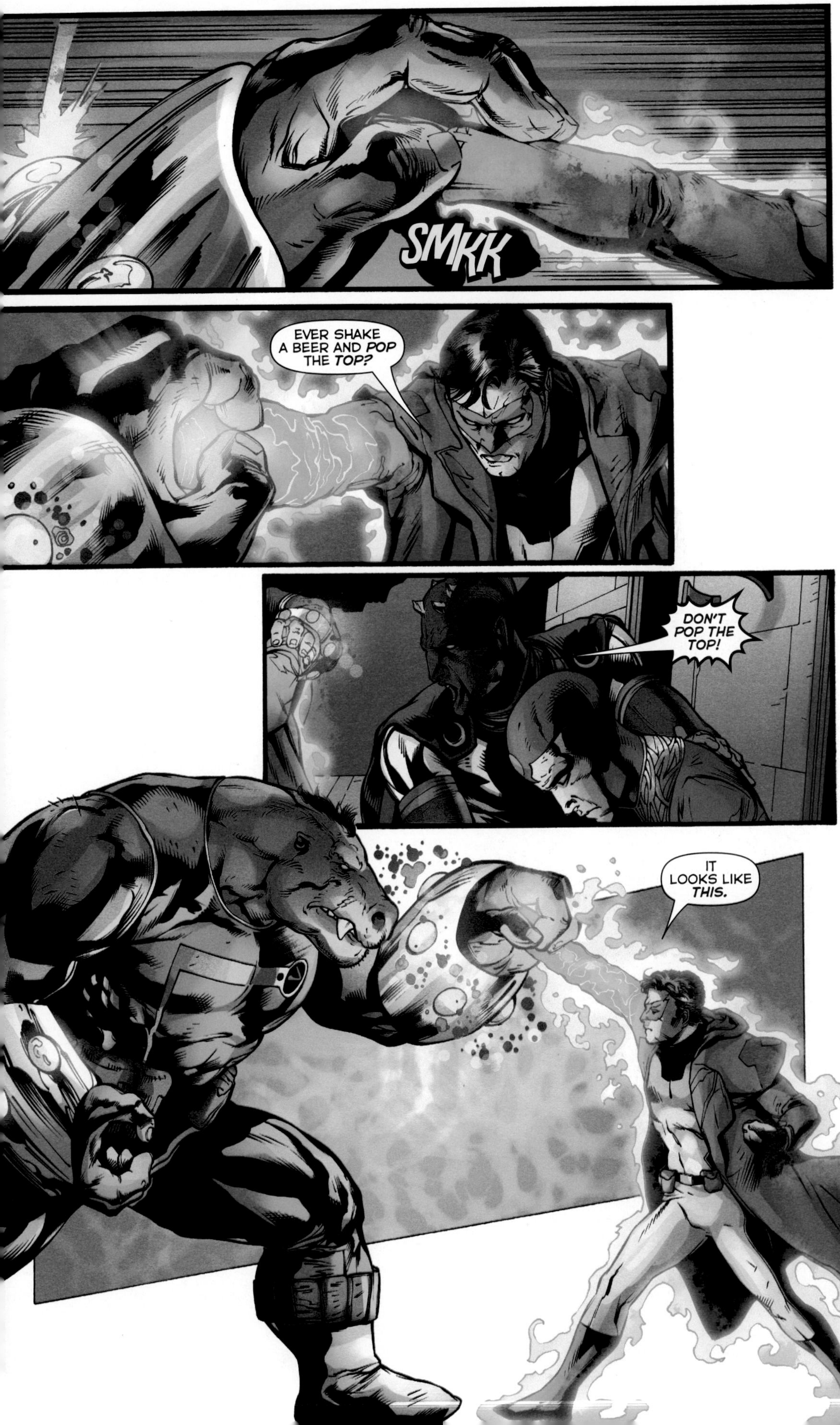
SMKK
EVER SHAKE A BEER AND POP THE TOP?
DON'T POP THE TOP!
IT LOOKS LIKE THIS.

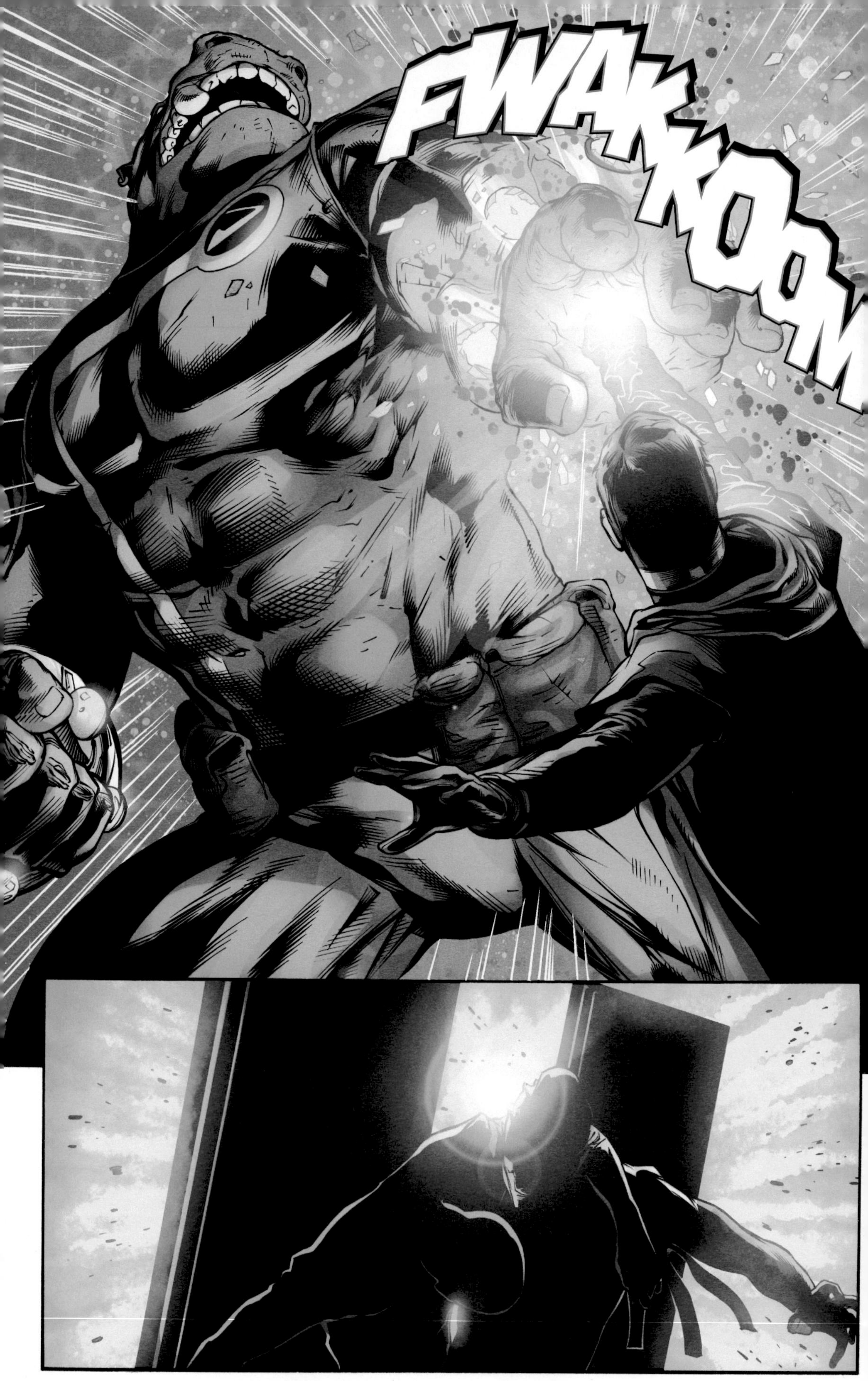
FWAKKOOM

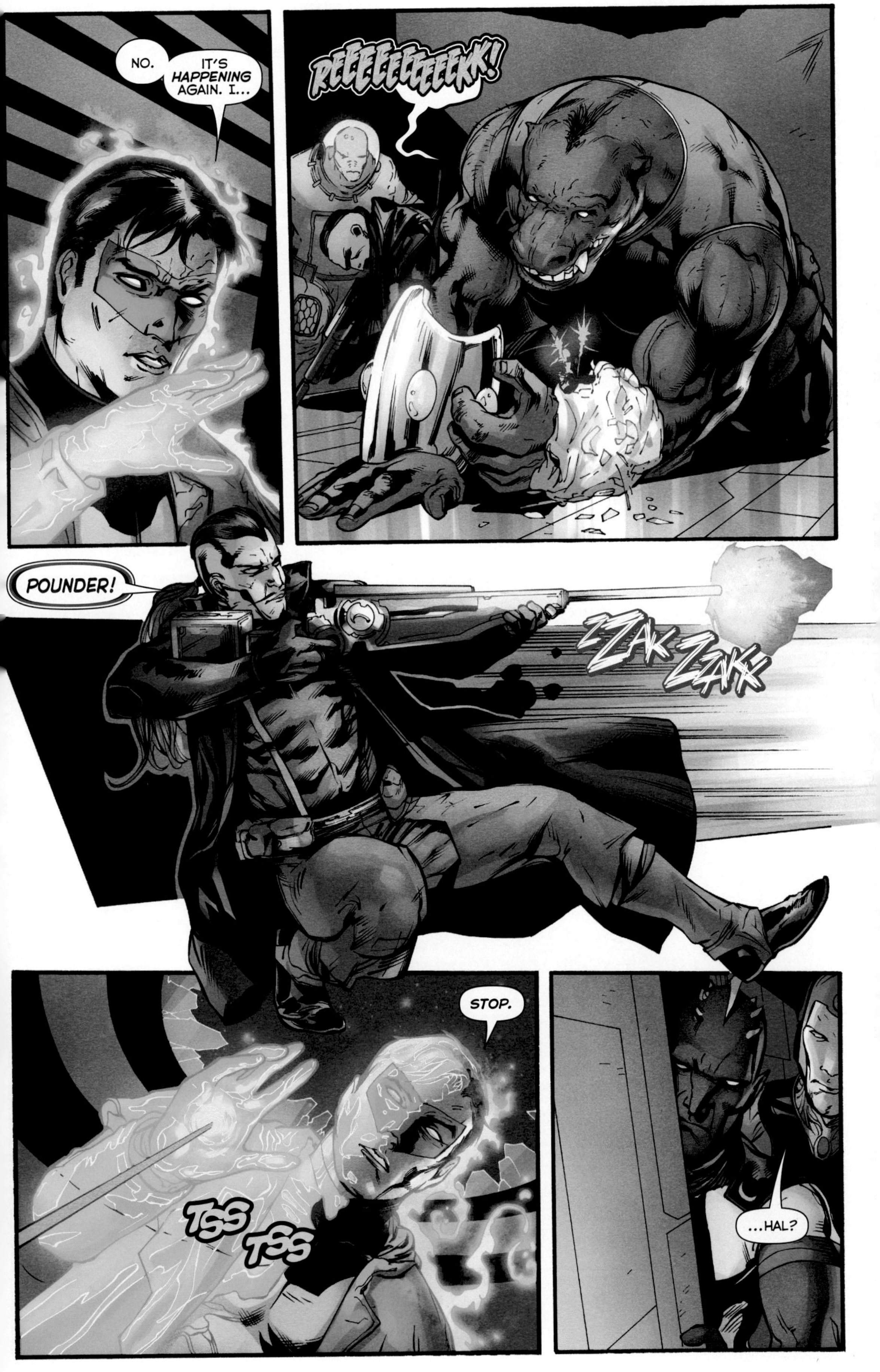
NO.
IT'S HAPPENING AGAIN. I...
REEEEEEEEEEEEKK!
POUNDER!
ZZAK ZZAKK
STOP.
TSS TSS
...HAL?

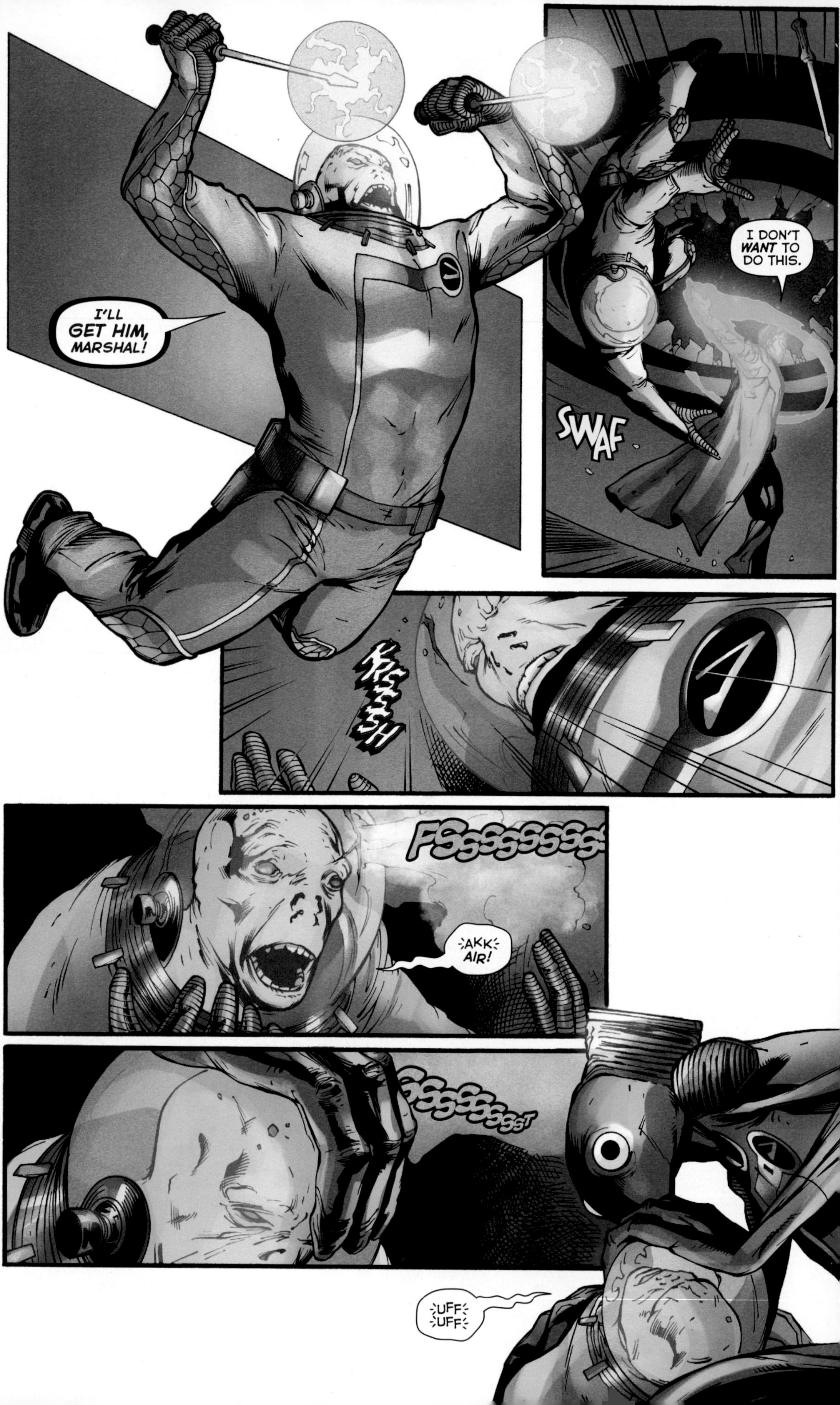
I'LL GET HIM, MARSHAL!
I DON'T WANT TO DO THIS.
SWAF
KRSSSH
FSSSSSSSSS
AKK AIR!
SSSSSSSSST
UFF UFF

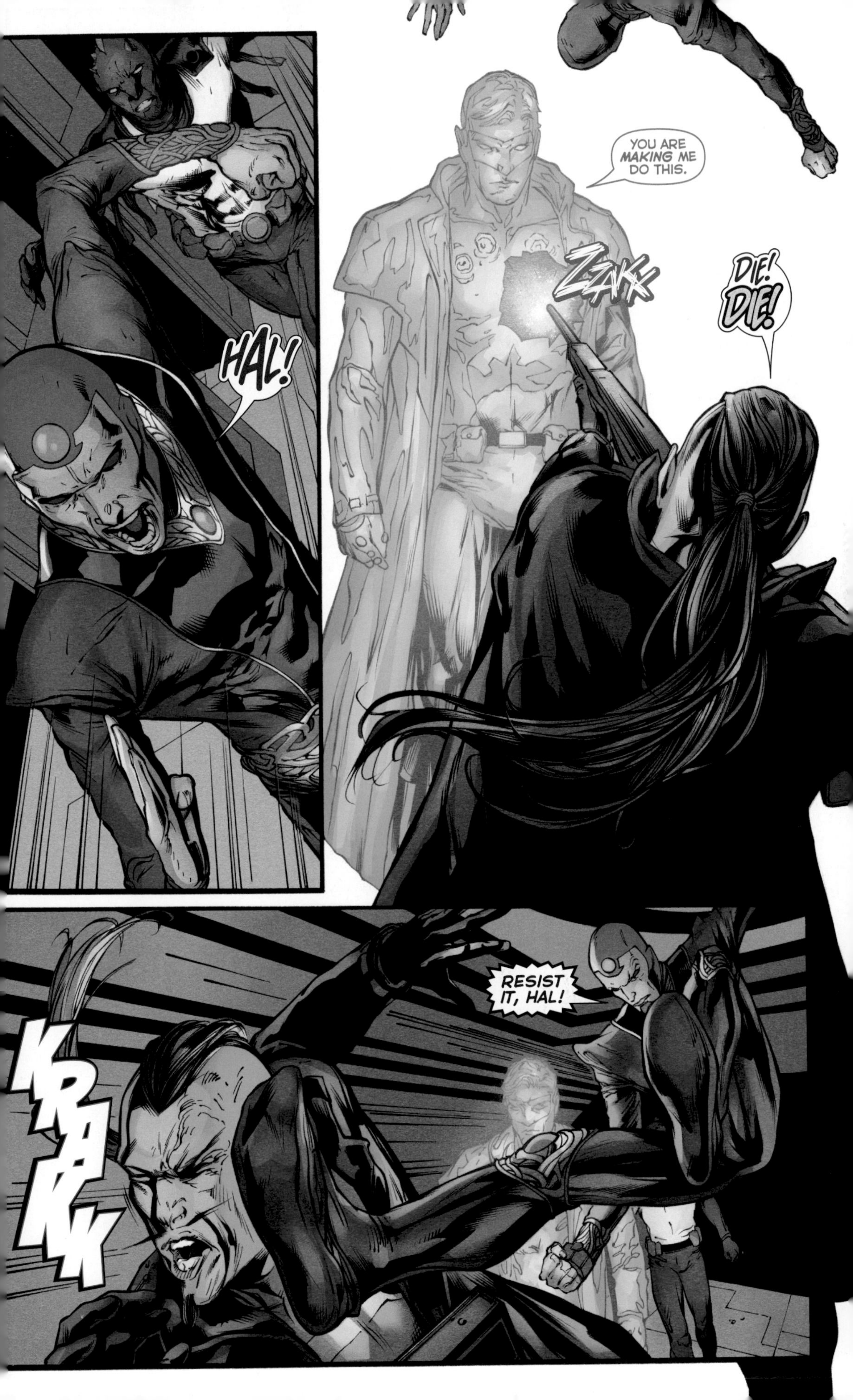
HAL!
YOU ARE MAKING ME DO THIS.
ZZAKK
DIE! DIE!
RESIST IT, HAL!
KRAKK

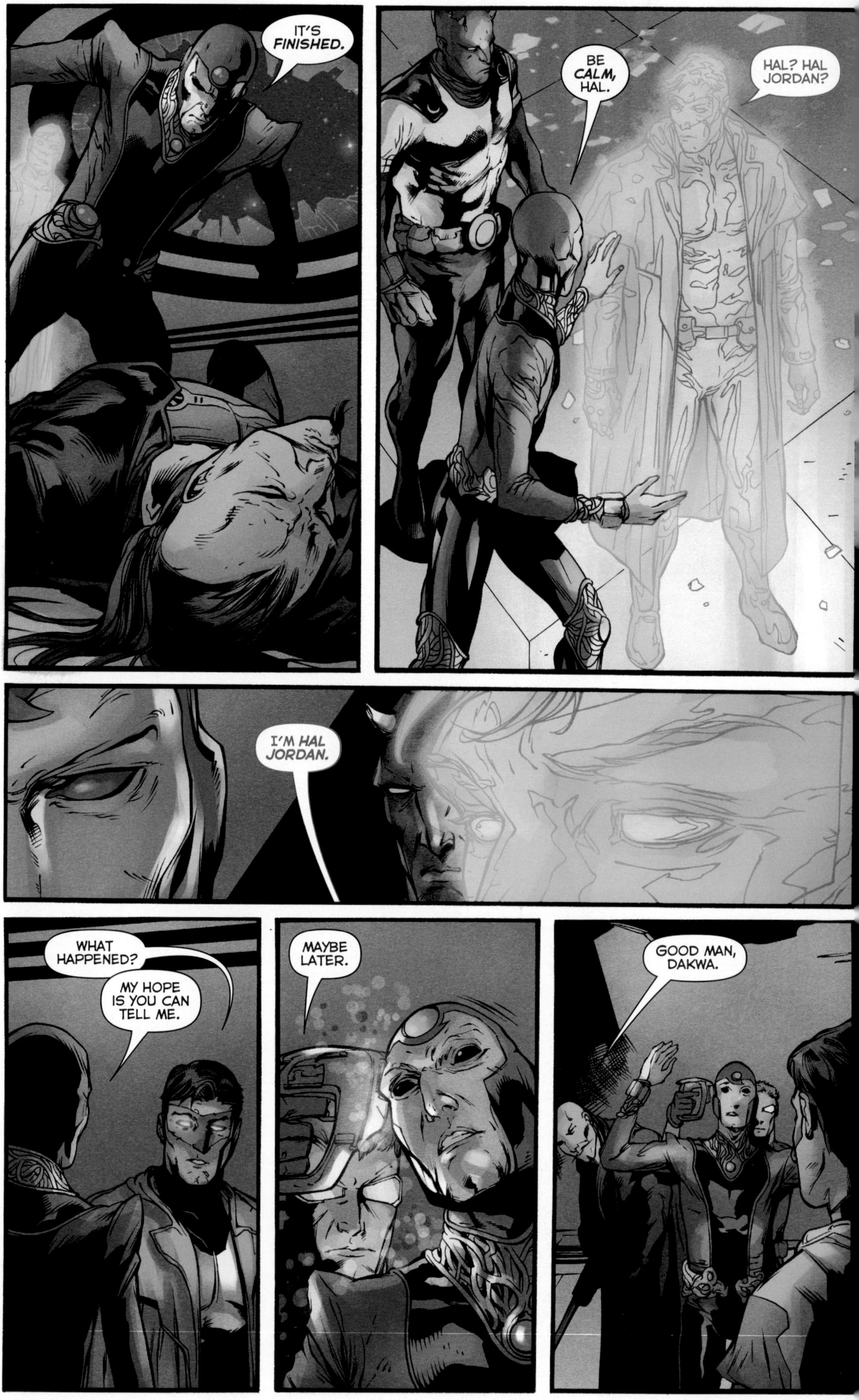
IT'S FINISHED.
BE CALM, HAL.
HAL? HAL JORDAN?
I'M HAL JORDAN.
WHAT HAPPENED?
MY HOPE IS YOU CAN TELL ME.
MAYBE LATER.
GOOD MAN, DAKWA.

YOU'RE **DONE**, JORDAN. TAKE OFF THE GLOVE, AND YOUR FRIEND LIVES. DON'T, HE **DIES**. THE REST SHAKES OUT HOW IT SHAKES OUT.

EASY ON THE TRIGGER, NOW.

WHAT'S THIS ABOUT, RANKK? WE CROSS PATHS SOMEWHERE AND I DON'T REMEMBER?

THE UNIVERSE IS UP FOR GRABS. THE GREEN LANTERN CORPS IS **GONE**.

MEANS THERE'S A **HOLE** WAITING TO BE FILLED. WE FILL IT, EVERYTHING IS OURS FOR THE TAKING. AND IT'LL BE **LEGAL**.

SPOKEN LIKE A TRUE **LAWMAN**.

YOU'RE THE UNIVERSE'S **MOST WANTED**, JORDAN. WE EXECUTE YOU ON LIVE VID FEED TO A **THOUSAND** WORLDS, PEOPLE WILL BEG TO HAVE A SQUAD OF GRAY AGENTS IN EVERY SECTOR. WE'LL RUN IT **ALL**.

QUESTION IS, ARE YOU **MAN** ENOUGH TO ACCEPT YOUR PUNISHMENT? OR ARE YOU GOING TO LET MR. BLUE DIE INSTEAD?

DON'T LISTEN, HAL. JUST **GO**.

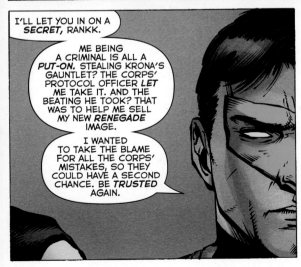

I'LL LET YOU IN ON A **SECRET**, RANKK.

ME BEING A CRIMINAL IS ALL A **PUT-ON**. STEALING KRONA'S GAUNTLET? THE CORPS' PROTOCOL OFFICER **LET** ME TAKE IT. AND THE BEATING HE TOOK? THAT WAS TO HELP ME SELL MY NEW **RENEGADE** IMAGE.

I WANTED TO TAKE THE BLAME FOR ALL THE CORPS' MISTAKES, SO THEY COULD HAVE A SECOND CHANCE. BE **TRUSTED** AGAIN.

DOESN'T MATTER IF YOU'RE A REAL CRIMINAL OR NOT. ALL THAT MATTERS IS THE UNIVERSE **THINKS** YOU ARE.

THAT'S THE ONLY **TRUTH** I NEED.

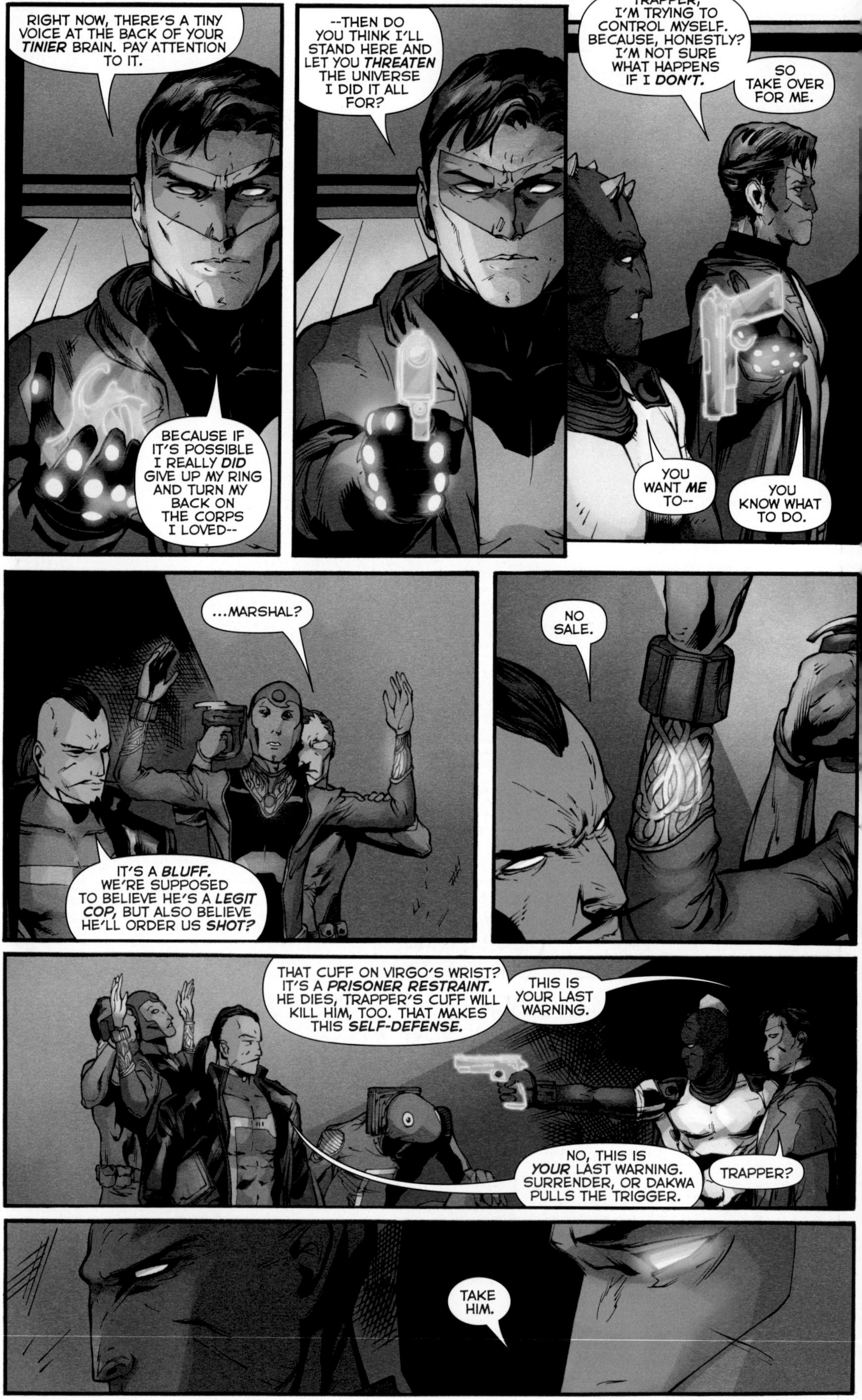
RIGHT NOW, THERE'S A TINY VOICE AT THE BACK OF YOUR TINIER BRAIN. PAY ATTENTION TO IT.
BECAUSE IF IT'S POSSIBLE I REALLY DID GIVE UP MY RING AND TURN MY BACK ON THE CORPS I LOVED--
--THEN DO YOU THINK I'LL STAND HERE AND LET YOU THREATEN THE UNIVERSE I DID IT ALL FOR?
TRAPPER, I'M TRYING TO CONTROL MYSELF. BECAUSE, HONESTLY? I'M NOT SURE WHAT HAPPENS IF I DON'T.
SO TAKE OVER FOR ME.
YOU WANT ME TO--
YOU KNOW WHAT TO DO.
...MARSHAL?
IT'S A BLUFF. WE'RE SUPPOSED TO BELIEVE HE'S A LEGIT COP, BUT ALSO BELIEVE HE'LL ORDER US SHOT?
NO SALE.
THAT CUFF ON VIRGO'S WRIST? IT'S A PRISONER RESTRAINT. HE DIES, TRAPPER'S CUFF WILL KILL HIM, TOO. THAT MAKES THIS SELF-DEFENSE.
THIS IS YOUR LAST WARNING.
NO, THIS IS YOUR LAST WARNING. SURRENDER, OR DAKWA PULLS THE TRIGGER.
TRAPPER?
TAKE HIM.

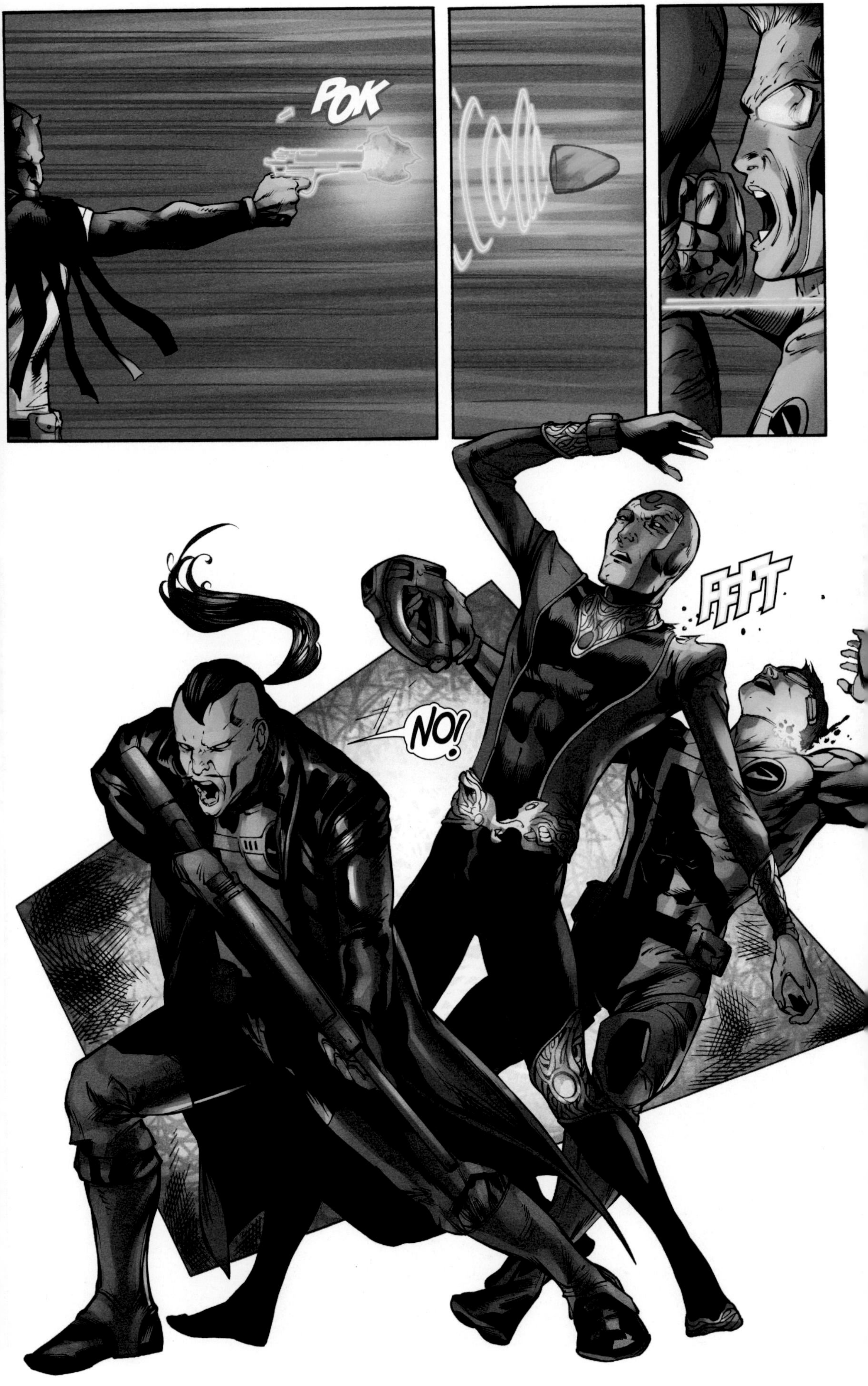
POK
NO!
FFFT

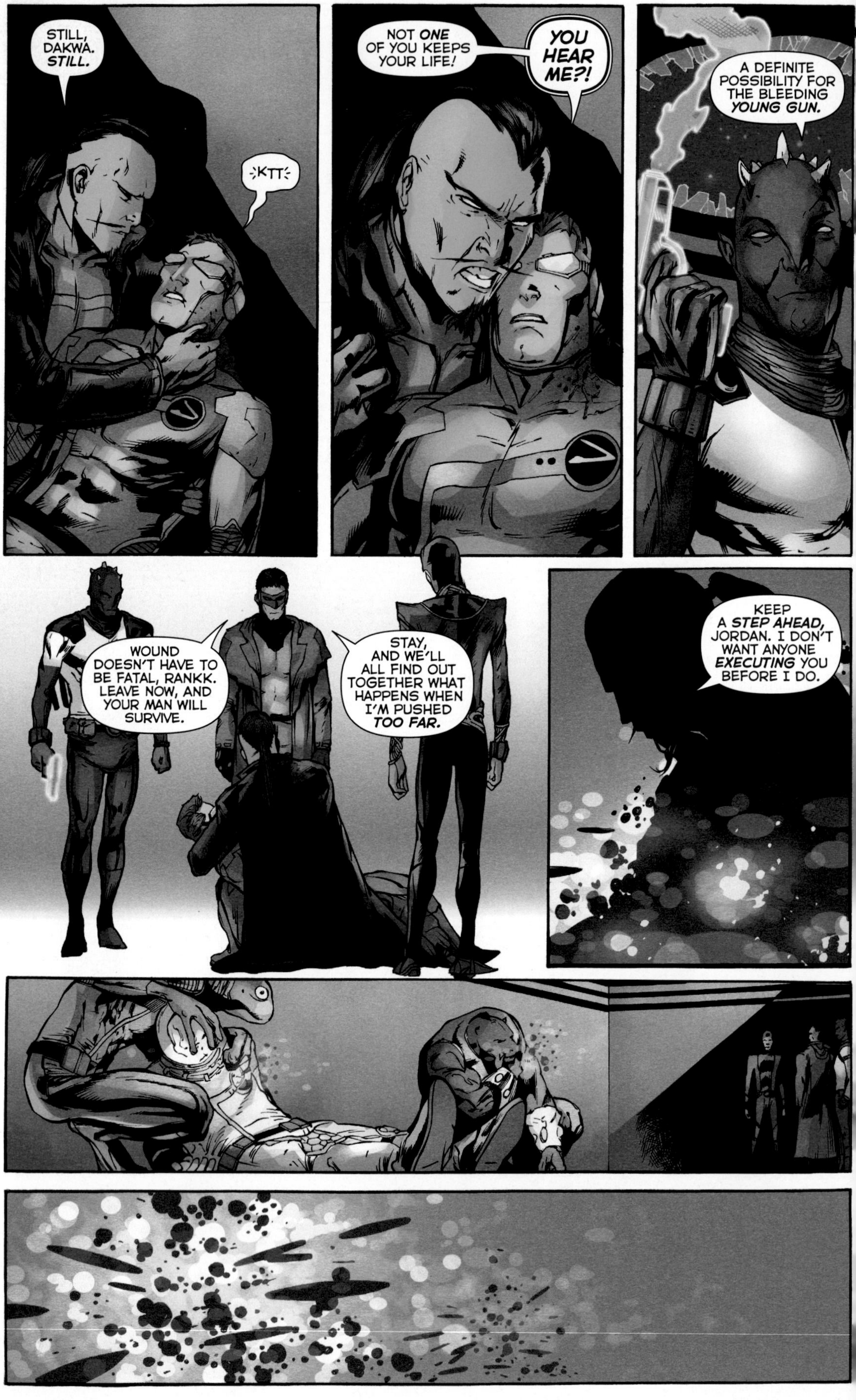
STILL, DAKWA. STILL.
KTT
NOT ONE OF YOU KEEPS YOUR LIFE!
YOU HEAR ME?!
A DEFINITE POSSIBILITY FOR THE BLEEDING YOUNG GUN.
WOUND DOESN'T HAVE TO BE FATAL, RANKK. LEAVE NOW, AND YOUR MAN WILL SURVIVE.
STAY, AND WE'LL ALL FIND OUT TOGETHER WHAT HAPPENS WHEN I'M PUSHED TOO FAR.
KEEP A STEP AHEAD, JORDAN. I DON'T WANT ANYONE EXECUTING YOU BEFORE I DO.

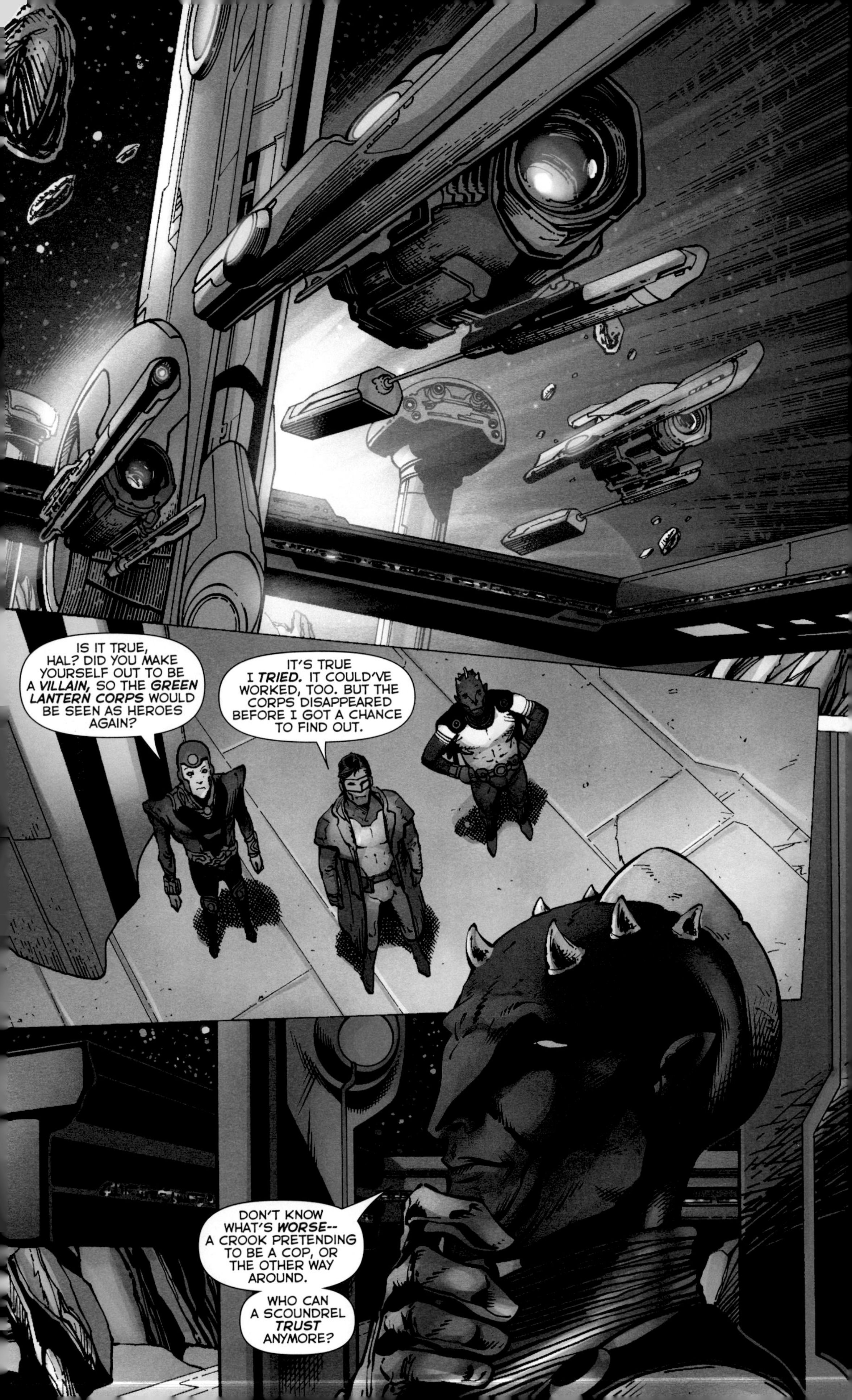
IS IT TRUE, HAL? DID YOU MAKE YOURSELF OUT TO BE A VILLAIN, SO THE GREEN LANTERN CORPS WOULD BE SEEN AS HEROES AGAIN?
IT'S TRUE I TRIED. IT COULD'VE WORKED, TOO. BUT THE CORPS DISAPPEARED BEFORE I GOT A CHANCE TO FIND OUT.
DON'T KNOW WHAT'S WORSE-- A CROOK PRETENDING TO BE A COP, OR THE OTHER WAY AROUND.
WHO CAN A SCOUNDREL TRUST ANYMORE?

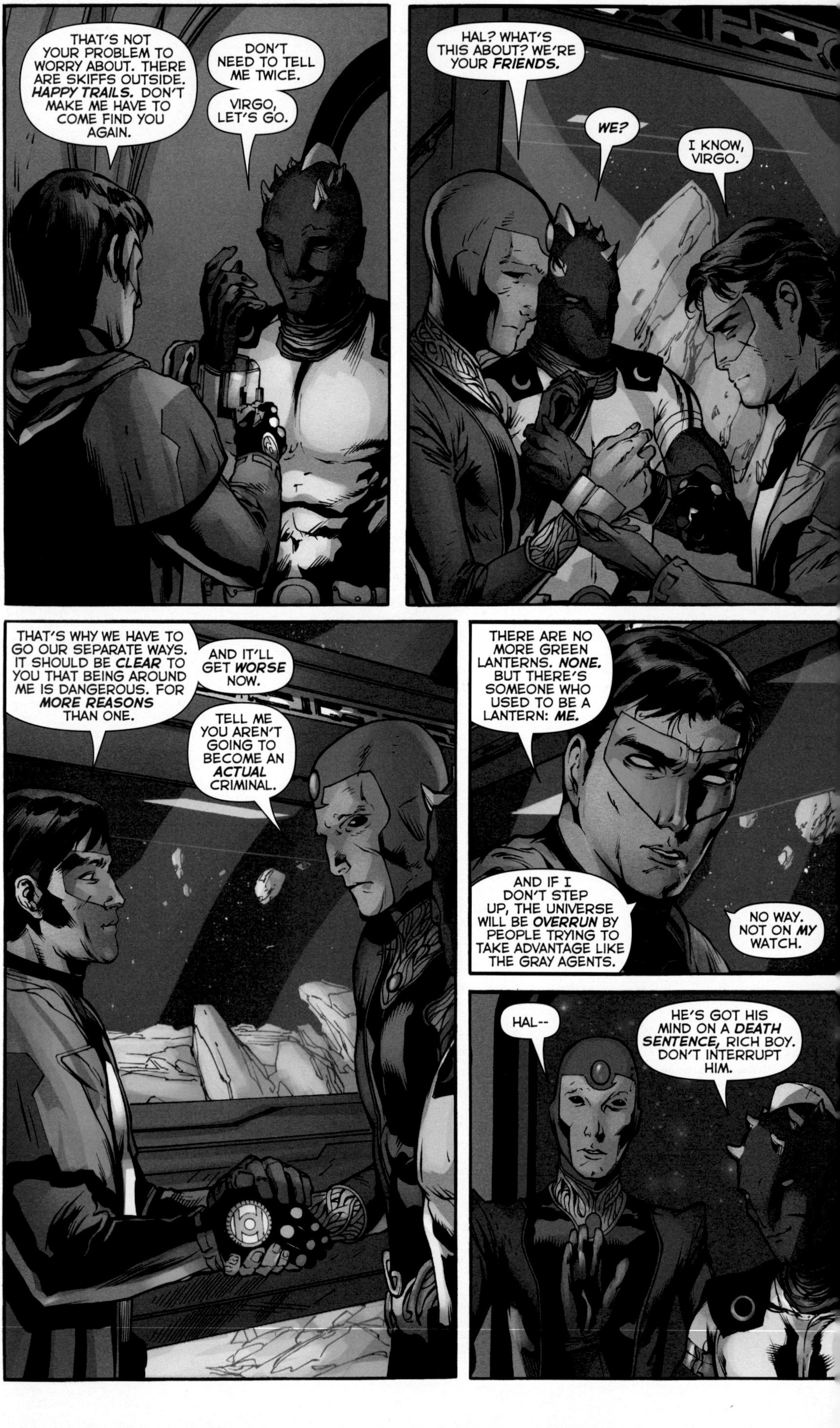
THAT'S NOT YOUR PROBLEM TO WORRY ABOUT. THERE ARE SKIFFS OUTSIDE. HAPPY TRAILS. DON'T MAKE ME HAVE TO COME FIND YOU AGAIN.
DON'T NEED TO TELL ME TWICE.
VIRGO, LET'S GO.
HAL? WHAT'S THIS ABOUT? WE'RE YOUR FRIENDS.
WE?
I KNOW, VIRGO.
THAT'S WHY WE HAVE TO GO OUR SEPARATE WAYS. IT SHOULD BE CLEAR TO YOU THAT BEING AROUND ME IS DANGEROUS. FOR MORE REASONS THAN ONE.
AND IT'LL GET WORSE NOW.
TELL ME YOU AREN'T GOING TO BECOME AN ACTUAL CRIMINAL.
THERE ARE NO MORE GREEN LANTERNS. NONE. BUT THERE'S SOMEONE WHO USED TO BE A LANTERN: ME.
AND IF I DON'T STEP UP, THE UNIVERSE WILL BE OVERRUN BY PEOPLE TRYING TO TAKE ADVANTAGE LIKE THE GRAY AGENTS.
NO WAY. NOT ON MY WATCH.
HAL--
HE'S GOT HIS MIND ON A DEATH SENTENCE, RICH BOY. DON'T INTERRUPT HIM.

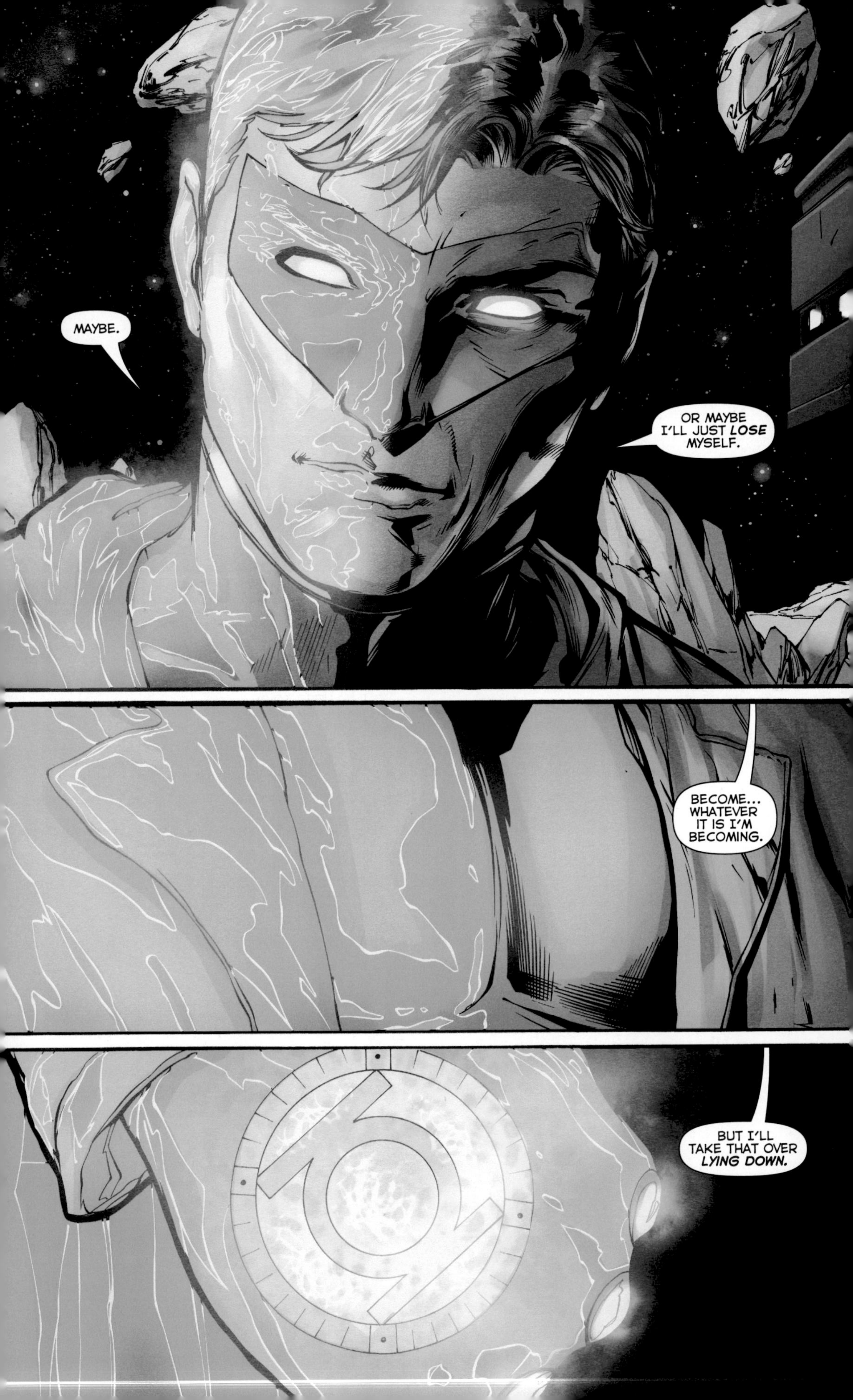
MAYBE.
OR MAYBE I'LL JUST *LOSE* MYSELF.
BECOME... WHATEVER IT IS I'M BECOMING.
BUT I'LL TAKE THAT OVER ***LYING DOWN.***

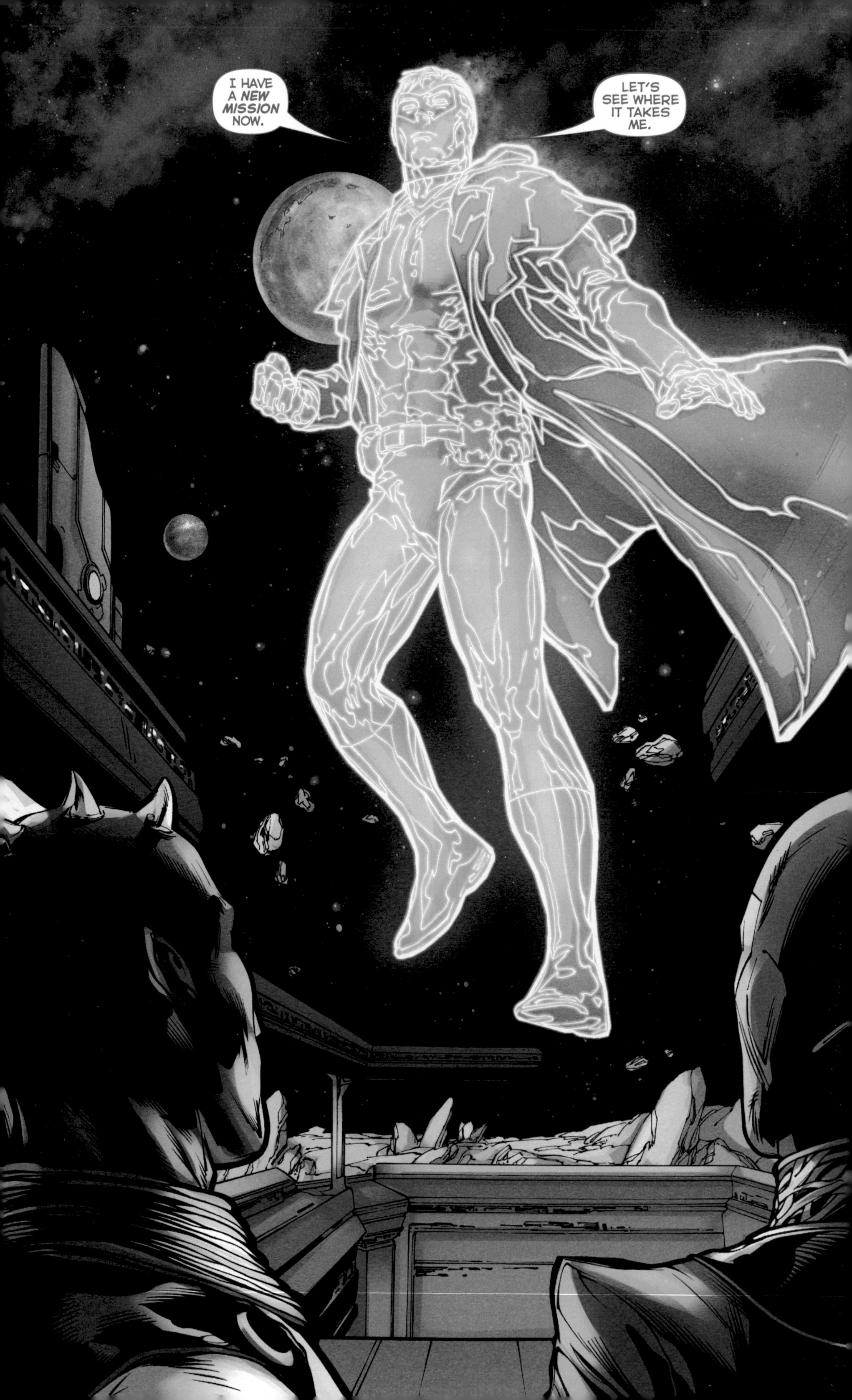
I HAVE A NEW MISSION NOW.
LET'S SEE WHERE IT TAKES ME.

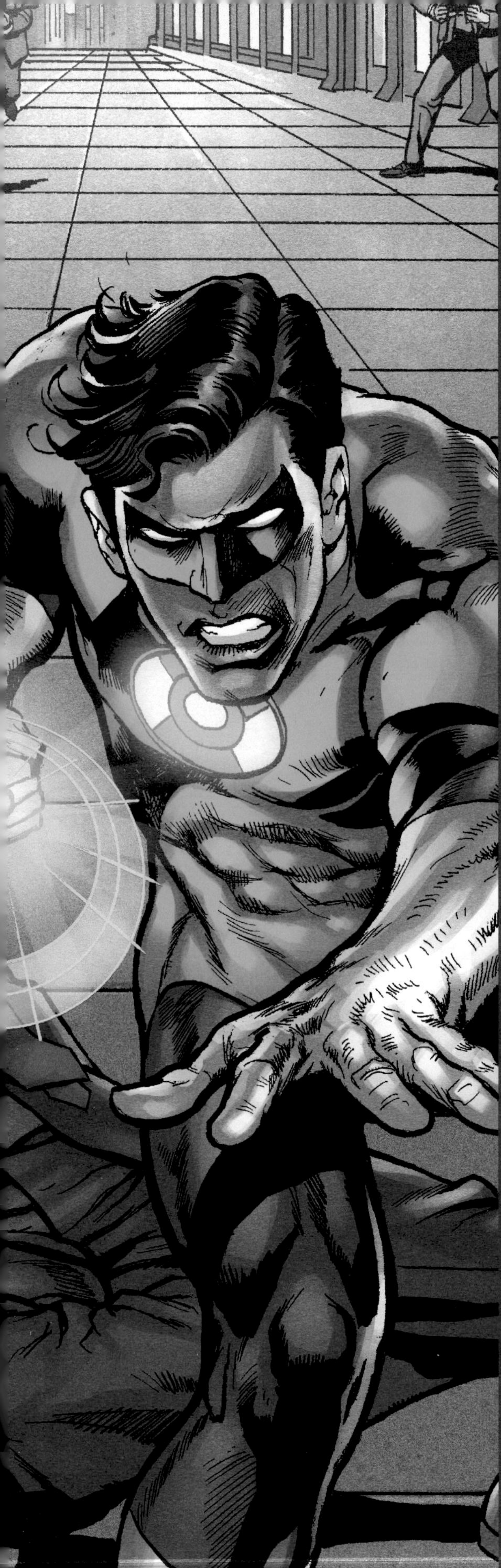

VARIANT COVER GALLERY

GREEN LANTERN #47
HARLEY'S LITTLE BLACK BOOK
VARIANT BY DARWYN COOKE

GREEN LANTERN #48
ADULT COLORING BOOK VARIANT
BY MIKE ALLRED

GREEN LANTERN #49
VARIANT BY NEAL ADAMS,
KEVIN NOWLAN & ALEX SINCLAIR

GREEN LANTERN #50
BATMAN V SUPERMAN VARIANT BY
DOUG MAHNKE,
SANDRA HOPE ARCHER
& DINISIO CARMINE MORENO

GREEN LANTERN #51
VARIANT BY JOHN ROMITA JR.,
KLAUS JANSON & LAURA MARTIN

GREEN LANTERN #52
THE NEW 52 VARIANT
BY BILLY TAN & ALEX SINCLAIR

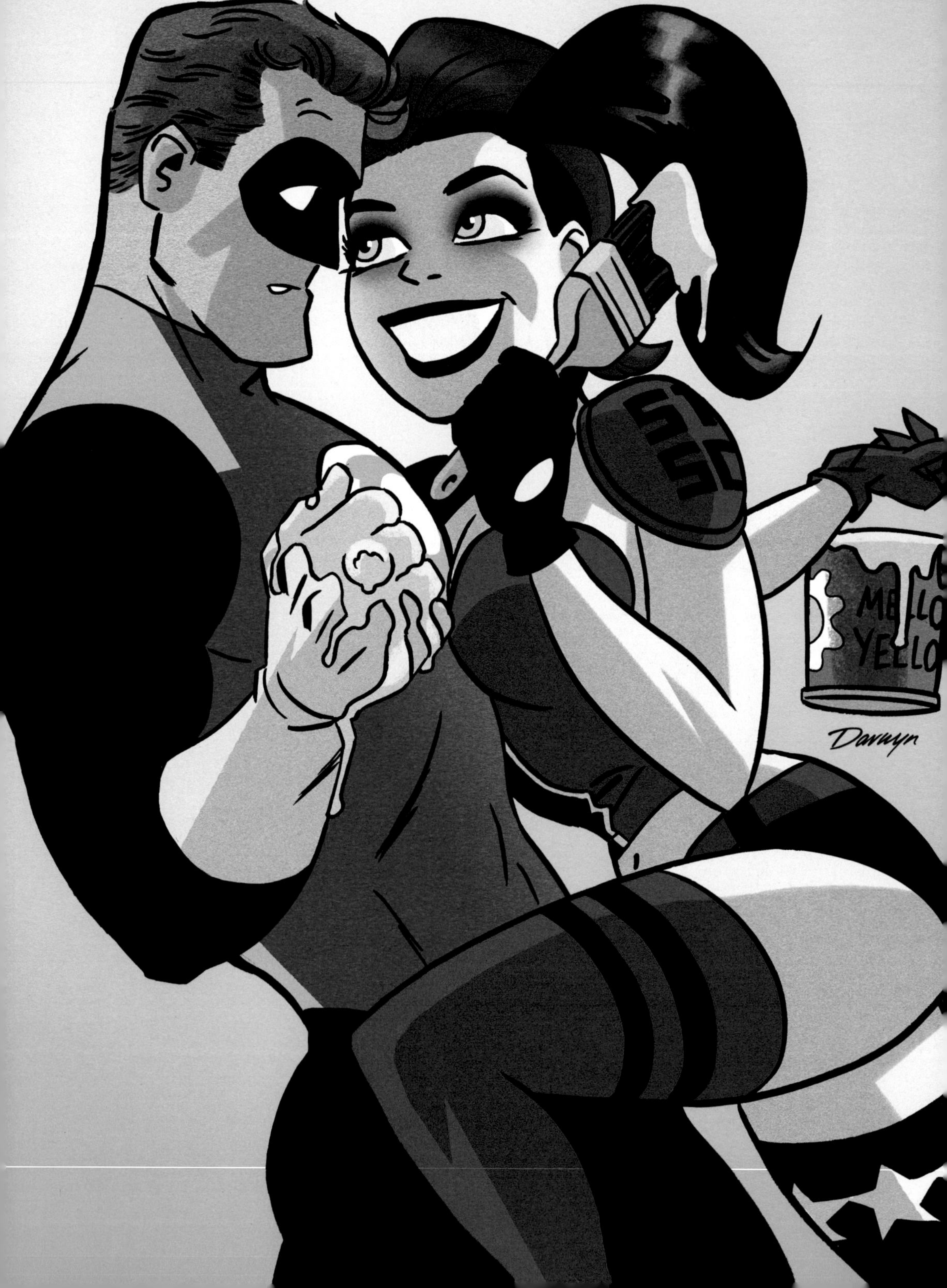

MELLO
YELLO
Darwyn

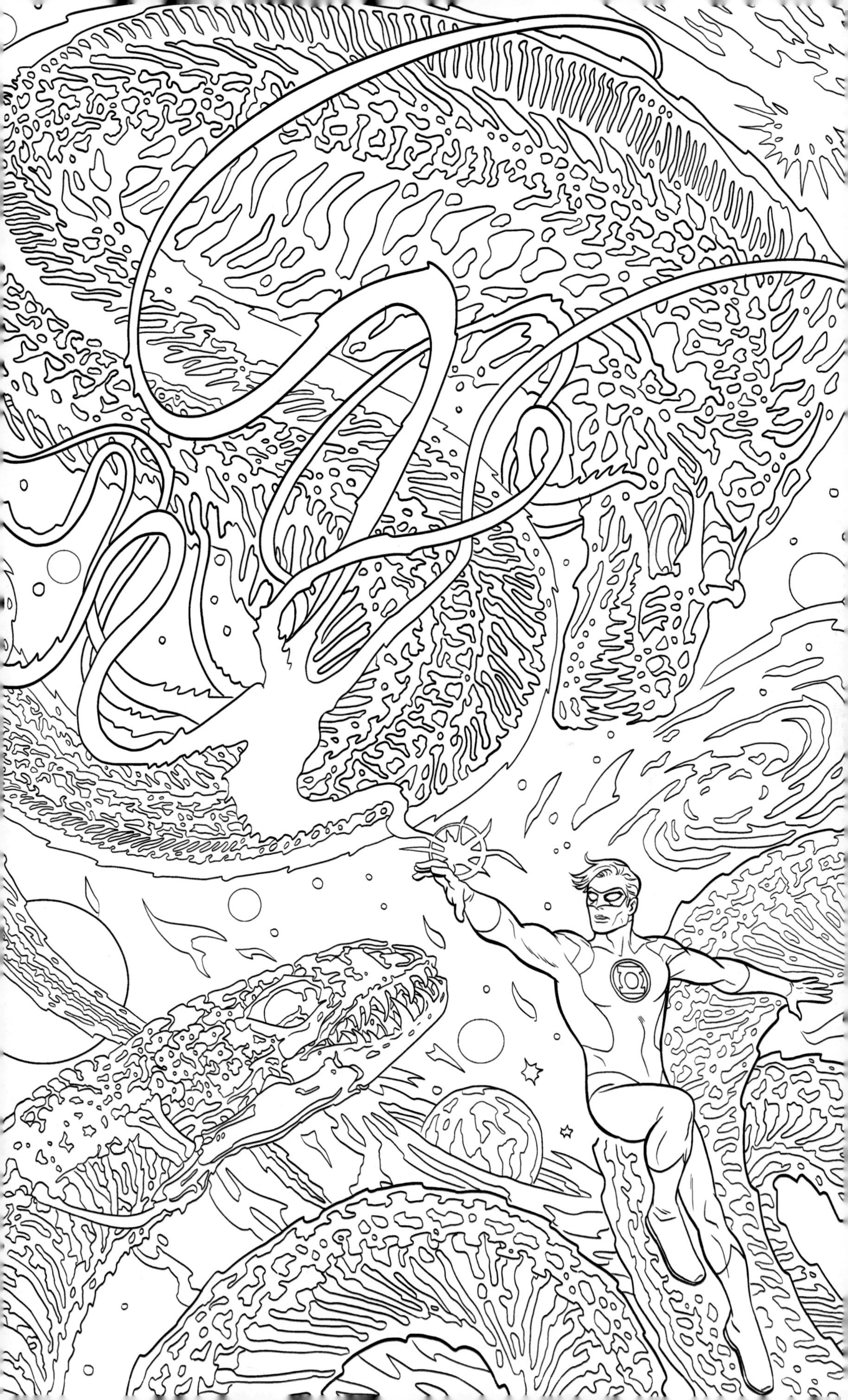

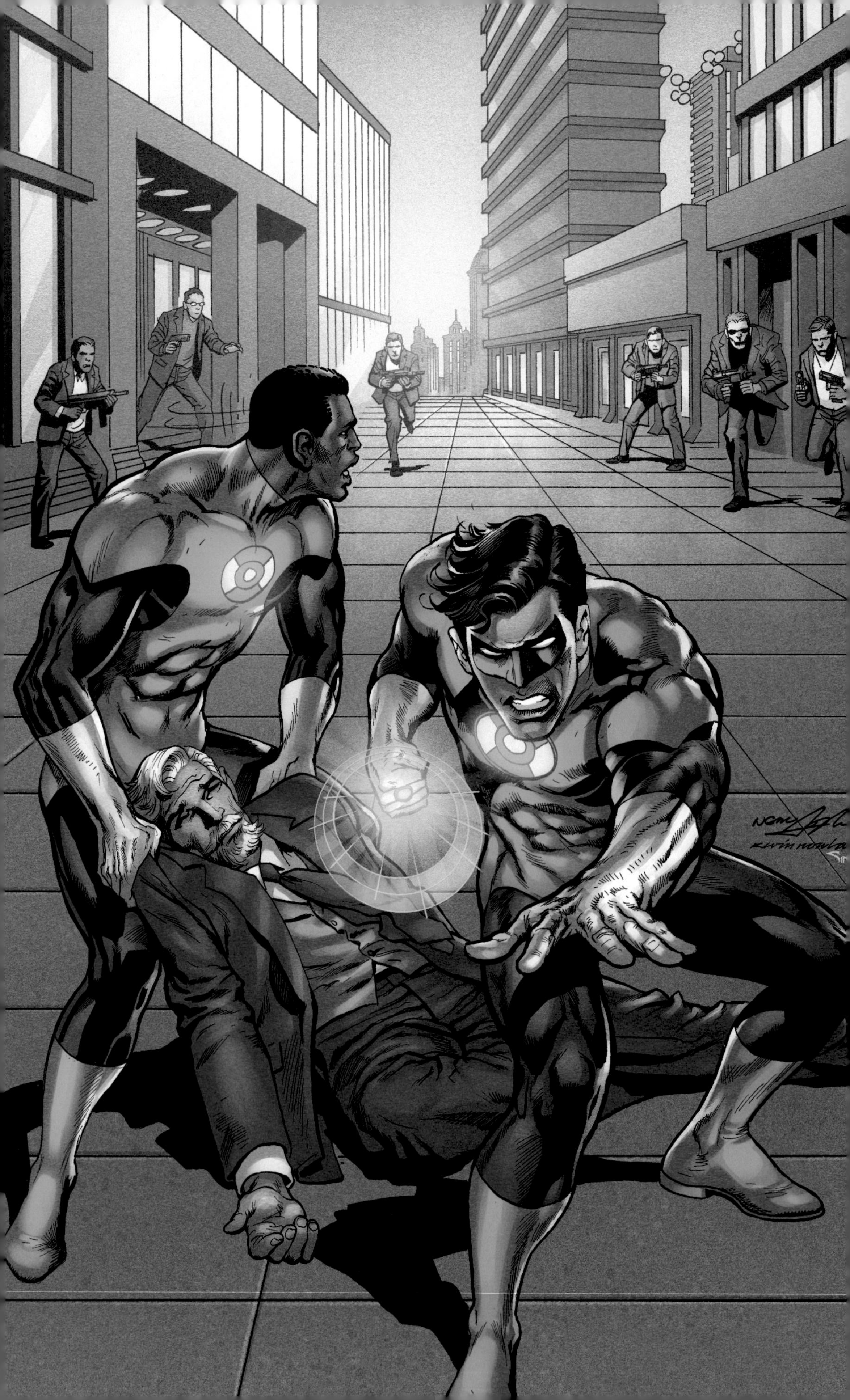

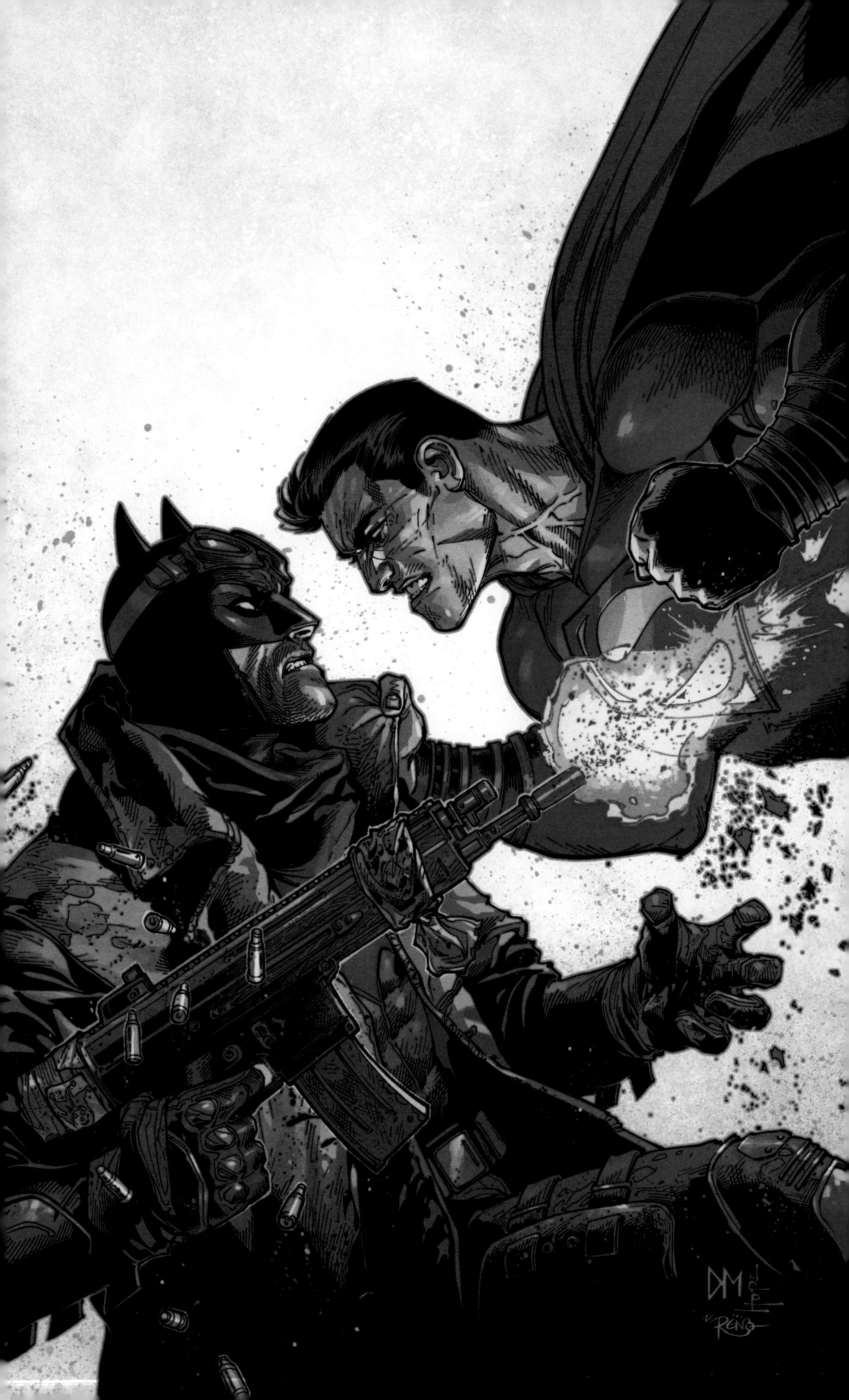

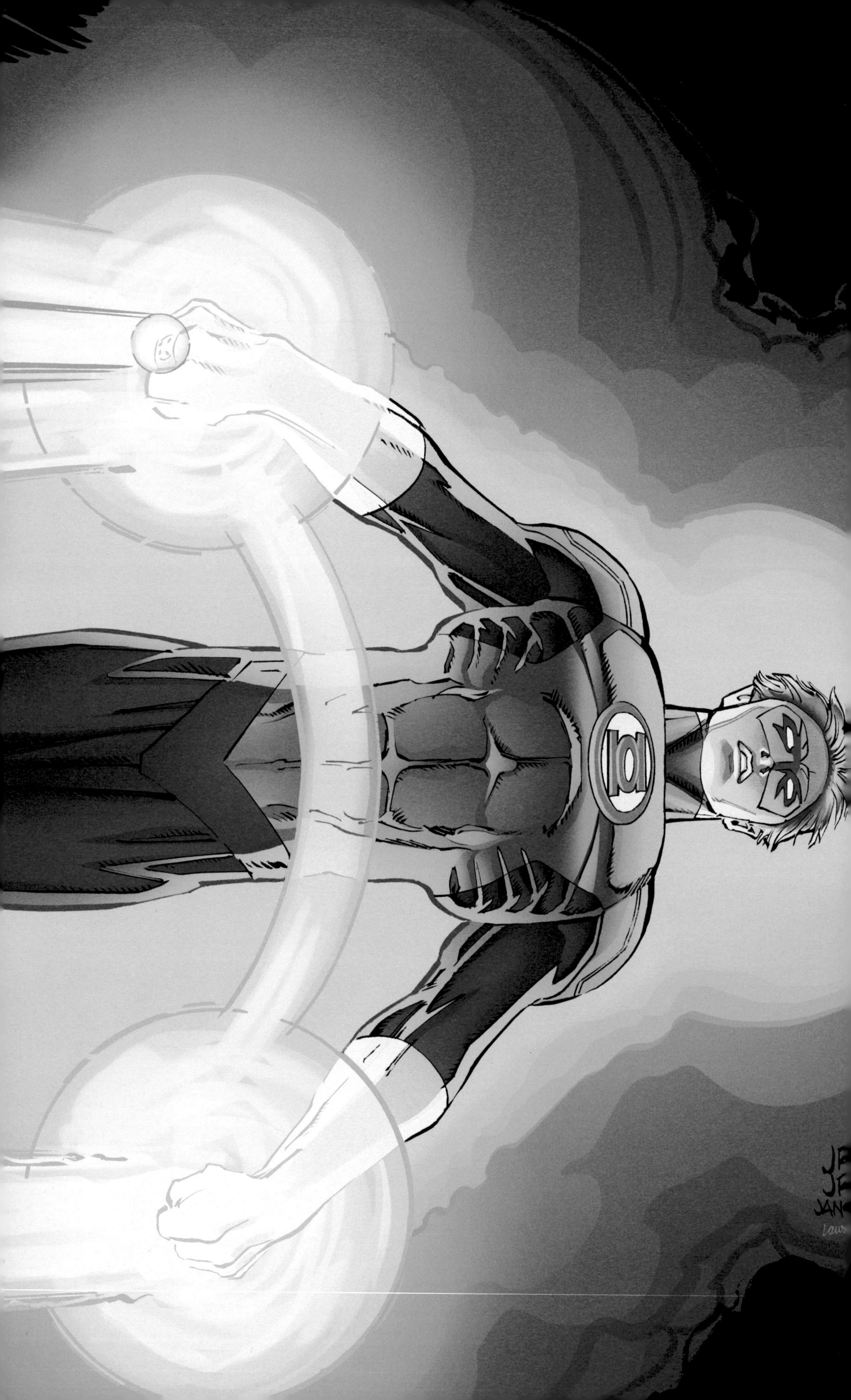

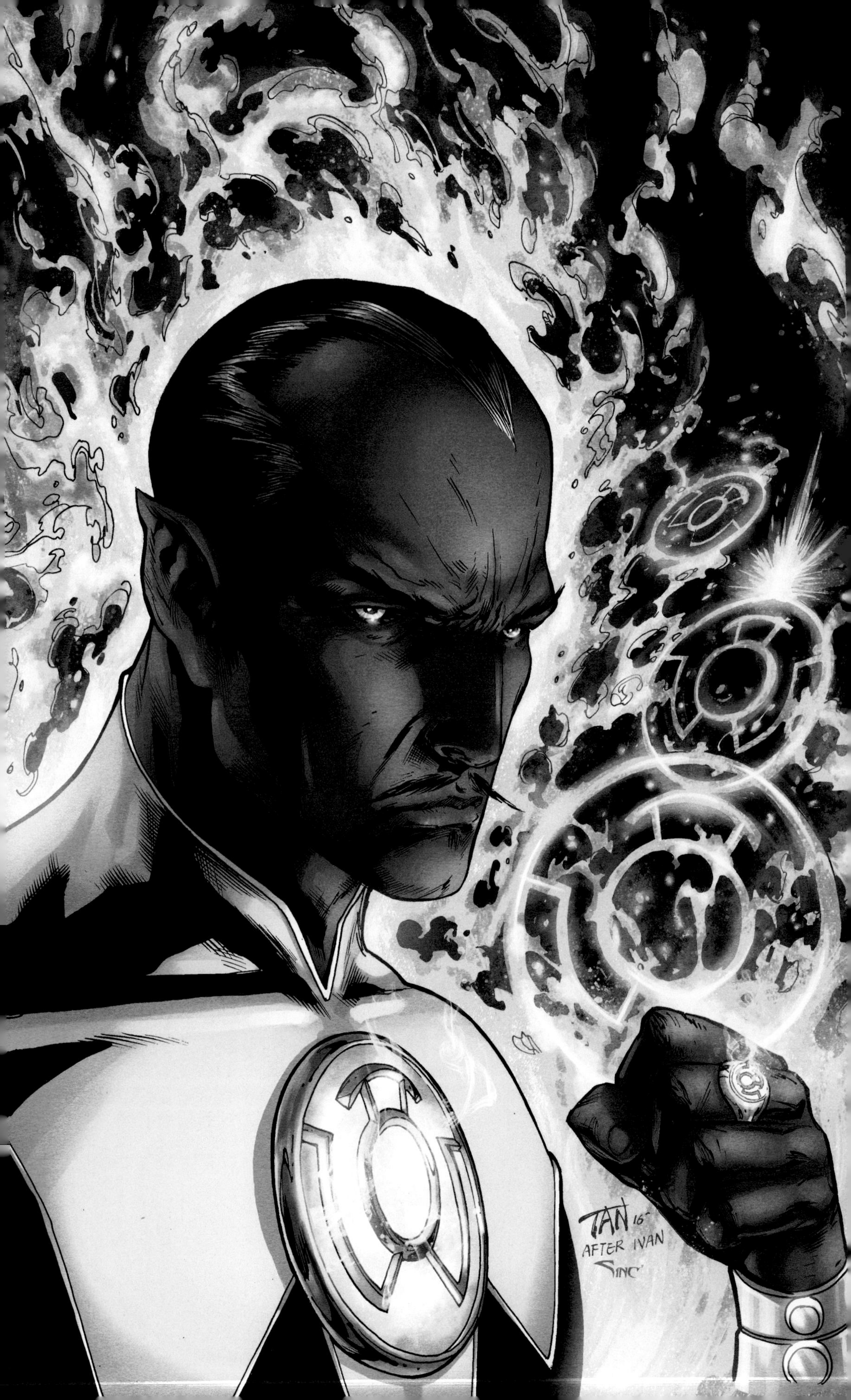
TAN 16'
AFTER IVAN
SINC'

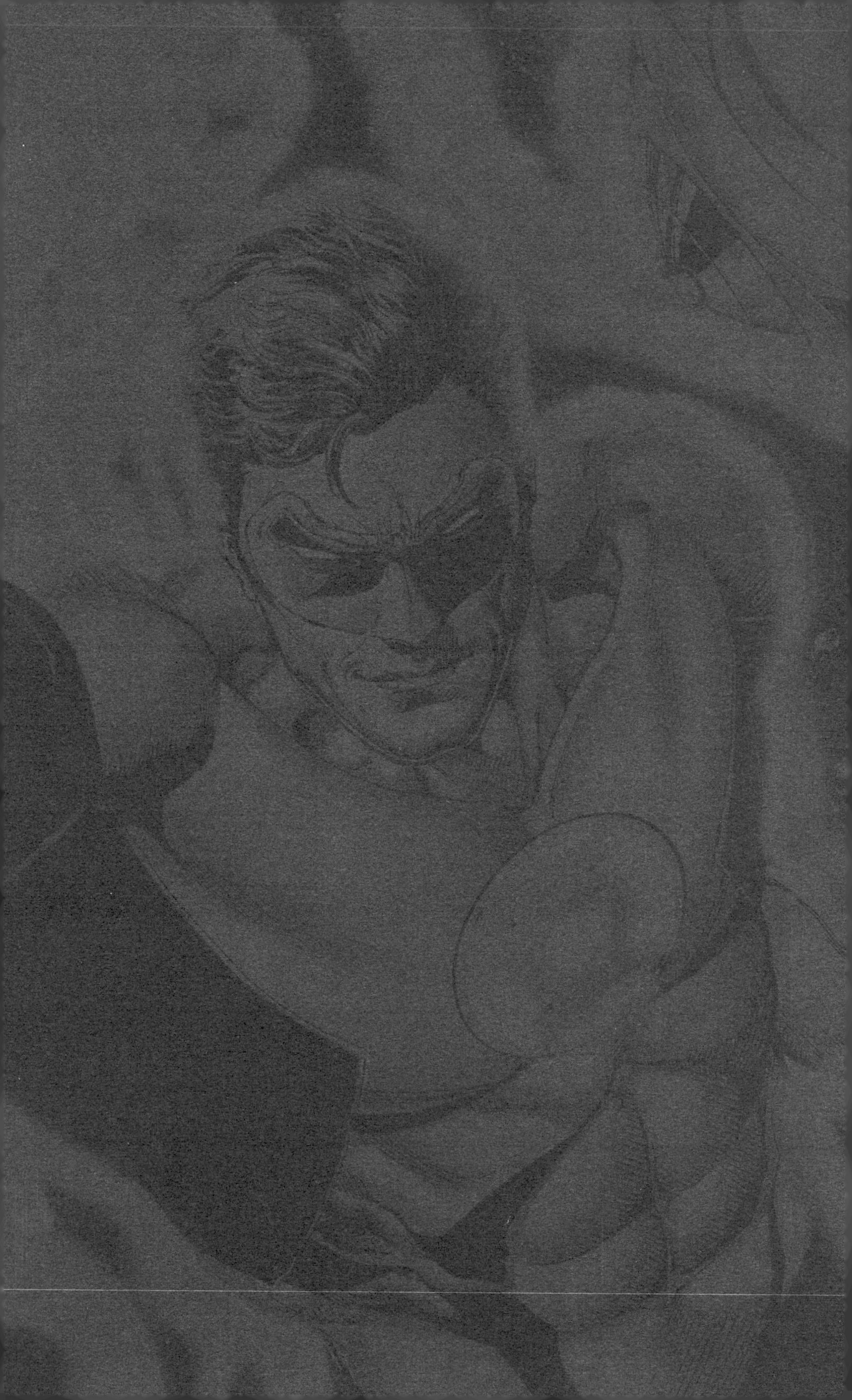

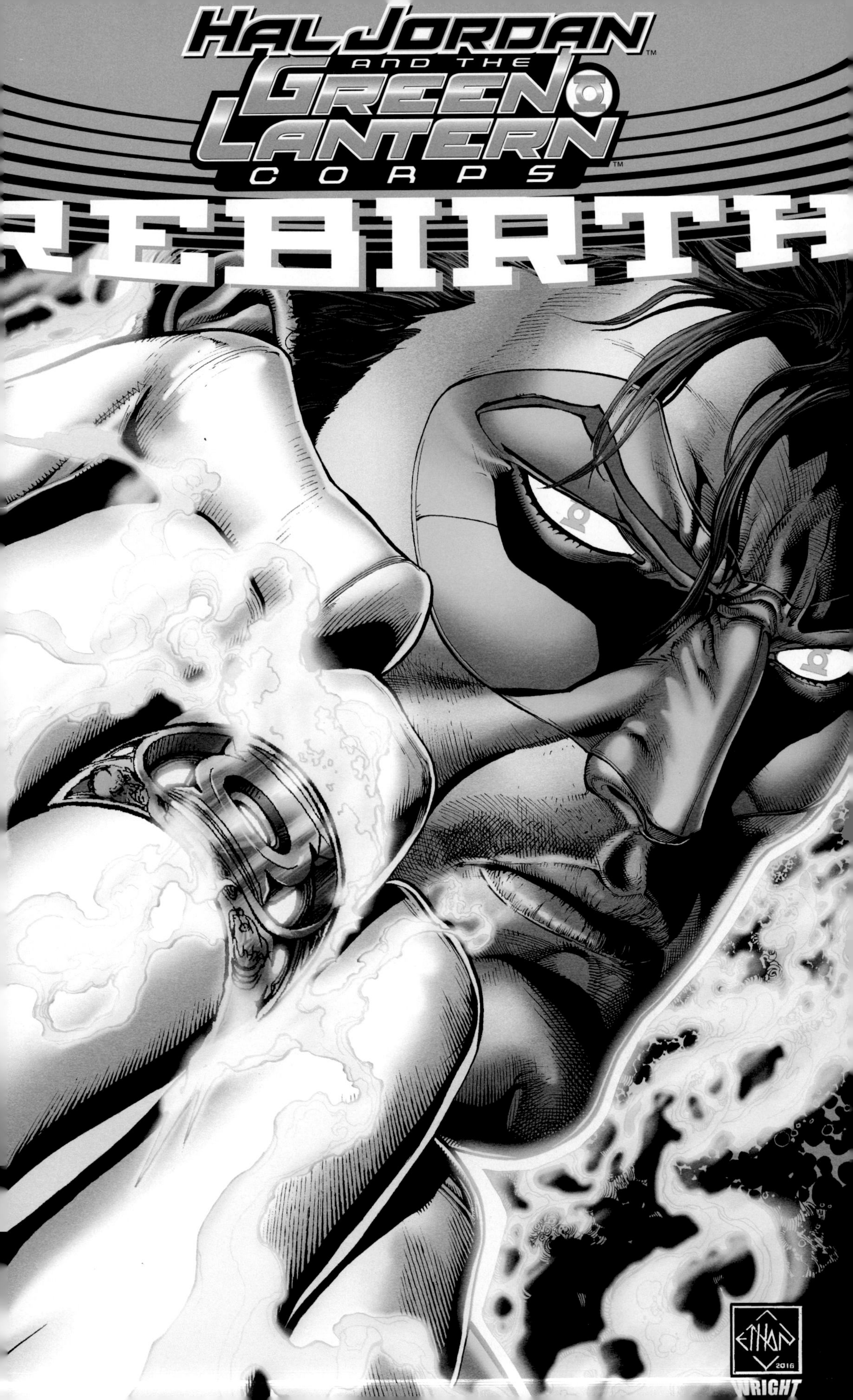
HAL JORDAN AND THE GREEN LANTERN CORPS
REBIRTH
WRIGHT

The future (and past) of the DC Universe starts with DC UNIVERSE: REBIRTH!

Explore the changing world of GREEN LANTERN in this special bonus preview of **HAL JORDAN & THE GREEN LANTERN CORPS: REBIRTH**!

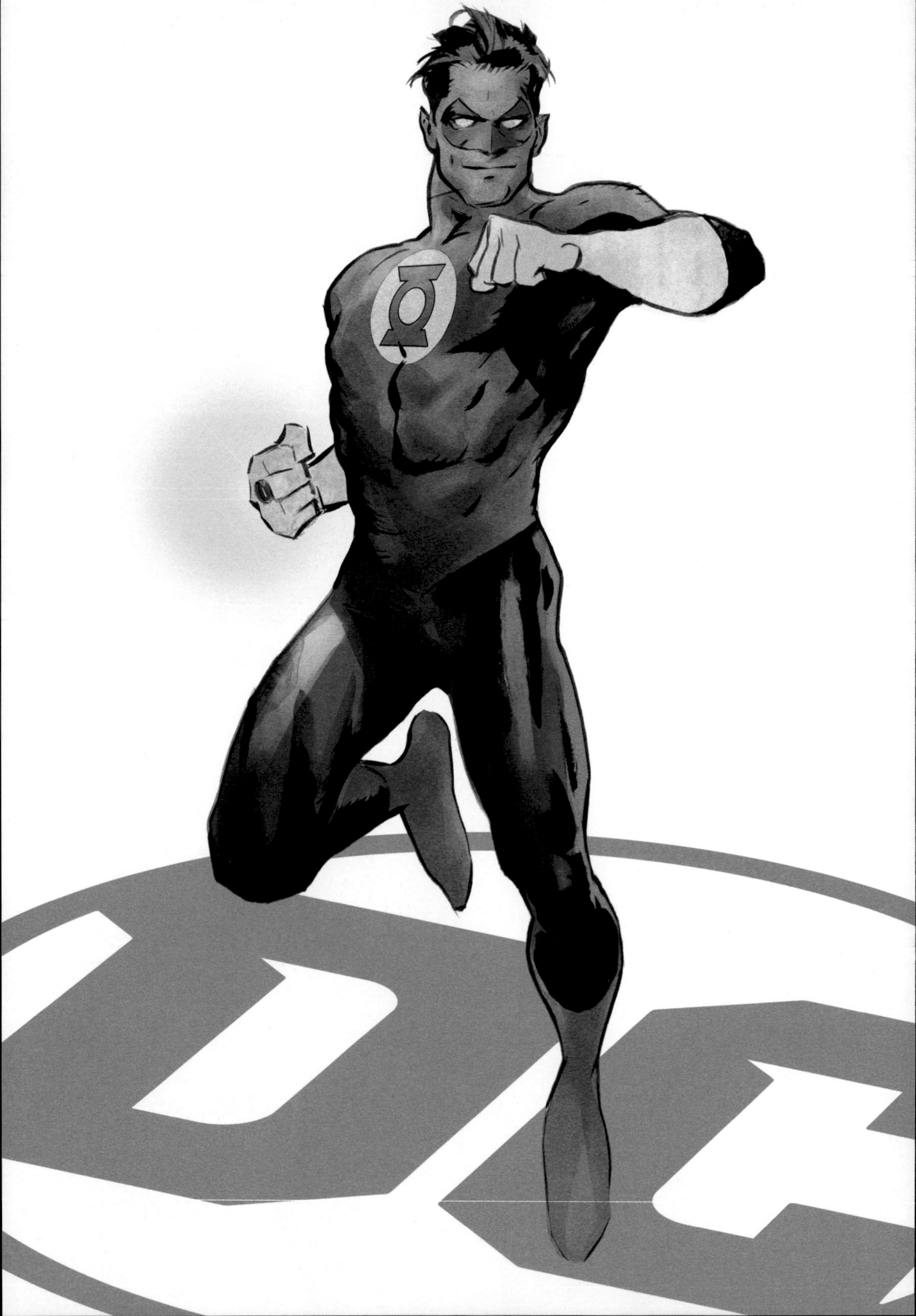

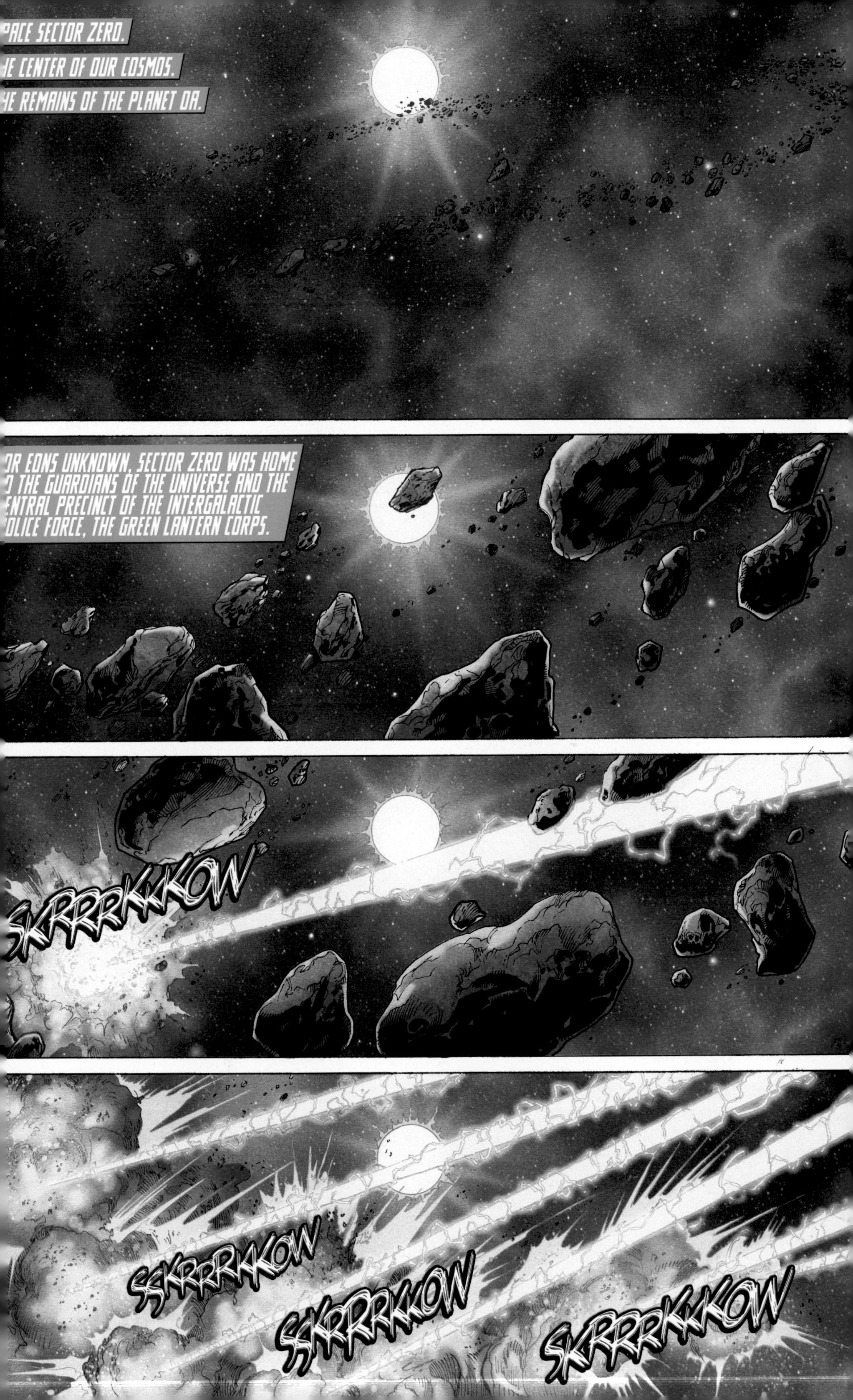
PACE SECTOR ZERO.
HE CENTER OF OUR COSMOS.
HE REMAINS OF THE PLANET OA.
OR EONS UNKNOWN, SECTOR ZERO WAS HOME
O THE GUARDIANS OF THE UNIVERSE AND THE
ENTRAL PRECINCT OF THE INTERGALACTIC
OLICE FORCE, THE GREEN LANTERN CORPS.
SKRRRKKKOW
SSKRRRKKOW
SSKRRRKKOW
SKRRRKKKOW

NOW IT IS UNDER THE CONTROL OF THE SUPREME FORCE OF ORDER IN THE UNIVERSE, THE SINESTRO CORPS.
SSKRRRKKOW
SSKRRRKKON
SSKRRRKKON
SSKRRRKKON
SKRRRKKKON

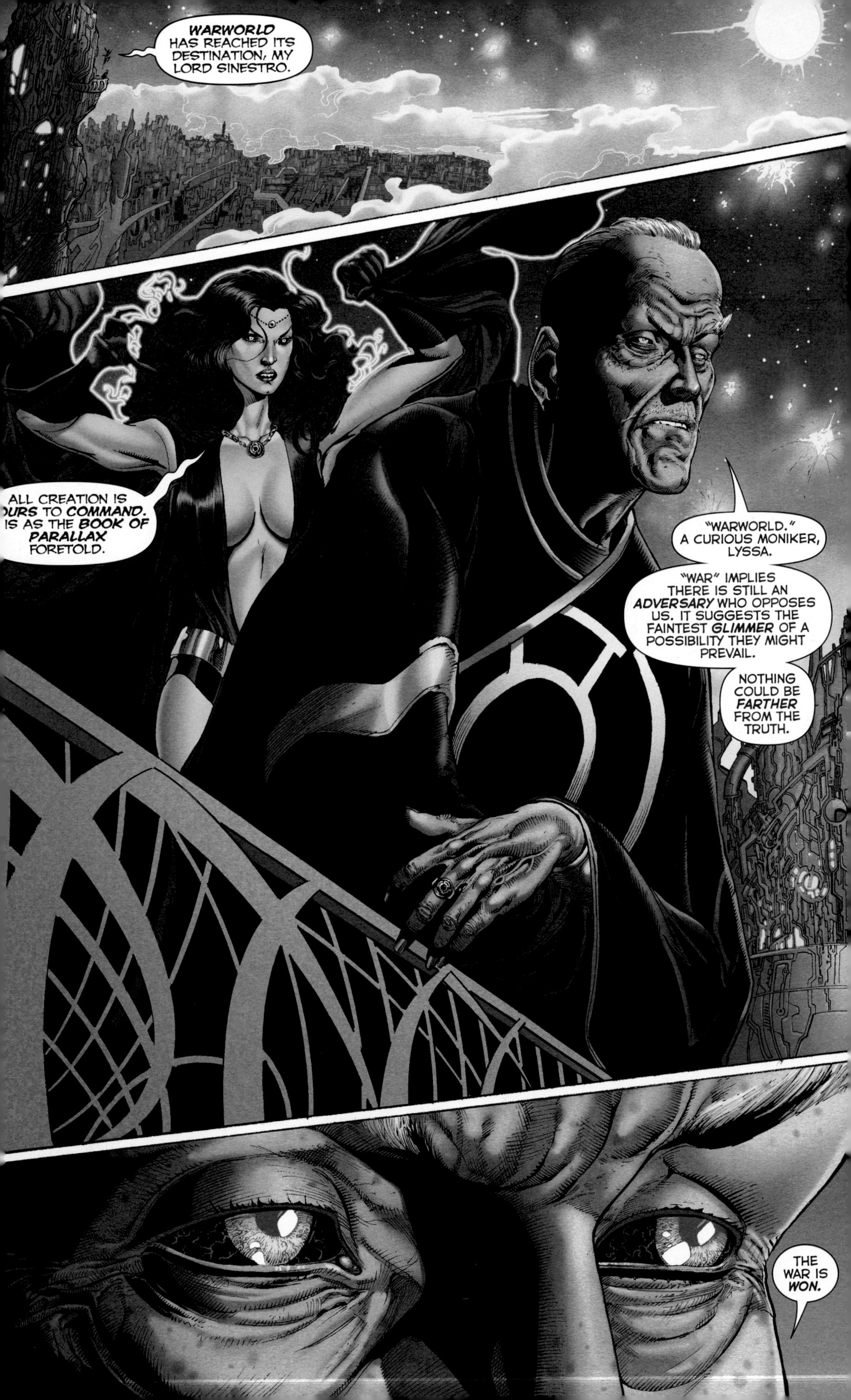
WARWORLD HAS REACHED ITS DESTINATION, MY LORD SINESTRO.
ALL CREATION IS OURS TO COMMAND. IS AS THE BOOK OF PARALLAX FORETOLD.
"WARWORLD." A CURIOUS MONIKER, LYSSA.
"WAR" IMPLIES THERE IS STILL AN ADVERSARY WHO OPPOSES US. IT SUGGESTS THE FAINTEST GLIMMER OF A POSSIBILITY THEY MIGHT PREVAIL.
NOTHING COULD BE FARTHER FROM THE TRUTH.
THE WAR IS WON.

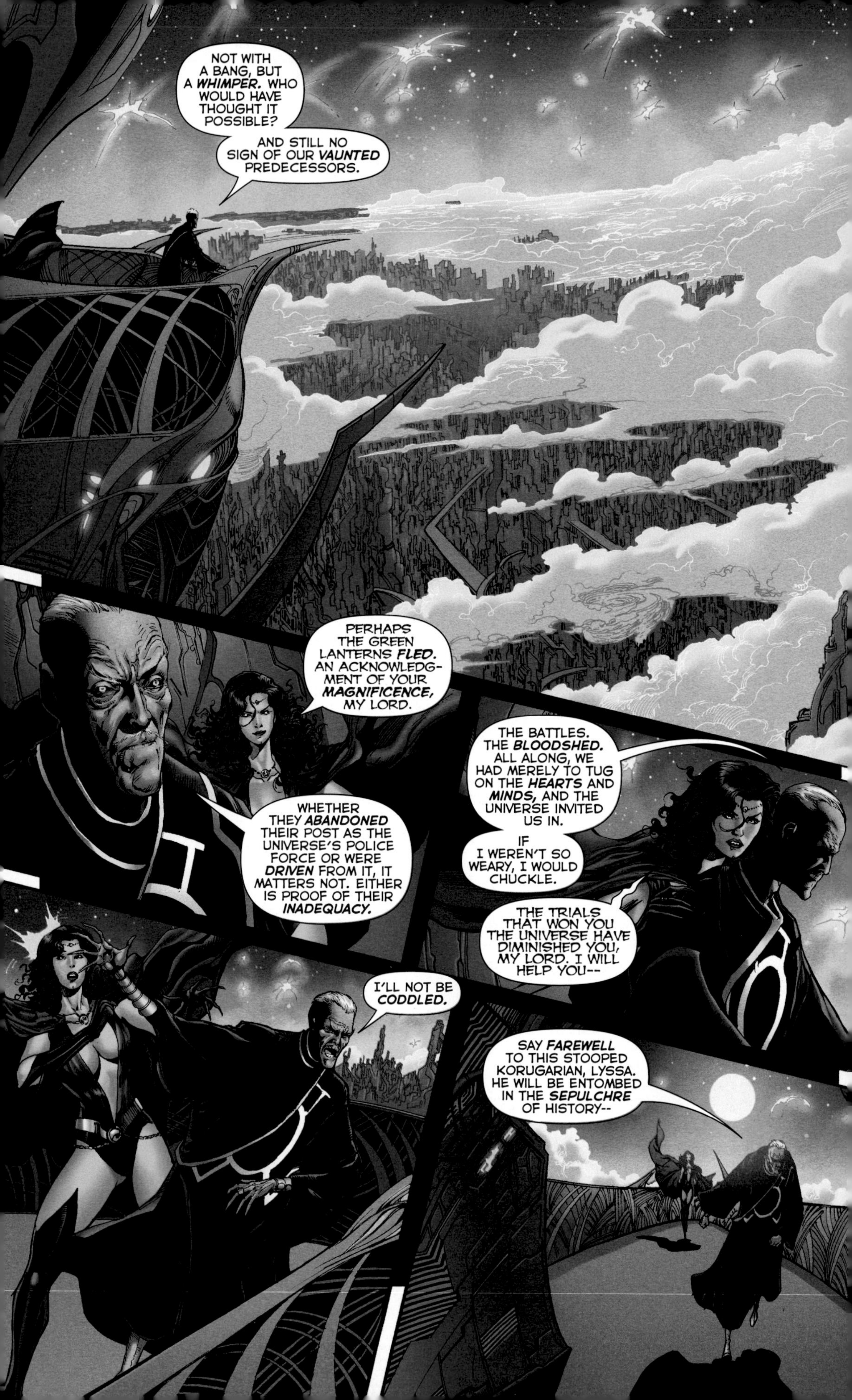
NOT WITH A BANG, BUT A WHIMPER. WHO WOULD HAVE THOUGHT IT POSSIBLE?
AND STILL NO SIGN OF OUR VAUNTED PREDECESSORS.
PERHAPS THE GREEN LANTERNS FLED. AN ACKNOWLEDG-MENT OF YOUR MAGNIFICENCE, MY LORD.
WHETHER THEY ABANDONED THEIR POST AS THE UNIVERSE'S POLICE FORCE OR WERE DRIVEN FROM IT, IT MATTERS NOT. EITHER IS PROOF OF THEIR INADEQUACY.
THE BATTLES. THE BLOODSHED. ALL ALONG, WE HAD MERELY TO TUG ON THE HEARTS AND MINDS, AND THE UNIVERSE INVITED US IN.
IF I WEREN'T SO WEARY, I WOULD CHUCKLE.
THE TRIALS THAT WON YOU THE UNIVERSE HAVE DIMINISHED YOU, MY LORD. I WILL HELP YOU--
I'LL NOT BE CODDLED.
SAY FAREWELL TO THIS STOOPED KORUGARIAN, LYSSA. HE WILL BE ENTOMBED IN THE SEPULCHRE OF HISTORY--

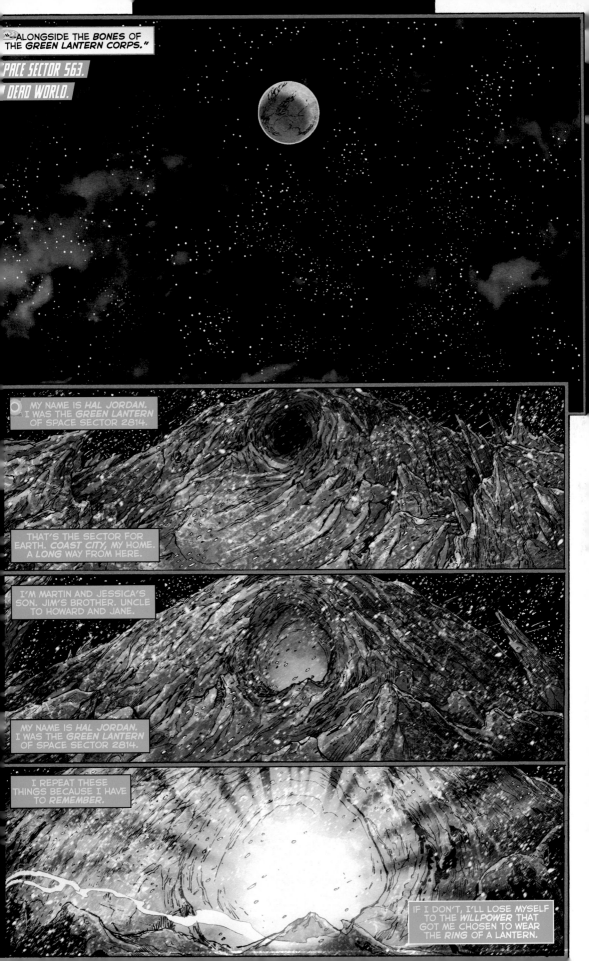

"--ALONGSIDE THE *BONES* OF THE *GREEN LANTERN CORPS.*"

PACE SECTOR 563.
DEAD WORLD.

MY NAME IS *HAL JORDAN.* I WAS THE *GREEN LANTERN* OF SPACE SECTOR 2814.

THAT'S THE SECTOR FOR EARTH. *COAST CITY,* MY HOME. A *LONG* WAY FROM HERE.

I'M MARTIN AND JESSICA'S SON. JIM'S BROTHER. UNCLE TO HOWARD AND JANE.

MY NAME IS HAL JORDAN. I WAS THE *GREEN LANTERN* OF SPACE SECTOR 2814.

I REPEAT THESE THINGS BECAUSE I HAVE TO *REMEMBER.*

IF I DON'T, I'LL LOSE MYSELF TO THE *WILLPOWER* THAT GOT ME CHOSEN TO WEAR THE *RING* OF A LANTERN.

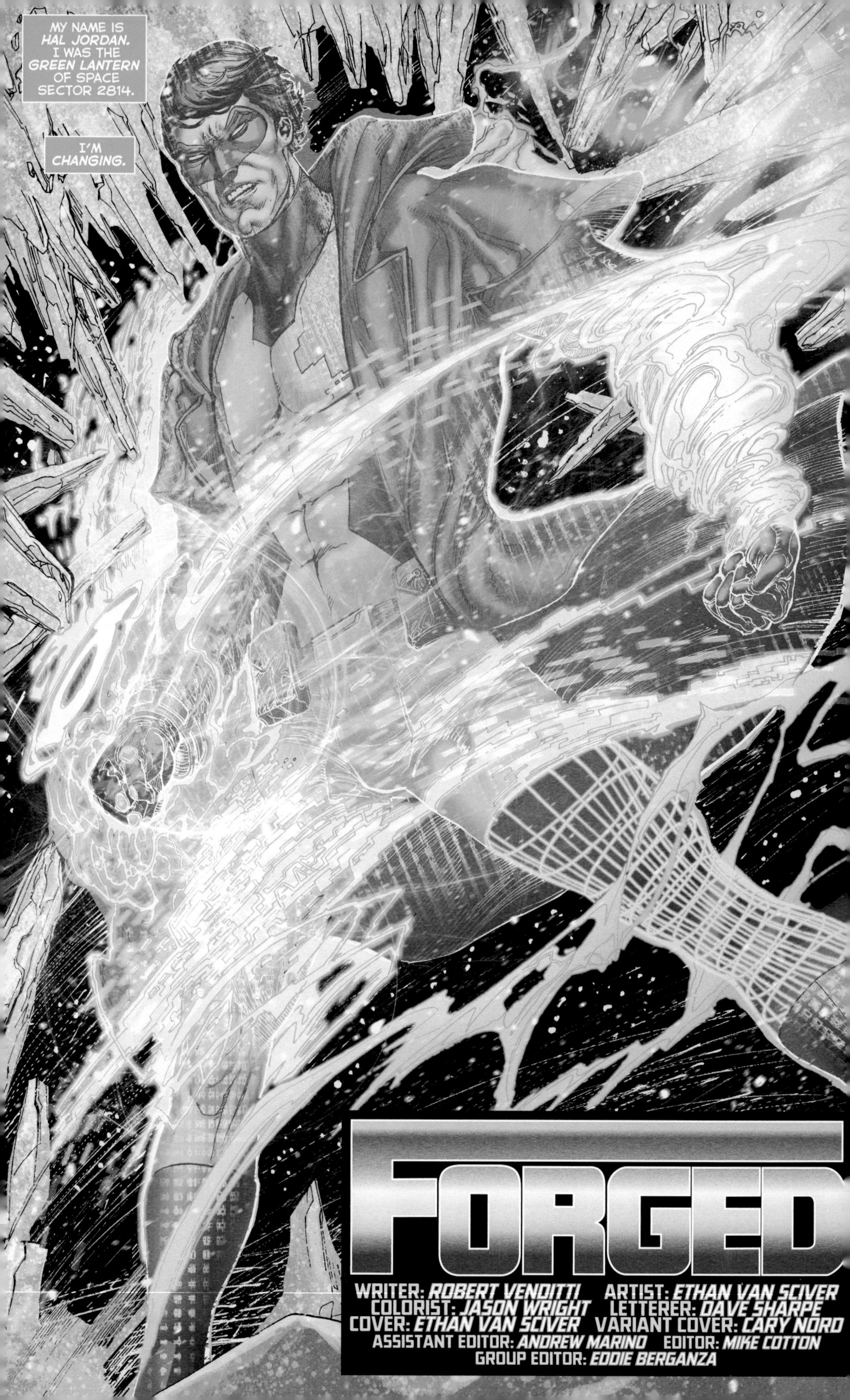
MY NAME IS HAL JORDAN. I WAS THE GREEN LANTERN OF SPACE SECTOR 2814.
I'M CHANGING.
FORGED
WRITER: ROBERT VENDITTI ARTIST: ETHAN VAN SCIVER
COLORIST: JASON WRIGHT LETTERER: DAVE SHARPE
COVER: ETHAN VAN SCIVER VARIANT COVER: CARY NORD
ASSISTANT EDITOR: ANDREW MARINO EDITOR: MIKE COTTON
GROUP EDITOR: EDDIE BERGANZA

MY DAD WAS A TEST PILOT. MY *HERO*.

WHEN I WAS JUST A KID, HE *CRASHED* AND *DIED* RIGHT IN FRONT OF ME.

I GREW UP AND BECAME A TEST PILOT, TOO.

A GREEN LANTERN NAMED *ABIN SUR* FOUND ME. CRASHED AND DYING, JUST LIKE DAD. HIS LAST ACT WAS TO GIVE ME HIS RING, SO I COULD TAKE HIS PLACE IN THE *GREEN LANTERN CORPS*.

THERE USED TO BE 7200 GREEN LANTERNS. IN TIME, I BECAME THEIR LEADER.

BUT WE WERE IN TROUBLE. *MISTRUSTED* AND *HATED* BY THE UNIVERSE WE'D SWORN TO PROTECT.

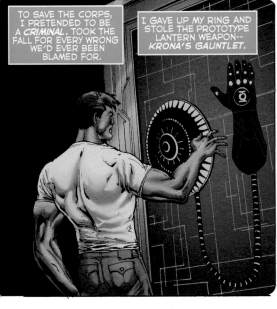

TO SAVE THE CORPS, I PRETENDED TO BE A *CRIMINAL*. TOOK THE FALL FOR EVERY WRONG WE'D EVER BEEN BLAMED FOR.

I GAVE UP MY RING AND STOLE THE PROTOTYPE LANTERN WEAPON-- *KRONA'S GAUNTLET*.

THEN I RAN...

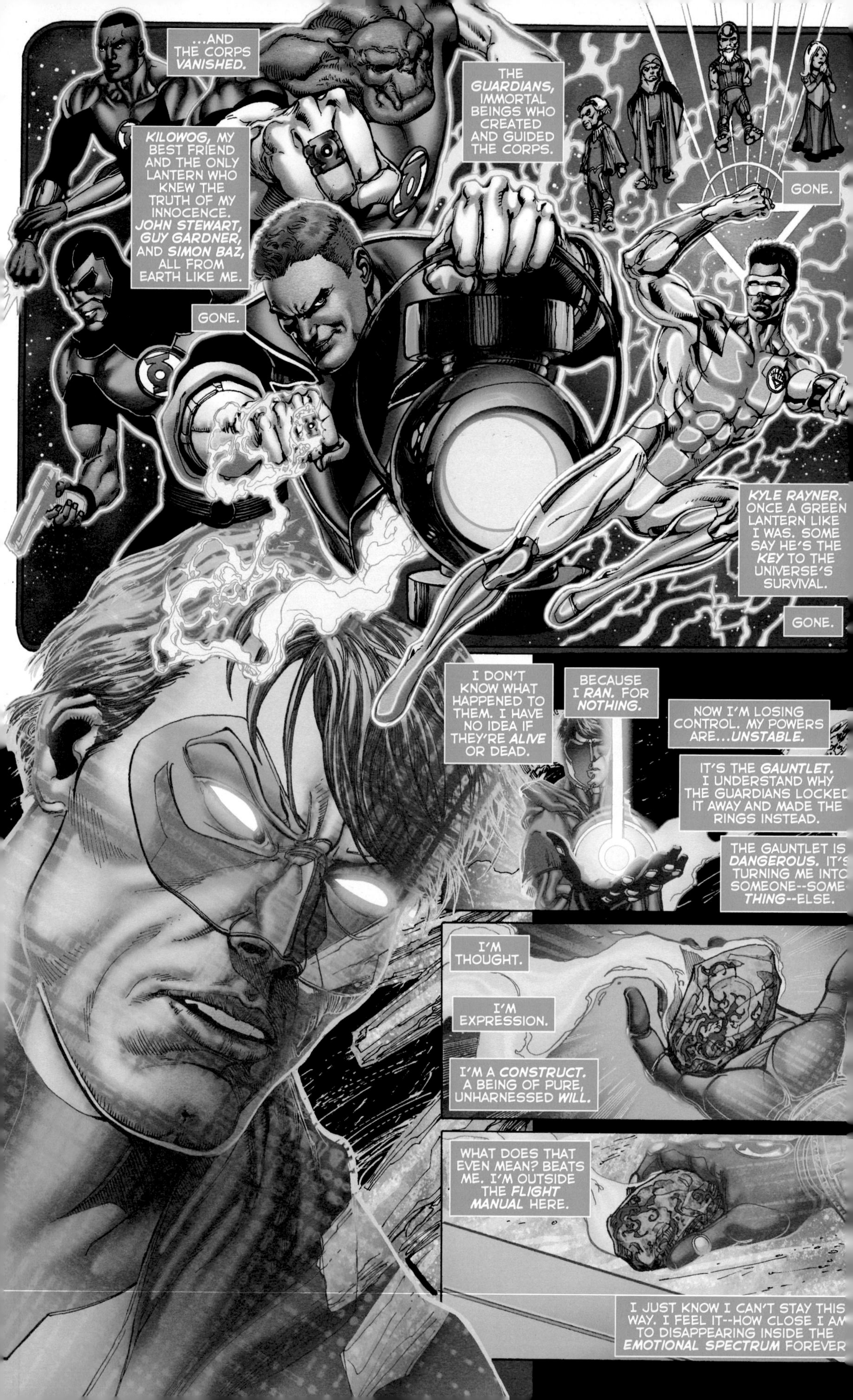
...AND THE CORPS VANISHED.
KILOWOG, MY BEST FRIEND AND THE ONLY LANTERN WHO KNEW THE TRUTH OF MY INNOCENCE. JOHN STEWART, GUY GARDNER, AND SIMON BAZ, ALL FROM EARTH LIKE ME.
GONE.
THE GUARDIANS, IMMORTAL BEINGS WHO CREATED AND GUIDED THE CORPS.
GONE.
KYLE RAYNER. ONCE A GREEN LANTERN LIKE I WAS. SOME SAY HE'S THE KEY TO THE UNIVERSE'S SURVIVAL.
GONE.
I DON'T KNOW WHAT HAPPENED TO THEM. I HAVE NO IDEA IF THEY'RE ALIVE OR DEAD.
BECAUSE I RAN. FOR NOTHING.
NOW I'M LOSING CONTROL. MY POWERS ARE...UNSTABLE.
IT'S THE GAUNTLET. I UNDERSTAND WHY THE GUARDIANS LOCKED IT AWAY AND MADE THE RINGS INSTEAD.
THE GAUNTLET IS DANGEROUS. IT'S TURNING ME INTO SOMEONE--SOMETHING--ELSE.
I'M THOUGHT.
I'M EXPRESSION.
I'M A CONSTRUCT. A BEING OF PURE, UNHARNESSED WILL.
WHAT DOES THAT EVEN MEAN? BEATS ME. I'M OUTSIDE THE FLIGHT MANUAL HERE.
I JUST KNOW I CAN'T STAY THIS WAY. I FEEL IT--HOW CLOSE I AM TO DISAPPEARING INSIDE THE EMOTIONAL SPECTRUM FOREVER.

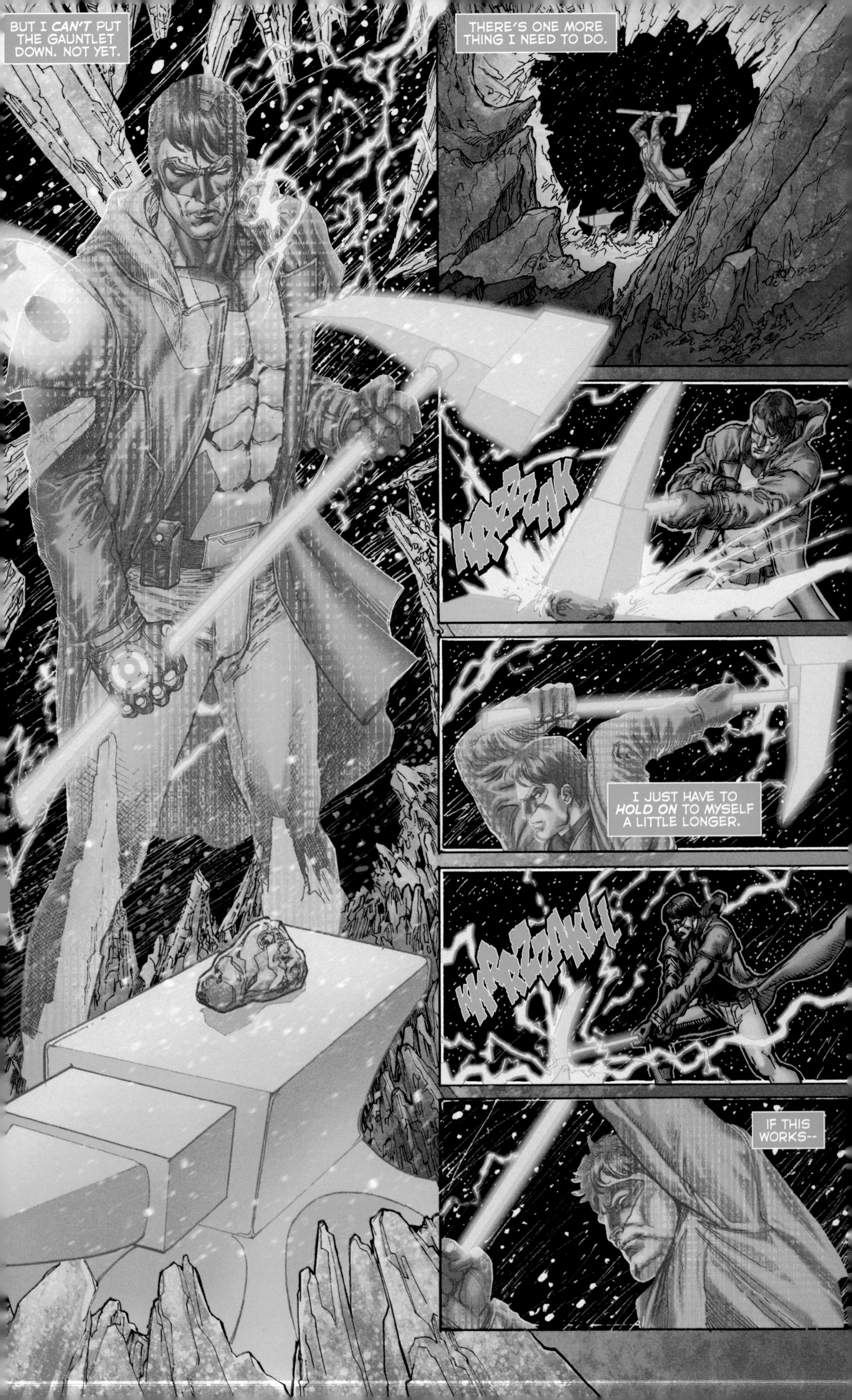
BUT I *CAN'T* PUT THE GAUNTLET DOWN. NOT YET.
THERE'S ONE MORE THING I NEED TO DO.
KRZZZAK
I JUST HAVE TO *HOLD ON* TO MYSELF A LITTLE LONGER.
KRRZZAKK!
IF THIS WORKS--

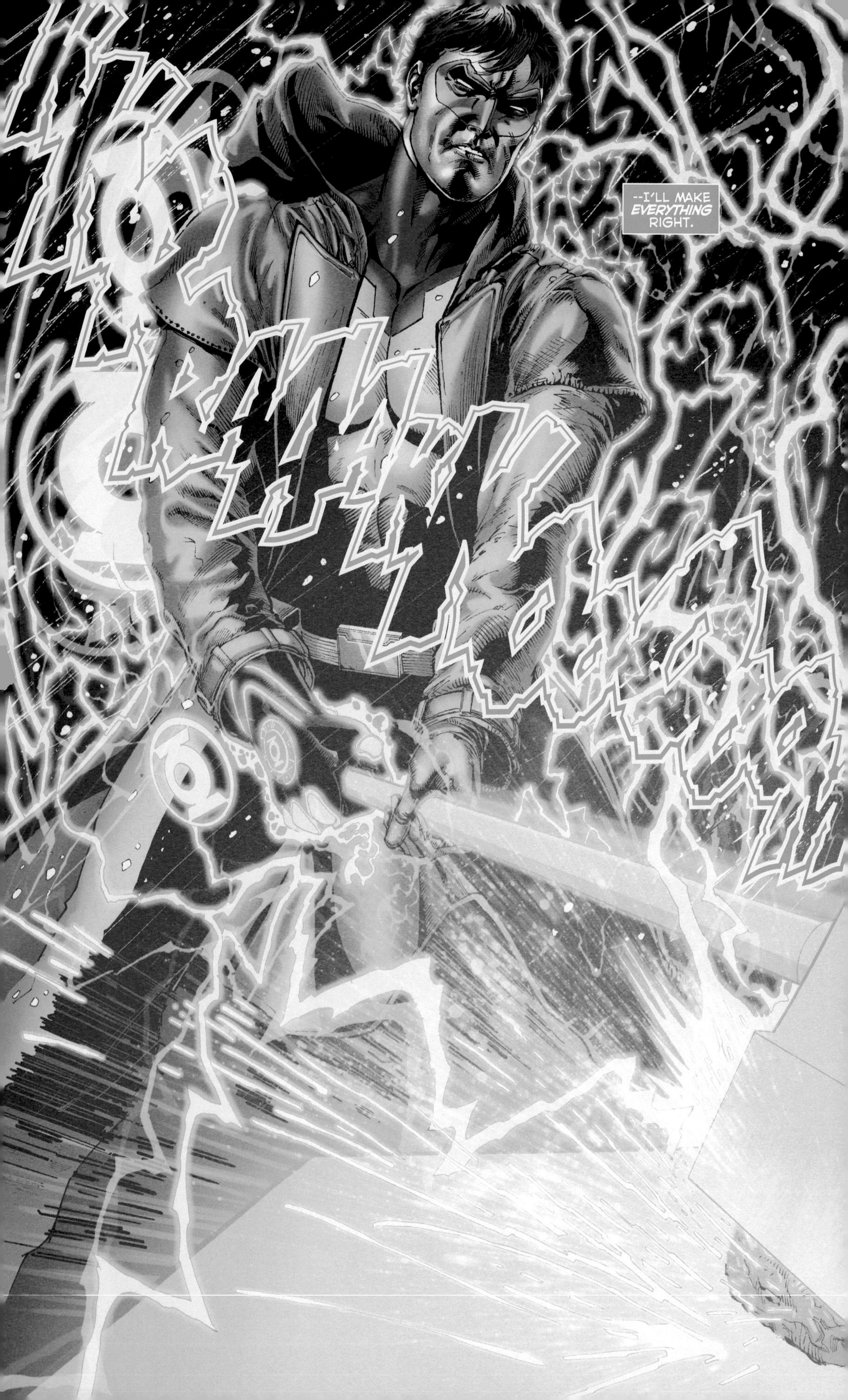
--I'LL MAKE EVERYTHING RIGHT.

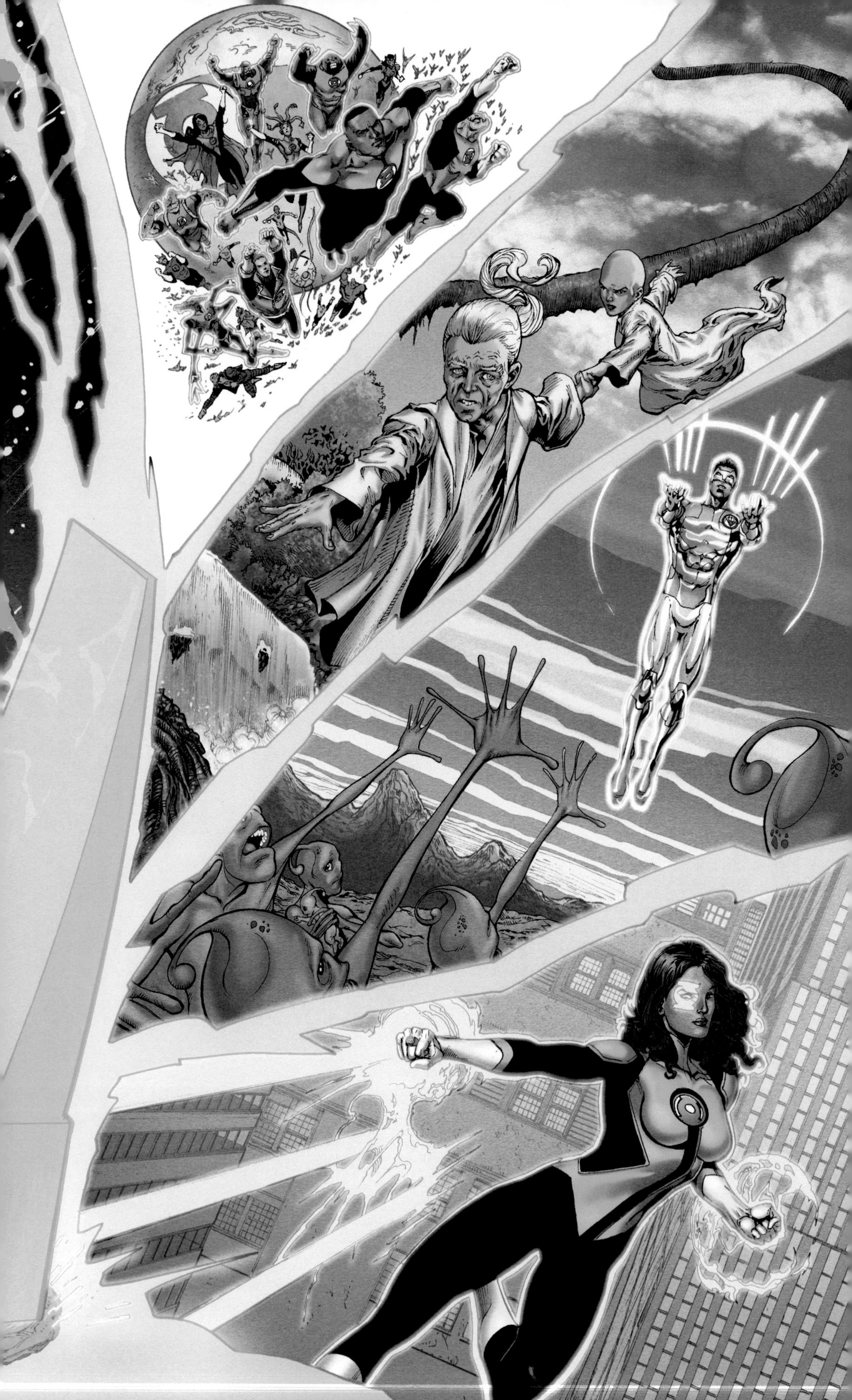

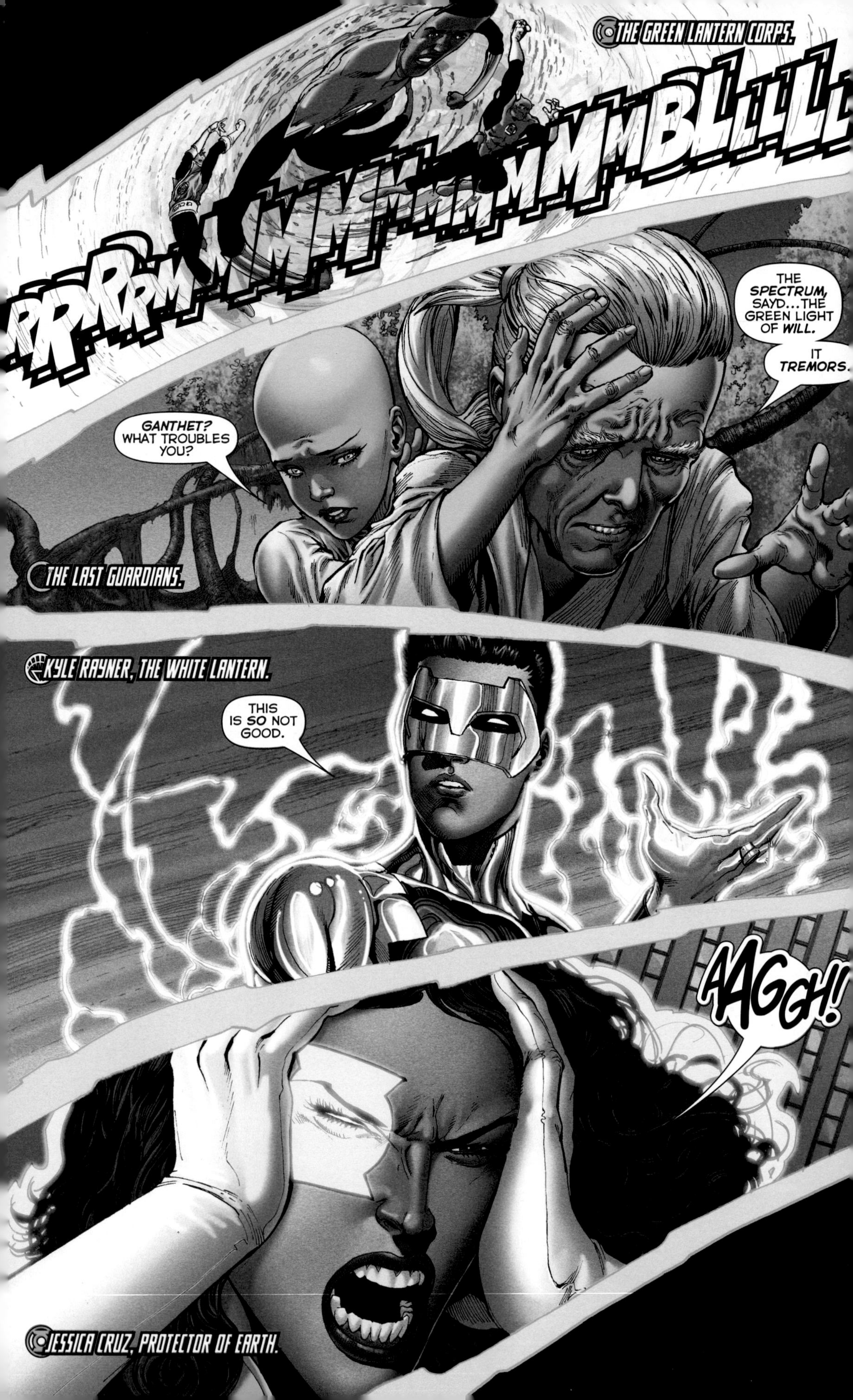
THE GREEN LANTERN CORPS.
PRRRMMMMMMMBLLLL
THE SPECTRUM, SAYD...THE GREEN LIGHT OF WILL.
IT TREMORS.
GANTHET? WHAT TROUBLES YOU?
THE LAST GUARDIANS.
KYLE RAYNER, THE WHITE LANTERN.
THIS IS SO NOT GOOD.
AAGGH!
JESSICA CRUZ, PROTECTOR OF EARTH.

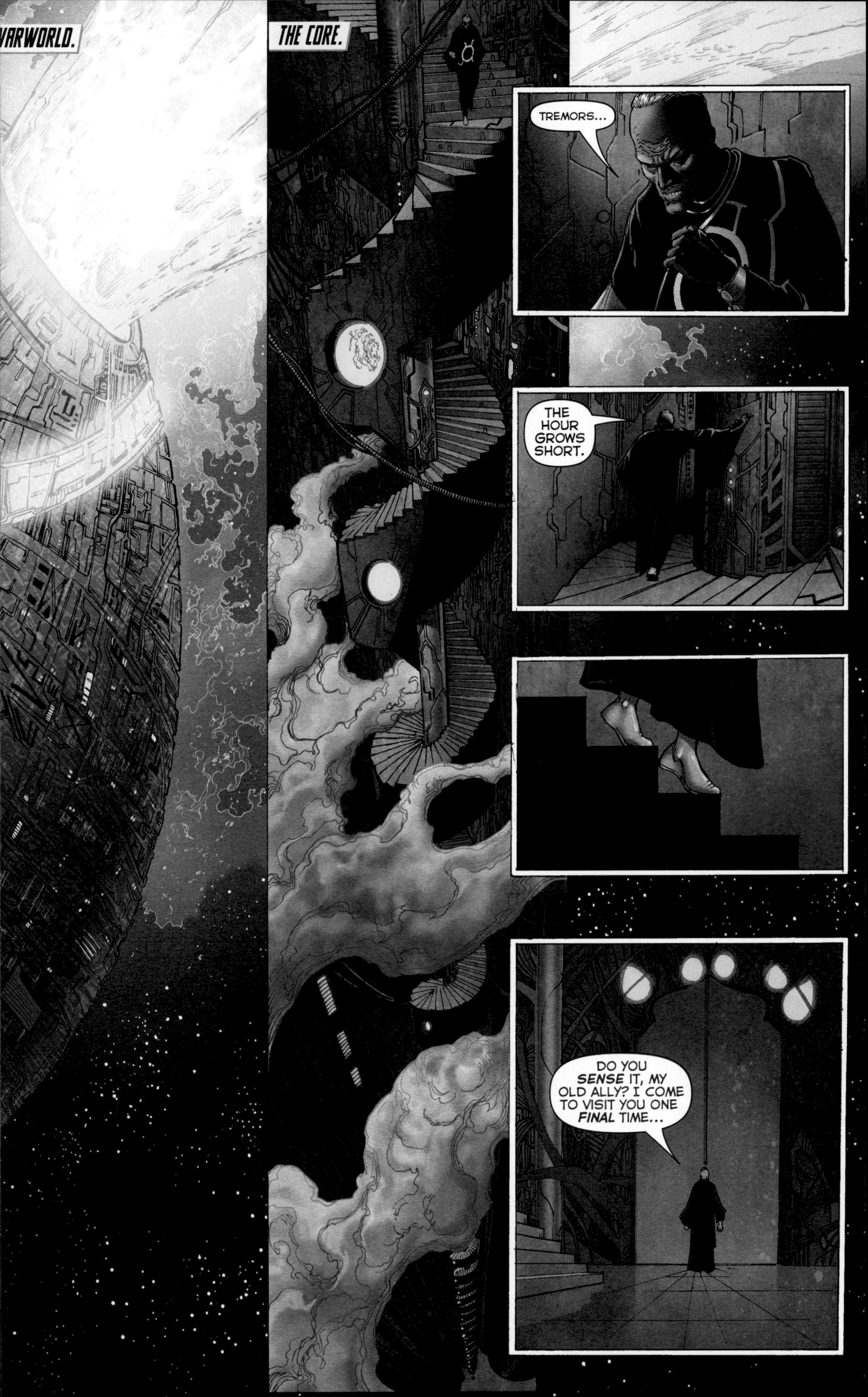
WARWORLD.
THE CORE.
TREMORS...
THE HOUR GROWS SHORT.
DO YOU SENSE IT, MY OLD ALLY? I COME TO VISIT YOU ONE FINAL TIME...

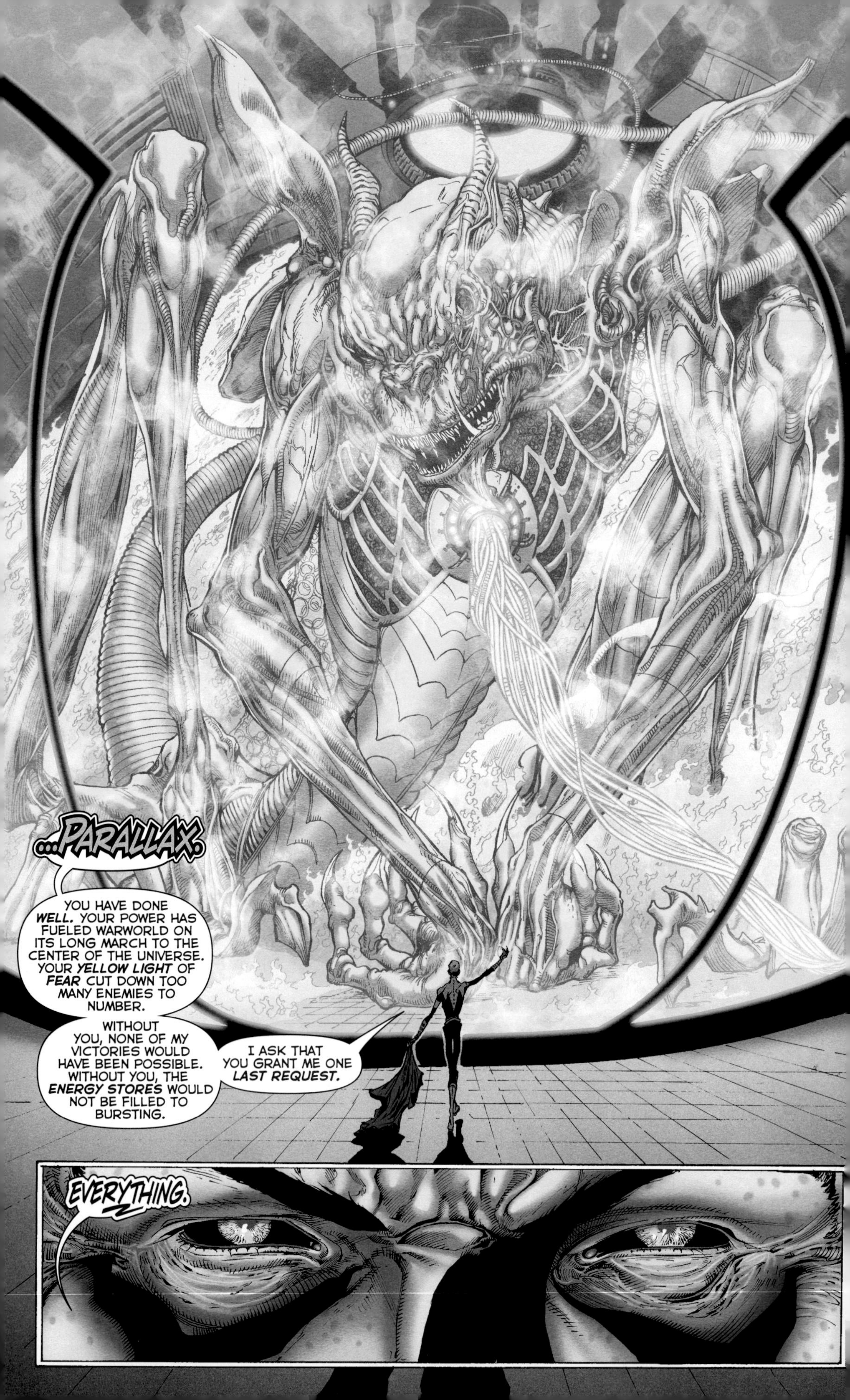

...PARALLAX.
YOU HAVE DONE WELL. YOUR POWER HAS FUELED WARWORLD ON ITS LONG MARCH TO THE CENTER OF THE UNIVERSE. YOUR YELLOW LIGHT OF FEAR CUT DOWN TOO MANY ENEMIES TO NUMBER.
WITHOUT YOU, NONE OF MY VICTORIES WOULD HAVE BEEN POSSIBLE. WITHOUT YOU, THE ENERGY STORES WOULD NOT BE FILLED TO BURSTING.
I ASK THAT YOU GRANT ME ONE LAST REQUEST.
EVERYTHING.

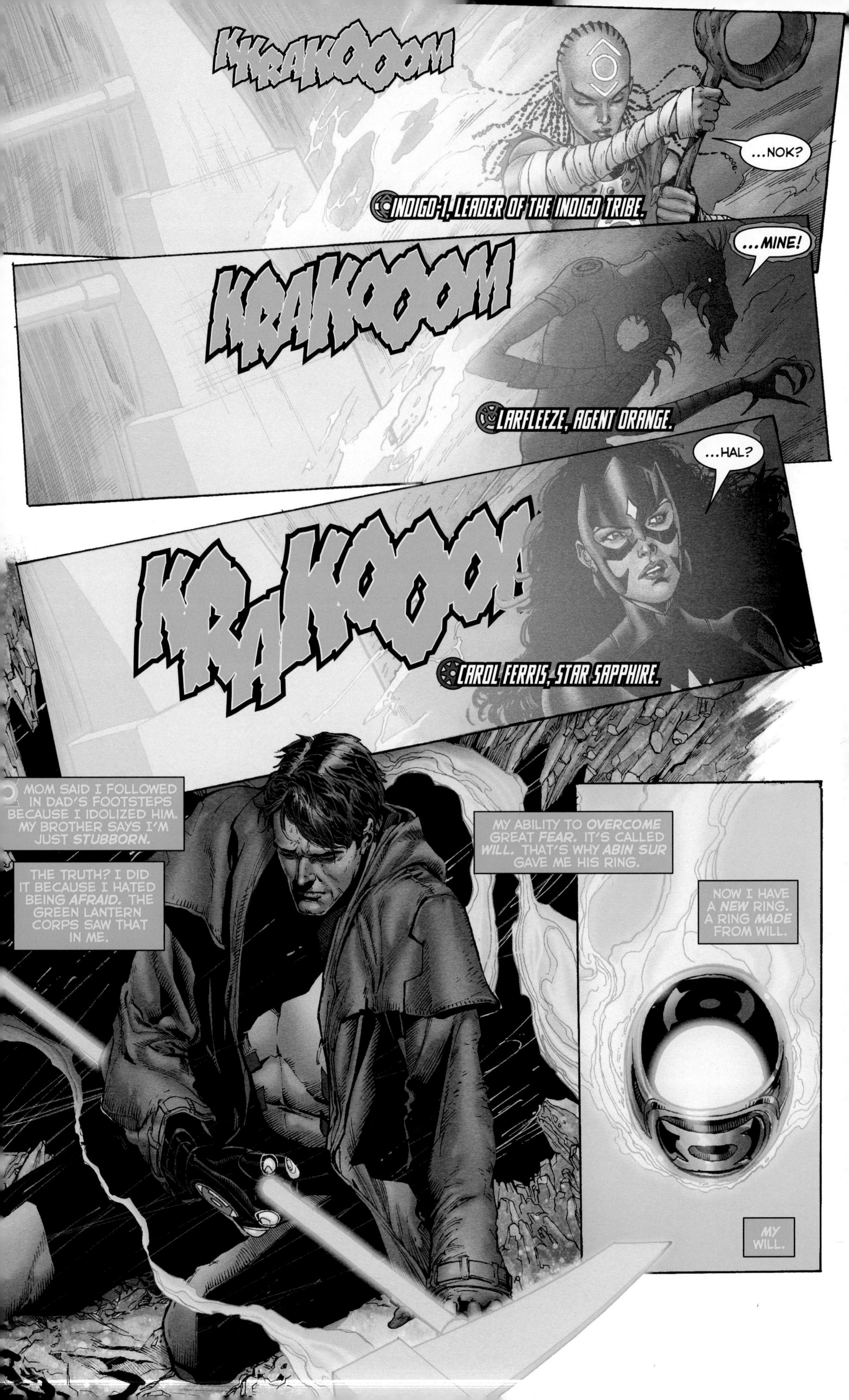
KKRAKOOOM
...NOK?
INDIGO-1, LEADER OF THE INDIGO TRIBE.
KRAKOOOM
...MINE!
LARFLEEZE, AGENT ORANGE.
...HAL?
KRAKOOO
CAROL FERRIS, STAR SAPPHIRE.
MOM SAID I FOLLOWED IN DAD'S FOOTSTEPS BECAUSE I IDOLIZED HIM. MY BROTHER SAYS I'M JUST STUBBORN.
THE TRUTH? I DID IT BECAUSE I HATED BEING AFRAID. THE GREEN LANTERN CORPS SAW THAT IN ME.
MY ABILITY TO OVERCOME GREAT FEAR. IT'S CALLED WILL. THAT'S WHY ABIN SUR GAVE ME HIS RING.
NOW I HAVE A NEW RING. A RING MADE FROM WILL.
MY WILL.

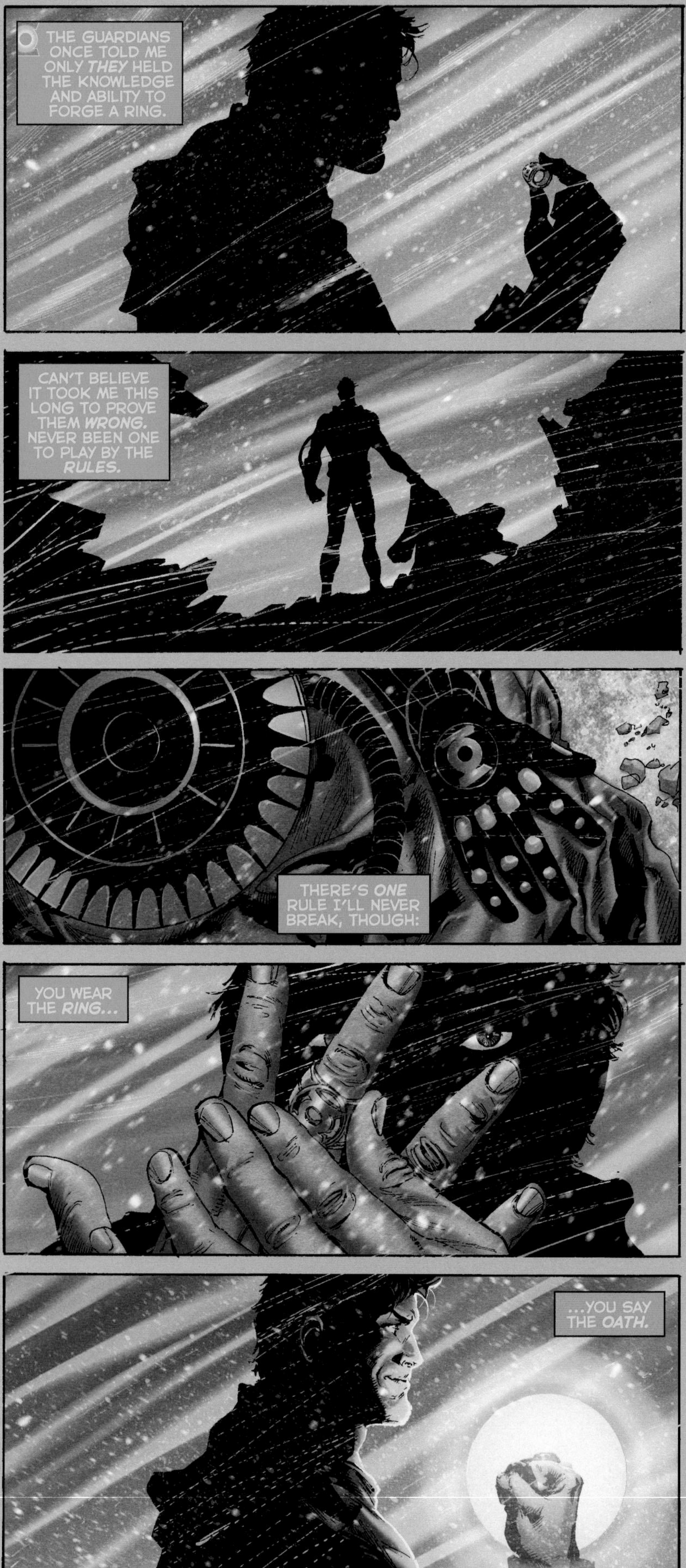
THE GUARDIANS ONCE TOLD ME ONLY *THEY* HELD THE KNOWLEDGE AND ABILITY TO FORGE A RING.
CAN'T BELIEVE IT TOOK ME THIS LONG TO PROVE THEM *WRONG.* NEVER BEEN ONE TO PLAY BY THE *RULES.*
THERE'S *ONE* RULE I'LL NEVER BREAK, THOUGH:
YOU WEAR THE *RING...*
...YOU SAY THE *OATH.*

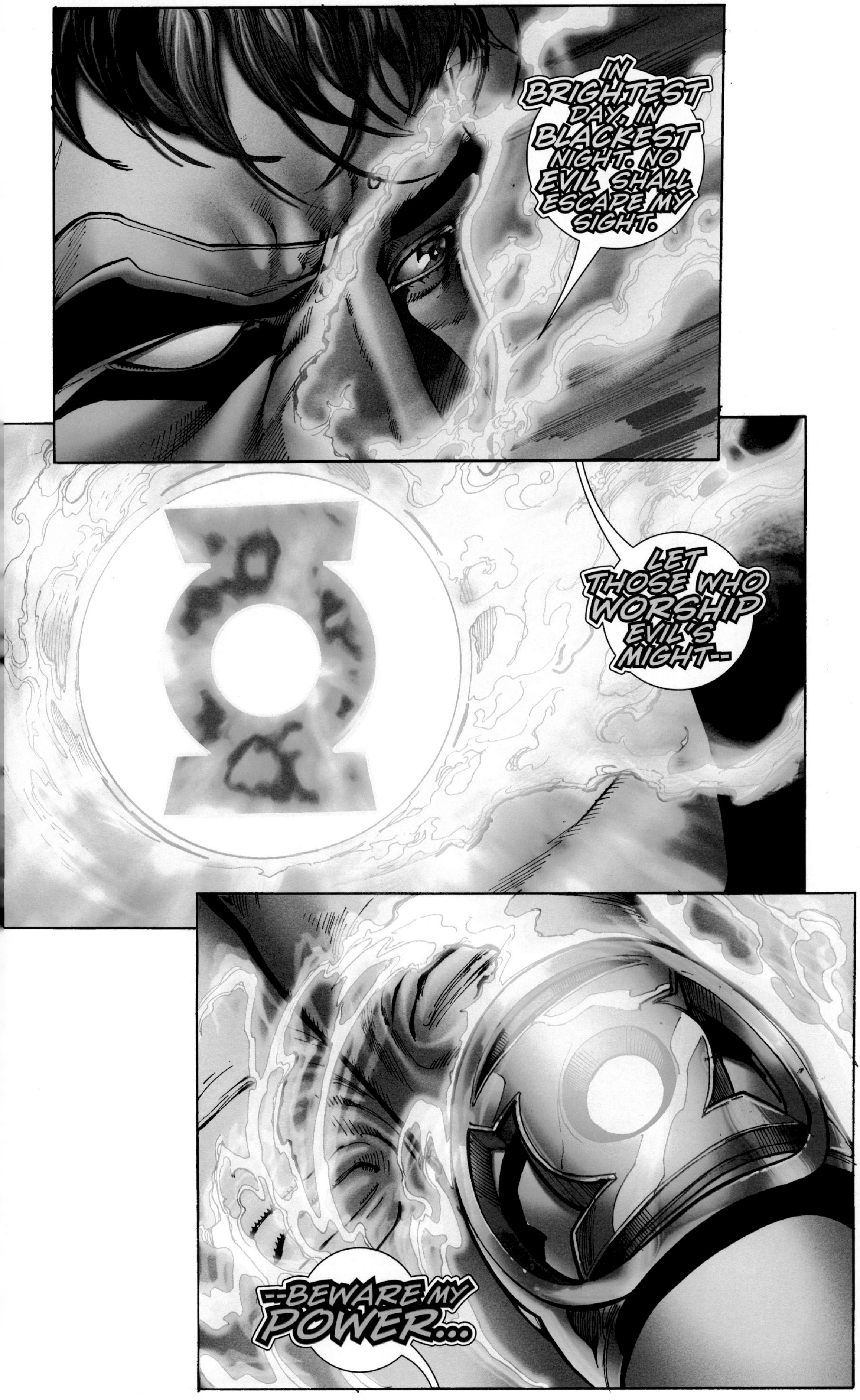
IN BRIGHTEST DAY, IN BLACKEST NIGHT. NO EVIL SHALL ESCAPE MY SIGHT.
LET THOSE WHO WORSHIP EVIL'S MIGHT--
--BEWARE MY POWER...

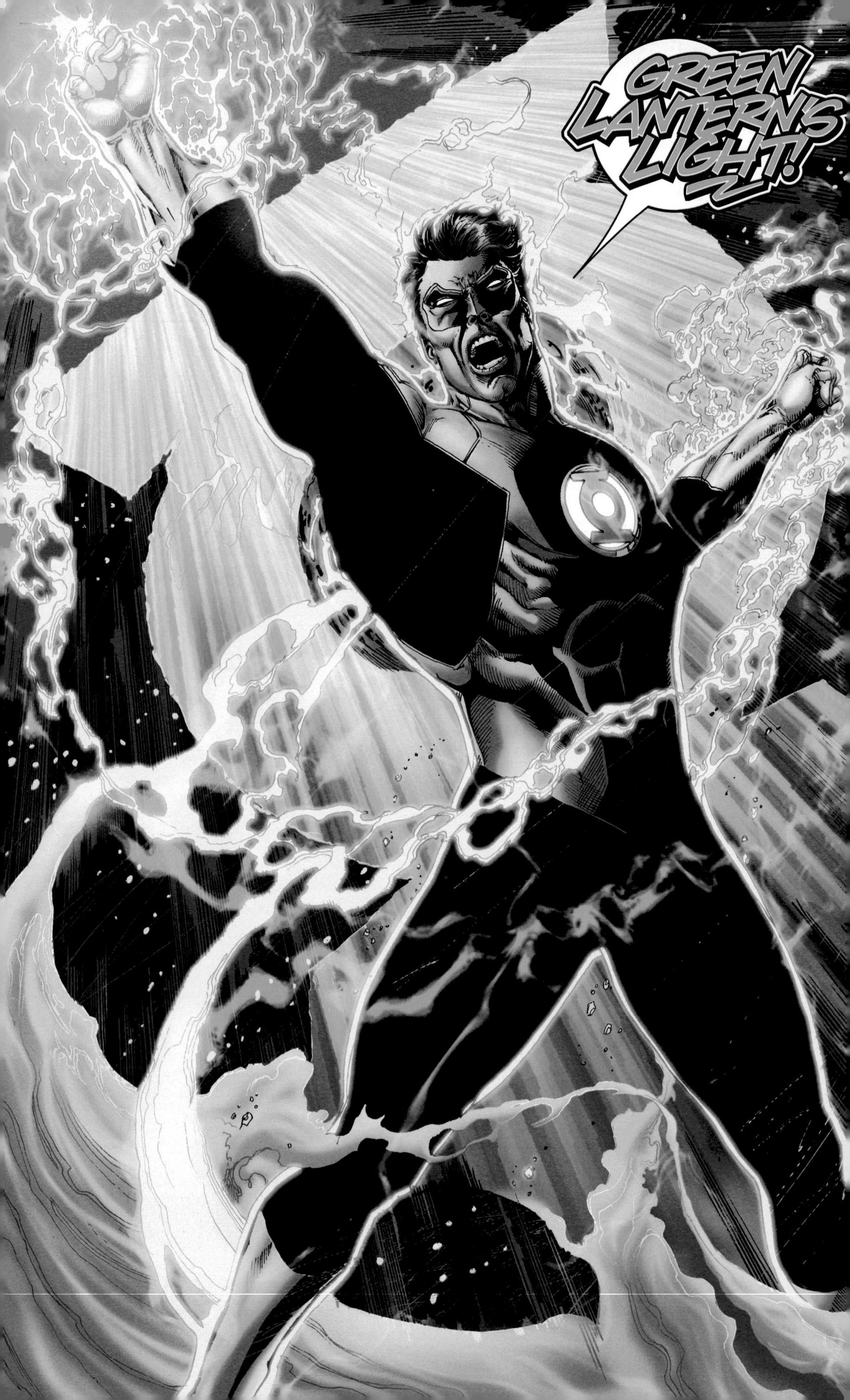
GREEN LANTERN'S LIGHT!

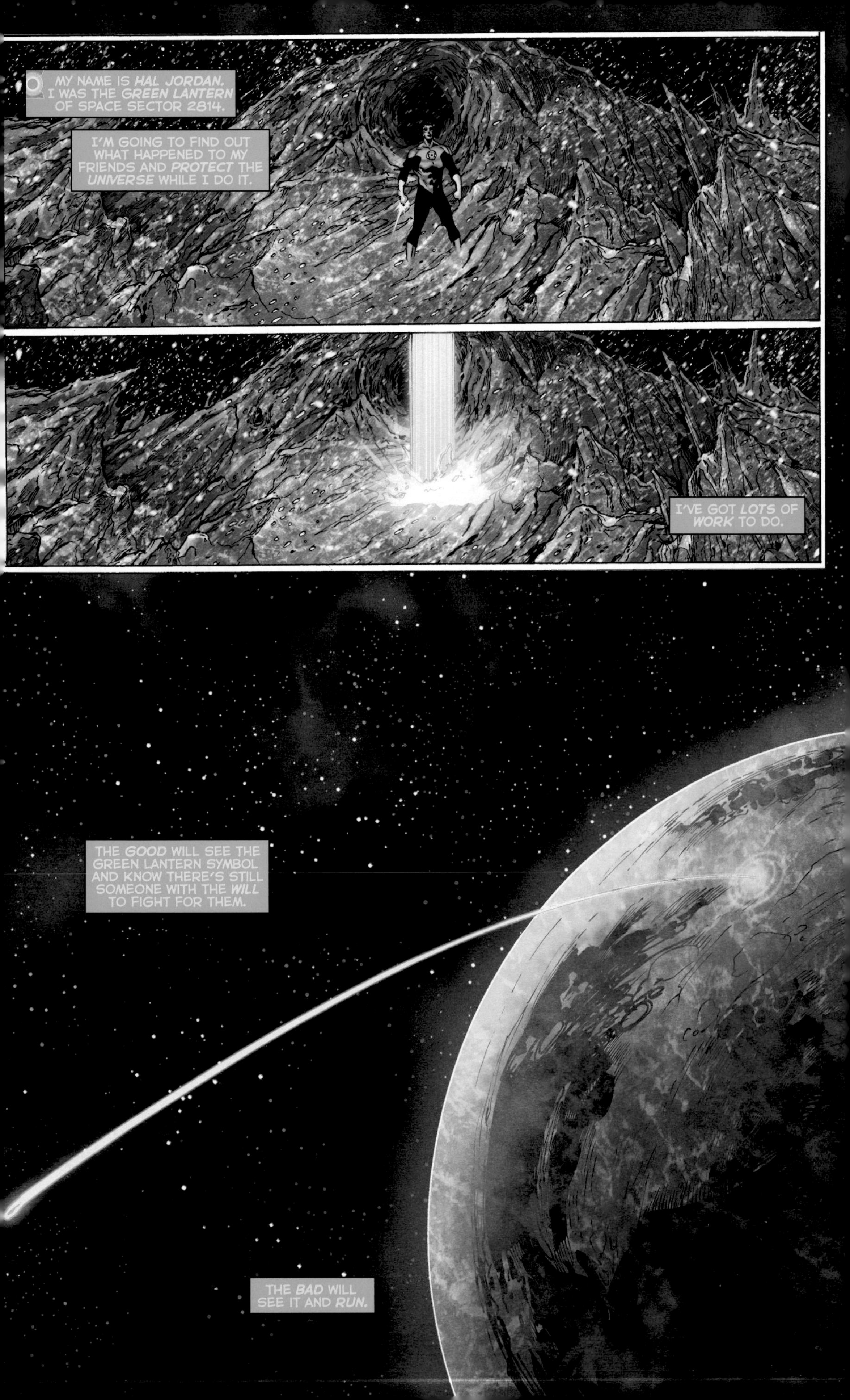
MY NAME IS HAL JORDAN. I WAS THE GREEN LANTERN OF SPACE SECTOR 2814.
I'M GOING TO FIND OUT WHAT HAPPENED TO MY FRIENDS AND PROTECT THE UNIVERSE WHILE I DO IT.
I'VE GOT LOTS OF WORK TO DO.
THE GOOD WILL SEE THE GREEN LANTERN SYMBOL AND KNOW THERE'S STILL SOMEONE WITH THE WILL TO FIGHT FOR THEM.
THE BAD WILL SEE IT AND RUN.

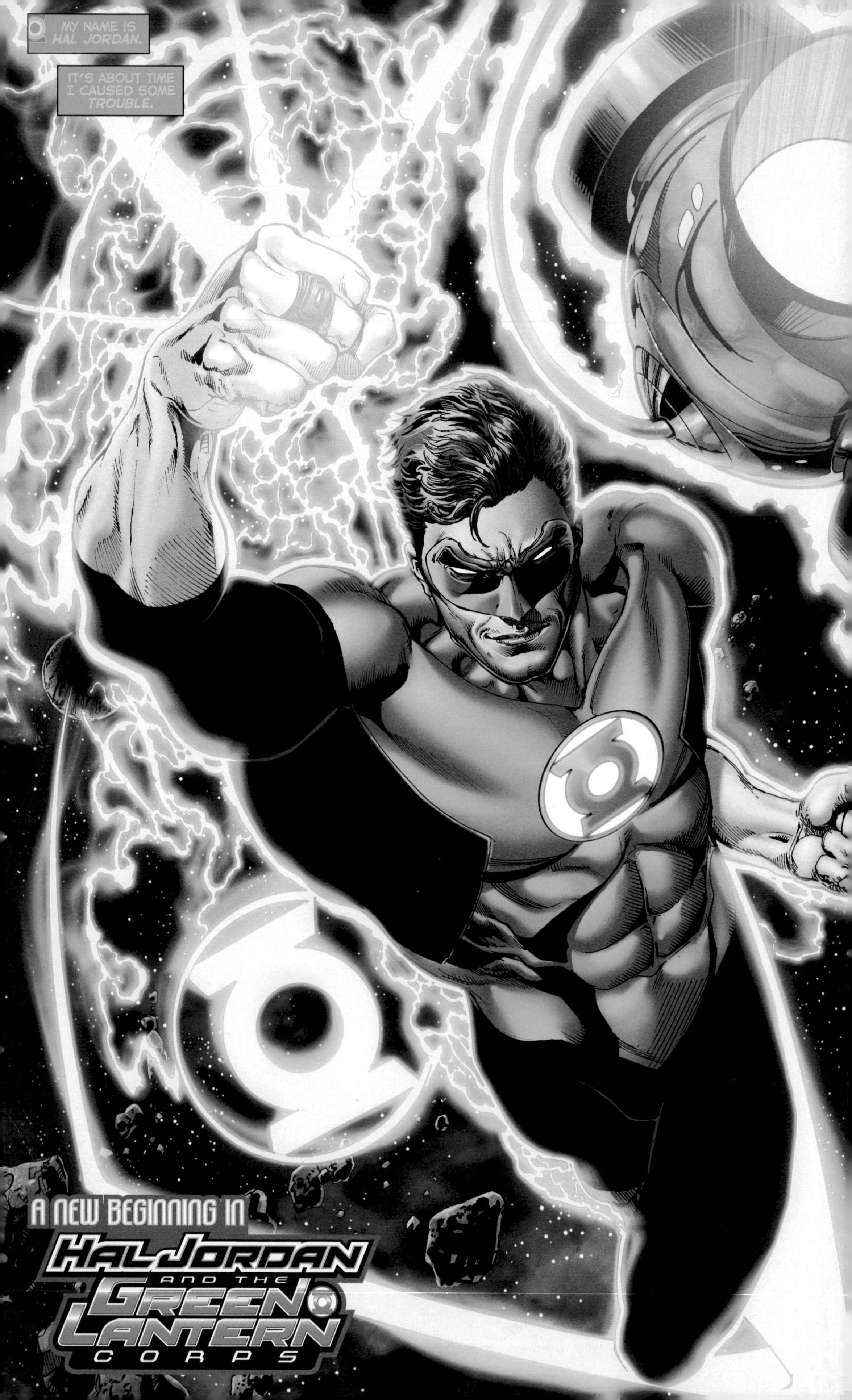

MY NAME IS HAL JORDAN.
IT'S ABOUT TIME I CAUSED SOME TROUBLE.
A NEW BEGINNING IN
HAL JORDAN AND THE GREEN LANTERN CORPS

"Consistently entertaining..."
—NEWSARAMA.COM

"This is comic book storytelling at its absolute finest."
—IGN

"If you've read a superhero comic book published by
DC Comics within the last few years, and were completely
blown away by it, there's a good chance that it was something written by Geoff Johns." —WASHINGTON EXAMINER

FROM THE WRITER OF *JUSTICE LEAGUE* AND *THE FLASH*

GEOFF JOHNS
GREEN LANTERN: REBIRTH

GREEN LANTERN:
BRIGHTEST DAY

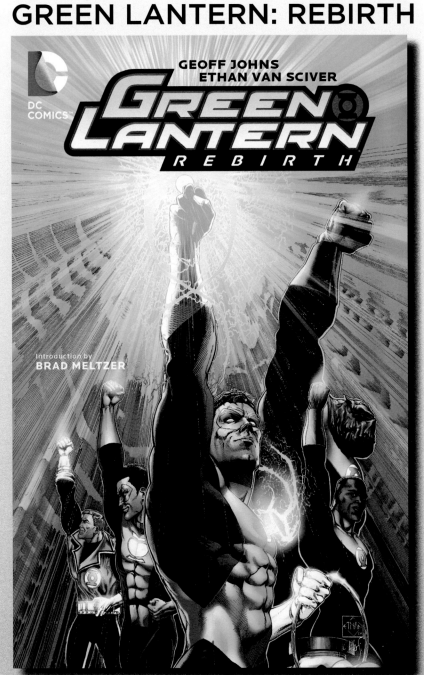

DC COMICS™

"This is the perfect place for people wary of the Gree
Lantern to start reading his adventures in order to see ju
how dynamic his world really is."—COMPLEX MAGAZIN

START AT THE BEGINNING!

GREEN LANTERN
VOLUME 1: SINESTRO

GREEN LANTERN VOL. 2: THE REVENGE OF THE BLACK HAND

GREEN LANTERN VOL. 3: THE END

GREEN LANTERN: RISE OF THE THIRD ARMY

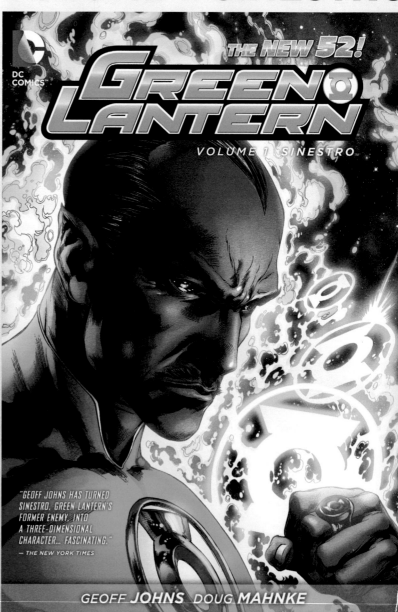